W9-CES-653

HANDBOOK
of
ENGLISH

James A. S. McPeek
PROFESSOR OF ENGLISH
UNIVERSITY OF CONNECTICUT

Austin Wright
PROFESSOR OF ENGLISH
CARNEGIE INSTITUTE OF TECHNOLOGY

THE RONALD PRESS COMPANY , NEW YORK

9

Library of Congress Catalog Card Number: 55-6817

PRINTED IN THE UNITED STATES OF AMERICA

PREFACE

This *Handbook of English* is intended to serve college students both as a text for class study and as a work of reference which will answer most of their questions about language and its usage. As a text for study and class assignment it is functionally organized. For the student the process of learning how to improve his writing is not merely one of mastering parts separately but one of relating parts to a whole; therefore this text first considers composition as a whole. After the student is made aware of the major aims of composition, he is ready to study its separate features, always, however, in relation to the whole.

It is both natural and logical to study the sentence first among these features; and study of the sentence leads inevitably to study of its parts. Experience has taught us that if a student is to learn how to recognize and eliminate his faults, he must know at least the basic facts about the parts of speech. Hence errors in grammar are not studied as isolated faults in this text, but are analyzed as they should be, in close association with the study of the grammatical features which they violate. The method used is positive and remedial: first the student learns the nature of some aspect of sentence structure; next he is given recognition exercises to test his knowledge; and then he examines the common errors that students commit in violation of the principle. The instructor of course must decide for himself whether his class needs an extensive study of these fundamentals—most classes do—or whether he will assign this material only to those students especially needing such instruction; but the information is at hand in this book for all students, to serve as a text and reference for those needing it and to clarify the understanding of the better students about points that may puzzle them.

To proceed from the study of the parts of the sentence and their relationships to the special rhetorical patterns of the sentence, and thence to punctuation, paragraphing, and diction, is also natural and sound; and the various chapters are so arranged that assignments can be easily made according to the present organization of the text. On the other hand, the chapters are so self-contained and linked by cross references that it is possible for any instructor who would rather begin with a study of diction or any other phase of composition to evolve his own organization of the material.

Since this text is planned for college freshmen, it is addressed to them throughout. We have not talked down to the students, nor have we assumed in them a sophistication that the majority of freshman English students do not possess. In short, this text does not need explanation; the information it gives is clearly accessible and never hidden in ambushes of rhetoric or wit aimed at the instructor rather than the student. The explanations are reasonably full and designed to teach: this is not a book of set rules or convenient generalities which the student may scan at a glance without considering their context, and forget as quickly as he refers to them. For the most part the explanations are so developed and arranged that the student will find it desirable and even necessary to read the discussions and illustrations in order to know the reasons for the rules as well as the rules themselves.

From the outset the student is made aware that language has many faces, that it is a diverse and changing instrument of expression. But though he learns that standard English has many varieties of expression and that each of these may borrow from all the others, the distinctions between the two large comprehensive classes, formal and informal English, are made sharply clear to him. Though he becomes aware of growth and change in language, he perceives also that for his lifetime there is at least the illusion of permanence. Change comes slowly; and even those who are closest students of the changing language, in discussing the symptoms of change write a language that is notably formal and traditional in all its aspects.

In the interpretation of rules of grammar and punctuation, the student will likewise find this book helpfully direct and unequivocal. Though he learns, for example, that some comma splices, incomplete sentences, and dangling modifiers are permissible and that some writers punctuate only to suit their own (often esoteric) standards of clarity, the student is steadily reminded that it is safer for him to follow generally accepted rules rather than exceptions to the rules.

The reference chart inside the front and back covers will enable the student to locate quickly the treatment of each main topic and of the most serious and frequently committed errors, and he will soon memorize the section numbers to which he is most often referred. But because most teachers usually prefer to prescribe their own system of correction symbols, no arbitrary list of such symbols has been provided. The index has purposely been made extremely full and detailed. Diagraming, which some teachers find valuable and others prefer to dispense with, is given concise treatment in an appendix.

Like all other authors of handbooks of English and texts in composition, we are indebted to many predecessors. Every student of grammar and usage must acknowledge general and often specific indebtedness to such authorities as Kittredge, Curme, Jespersen, Fries, Pooley, Hook, and Kennedy. Moreover, numerous other scholars who must remain unnamed have helped to shape our approaches to various problems through their contributions to various journals. So far as we could, when we were aware of a specific debt we recorded the fact at the appropriate place. But the obligations that we owe to the authors of many books that have helped to shape our views of composition over many years, and to our colleagues from whose wisdom we have also profited, are hard to pin down and, though large, cannot be specifically acknowledged.

We must, however, express our gratitude to professors over the country who read and criticized the work in manuscript. Much that is good in this book results from their suggestions. We confess the faults as our own. We are grateful to the staffs of the Library of Carnegie Institute of Technology and the Library of the University of Connecticut for advice and help of varied kinds generously given. Finally we thank our wives, Gertrude C. Wright and Kathleen Gibson McPeek, and L. Maeve McPeek Ward, who have suffered with us from the inception of the work and who have helped us with valuable criticism and other aid in various parts of the book.

James A. S. McPeek
Austin Wright

Storrs, Conn.
Pittsburgh, Pa.
December, 1955

ACKNOWLEDGMENTS

The authors are grateful to various publishers and persons for permission to reproduce material as follows:

George Allen & Unwin Ltd.: For the quotations from *Education and the Social Order, Mysticism and Logic,* and *Sceptical Essays* by Bertrand Russell. Used by permission of George Allen & Unwin Ltd.

The American Magazine: For the quotation from "All Arted Uppe" by Don Marquis from *The American Magazine*, January, 1929. Used by permission of *The American Magazine.*

The American Scholar: For the quotation from "The American Student as I See Him" by Gilbert Highet from *The American Scholar*, Autumn, 1941. Used by permission of *The American Scholar.*

American Technical Society: For the quotation from "The Gettysburg Address Rephrased" from *Tech Training.* Used by permission of the American Technical Society.

Appleton-Century-Crofts, Inc.: For the quotation from *Teaching English Usage* by Robert C. Pooley. Copyright 1946 by The National Council of Teachers of English (English Monograph No. 16). Used by permission of Appleton-Century-Crofts, Inc.

The Atlantic Monthly: For the quotation from "If the Atomic Bomb Had Not Been Used" by Karl T. Compton from *The Atlantic Monthly*, December, 1946. Used by permission of *The Atlantic Monthly.*

Brandt & Brandt: For the quotation from "Enoch Soames" in *Seven Men* by Sir Max Beerbohm. Published by Alfred A. Knopf, Inc. Copyright 1920 by Max Beerbohm. Used by permission of Brandt & Brandt.

Cambridge University Press: For the quotation from *A Mathematician's Apology* by G. H. Hardy. Used by permission of Cambridge University Press.

Chatto and Windus Ltd.: For the quotation from *Eminent Victorians* by Lytton Strachey. Used by permission of Chatto and Windus Ltd.

Columbia University Press: For the quotations from *Modern Science and Modern Man* by James B. Conant. Used by permission of Columbia University Press.

Henry Steele Commager: For the quotation from "Still 'The Hope of the Human Race'" by Henry Steele Commager from *The New York Times Magazine*, July 20, 1941.

Acknowledgments

William H. Cornog: For the quotation from "Bread and Hyacinths" by William H. Cornog from *School and Society*, July 8, 1950.

Coward-McCann, Inc.: For the quotation from *All Sorts and Kinds* by Christopher La Farge. Copyright 1940, 1942, 1943, 1945, 1948, 1949 by Christopher La Farge. Used by permission of Coward-McCann, Inc.

Doubleday & Company, Inc.: For the quotations from *The Old Wives' Tale* by Arnold Bennett, copyright 1911 by Doubleday & Company, Inc., *Fifty Modern English Writers* by W. Somerset Maugham, copyright 1933 by Doubleday & Company, Inc., and "All Arted Uppe" by Don Marquis from *The American Magazine*, January, 1929. Used by permission of Doubleday & Company, Inc.

The Dryden Press, Inc.: For the quotations from *The Analysis of Propaganda* by William Hummel and Keith Huntress. Copyright 1949 by William Hummel and Keith Huntress. Reprinted by special permission.

E. P. Dutton & Co., Inc.: For the quotations from *The Private Papers of Henry Ryecroft* by George Gissing, Everyman's Library, published by E. P. Dutton & Co., Inc., and *The Flowering of New England* by Van Wyck Brooks, American Edition Everyman's Library, published by E. P. Dutton & Co., Inc. Copyright 1936, 1952, by Van Wyck Brooks.

Faber and Faber Limited: For the poem "Morning Sun" from *Collected Poems 1925–1948* by Louis Macneice. Used by permission of Faber and Faber Limited.

Fortune: For the quotations from *Fortune*, October, 1930, and February, 1940, copyright 1930, 1940 by Time, Inc. Used by permission of *Fortune.*

Harcourt, Brace and Company, Inc.: For the quotations from *Three Plays* by William Saroyan, copyright 1939, 1940, *Like Summer's Cloud* by Charles S. Brooks, *Main Street* by Sinclair Lewis, *Language in Thought and Action* by S. I. Hayakawa, *Eminent Victorians* and *Queen Victoria* by Lytton Strachey, *Saints and Strangers* by George F. Willison, *The Death of the Moth and Other Essays* and *To the Lighthouse* by Virginia Woolf. Used by permission of Harcourt, Brace and Company, Inc.

Harper & Brothers: For the quotations from *This Shakespeare Industry* by Ivor Brown and George Fearon, "Who Is Loyal to America?" by Henry Steele Commager from *Harper's Magazine*, September, 1947, *The Unquiet Grave* by Cyril Connolly, *Music at Night* by Aldous Huxley, *On Living in a Revolution* by Julian Huxley, "When Squirrel Meets Squirrel" by Burgess Johnson from *Harper's Magazine*, January, 1938, *The Mind in the Making* by James Harvey Robinson, *One Man's Meat* by E. B. White, *You Can't Go Home Again* by Thomas Wolfe. Used by permission of Harper & Brothers.

Harvard University Press: For the quotations from *Education in a Divided World* by James Bryant Conant, copyright 1948, *Education and World Tragedy* by Howard Mumford Jones, copyright 1946, *Chaucer and*

His Poetry by George Lyman Kittredge, copyright 1915, 1946. Copyright by the President and Fellows of Harvard College. Reprinted by permission of Harvard University Press.

William Heinemann Ltd.: For the quotation from "Enoch Soames" from *Seven Men* by Sir Max Beerbohm. Used by permission of William Heinemann Ltd.

Houghton Mifflin Company: For the selections from *Damaged Souls* by Gamaliel Bradford, "Small-Town Middle-Westerner" by Willis Fisher from *Who Owns America?* edited by Herbert Agar and Allen Tate, and *The Road to Xanadu* by John L. Lowes. Used by permission of Houghton Mifflin Company.

William Hummel and Keith Huntress: For the quotations from *The Analysis of Propaganda* by William Hummel and Keith Huntress. Copyright 1949 by William Hummel and Keith Huntress.

Alfred A. Knopf, Inc.: For the quotations from *The American Experience* by Henry Bamford Parkes, and *Lincoln and His Generals* by T. Harry Williams. Used by permission of Alfred A. Knopf, Inc.

Little, Brown & Company: For the quotations from *Origins of the American Revolution* by John C. Miller. Used by permission of Little, Brown & Company.

Liveright Publishing Corporation: For the quotation from *Education and the Good Life* by Bertrand Russell, copyright R-1953 by Bertrand Russell. Used by permission of Liveright Publishers.

Macdonald & Company (Publishers) Ltd.: For the quotation from *Guy and Pauline* by Sir Compton Mackenzie. Used by permission of Macdonald & Company (Publishers) Ltd.

The Macmillan Company: For the quotations from *American Government and Politics* by Charles A. Beard, copyright 1944, and *The Meeting of East and West* by F. S. C. Northrop, copyright 1946. Used by permission of The Macmillan Company.

W. Somerset Maugham: For the quotation from *Fifty Modern English Writers* by W. Somerset Maugham. Used by permission of W. Somerset Maugham.

McGraw-Hill Book Company, Inc.: For the quotation from *Crisis in Education* by Bernard Iddings Bell, copyright 1949 by Bernard Iddings Bell. Used by permission of McGraw-Hill Book Company, Inc.

G. & C. Merriam Company: For the quotations from *An Outline for Dictionary Study*, copyright 1954, and *Webster's New Collegiate Dictionary*, copyright 1949, 1951, 1953. Used by permission of G. & C. Merriam Company.

William Morrow & Company, Inc.: For the quotations from *Atoms in Action* by George Russell Harrison, copyright 1937, 1938, 1939, 1941, 1949 by George Russell Harrison. Used by permission of William Morrow & Company, Inc.

The New York Times: For the quotations from "Canada's Stratford" by Brooks Atkinson from *The New York Times,* July 19, 1953, and "Still 'The Hope of the Human Race'" by Henry Steele Commager from *The New York Times Magazine,* July 20, 1941. Used by permission of *The New York Times.*

The New Yorker: For the quotations from "Soapland" by James Thurber, copyright 1948 by James Thurber, "Farewell, My Lovely" by Lee Strout White, and "The Talk of the Town," January 3, 1953. Used by permission of *The New Yorker.*

W. W. Norton & Company, Inc.: For the quotations from *The Way of an Investigator* by Walter B. Cannon and *Mysticism and Logic* and *Sceptical Essays* by Bertrand Russell. Used by permission of W. W. Norton & Company, Inc.

Oxford University Press, Inc.: For the quotations from *The Sea Around Us* by Rachel L. Carson, copyright 1951 by Rachel L. Carson, *A Dictionary of Modern English Usage* by H. W. Fowler, *Poetry for You* by C. Day Lewis, and *Civilization on Trial* by Arnold J. Toynbee. Used by permission of Oxford University Press, Inc.

The Pennsylvania State University: For the quotations from *Penn State Yankee: The Autobiography of Fred Lewis Pattee.* Used by permission.

G. P. Putnam's Sons: For the quotation from *Night Club* by Katharine Brush, copyright 1929 by Katharine Brush, published by Minton Balch Co., and *Blood, Sweat, and Tears* by Winston S. Churchill, copyright 1941 by Winston S. Churchill. Used by permission of G. P. Putnam's Sons.

Random House, Inc.: For the poem "Morning Sun" from *Poems, 1925–1940* by Louis Macneice, copyright 1937 by Louis Macneice. Used by permission of Random House, Inc.

Rinehart & Company, Inc.: For the quotations from the Introduction by Rodman W. Paul to the Rinehart Edition of *Roughing It* by Mark Twain, copyright 1953 by Rodman W. Paul, and "Golden Wedding" from *Iowa Interiors* by Ruth Suckow. Used by permission of Rinehart & Company, Inc.

Charles Scribner's Sons: For the quotations from *Man, Real and Ideal* by Edwin Grant Conklin, *The Enjoyment of Poetry* by Max Eastman, *R. E. Lee: A Biography,* Vol. III, by Douglas Southall Freeman, *Virginibus Puerisque and Other Papers* by Robert Louis Stevenson, and *Of Time and the River* by Thomas Wolfe. Used by permission of Charles Scribner's Sons.

The Society for the Advancement of Education: For the quotation from "Bread and Hyacinths" by William H. Cornog from *School and Society,* July 8, 1950. Used by permission of The Society for the Advancement of Education.

Simon and Schuster, Inc.: For the quotation from *How to Read a Book* by Mortimer J. Adler. Used by permission of Simon and Schuster, Inc.

James Thurber: For the quotations from "Soapland" by James Thurber, from *The New Yorker*, copyright 1948 by James Thurber.

The Viking Press, Inc.: For the quotations from *Modern Man Is Obsolete* by Norman Cousins, *A Portrait of the Artist as a Young Man* by James Joyce, and *Science Today and Tomorrow* by Waldemar Kaempffert. Used by permission of The Viking Press, Inc.

A. P. Watt & Son: For the quotation from *The Old Wives' Tale* by Arnold Bennett, used by permission of the Public Trustee, and for the quotation from *Fifty Modern English Writers* by W. Somerset Maugham, used by permission of W. Somerset Maugham.

G. P. Wells: For the quotation from *The Outline of History* by H. G. Wells. Used by permission of G. P. Wells.

Leonard Woolf: For the quotation from "Street Haunting" from *The Death of the Moth and Other Essays* by Virginia Woolf. Used by permission of Leonard Woolf.

Yale University Press: For the quotation from *The English Dramatic Lyric, 1603–1642* by William R. Bowden. Used by permission of Yale University Press.

Acknowledgments

Simon and Schuster, Inc.: For the quotation from *How to Read a Book* by Mortimer J. Adler. Used by permission of Simon and Schuster, Inc.

James Thurber: For the quotation from "[illegible]," by James Thurber; © 1948 *The New Yorker*, copyright 1948 by James Thurber.

The Viking Press, Inc.: For the quotations from *Modern Man Is Obsolete* by Norman Cousins; *A Portrait of the Artist as a Young Man* by James Joyce; and *Science Today and Tomorrow* by Waldemar Kaempffert. Used by permission of The Viking Press, Inc.

A. P. Watt & Son: For the quotation from *The Old Wives' Tale* by Arnold Bennett, used by permission of the Public Trustee; and for the quotation from *Fifty Modern English Writers* by W. Somerset Maugham, used by permission of W. Somerset Maugham.

[illegible]: For the quotation from *The Outline of History* by H. G. Wells. Used by permission of G. P. Wells.

Leonard Woolf: For the quotation from "Street Haunting" from *The Death of the Moth and Other Essays* by Virginia Woolf. Used by permission of Leonard Woolf and [illegible].

Yale University Press: For the quotation from *The English Dramatic Lyric, 1603–1642* by William R. Bowden. Used by permission of Yale University Press.

CONTENTS

Chapter I: THE WHOLE COMPOSITION

Chapter 2: STRUCTURE OF SENTENCES

Chapter 3: PARTS OF SPEECH AND SENTENCE STRUCTURE

Chapter 5: PUNCTUATION AND MECHANICS

Chapter 6: THE PARAGRAPH

Chapter 7: DICTION

Chapter 8: SPELLING

Chapter 9: USE OF THE LIBRARY

Chapter 10: THE RESEARCH PAPER

Chapter 11: LETTER WRITING

HANDBOOK OF ENGLISH

Chapter I

THE WHOLE COMPOSITION

The use of words is the great social art, and we spend all our lives practicing it. Whether we use words poorly or effectively depends to a great extent on our training. The purpose of this book is to help you in learning how to use words effectively. Training in basic principles and rules, knowledge of words and the ways they function, and continual practice are needed for this subject. The results of such discipline for you as a student will be found in an increased understanding of other people and their ideas, a richer grasp of the meaning of literature of all sorts, and more effective communication of your own thought.

The importance of mastering this art of expression cannot be overemphasized. Your use of language in writing and speaking indicates your place in society. It not only tells others what you are thinking but also tells them what you are. Words and the ways you use them are the clothing of your personality. Just as you aspire to dress correctly, so you try to use words acceptably. Custom prescribes manners of dress for various times and places; it likewise prescribes certain styles in speech and writing, formal and informal. Within these limits, within the framework of the rules, there is still room for the expression of the self. To learn the rules of generally approved expression in writing and speaking,

NOTE: The student will find many aids to mechanics of style and good usage in style manuals and dictionaries, and will learn for himself that neither style nor usage is rigidly fixed: both dictionaries and style manuals disagree on certain points or admit varying conventions. But everyone can achieve a desirable consistency by selecting and always using one particular choice among those conventions. This text follows, in the main, *Webster's New International Dictionary* and *A Manual of Style* (Chicago, 1949).

and to express your own nature within the compass of these rules, should be your aim in the study of English composition.

Your experience in using language in college will be both individual and social, personal and impersonal. In particular, you will find it necessary to do many sorts of writing, varying from relatively informal letters and biographical themes to formal investigative reports and letters of application. A great part of your expression in the writing of many themes as well as in most of your social relationships will be colored by your personality. In a careful report of fact your personality may show to advantage only in exact choice of words and good organization; but in general it may be said that all writing is a product of what a person is, modified by his understanding of his subject matter.

1. YOU AND YOUR SUBJECT

"What shall I write about?" The answer to this question will be given in part by your instructor. But after he has assigned a general or even a specific subject and discussed it, the problem of what you will say remains with you. In a large view you have two sources of subject matter, your inner world and the outer world, and you will find constant occasion to draw upon both.

Your inner world is the one world you know better than anyone else can. Though there may be others somewhat like you, there is only one you, seeing the world with your sensibilities, from your standpoint. You have already acquired certain tastes and opinions that, with your inherited characteristics, have made you what you are. Now is a good time to take stock of yourself, of that inner world. What sort of person are you? What are your tastes in sports, in music, in reading? What are your hobbies, your avocations? What is your fundamental outlook on life? Are you deeply religious? philosophical? What are your aims and how far have you come toward realizing them? To ask (and answer) these and like questions will serve not only to help orient you but also to uncover an abundant store of subject matter waiting for you to impose limits on it and to give it form.

Your second source of subject matter, the outer world, is of course everything else. The outer world is the contemporary scene, political, social, scientific, economic, religious, artistic. It is the historic past and the visionary future. This subject matter is limitless in extent or bounded only by your vision. It is the great telescope at the Palomar Observatory, the ship of a Pharaoh centuries buried. It is a presidential election, a college tea, the latest football game, the World Series, your favorite comedian or choice in dance bands. It is a poet or statesman. It is fiber, diamonds, heavy water in chemistry, atomic power for automobiles. It is ideas, problems, world issues. There is no lack of things to write about: your task is to select those subjects that are most interesting to you and your potential reader, to gather exact information about them, to organize that information, and finally to reflect in your own words your responses or opinions in writing about them.

Observe that though everyone is fascinated by the strange and unfamiliar, novelty is not essential. The very familiar may be a good subject if looked at with fresh insight. Sir Walter Scott once wrote that he was able to do the "Big Bow-wow strain" himself—in other words to write the startling or sensational—but that Jane Austen could make interesting even the commonplace. Few are geniuses, but each of you knows certain things well; and you will do well to write about those things rather than about things remote from your experience. What is essential for good writing is the proper limitation of your subject and the selection of significant detail within the limits of that subject.

1A. Limiting Your Subject: Unity and the Controlling Idea or Thesis

Your experience, reading, and observation will furnish you with ample subject matter—an endless store of raw material. For comprehension, this subject matter must be limited to specific units, each one, as the word *unit* implies, complete in itself. All writing should have unity, from the largest work that the mind can conceive down to the smallest unit of discourse; and all the best works do have unity, an organic unity like that of a living body in which each part and every cell help to constitute the whole being. This means, in practice, that you must think carefully what part of your experience or what aspect of a subject you are going to write about, and then you must concentrate on that, making use of other material only when it validly illustrates your subject. This is the first step in writing any expository work, whether it be an essay, a report, an application for a position, an answer to an examination question, or a theme. The procedure in writing a poem or a story may vary somewhat, but the end is the same: a unity of concept or idea must be achieved. This is, indeed, the meaning of *theme*: the various compositions you will be asked to write are called *themes* because they are supposed to be devoted to one concept, limited to one controlling idea. If you can express your controlling idea or thesis in one sentence, and if all the thought of the theme helps to develop that idea cogently, your theme will have unity in the large sense. It is often desirable to state this controlling idea at some point in your opening paragraph, as we shall shortly see; but sometimes this controlling idea is implied by the nature of the subject matter rather than directly stated. But it must be evident: any reader must be able to grasp your controlling idea without difficulty regardless of the means by which it is expressed.

There is a great difference, then, between subject matter and a subject for a theme. Thus "Collecting" cannot be considered as a subject for a theme; but it suggests many subjects, any one of which may be large enough (or too large) for a short theme. It would be dull and absurd to attempt a theme listing types of collections from butterflies to taxes. Even topics like "Collecting Antiques" or "Collecting Stamps," though more limited, still present fields too large for any short composition. "My Collection of Stamps" or "My Collection of Clocks" or similar topics bearing on special collections of miniature animals, ship models, matchboxes, marbles, calendar girls, or blue bottles may, with judicious selection and arrangement, afford good subject matter for a theme. But even when the subject matter is thus reduced, when you begin planning your theme you may find it desirable to limit that material still further—perhaps to certain choice specimens. Not everything will fit the controlling idea that has begun to take shape in your mind.

1B. The Title

Once you have your limited subject, you may begin thinking about an effective title. The right title will probably not occur to you immediately. The mere subject itself as a title may not attract the attention of a reader. Neither "My Stamp Collection" nor any of its wooden variants ("Why I Like to Collect Stamps," "My Interest in Stamp-Collecting," "My Hobby") will spark a gleam of anticipation in a reader's eye. Perhaps a title like "A One-Inch-Square Magic Carpet" or "A Gateway to Contentment" may challenge him. A title need not be startling (consider the titles of the various works you read); but it should, if possible, engage interest, and it must fit the subject matter.

Do not use a pronoun to refer to your title in the opening sentence of any piece of work. Do not say, "This is a subject that has interested me for several years," or, "I have been interested in this subject . . ." If you must begin so baldly (there are better openings), use the key words of the subject matter itself: "My stamp collection has taken a great part of my spare time . . . ," or, "I have collected stamps ever since . . ."

EXERCISES

1. Limiting the subject. The following subjects might possibly be suitable for works of book length but are much too large for either long or short themes. Select five of these and, choosing certain aspects of each, limit them in size first to subjects that could be handled in long themes of two to three thousand words and then to subjects suitable for short themes of around five hundred words. For example, the general subject of *radio* could be developed in a work of book length; a theme on the topic, even a long theme, would be too general to be of value. Long themes could be written on various aspects of the subject, such as the invention of the radio, radio advertising, the radio and education. But all these in turn are too extensive for short themes. Short themes

could be written on such topics as a favorite radio program, a radio detective, the five-minute commercial.

Architecture
The Red Cross
Teachers
The United Nations
The Art of Painting (Water Colors)
Abraham Lincoln
The Korean War
American Wild Flowers (Birds)
College Fraternities
Reading
Religion
The Community Chest
Tobacco (Tomatoes, Corn, Apples)
Football
Aviation
Television

2. Assume that you are going to write a series of themes based on your own experience. Select and properly limit those subjects that would be most likely to interest your readers. In making up your list, consider such points as your family, your character, your schooling, your tastes, your reasons for coming to college.

3. What is the controlling thesis of Miss Carson's "Petroleum: A Legacy of Ancient Seas" (p. 35 of this text)? Is the idea specifically expressed anywhere in this essay? Can you phrase it in one sentence?

4. Study the titles of the several articles in the current issue of *Harper's* or the *Atlantic* in your library.

a) Which two have the most attraction for you? Why? Which two do you like least?

b) Read the two essays with the attractive titles. Are the titles well chosen? Why?

5. Devise titles more expressive of the subject and more attractive to the reader to replace the following vague titles:

My Hobby (or Avocation)
My Pet Aversion
My Interest in Music
My Religion
My Life Story
My Favorite Reading
My Travels
My High-School Memories

2. YOU AND YOUR READER

Every real work of art looks as if it were made by one person for another.—W. R. LETHABY.

Every successful effort at communication carries the feeling of being particular and personal. Practically everything you write should be aimed directly at a reader, and for you to ignore that reader would be as foolish as for a manufacturer to ignore the tastes of the buying public. No matter how much your own work may please you, no matter how carefully thought out or how beautifully phrased it may seem to you, it is a failure if it does not produce the desired effect on your reader.

One of your most important concerns in writing must be this intended reader, the audience for whom your work is planned. Thus if on a visit home you are invited to address a high-school class, you will talk, not down to them, nor in terms of slang, but in good clear English that they will understand; you will not antagonize them by talking over their heads. If you sometime write an article for a learned journal, you will carefully avoid saying the obvious about your subject or loading it down with information already available. Every writing or speaking assignment is a problem in communication, a problem of psychological approach of writer to reader, of speaker to audience. Again and again you will be required to write on one occasion for a special reader, a reader quite different from the one addressed on another occasion.

In order to communicate effectively with your reader, you must try to understand him. Tabloid newspapers are written for the type of reader who sits in the subway and likes sensationalism with pictures. More sedate newspapers, like *The New York Times,* are written for people who like thoughtful editorials, stock reports, and "all the news that's fit to print." All magazines, books, articles, and stories are written for specific audiences. Who is the reader whose attention you are trying to reach? What are his interests? What is his cultural level? What is his relationship to you? Are you buying something from him or selling to him? What is his emotional state?

After you have answered (in your own mind) some of these questions about your reader, you may begin thinking about the approach best designed to win his attention, and new questions will occur to you: Should you start with the most important details first (as in news stories), or can you think of some interesting point perhaps tied in with his hobbies or special interests that may appeal to him? Should your approach be pleasantly informal or serious and dignified? What sort of language should you use? What organization of your thought will be most effective in holding his interest after you have caught it? The answers to all these questions depend on the nature of the reader, the subject matter, and the occasion.

Of course much of your writing in freshman English composition will be aimed at a specific reader, your instructor. But it is inhibiting to write always thinking of the one reader. You can please your instructor by writing with other audiences in mind. For example, think of yourself addressing an engineering or philosophy club or the student senate, or writing an essay or article for *Field and Stream, Nature Study, Holiday,* or any other magazine of special interest to you. Here once more you will have to study carefully the nature of the publication and fit your subject matter and style to its audience.

2A. Tone

This concern with subject matter and audience will determine the tone of your writing. Tone may be defined as a writer's attitude toward his subject and toward his audience as reflected in his work. Just as a tone of voice may modify meaning, so a piece of writing carries with it as part of its texture a tone that reflects the intention of the writer. The writing of letters offers a simple but effective illustration: think of the differences in tone between a letter to a girl or boy you have just met and wish to impress and a letter to your sister or brother; between a letter to a friend and a letter of application; between a letter to your roommate and one to the president of your college; between a letter of congratulation and one of condolence. Successful writers and speakers always adjust their tone to fit both their audience and their subject matter. A grave and dignified occasion calls for a serious, formal tone of address; a festive occasion calls for a tone of good fellowship. In considering your reader then, in writing any theme, you will be governing the tone of what you write. Unless you have a gift for humor and irony, it would be better not to attempt a humorous or ironic tone. Again, try to sustain the tone you have chosen. If your paper is formal, maintain the same tone throughout the whole work; if it is informal, keep it informal: do not suddenly change to a formal style. (For further consideration of the nature of tone, and illustrative paragraphs, see The Paragraph, Chapter 6.)

2B. Tone and Diction

Tone depends on diction—that is, the language you use and the ways you use it. To write effectively, you must learn to choose the right word for the right place. This aim involves for everyone a continuing study of the best uses of words—a continuing study in the sense that you began it when you first learned to talk and will finish it only when you have no need for further expression. Already you are well aware that there are certain kinds of speech that educated people must avoid or use with discretion. In learning to select the right word for the right place, you must become yet more aware of the differences in the various types of speech that compose our language.

2B 1. Levels and Varieties of English. Broadly speaking, there are from a cultural point of view two main levels of English writing and speaking, namely, standard English and nonstandard English.[1] Standard English, the language of educated writers and speakers, embraces several functional and interrelated varieties of language, such as standard colloquial English, letter writing, public speaking, expository writing, criticism, and literary writing. These varieties, depending on their degree of formality or familiarity, fall roughly into two classes of expression, namely, formal and informal English. Thus standard colloquial English (that is, literally, conversational English), though it may become highly formal in certain situations (as in a Senate debate), is generally informal in manner and, as usually defined, is the language

[1] The authors are specially indebted in this discussion of the levels of English to Professor John S. Kenyon's excellent article, "Cultural Levels and Functional Varieties of English," *College English,* X (1948–49), pp. 31–39.

of familiar conversation, ways of expression acceptable for educated speakers but not suitable in formal writing. Letter writing varies from the familiarity of a friendly letter to the dignified reserve or formality of many business letters and letters of application. Similar variation from the informal to the formal exists in all varieties of standard English. It must always be remembered that both formal and informal English are good English when used in the right places. Appropriateness is the only measure.

2B 2. Standard Formal English. Standard formal English follows rather precise rules—always, of course, as with all kinds of language, subject to change with the passing of time. Its sentences tend to be long and often complex in structure. It usually avoids elliptical constructions, the use of the second person, and contractions. Its vocabulary is often learned, though some of the best formal literature, as in the Psalms of the Bible and Lincoln's Gettysburg Address, has very simple diction. It avoids familiar expressions and makes little or no use of slang or of dialect terms. [This paragraph and the preceding one show characteristics of formal English.]

2B 3. Standard Informal English. Standard informal English offers you more freedom of expression. But don't take a chance on using slang freely or on slipping often into dialect or folkways of speaking except when you wish to represent a character who is using nonstandard speech. Use contractions, elliptical constructions (with judgment), and the second person. Talk naturally, and write more or less as if you were talking. [This paragraph has some of the marks of informal English. Notice that the change from the formal style of the preceding two paragraphs (or, in reverse, from the informal style of this paragraph to the style of the preceding two) is not pleasing: tone is violated. You may mix the two styles to some degree, as is done in this textbook and many others; but in general avoid changing completely from one style to the other in the same piece of writing.]

2B 4. Nonstandard English. Nonstandard English is a term describing the varieties of language used by the careless, the poorly educated, and the illiterate. The varieties of nonstandard English, such as narrowly dialectal English, slang (used in excess), and illiterate English, have their own ways of expression, which though acceptable on their own level, are not appropriate to the level of standard English. Persons who habitually use nonstandard English cannot expect to be successful in most professions. As you study the most effective ways of writing and speaking, you must learn to avoid the slang and the speech habits of the nonstandard level. (For further consideration of the levels of usage and passages illustrating their natures, see Diction, Chapter 7.)

3. THE WELL-ORDERED THEME: UNITY THROUGH COHERENCE

From the time when you first heard "The Farmer in the Dell" with its unbroken chain of relationships from the farmer to the cheese, you have been aware of the advantages of order. If you did not always docilely put the round peg in the round hole, you seldom put in the square peg without being aware of what you were doing. Order beats in our blood and brain, and our lives are a long attempt to reshape the chaos of things to our personal concept of what they ought to be. Hence in ordering your ideas in writing, you are merely following a natural bent. A well-ordered theme is like a well-planned house. Just as each room has its special purpose in relationship to the whole, so each paragraph (see The Paragraph, Chapter 6) has its special function in relationship to the whole theme. Order in a theme is often spoken of as coherence. In a well-ordered theme all the parts cohere; that is, they stick together to form unity. Paragraph leads to paragraph and sentence follows sentence in a chain of thought broken only by punctuation. Coherence is one of the main ways of securing unity.

3A. Methods of Coherence

In ordering the thought of a theme we may use several schemes of arrangement. If our theme is narrative, as for example a biographical sketch, we may follow the natural time order of events, telling each event as it occurs, though we may vary this pattern somewhat by beginning near the middle of the complete story and summing up the early events through recollections (the flashback device of the moving pictures). If our theme is the explanation of a process—for example, making a model airplane, cooking a steak, growing tomatoes—we shall also use the time order of the steps in the process. If our theme is the explanation of an opinion or an idea—for example, the use of federal funds in education, or the meaning of democracy—we may arrange our thought in different ways, depending on the controlling idea of the theme and the subject matter. Ordinarily, in such themes, we shall arrange the various divisions of our thought in climactic order, proceeding from the less important to the more and most important ideas. Or we may proceed from cause to a study of effects, as when John Hersey wrote his great narrative on the destruction of Hiroshima, or from effect to cause, as in many investigations in our conquest of diseases or in detective fiction. We may proceed by comparison and contrast, as in a theme comparing and contrasting the respective skills needed in playing ping-pong and tennis, or by presenting positive and negative views of an idea, as in some editorials. We may proceed by analysis, breaking our idea down into its component parts, as when a historian explains the separate elements that make up the Bill of Rights; or by illustration, citing examples of the situation or condition presented in the controlling thesis. Or our subject matter may invite a combination of these methods. The subject matter and the purpose of the theme will dictate the methods used. This careful organization of the thought structure of a theme is carried over, of course, into its separate paragraphs, the material of each paragraph being organized in schemes like those described above. You will find it helpful to study these schemes of thought arrangement in the chapter on paragraphing (Chapter 6).

Lack of careful attention to the demands for unity and careful organization results in a performance bewildering to the reader—if he is patient enough to continue reading. Here is a student theme that fails to meet these demands:

NEW HAVEN

Unless some unpleasant happening is connected with your home town, the place of a person's birth always remains more or less dear to him. Such is true with me. Although I was not born in New Haven, it is my home town by adoption. I was born in New York City but I only lived there for the first two years of my life. During my pre-army life, I took New Haven for granted. I never gave it much thought other than it was the city where I lived. Then other cities looked greener to me. Now I really like New Haven and not only because it is where I live.

Looking at New Haven, not as a native but as a prospective buyer of property, let me evaluate its good points and its poor points. New Haven is a city with approximately 165,000 people. The population increased during the war due to the influx of war workers. New Haven is governed by a Mayor and a Board of Aldermen. The mayor, aldermen, and other city officials are elected every two years by popular vote. The mayor receives a yearly salary of 10,000 dollars. The aldermen receive no compensation other than the honor of their position. (Also the opportunity to tear up a traffic ticket.) Politically New Haven is not very progressive. Until November 1945, New Haven had the same mayor for fourteen years. Personally I think that fourteen years is too long for any one person to be in office. There is the temptation to grow lax, to worry about the election.

New Haven is well planned. The streets radiate from a central hub to the outskirts of the city. Most of the streets are paved with macadam and are in good repair. But there are several streets that are in terrible shape. Sylvan Avenue, for example, is a hazard for the motorist. The main fault with New Haven's streets are the trolley tracks. Not only do the shiny rails offer an excellent surface for skidding, but the edge of the road around the rail is continually chipping and causing holes in the pavement to form. Then too the policy of the street department seems to be in repairing only the main streets and those running through the wealthy sections. New Haven has its slums and its "Nob Hill" sections. The slum districts are not very extensive but what the slums lack in area they make up in intensity. These slum areas should all be razed and new homes built. The residential sections are very nice and are in different parts of the city. There are only a few large estates in New Haven as most of the homes are small. Yale University adds much beauty with its Gothic buildings. New Haven has many large and beautiful parks that are scattered throughout its entirety. Though known as the "Elm City," New Haven does not have many of the majestic and stately elms left. The hurricane of 1939 finished those that managed to escape the march of civilization.

At present New Haven is conducting a survey of its educational system. About time! for New Haven is in a deplorable condition educationally There is only one high school that offers academic courses in New Haven. To accommodate all the students, it is necessary to divide the student body. Seniors and juniors go to school during the morning and freshmen and sophomores go during the afternoon. The teachers are underpaid. (That is what they say.)

As I like what I see in New Haven, I am going to buy a home and settle there. That is if it is possible to find a house.

This theme begins with a title that needs a book for its development. The student's guiding purpose is somewhat uncertain. After an opening paragraph with a personal approach centered around his liking for New Haven as his adopted home town, he discards that approach for a new one, that of a nonnative prospective buyer of property, reviewing the good and the bad points of the city.

This appears to be his guiding purpose. But he does not make clear whether he regards the size of the city and its political system as essentially good or bad points. He then starts to tell us that New Haven is well planned, but gets lost on the shiny trolley tracks and in a maze of slums, fine residences, and Yale University. To be sure, slums often abut on good residential sections, but the writer observes that the slums are in a different part of town. In any event, none of these details has any relation to his supposed paragraph topic, the plan of the city, which is discarded after the first two sentences in the paragraph. In the end, when he tells us that he likes what he sees, he leaves us to assume that he likes the good features of the city, not the bad. A little care in marshaling the good points of the city as opposed to the bad could have made this into a well-organized theme.

And now let us look at a theme that shows evidence of careful planning:

OAKWOOD HALL FIVE YEARS AGO

Oh, the heartbreak of being left alone in a strange place at the tender age of fourteen! Make no mistake—these were not my sentiments, but those of my mother. My only acquaintance at school was of the same mind as I. We wished to establish ourselves immediately and get our families started on their homeward journey as soon as was decently possible. It was their opinion that we were being brave and unselfish by wishing to spare them a tedious parting scene. In reality we were eager to be on our own, to be independent, to seek adventure in our new environment. This adventurous spirit was short-lived. At the end of a week we had learned that our own private worries were not the only concern of the headmistress; we had learned that the odor of frying hamburgers rising from the kitchen meant that it was Wednesday, and that no odor at all meant a cold Sunday night supper.

The food was our greatest problem. If it was bad there would be talk of a hunger strike; if it was good there were complaints about the weight gained. Although I never had the pleasure of meeting the cook, I know she was one of those fortunates or unfortunates, according to one's lights, possessing a one-track mind. For days at a time we would have grapefruit, for example, for breakfast, lunch, and dinner; other times every dish from the soup to the dessert would be sprinkled with nuts, or garnished with whipped cream, or flavored with onions, according to the school of cookery to which she had dedicated herself that week. We were permitted to keep fruit and plain crackers in our rooms to satisfy our appetites between meals. The great game of student against proctor was to see how much contraband food we could smuggle in without detection. Any pounds added as a result of eating forbidden cakes and pies were considered worth the price.

Rule-breaking was the main recreation and occasional ruination of many a true Oakwood Haller. To appreciate the rare skill required to make a success of this perilous game, one must have a fundamental knowledge of the laws of the institution. They were for the most part negative: no getting up and no talking after "lights out," no smoking, no "young gentlemen callers," no visiting at the homes of the day-students, no chewing gum, no cosmetics, and a minimum of noise in the building. The relatively few positive rules required the wearing of a hat and gloves off campus, promptness for meals, classes, and assemblies, keeping uniforms immaculate, and strict observance of all rules of etiquette.

Wednesday afternoon, when permission was granted to go into the village unchaperoned for incidental shopping, was considered the proper time to indulge in a little freedom. With the willing and able help of the day-students, it became a simple matter to visit their homes, smoke a forbidden cigarette, perhaps meet a "town boy," or put on a little lipstick for a short time just to get the feel of it again. The danger and excitement of dodging people connected with the school usually proved so exhausting that the tamer pastime of breaking "light" rules was more popular. Few people were ever ready for bed when the bell rang, and I, for one, soon learned to perform almost any task in the dark. I could scrub my teeth, take a bath, put up my hair, and even write in total blackness. In fact I think I have an overdeveloped sense of touch and of hearing as a result of my nocturnal adventures. Conversation went on far, far into the night. After the hour of 10:00 P.M. roommates took it upon themselves to settle the problems of this world and of the world at large. After "lights," prowling was undertaken for all purposes from getting a fourth for bridge (played with the aid of a flashlight) to indulging in a feast of grilled cheese and olive sandwiches. If one was caught the punishment was "on campus" or "early lights."

The faculty was a worthy body with a variety of idiosyncrasies and accents, but with a remarkable similarity of reactions and purposes. Madame S—— was a slightly wicked old Frenchwoman, the only one of the entire group who had made the mistake of getting married. She had lived in Russia for some time and she spoke English with a German accent—a true internationalist. Her French blood cropped out in her extreme shoes and silly little hats, in her closely-curled, henna-ed hair, and in her delightfully risqué sense of humor. Our other friend from across the seas came from Manchester, England. As far as Miss R—— of the baggy tweeds, English complexion, and straying hair, was concerned, the American Revolution had never taken place, and American writers might just as well have written in invisible ink. But a more thorough drilling in English literature could not be obtained between here and London. The "Old South" was well represented, as were New York, New England, and the Middle West. Three slightly younger teachers, bitter, frustrated, and disappointed though they were, tried to bring a few modern methods into the tradition-bound system of teaching science, Latin, and art. They were hindered, however, by Miss B——, the old school retainer. Since she had been there twice as long as any of the others, the whole teaching body stood in fear of her. She would have none of your new-fangled ideas of education, but she succeeded in teaching many things besides mathematics in her classroom. The last member of our strange assembly, the headmistress, towered above the others both in stature and intellectual capacity. Six feet tall, she added to her height by screwing up her white hair in a knob at the crown of her head. Although she was brilliant, her intolerance, her brutal lack of tact, and her ironbound New England conscience did not fit her for the role of an understanding guide for a group of young girls.

The only recreation provided by the school itself consisted of a series of concerts and lectures, with compulsory church attendance every Sunday just to break the monotony. If a speaker or musician of the male sex was scheduled to make an appearance, a flurry of preparation occupied the faculty for days in advance of the event. When they finally gathered to meet the guest, there was present a peculiar mixture of humor and pathos. Well-worn dinner dresses had been aired and pressed into condition; the art of the local beauty parlor was apparent in the plastered-down, zig-zag coiffures; an air of brightness, expectancy, and coquetry pervaded the atmosphere.

However, it is the friendships one makes which are the lasting influences of school days—friends one sees frequently or those now scattered country wide, that come to mind in brief, poignant moments. Nostalgia for irretrievable pleasures, the possibility of meeting again, the joy of reminiscences, even in letters—all these add happiness to life throughout later years.

The controlling idea of this theme is suggested by the title. We are prepared by it for reminiscences of a school experience. The central idea is not stated at the outset, but its implication is clear and it shapes the whole: one has no doubt about the intentions of the writer.

Notice that this student has a definite plan. First she considers the adventure of coming to a new school, then, in successive paragraphs, the problems of food, the rules of the school and rule-breaking (two paragraphs), the faculty, the formal recreation provided by the school, and school friendships. And observe also how each division coheres, that is, naturally leads to the next: mention of the cold Sunday-night supper leads to the problem of food; contraband food suggests the breaking of rules as a recreation (a topic carried through two paragraphs); punishment for infraction of rules suggests authority, the faculty (and with what care the writer briefly sketches them all!); the faculty suggests an account of the school's concerts and lectures; and the last idea, that of friendships, is tied in with a statement of the controlling thesis, the pleasure of reminiscences.

EXERCISE

The following student theme lacks both unity and coherence. First, read it over to find out the main idea that the student had in mind. Using this as your controlling thesis, rewrite the theme entirely, organizing it to achieve unity of idea and coherent development of thought. Eliminate all the unnecessary detail and add details of your own invention if necessary to achieve a good organization. Give the theme a proper title.

JOB CONTRACTING

Many people consider a laborer as a person lacking so in education, ambition, and common ordinary sense that he is unable to do any other kind of work.

True, there are men like that in the construction field as well as any other. There are also the men to whom the tools of their profession are something to be skillfully mastered. These men use their picks and shovels with the same pride of craftsmanship as the artist uses his brushes.

Many of these skilled laborers are not content to work by the hour or day for a large company. They prefer to make contracts for small jobs they can do by themselves. Some laborers even have specialties and strive to become well known for them.

If a man's specialty is ditch digging he will try to confine his work to that line. When there is a job of his type open he will inspect the area to be excavated. This inspection will determine whether he will submit a bid on a job or not. If he decides to bid the inspection will tell him what points he must stipulate in his contract. The bid is the most important part of the job and if correctly made will see that the worker makes a profit. If the bid doesn't take into account such important things as early freezes in the fall and heavy rains in the spring the laborer is sure to lose money. Even the depth of the ditch must be taken into account and maps consulted to make clear the position of any underwater streams.

Some jobs have many small extra jobs that are tied to it. One extra on the digging of a ditch would be the removal of the dirt and debris after the completion of the digging. Many people want this soil for fill and if it is good top soil farmers pay high prices for it. The profit from the sale of this earth goes to the laborer and not the owner of the land. The extras on a contract tend to raise the hourly rate of pay for the laborer and he welcomes as many of them as he can get.

After the prospective bidder has taken into account all these factors he will estimate the cost of the job.

This estimate is usually, unless the bidding is very close, made to include a ten per cent profit.

From this estimate a bid is made and the lowest bidder is usually the winner of the contract. After securing the contract it is reviewed by the employer and the contractor to dispose of any questions which may arise about job method. When these preliminaries are worked out the laborer is ready to commence the job from which he derives his name.

3B. Transitional Devices and Coherence

A proper ordering of your thought is the best way to achieve coherence. But there are some helpful means of linking paragraph to paragraph and sentence to sentence that deserve your careful study. One of these is the repetition of key words and phrases, as in the following passages. These repetitions are italicized to show the use of the device. (For more extensive discussion of repetition, see Repetition, Sections 4B 1 and 65A.)

The core of the American philosophy of *government* is the *individual.* The *individual* is the source of *government,* he *makes government,* he can *unmake government.* The *individual* has *rights* and *liberties—rights* and *liberties* in society to be sure, but nevertheless *individual rights*: the *right* to worship, to speak, to write, to go about his own affairs undisturbed by the State.—HENRY STEELE COMMAGER, "Still 'The Hope of the Human Race,'" *The New York Times Magazine.*

But *power*, like control, cannot be isolated, nor is it desirable except under carefully defined circumstances. *Power* must be subordinate to *law*, unless it is to take the form of brute, irresponsible force. Here, too, we are involved in an important interrelationship, because *law* can only be derived through *government. Law* is a product of moral, judicial, executive, legislative, and administrative sanction—all of which adds up to *government.* And *government* means what it says—the process of governing.—NORMAN COUSINS, *Modern Man Is Obsolete.*

An even more common linking device is the use of pronouns, a device so familiar as hardly to need illustration. (For definition of the pronoun, its kinds and functions, see Section 14.) The use of the personal pronoun as a linking device may be seen in the first passage above, in which the pronoun *he,* with its possessive form *his,* refers to the antecedent *individual.* Consider also the use of the indefinite pronoun *some* in the following passage:

Small-town people, however, vary considerably in the amount of attention they devote to each other. *Some* of them are snoopers and gossips; *some*, but not all. *Some* have only a mild and fitful interest in even the misdeeds of their neighbors. *Some* are too tightly shut up in private worlds of their own to be vividly conscious of any one else.—WILLIS FISHER, *Who Owns America?*

Yet another linking device is the use of conjunctive adverbs (*however, moreover, accordingly, consequently, therefore,* etc.) and similar connective and directive words, and phrases or clauses such as *for example, on the other hand, in fact, in the first place, first, second, last, I think, we are told, that is, let me explain, as we see.* (See Conjunctive Adverbs, Section 17D 2.) These connectives may be helpful in establishing a well-ordered structure, but they should not be used unless the structure and the situation really call for them. Their frequent use makes style heavy, and the element of order too obvious. Order should be pleasingly manifest but not obtrusive. Exceptions may be made, however, for such writing as laboratory experiments, or abstract writing in which the obvious framework of order is helpful.

EXERCISES

A. Study the organization of Miss Carson's "Petroleum: A Legacy of Ancient Seas," on pp. 35–38.

1. By what principal means does Miss Carson achieve coherence?
2. Can you find any examples of space- or time-order?
3. Does she make use of conjunctive adverbs or directive phrases? List any that you can find.
4. What lesson does the comparative lack of these devices in this essay have for a beginner in composition?

B. Read the following paragraphs in The Paragraph, Chapter 6: Nos. 19, 20, 28, 55. Make a list of the conjunctive adverbs and directive phrases used by the authors to improve coherence. Try reading the various paragraphs with these words eliminated and decide whether these helps to coherence aid the thought, and if so, why.

4. THE WELL-ORDERED THEME: COHERENCE THROUGH EMPHASIS

The well-ordered theme has not only unity and coherence, but also emphasis. Emphasis is not simply emphatic statement. It is also a matter of form, an important means for securing coherence.

It is to be seen in the structure of the completed work, of the paragraphs, of the sentences. In all three, one principle holds for most writing: the beginning and the end are places of chief importance. In the beginning of a theme we must secure the reader's attention by a clear statement or suggestion of the controlling idea. In the body of the theme it is desirable to achieve emphasis, if possible, by the careful arrangement of the main divisions of thought (in a short theme, the paragraphs) in climactic order, proceeding from the least to the most important. If such procedure is not permitted by the nature of the material, emphasis can still be secured by clearly stating the topic of each paragraph. The conclusion of a theme is no less important than the beginning, and hence must be designed with care. In a long theme the conclusion may summarize briefly what has been said or draw inferences from the evidence presented. In a short theme the conclusion may correspond with the last important idea of the theme. It should not in any case be a formal recapitulation of the several main ideas, for such summing up is not necessary in a short paper.

4A. Proportion

A second way of securing the right emphasis of thought and structure in a theme is through attention to the proportion of the main divisions of your thought. Important ideas deserve full treatment; minor ones should be given less space. The beginning, though important, should be brief; the body should be the main substance of the paper, with the conclusion (in a short theme) merely completing the body. No yardstick can be offered to measure the parts, but in a six-hundred-word theme, the introduction should ordinarily not exceed one hundred and fifty words, and the conclusion should be less than one hundred words, though, as has been said, the conclusion may well be simply the last part of the body.

4B. Other Devices of Emphasis

Other means of securing emphasis are repetition, hyperbole, and the use of imagery.

4B 1. Repetition. Repetition, which may often be a fault (see Section 65B), may be a very effective means of emphasis when used with judgment. Prime Minister Churchill rallied the British people in the darkest hour of the Second World War with a speech richly employing this device:

> You ask, what is our policy? I say it is to wage war by land, sea, and air. War with all our might and with all the strength God has given us, and to wage war against a monstrous tyranny never surpassed in the dark and lamentable catalogue of human crime. That is our policy.
>
> You ask, what is our aim? I can answer in one word. It is victory. Victory at all costs—victory in spite of all terrors—victory, however hard and long the road may be, for without victory there is no survival. Let that be realized. No survival for the British Empire, no survival for all that the British Empire has stood for, no survival for the urge, the impulse of the ages, that mankind shall move forward towards his goal.—WINSTON CHURCHILL, *Blood, Sweat, and Tears.*

Notice how the speaker repeats important key words (*policy, war, victory, survival, British Empire*) and how he repeats phrases, always with new meaning for each repetition: *to wage* war *by land, sea, and air . . . to wage* war *against a monstrous tyranny; victory at all costs . . . victory in spite of all terrors; no survival for the British Empire . . . no survival for all the British Empire has stood for,* etc. Notice also the large topical repetition of structure: *You ask, what is our policy? . . . You ask, what is our aim?*

4B 2. Hyperbole. Hyperbole, or overstatement, is a much less effective means of securing emphasis. Sir Francis Bacon says: "The speaking in perpetual hyperbole is comely in nothing but in love." The hyperbole addict sees everything on a grand scale. He knows no moderation. Everything he likes is "great," "terrific," "colossal," "perfectly wonderful," "simply lovely," and when he comes upon a larger experience, he is at loss for words, or he piles superlative on superlative (*supercolossal, absolutely marvelous*), or he plunges into the sea of slang to give expression to his "perfectly tremendous" emotions. As a general rule, avoid hyperbole.

4B 3. Imagery. Imagery, on the other hand, is a very important means of emphasis, one of the best ways of giving color and life to what might otherwise be a drab piece of writing (see Imagery, Section 62).

5. ORGANIZATION OF A THEME

All themes, as we have seen, like all other units of writing, must have a beginning, a middle, and an end.

5A. Beginning

The beginning is, for most writers, the hardest part of a theme, because at the beginning one has to decide from what point to start, in what direction to go, what method of many to use, and how to win attention. And of the beginning, the first sentence is always the hardest to write. Though there is no limit to the variety of opening sentences, most function in one of the following ways:

(1) they state a problem to be examined;
(2) they directly state the controlling idea or thesis of the theme;
(3) they suggest the thesis or some aspect of it, by using some important fact or idea;
(4) they indicate the division of the subject;
(5) they suggest the thesis by an image or an analogy;
(6) they make use of an apt quotation or anecdote.

Each of these openings is, of course, meant to win attention. Let us look at a few examples.

BEGINNING WITH THE STATEMENT OF A PROBLEM: Is the United States a nation composed chiefly of people who have not grown up, who think and act with the impulsiveness of adolescents?—BERNARD IDDINGS BELL.

A fresh criticism of religion is afoot, the subtlety of which makes it difficult to counter. The gist of the contention is that religion is a comforting fantasy.—HARRY EMERSON FOSDICK.

STATEMENT OF THESIS: Ideals are not merely ways of escape from hard realities; what is much more important is that they are stimuli to work for goals that have not yet been reached.—EDWIN GRANT CONKLIN.

If any human being brought up in the tradition of western civilization could, by some miracle, step outside the familiar patterns of that culture, if history could come to him with the same shock of surprise that a new and stimulating novel brings him; if, in sum, retaining the moral idealism of western civilization, he could yet discover for the first time what has happened to mankind in the last fifty years, such a person would, I think, be overwhelmed by a single tragic conviction; namely that the history of mankind for the last half century has been a history of deepening horror. —HOWARD MUMFORD JONES, *Education and World Tragedy.*

You now know the recipe for simplicity: Talk about people in short sentences with many root words. Here is an easy trick for killing these birds with one stone: Use verbs. Let me repeat that: Use verbs.—RUDOLF FLESCH.

IMPORTANT FACT OR IDEA ILLUSTRATING THE THESIS: When you realize that the American public has paid Pullman porters over $150,000,000 in small change since the invention of the sleeping car, you begin to understand something of the tremendous volume of business grossed each year in tips.—CHARLES W. FERGUSON.

For a quarter of a century now I have held a great affection for rain.—RICHARDSON WRIGHT.

The great age of invention was in prehistoric times, long ago.—CLARENCE DAY.

The cool earth presses down upon him, and is under him and bears upon his tiny flanks. The Mole rests.—ALAN DEVOE.

STATEMENT OF THE DIVISIONS OF A SUBJECT: The fabric of the American system of education has been woven with four distinct threads of different hue: two representing the aristocratic traditions of the old world, two the democratic forces unleashed on a new continent.—JAMES BRYANT CONANT.

There are three things about the churches which seem lacking to the men who are undergoing the tough discipline of training camps or are stripped to essentials on the various fronts or at sea. They deplore the absence of Simplicity, Sincerity, and Sympathy.—BERNARD IDDINGS BELL.

THE USE OF AN IMAGE OR ANALOGY: This afternoon I watched a squirrel on our front lawn under the oaks collecting acorns and burying them. For a time he carried them one by one to some cache; but now he was burying each where he found it, without bothering to mark the spot. I watched him with a sort of amused pity. Of course there was no need to mark the spot. He wouldn't need those acorns. He had enough in his cache for a hard winter and he was saving these others just because he couldn't help it. I ought to know; because in these moments of brutal self-analysis I must admit that I too am a squirrel—of sorts.—BURGES JOHNSON, "When Squirrel Meets Squirrel," *Harper's Magazine.*

For another example of the use of imagery, see the sentence by Mr. Conant above.

Some of these introductory sentences, especially those by Mr. Jones and Mr. Conant, manifestly begin long and carefully elaborated essays; but most in their simplicity of phrasing and idea could very well have introduced short themes.

Once you have written your opening sentence, deciding the direction of your thought, the rest of the brief introductory paragraph will suggest itself. It may be an amplification of the opening topic, making the controlling idea more definite. Or it may, especially in the discussion of a person, seize upon one of his traits and illustrate it, in which case the introduction is fused with the body. In an expository theme developing a process, it may list the equipment needed for the process or the method used in an experiment. In an exposition of an idea or problem, it may define or explain the idea or suggest the solution which is to be developed in the body.

Just how long is a beginning? The answer, as said before, cannot be exact. In a short theme it should usually be limited to a short paragraph, and this paragraph may present at the same time the first division of the body of the theme. In general, the beginning of a theme is limited by its function, the introduction of the controlling idea. As works grow longer, introductions usually become more elaborate until we find whole chapters introducing various books.

5B. Body of the Theme

The nature of the body of the theme is determined by the controlling idea. If the controlling idea is one of many implications, the body of the theme will necessarily be long. For a short theme the controlling idea must be suitably limited, as we have seen. Once the theme is properly limited in subject matter, the next requirement is that it shall be well arranged and coherent (see Coherence, Section 3). The nature of the controlling idea will dictate the method of arrangement. As always, you must remember that you are trying to interest a reader who will need to be guided from point to point, and who cannot be informed or entertained by a mere listing of details or experiences. Thus if you are writing on the subject of your travels, a superficial account of your journey to Singapore or Sumatra or a listing of the places you have seen is not enough to hold interest in a short theme. The short theme allows space for an account of only one of these excursions, and, very likely, only a limited aspect of that one excursion. You have not been anywhere unless you can recount what you saw there in rich, well-selected detail.

You must be careful to avoid excessive paragraphing. A long theme will of necessity have several paragraphs. A short one ordinarily should have very few, usually not more than four or five, and two or three may well be enough. A good practice is to make your paragraph divisions correspond to the main divisions of your thought in a short theme. If you have many divisions, your short theme will probably be poorly organized.

Finally, the body must fulfill the promise of the introduction. If in the development of your theme you find that you have strayed from the intentions of the beginning, you must change either the body itself or the introduction to secure unity.

How long should the body of a theme be? Once more, no positive answer can be given. A satisfactory development of each division of the body is clearly necessary for a good theme; and the body should be, as a rule, much more extensive than the introduction, which, as observed above, may even be fused with the body. In a short theme with an introduction of one hundred to one hundred fifty words, one would expect to have a body at least three or four times as long as the introduction; and it might be much longer. If your instructor assigns a word limit for the whole theme, one of your main tasks will of course be the limiting of your subject to a size that can be adequately handled in the number of words assigned. If you find that the first draft of a theme exceeds the assigned limit, sometimes you will be able to reduce it successfully by eliminating unneeded detail or unneeded repetitions or amplifications of ideas; at other times, however, you may find it necessary to eliminate one or more divisions of the body.

After such excision you will revise your title (if necessary) and the introduction to correspond with the changes.

5C. Ending

The end of a theme is your exit from the stage of the reader's attention. It should be both graceful and satisfying. It should not be elaborate. You have already given the reader your impressions, your ideas, your information (the ending is not the place for details or afterthoughts which you forgot to include where they belonged in the body). All that remains is to conclude your theme in a sentence or a few sentences at most. Do not use the words *conclusion* or *in conclusion* in the final sentence or sentences.

In a long theme it may be well to summarize briefly the important points that you have made, or to attempt a neat restatement of the theme to help secure a general effect of unity. Thus Mr. Conant starts the final paragraph of the essay whose beginning is quoted above as follows:

> The four threads of the American educational fabric are knotted together in our great centers of learning. In the future, as in the past, the aristocratic and the democratic traditions must be united in correct proportions . . .

This device of the repetition of his theme and imagery, together with a few more sentences of general summation, makes a pleasing conclusion for a long and serious essay, "The Future of Higher Education."

But in a short theme, conclusions should be less formal. Avoid summarizing or listing the points you have discussed. The last point examined in the body of the theme, especially if that point emphasizes an important aspect of the theme, may well be a good ending. In a word, don't try to achieve what one student called a "golden dome of conclusion" for a theme as simple in structure as a Cape Cod cottage. When you have finished the last point you were trying to develop, stop. Don't worry about writing a rich final sentence. If you find yourself trying to add such a sentence without success, the chances are that you have already completed your theme without realizing it.

6. THE OUTLINE

6A. Definition

An outline is a summary of the important features of any composition. It may be a loose jotting of outstanding details, commonly called an inventory outline, or it may be formally organized into main headings and subheadings, as in the noun-phrase and sentence outlines, or main headings alone, as in the paragraph outline. Inventory outlining is helpful in all kinds of writing and is a useful preliminary to the building of the more formal types of outlines. Noun-phrase, sentence, and paragraph outlines are useful in organizing themes or studies that explain ideas or processes; they are less useful in organizing the structure of a story or any writing expressing a mood.

One of the best ways to achieve a good organization of a theme explaining an idea or a process, indeed the only sure way, is to outline your theme. Though many prefer to write their first drafts without outlines, no one ever writes a well-organized theme or any other work without rearranging and revising his work to make it conform to an outline that he has in mind, if not actually written down; and some writers actually outline their work in advance of writing the text itself. For this reason it is both desirable and necessary for you to know the principles of outlining.

6B. Symbols and the Arrangement of Formal Outlines

Before writing a noun-phrase, sentence, or paragraph outline, you should be familiar with the system of symbols and arrangement used in such writing. All major points, the grand divisions of your subject matter, are indicated by capital Roman numerals, I, II, III, and so on. Since a subject cannot be divided into fewer than two parts, a short theme will have at least two main points, but rarely more than four or five.

Subdivisions of these major divisions are indicated by capital letters, A, B, C, and subsequent letters. Some of the major points may have three or four or more of these subdivisions; others may have only two or even none. No one of these subdivisions, if divided at all, will have fewer than two points. Single supporting details can be combined with preceding headings or omitted.

If these subdivisions in turn are divided into parts, these parts are indicated by Arabic numerals, 1, 2, 3, and so on. As above, there may be two or more such parts, but never fewer than two. It is usually not necessary to resort to further subdivision, particularly in a short theme; but if it seems called for, the symbols *a, b, c,* and subsequent letters and (1), (2), (3), and so on may be used for new divisions in the same fashion as those already discussed.

This arrangement and subordination of material by means of symbols is further indicated by the parallel arrangement of ideas of equal rank and the increasing indention of each new subdivision on the page. Here is a pattern of an arrangement of the symbols and the indention:

```
I. ________________________________
   A. _____________________________
      1. __________________________
         a) _______________________
            (1) ___________________
                (a) _______________
                    i) ____________
                   ii) ____________
                (b) _______________
            (2) ___________________
         b) _______________________
      2. __________________________
   B. _____________________________
II. _______________________________
```

This parallelism of arrangement is carried throughout the outline. Successive lines of any division have their left margin established by the first word following the symbol and assume a block form, as illustrated in the sentence outline on pages 39–41.

6C. Types of Outlines

There are four types of outlines: namely, the inventory, the noun-phrase outline, the sentence outline, and the paragraph outline.

6C 1. Inventory. The inventory is a jotting down, without any special reference to order, of all the ideas and information that you can bring to bear on your subject. This is a good device for any student to use as a preliminary step in writing a theme, preferably after he has limited his subject and decided on his controlling idea, though a quick inventory of his general subject may help him limit his subject. This inventory is a mere jotting of words and phrases in any form that occurs to the writer. As you make this list, you will gradually become aware of certain outstanding ideas to which most of the others can be related. These outstanding ideas will serve as the main divisions of your phrase, sentence, or paragraph outline, which you will then be ready to develop.

6C 2. Noun-Phrase Outline. The noun-phrase outline is, as the name suggests, made up exclusively of noun phrases. Noun phrases must not be confused with verb phrases (a verb and its modifiers: see Section 11A 2) or prepositional phrases (see Section 19A 1). The noun phrase used in outlining is composed of a noun and its modifiers (see Sections 13A, 16A, 16D). "The colors of the rainbow" is a noun phrase, consisting of the basic noun "colors" and its modifiers—the definite article "the" and the adjectival prepositional phrase "of the rainbow." The headings of the various divisions of this text are noun phrases. "Ran for the student senate" is a verb phrase, made up of the verb "ran" and the adverbial prepositional phrase "for the student senate," which modifies "ran." Neither verb phrases nor prepositional phrases should be used in noun-phrase outlines. The idea implied in "Ran for the student senate" could be expressed in a noun phrase as "His candidacy for the student senate."

The noun-phrase outline, unlike the inventory, must be well ordered. After you have developed your inventory and have rearranged its material under a few main headings (in a short theme, rarely more than four or five) and have these headings in the best possible order, you are ready to build a noun-phrase outline.

These noun phrases, so far as possible, should reveal your actual subject matter. A noun-phrase outline that does not give specific information may have some value to the writer but will mean little to the reader. Your purpose is to communicate thought, not to conceal it. The noun-phrase outline should tell us what you are going to say in your theme, so far as it is possible to convey that information by nouns. Consider the following partial outlines on the theme of a student's early life:

VAGUE:

I. My birth and parentage
  A. My birth in a foreign land
  B. My parents
II. My early schooling

INFORMATIVE:

I. My birth and parentage
  A. My birth on January 1, 1934, in Manila
  B. My parents of French-Irish ancestry
II. My early schooling in Manila from 1938 to 1946

Make your outline informative, like the second one above. Observe that since these are noun phrases, not sentences, no periods follow the separate phrases.

All carefully organized themes, as has been observed, are either written from a well-organized outline or made to conform to one after they are first composed. Here is a noun-phrase outline of the student theme, "Oakwood Hall Five Years Ago," printed on pages 16–19:

OAKWOOD HALL FIVE YEARS AGO

I. Our attitude toward going to Oakwood Hall
  A. Its difference from my mother's
  B. Our anticipation of school as an adventure
    1. The waning of this view
    2. Our accommodation to life in a school
II. The problem of food
  A. The one-track mind of our cook
    1. The monotony of her menus
    2. Her ideas of variation
  B. Our contraband food

III. Our recreation of rule-breaking
   A. The rules of Oakwood Hall
      1. The negative rules
         a) The rule against talking after "lights out"
         b) The rule against smoking
         c) The rule against receiving young gentlemen callers
         d) The rule against visiting homes of day students
         e) Rules forbidding chewing gum and cosmetics
         f) Rules against noise in the building
      2. The positive rules
         a) The rule requiring the wearing of a hat and gloves off campus
         b) The rule requiring promptness at meals, classes, assemblies
         c) The rule requiring immaculate uniforms
         d) The rules of etiquette
   B. Our violation of these rules
      1. The opportunities offered by our Wednesday afternoons
         a) Our breaking of nearly all the negative rules
         b) The excitement of this pastime
      2. Our violation of the "lights out" rules
         a) Our skill in performing tasks in the dark
         b) Our development of acute senses of touch and hearing
         c) Our entertainment after "lights out"
            (1) Conversation
            (2) Bridge by flashlight
            (3) Feasts
   C. Punishment for the violation of rules
      1. Restriction to the campus
      2. "Early lights"

IV. The faculty
   A. Our French teacher
   B. Our English teacher
   C. Our teachers of science, Latin, and art
   D. Our mathematics teacher
   E. The headmistress

V. The school concerts and lectures
   A. The preparation for the coming of a male performer
   B. The pathos and humor of the occasion

VI. The nostalgia for the past
   A. The lasting influence of school friendships
   B. The pleasure of reminiscences

6C 3. Sentence Outline. The most informative of all outlines, and the one which will best help you to arrange your thoughts effectively, is the sentence outline. The sentence outline may be regarded as a noun-phrase outline converted into complete sentences (see Section 10A for the definition of a complete sentence). All the separate parts of a sentence outline must be complete sentences or parts of complete sentences. Never use noun phrases or verb phrases as separate parts of a sentence outline. Prepositional phrases may be used as parts if they are properly subordinated to a preceding sentence structure. As in the noun-phrase outline, you must be careful in selecting the main headings and make sure that all minor points are properly subordinated.

The sentence outline is the skeleton outline of all the important information you are going to present in your theme. Even more than the phrase outline, it states exactly what you are going to say. How long should the sentence outline be? There is no rule, but ordinarily it should be from a fourth to a third as long as the completed theme itself. For an essay involving many facts and specific details it may be almost as extensive as its theme, as in the example given below.

Nearly all good expository writing shows the careful articulation of parts that is to be found in a well-ordered sentence outline. Study, for example, with careful attention to its organization, the following essay excerpted from Miss Rachel L. Carson's *The Sea Around Us.*

PETROLEUM: A LEGACY OF ANCIENT SEAS [2]

Of all legacies of the ancient seas the most valuable is petroleum. Exactly what geologic processes have created the precious pools of liquid deep within the earth no one knows with enough certainty to describe the whole sequence of events. But this much seems to be true: Petroleum is a result of fundamental earth processes that have been operating ever since an abundant and varied life was developed in the sea—at least since the beginning of Paleozoic time, probably longer. Exceptional and catastrophic occurrences may now

[2] *The Sea Around Us* by Rachel L. Carson. Copyright 1951 by Rachel L. Carson. Reprinted by permission of Oxford University Press, Inc. The title of this essay is supplied by the authors of this text.

and then aid its formation but they are not essential; the mechanism that regularly generates petroleum consists of the normal processes of earth and sea—the living and dying of creatures, the deposit of sediments, the advance and retreat of the seas over the continents, the upward and downward foldings of the earth's crust.

The old inorganic theory that linked petroleum formation with volcanic action has been abandoned by most geologists. The origin of petroleum is most likely to be found in the bodies of plants and animals buried under the fine-grained sediments of former seas and there subjected to slow decomposition.

Perhaps the essence of conditions favoring petroleum production is represented by the stagnant waters of the Black Sea or of certain Norwegian fiords. The surprisingly abundant life of the Black Sea is confined to the upper layers; the deeper and especially the bottom waters are devoid of oxygen and are often permeated with hydrogen sulphide. In these poisoned waters there can be no bottom scavengers to devour the bodies of marine animals that drift down from above, so they are entombed in the fine sediments. In many Norwegian fiords the deep layers are foul and oxygenless because the mouth of the fiord is cut off from the circulation of the open sea by a shallow sill. The bottom layers of such fiords are poisoned by the hydrogen sulphide from decomposing organic matter. Sometimes storms drive in unusual quantities of oceanic water and through turbulence of waves stir deeply the waters of these lethal pools; the mixing of the water layers that follows brings death to hordes of fishes and invertebrates living near the surface. Such a catastrophe leads to the deposit of a rich layer of organic material on the bottom.

Wherever great oil fields are found, they are related to past or present seas. This is true of the inland fields as well as of those near the present seacoast. The great quantities of oil that have been obtained from the Oklahoma fields, for example, were trapped in spaces within sedimentary rocks laid down under seas that invaded this part of North America in Paleozoic time.

The search for petroleum has also led geologists repeatedly to those "unstable belts, covered much of the time by shallow seas, which lie around the margins of the main continental platforms, between them and the great oceanic deeps."

An example of such a depressed segment of crust lying between continental masses is the one between Europe and the Near East, occupied in part by the Persian Gulf, the Red, Black, and Caspian Seas, and the Mediterranean Sea. The Gulf of Mexico and the Caribbean Sea lie in another basin or shallow sea between the Americas. A shallow, island-studded sea lies between the continents of Asia and Australia. Lastly, there is the nearly landlocked sea of the Arctic. In past ages all of these areas have been alternately raised and depressed, belonging at one time to the land, at another to the encroaching sea. During their periods of submersion they have received thick deposits of sediments, and in their waters a rich marine fauna has lived, died, and drifted down into the soft sediment carpet.

There are vast oil deposits in all these areas. In the Near East are the great fields of Saudi Arabia, Iran, and Iraq. The shallow depression between Asia and Australia yields the oil of Java, Sumatra, Borneo, and New Guinea. The American mediterranean is the center of oil production in the Western Hemisphere—half the proved resources of the United States come from the northern shore of the Gulf of Mexico, and Colombia, Venezuela, and Mexico have rich oil fields along the western and southern margins of the Gulf. The Arctic is one of the unproved frontiers of the petroleum industry, but oil seepages in northern Alaska, on islands north of the Canadian mainland, and along the Arctic coast of Siberia hint that this land recently raised from the sea may be one of the great oil fields of the future.

In recent years, the speculations of petroleum geologists have been focused in a new direction—under sea. By no means all of the land resources of petroleum have been discovered, but probably the richest and most easily worked fields are being tapped, and their possible production is known. The ancient seas gave us the oil that is now being drawn out of the earth. Can the ocean today be induced to give up some of the oil that must be trapped in sedimentary rocks under its floor, covered by water scores or hundreds of fathoms deep?

Oil is already being produced from offshore wells, on the continental shelf. Off California, Texas, and Louisiana, oil companies have drilled into the sediments of the shelf and are obtaining oil. In the United States the most active exploration has been centered in the Gulf of Mexico. Judging from its geologic history, this area has rich promise. For eons of time it was either dry land or a very shallow sea basin, receiving the sediments that washed into it from high lands to the north. Finally, about the middle of the Cretaceous period, the floor of the Gulf began to sink under the load of sediments and in time it acquired its present deep central basin.

By geophysical exploration, we can see that the layers of sedimentary rock underlying the coastal plain tilt steeply downward and pass under the broad continental shelf of the Gulf. Down in the layers deposited in the Jurassic period is a thick salt bed of enormous extent, probably formed when this part of the earth was hot and dry, a place of shrinking seas and encroaching deserts. In Louisiana and Texas, and also, it now appears, out in the Gulf itself, extraordinary features known as salt domes are associated with this deposit. These are fingerlike plugs of salt, usually less than a mile across, pushing up from the deep layer toward the earth's surface. They have been described by geologists as driven up through 5,000 to 15,000 feet of sediments by earth pressures, like nails through a board. In the states bordering the Gulf such structures have often been associated with oil. It seems probable that on the continental shelf, also, the salt domes may mark large oil deposits.

In exploring the Gulf for oil, therefore, geologists search for the salt domes where the larger oil fields are likely to lie. They use an instrument known as a magnetometer, which measures the variations in magnetic intensity brought about by the salt domes. Gravity meters also help locate the domes by measuring the variation in gravity near them, the specific gravity of salt being less than that of the surrounding sediments. The actual location and outline of the dome are discovered by seismographic exploration, which traces the inclination of the rock strata by recording the reflection of sound waves produced by dynamite explosions. These methods of exploration have been used on land for some years, but only since about 1945 have they been adapted to use in offshore Gulf waters. The magnetometer has been so improved that it will map continuously while being towed behind a boat or carried in or suspended from a plane. A gravity meter can now be lowered rapidly to the bottom and readings made by remote control. (Once an operator had to descend with it in a diving bell.) Seismic crews now shoot off their dynamite charges and make continuous recordings while their boats are under way.

Despite all these improvements which allow exploration to proceed rapidly, it is no simple matter to obtain oil from undersea fields. Prospecting must be followed by the leasing of potential oil-producing areas, and then by drilling to see whether oil is actually there. Offshore drilling platforms rest on piles that must be driven as far as 250 feet into the floor of the Gulf to withstand the force of waves, especially during the season for hurricanes. Winds, storm waves, fogs, the corrosive gnawing of sea water upon metal structures—all these are hazards that must be faced and overcome. Yet the technical difficulties of far more extensive offshore operations than any now attempted do not discourage specialists in petroleum engineering.

A careful analysis of this essay reveals that Miss Carson has planned and built it as a skillful builder constructs a house. There is nothing of chance in the whole structure. Though she does not number the parts stiffly and formally, her plan is clear and can be reduced to the following sentence outline. We may conclude either that she wrote the essay after developing such an outline as the one presented below or that she made her material correspond finally in structure to such an outline.

As you study the outline and compare its structure with that of the essay, you will observe that though this is the essential frame of Miss Carson's thought, she is not enslaved by the structure. For example, she writes two or three introductory sentences before stating her first main point; and at various places she amplifies or condenses material in a way that shows that though she is following a well-conceived plan, she is master of the plan, developing its parts with variety and color. But the plan is there, as the following sentence outline shows:

PETROLEUM: A LEGACY OF ANCIENT SEAS

I. Petroleum seems to be a result of earth processes operating since the beginning of Paleozoic time or earlier.
  A. Exceptional occurrences may aid in its formation but are not essential.
  B. The mechanism generating petroleum consists of the normal processes of earth and sea, namely,
    1. living and dying of creatures,
    2. deposit of sediments,
    3. advance and retreat of the seas, and
    4. upward and downward foldings of the earth's crust.
  C. The theory linking the origin with volcanic action has been largely abandoned.
  D. The origin seems to lie in decomposition of plants and animals under the sea.

II. Conditions favoring petroleum production may possibly be seen today in certain regions.
  A. The stagnant waters of the Black Sea offer favorable conditions.
    1. The upper layers swarm with life.
    2. The deeper waters are devoid of oxygen and often permeated with hydrogen sulphide.
      a) No scavengers can live in these waters.
      b) Animal bodies drifting down are buried here in sediment.
  B. The waters of many Norwegian fiords offer like conditions.
    1. They are stagnant because they are cut off from the open sea by a shallow sill.
    2. The bottom layers are poisoned by decaying organic matter.
    3. Storms from the ocean stir up these waters and poison surface life.
    4. The result is a new layer of organic matter on the bottom.

III. Great oil fields are all related to past or ancient seas.
   A. This is true of inland fields, like those of Oklahoma.
      1. Seas invaded this part of America in Paleozoic time.
      2. Quantities of oil were trapped in sedimentary rock under these seas.
   B. It is also true of coastal fields, including the unstable belts covered much of the time by shallow seas.
      1. There are several such regions.
      2. In the past all these areas have been alternately raised and depressed.
      3. During their period of submersion they have had the right conditions for oil formation.
      4. Vast oil deposits have been found in all these areas.

IV. Recently speculation about oil deposits has been focused in a new direction—under sea.
   A. Oil is already being produced from offshore wells near California, Texas, and Louisiana.
   B. The most active American exploration has been centered in the Gulf of Mexico, a region of rich promise.
      1. For eons of time this gulf was either dry land or a very shallow sea.
      2. In the Cretaceous period the Gulf sank under its load of sediment and became a deep basin.
      3. Exploration shows that the layers of sedimentary rock of the coastal plains tilt downward under the Gulf.
         a) In the layers deposited in the Jurassic period there is a thick salt bed.
         b) The salt domes in this deposit probably indicate oil.

V. In exploring the Gulf for oil, geologists search for the salt domes where the larger oil fields are likely to lie.
   A. To find them they use two instruments, the magnetometer and the gravity meter.
      1. The magnetometer measures the variations in magnetic intensity produced by the salt domes.
      2. The gravity meter locates the domes by measuring the variations in gravity near them.
   B. These instruments have been adapted since 1945 for use in the Gulf.
      1. The magnetometer will now map continuously as it is towed from a boat or suspended from a plane.
      2. The gravity meter can now be lowered to the bottom and read by remote control.

3. Seismic crews can make their recordings while boats are under way.

VI. Despite these improvements, it is not easy to obtain oil from undersea fields, but experts refuse to be discouraged.
   A. After prospecting and leasing the areas, the companies must drill under difficult conditions to find whether oil exists.
      1. Offshore drilling platforms rest on piles driven as far as 250 feet deep.
      2. These must withstand waves of hurricane force.
   B. Many hazards must be met and overcome.
      1. Winds, storm waves, and fogs must be contended with.
      2. The corrosion of sea water on metal structures is a constant problem.
   C. These difficulties do not discourage the specialists in petroleum engineering.

6C 4. Paragraph Outline. The paragraph outline is also a sentence outline, but a brief one, not unlike a summary or précis of an essay or theme. In building a paragraph outline of any piece of work, look for the topic sentences of the paragraphs (see Section 49A). Sometimes these topic sentences begin paragraphs; they may follow an introductory sentence; they may come at the end of a paragraph. Sometimes the topic sentence is not given but may be inferred from the sense of the paragraph. Yet again, two or more paragraphs may relate to one topic sentence. When you have found the topic sentences, reduce them (if necessary) to their essential structure by stripping away any unneeded modifiers, assemble them with Roman numerals, and your task is done. This type of outlining is valuable in studying assignments of expository reading. If you can learn to grasp quickly the sense of a paragraph as suggested by its topic, you have mastered an effective method of study.

6D. Common Faults in Outlining

6D 1. Mixing of Types. A sentence outline is written in sentences and a phrase outline is written in noun phrases. Do not mix the types. Consider the mixture of types in the following incomplete section of an outline entitled "The Aurora Borealis."

I. Men have speculated about the nature of the aurora borealis for centuries. (Sentence)
   A. Aristotle's reference to auroras (Noun phrase)
   B. Seneca offers a vivid description of them. (Sentence)
   C. In the late Renaissance auroras confused with comets. (Elliptical sentence; verb missing)
   D. Superstitious people have always considered them supernatural. (Sentence)
   E. Critical examination of the aurora in the eighteenth century (Noun phrase)

II. The three main classes of the aurora borealis (Noun phrase)
   A. Without ray structures (Prepositional phrase)
      1. Homogeneous arcs the most common form. (Elliptical sentence)
         a) Various breadths (Noun phrase)
         b) Parallel arcs like rainbows (Noun phrase)
         c) Appearing of isolated parts (Participial or gerund phrase)
         d) Lower border sharply defined. (Elliptical sentence)
         e) The upper arcs may curve back to form lower arcs. (Sentence)
         f) They may pulsate rhythmically. (Sentence)

This outline clearly needs revision into either a complete-sentence or a noun-phrase outline. Here is the same material developed by a student in sentence form:

I. Men have speculated about the nature of the aurora borealis for centuries.
   A. Aristotle realized the auroras were natural phenomena.
   B. Seneca offers a vivid description of them.
   C. In the late Renaissance they were confused with comets.
   D. Superstitious people have always considered them supernatural.
   E. Critical examination of the auroras began in the eighteenth century.

II. The aurora borealis has three main classes of forms.
   A. One class is without ray structure.
      1. Of this type, homogeneous arcs are the most common form and have the following structure.
         a) The arcs have various breadths.
         b) They may extend in parallels like rainbows across the sky.
         c) Isolated parts may appear.
         d) Their lower border is often sharply defined, but the upper limits are diffused.
         e) Upper arcs may curve back on themselves to form lower arcs.
         f) They may pulsate rhythmically.

(For a complete development of this outline, see pp. 475–81.)

6D 2. Lack of Parallelism. The members of divisions of the same rank in phrase outlines should be parallel in structure. (For a discussion of parallelism, see Section 24.) If sentence structures are subdivided in sentence outlines, the divisions must also be parallel.

Lack of parallelism in a noun-phrase outline:

II. The forms of the aurora borealis (noun phrase)
  A. Without ray structure (prepositional phrase)
    1. Homogeneous arcs being the most common form (absolute construction)
      a) Various breadths (noun phrase)
      b) Extending in parallels (participial or gerund phrase)
      c) Appearing of isolated parts (participial or gerund phrase)
      d) With lower borders sharply defined (prepositional phrase)
      e) With diffused upper limits (prepositional phrase)
      f) Pulsating rhythmically (participial phrase)

Revised into a noun-phrase outline of parallel forms:

II. The forms of the aurora borealis
  A. The forms without ray structure
    1. The homogeneous arc type and its characteristics
      a) Its various breadths
      b) Its extension in parallels
      c) Its appearance in isolated parts
      d) Its sharply defined lower border
      e) Its diffused upper limits
      f) Its rhythmical pulsation

6D 3. Illogical Subordination. Subordinations must be logical. Minor points must be subordinate to major points, and major points must not be subordinate to minor ones. Now and then a very serious idea may be used in a minor relationship, but its subordination must be logical.

Consider the lack of logic in the following section of an outline on the life of Emile Zola:

II. Emile Zola was a greatly spoiled child.
  A. He was sickly as a young child.
  B. He was happy playing outdoors by himself.

C. The death of Francisco Zola left the family in a state of poverty and debt.

D. His mother and grandfather pampered Emile because of his misfortune.

Revised:

II. Though sickly as an infant, Zola spent a happy, pampered childhood.
   A. Except for a serious illness at the age of two, he enjoyed good health.
   B. He was happy playing outdoors by himself.
   C. He was too young at seven to realize the meaning of his father's death.
   D. His mother and grandfather pampered Emile.

III. The death of his father left the family in a state of poverty and debt.

Study also the lack of logic in this example:

B. Francisco Zola was trained for a military career.
   1. After Napoleon's fall he became a qualified engineer.
   2. Soon he undertook the role of wanderer and adventurer.
   3. After a while he became a civil engineer.

Revised:

B. Francisco Zola had a varied career.
   1. At the age of seventeen he was commissioned in the Royal Italian Artillery and fought for Napoleon.
   2. After Napoleon's fall, he studied mathematics and engineering.
   3. Subsequently he became an adventurer and joined the Foreign Legion.
   4. On his return from this service, he became a civil engineer.

6D 4. Faulty Indention. Indent all members of subdivisions to indicate their subordination. The margin of each new subdivision must be carefully kept, as in the sentence outline in Section 6C 3 above.

WRONG: III. Attempts to control malaria began early.
A. The first successful attempt occurred in America.
1. Jesuit missionaries in Peru found the Indians using cinchona bark for the disease.
2. They brought the method to Spain in 1632.
3. The treatment was generally adopted by 1640.
B. Pelletier and Coventon, French scientists, isolated quinine in 1820.

RIGHT: III. Attempts to control malaria began early.
  A. The first successful attempt occurred in America.
    1. Jesuit missionaries in Peru found the Indians using cinchona bark for the disease.
    2. They brought the method to Spain in 1632.
    3. The treatment was generally adopted by 1640.
  B. Pelletier and Coventon, French scientists, isolated quinine in 1820.

6D 5. Faulty Division.

a) Members of divisions, major or minor, should be of the same category or type. Pair place with place, time with time, etc.

WRONG: II. My college before 1900
  A. Early presidents
  B. Before 1870
  C. Its expansion from 1870 to 1900

RIGHT: II. My college before 1900
  A. Its founding in 1830
  B. Its development from 1830 to 1870
  C. Its expansion from 1870 to 1900

b) Subject matter cannot be divided into one point. If your outline has one heading marked I, there must be at least a second main division marked II; if it has an A, there must be a B; if it has 1, there must be 2, and so on. Single illustrations of an idea, which may seem at first glance like subdivisions, can be merged with preceding headings, as in the following example:

WRONG: II. Rayon has numerous advantages as a fabric.
  A. It has four special qualities.
    1. Rayons are not weakened by perspiration.
    2. White rayons will not turn yellow with age or washing.
    3. Rayon does not mildew easily.
    4. Rayon is a better conductor of heat than silk.
III. Rayon fabrics have a bright future.

RIGHT: II. Rayon has four special advantages as a fabric.
  A. Rayons are not weakened by perspiration.
  B. White rayons will not turn yellow with age or washing.
  C. Rayon does not mildew easily.
  D. Rayon is a better conductor of heat than silk.
III. Rayon fabrics have a bright future.

EXERCISES

1. Make the noun-phrase outline of "Oakwood Hall Five Years Ago" on pages 33–34 into a sentence outline.

2. Make the outline referred to in Exercise 1 into a paragraph outline.

3. The following student outline violates a large number of the rules for outlining. How many errors can you discover in it? List these and the rule or principle violated. Then revise the outline into a noun-phrase outline.

ATOMIC ENERGY

I. A historical survey of the first work on atomic energy.
   A. Discovery of fission or release of certain amounts of energy
      1. Uranium atom first used for observation of fission.
   B. Countries all over the world contributed in experimenting with fission.

II. The first possibility in breaking the atom by Becquerel.
   A. In 1896 the physicist Becquerel found radium to emit radiation.
   B. In 1902 Rutherford and Soddy suggested that elements were constantly breaking up.
      1. Alpha particles carried helium atoms positively charged.
   C. In 1911 Rutherford discovered that each atom had a nucleus carrying a positive charge.
   d. In 1913 Neils Bohr of Copenhagen combined his theory with that of Rutherford.

III. In 1932 Urey and Brickwedde discovered isotopes.
   A. Lawrence developed the cyclotron the same year.

IV. By 1939 scientists believed that atomic energy could be produced.
A. In 1941 it was believed that atomic energy could be produced for the war.
   a. Albuquerque, New Mexico, was the scene of the first explosion, July 16, 1945.
   b. The Atomic Bomb Project was headed by General Leslie Groves and directed by Dr. J. R. Oppenheimer.
   c. Great care was taken in handling the bomb.
V. The explosion at 5:30 A.M.
   A. The project a success.

7. COMPLETING THE THEME: ITS WRITING, REVISIONS, AND FINAL FORM

7A. Writing the First Draft

The nature of the first draft of your theme will depend on whether you compose it with a well-shaped plan in mind or whether you shape it as you write. If you have a good plan in mind, your work of imparting order to the theme is done before you begin the theme itself. If you prefer to shape your material as you write, you will of course have to make sure of the correct organization of your theme. If you write from a written plan, follow it with care, but at the same time clothe the plan with such variety as the material may suggest. Remember that even a good sentence outline is not a theme. Details must be filled in, all in their planned places, to be sure, but monotony can be avoided in handling them. Though the structure of the outline must be essentially followed, variation in the use of topic sentences is possible and even desirable. For example, in the outline your topic sentences, the main headings, always come first. In the actual writing of the theme, you may choose to put a topic sentence first, in the middle, at the end of a paragraph, or occasionally let the material itself imply the topic sentence without any formal statement. Or you may find it desirable to unite into one paragraph all the material under one main division of your outline (that is, for example, all the material numbered II, A, B, C, D), and use two or three paragraphs to express the separate aspects of the idea of another main division. Ordinarily, however, in a short theme your paragraph divisions will correspond to the main divisions (I, II, III, etc.) of your outline.

Remember finally that your outline and your theme must correspond in subject matter. If the process of writing your theme shows you the desirability of adding to or altering your plan, revise your outline accordingly, and, of course, your controlling idea if it needs change.

At this time it is good once more to consider the number of your paragraphs. In general, short themes should not have more than four or five paragraphs. You may use fewer (two or three), but if you have more than five, it is advisable to ask yourself if some of them cannot be effectively combined under one topic sentence.

7B. First Step in Revision

Revision is an ugly word to most of us, because we are fundamentally lazy or are so wedded to what we have first written that we are unwilling to change it. But make no mistake: nearly all good writing is the result of much revision. You are not naïve enough always to believe the student who tells you that he wrote his *A* theme in fifteen minutes any more than you believe the one who tells you that he made a good mark in a test without ever cracking a book. Good sense tells you that if the theme was written with such speed, it was written as a result of earlier planning and reflection, that the student was developing material to which he had given careful thought at some time in the past, and that by practice he had learned the art of careful organization. Even those specially gifted with words find it necessary to revise with care all the work they write. John Gould Fletcher tells of one poet who revised a poem as many as twenty times before he submitted it for publication. Do not be afraid to change what you have written: it can nearly always be improved if you give it your full attention.

If possible, you will find it helpful to let a day or two pass between the first draft of your composition and the time when you give the copy its final revision before submitting it to your instructor.

7C. Testing Your Theme

In revising the theme, you should read and reread it several times with one specific thing in mind in each reading. This process of rereading several times will not take long, and it is your best hope for securing satisfactory results. Do not attempt to detect all possible errors in one or two hasty readings. Revise in a methodical way. Look first to make sure of the unity of your theme. Then examine it for coherence. Consider your paragraphs, their topic sentences, and the order of their thought. Are all your sentences truly sentences? Are they sufficiently varied? Does your diction fit your subject matter? Are you sure of your punctuation? and your spelling? One cannot eliminate all faults, but by painstaking revision he can hope to get rid of most of them. Here is a list of questions by which you may test the quality of your theme. You are not expected to be able to answer all these at the beginning of the course, but answer all that you can, and get the habit of looking up some of these points for yourself by consulting the index. Do not wait for the instructor to refer you to them. Observe that some of these questions overlap. This is necessary because the same matter is being considered from several points of view.

A TEST FOR THEMES

I. Is my theme unified?
   A. Is my subject matter properly limited or too extensive?
   B. Have I stated my controlling thesis sharply: can the central thought of my theme be reduced to a single sentence?
   C. Is every part of my theme provided for in this controlling idea?

II. Is my theme coherent?
   A. Are my main points organized either naturally or logically?
   B. Does the thought of my theme move smoothly from sentence to sentence?

III. Are my thoughts rightly emphasized?
   A. Are my main thoughts arranged in a climactic order?
   B. Are they rightly proportioned?
   C. Does my theme maintain its tone?

IV. Is my paragraphing satisfactory?
   A. Does each paragraph have an effective topic sentence governing its thought?
   B. If not, is the topical idea clearly indicated by the material itself?
   C. Is each paragraph carefully organized?
   D. Do I have too many paragraphs?

V. Are my sentences effective?
  A. Have I sufficiently varied my sentence types?
  B. Have I used any sentence fragments?
  C. Do my verbs agree in number with their subjects?
  D. Have I made any errors in the use of case?
  E. Do my pronouns agree with their antecedents?
  F. Have I used a weak passive verb where I should use an active verb?
  G. Have I any dangling modifiers?

VI. Is my diction effective?
  A. Have I avoided slang? clichés? jargon?
  B. Does my diction suit its subject?
  C. Are my sentences wordy? Can I reduce any of them effectively?
  D. Have I misspelled any words?

VII. Is my punctuation correct?
  A. Have I used periods after declarative sentences and after abbreviations?
  B. Have I used question marks after questions?
  C. Have I avoided the comma splice?
  D. Have I punctuated my nonrestrictive clauses with commas?
  E. Have I used commas where they are needed for clarity?
  F. Have I used apostrophes correctly with all my possessive nouns?

VIII. Is my theme interesting?
  A. Does my title not only sufficiently indicate my subject matter but also invite reading?
  B. Can I improve my introduction?
  C. Does the body of my theme maintain the interest aroused by the introduction?
  D. Is my conclusion short and emphatic or vague and indefinite?
  E. Would more imagery help to convey my ideas more effectively?

8. THE MANUSCRIPT

8A. Preparation of the Final Copy

After revising your theme as thoroughly as you can, you are ready to prepare a copy for your instructor. This copy should be written on the usual ruled theme paper, 8½″ x 11″, or, if you use a typewriter, on a good grade of typewriting paper of the same size. Do not use the onionskin type or any other thin paper. Do not use notebook paper: its lines are too close for the effective revision of errors. Use only black or blue-black ink. Do not use pencil.

Write legibly. Cross your *t*'s, dot your *i*'s, join the letters of all words, and avoid any decorative flourishes. Write as simple and as clear a hand as you possibly can. If you type, always double-space, except when quoting the writing of others. Such quoted matter should be single-spaced and set apart from your own writing if the quoted passage is more than two lines long. Shorter quotations (of one or two lines) should ordinarily be double-spaced and not set apart. (For discussion of handling of quotations, see Sections 41, 83A 2.)

8A 1. Margins. Observe margins carefully. For a handwritten theme on ruled theme paper, observe a margin of an inch and a half at the left of the page. On the right side a half-inch margin is sufficient. At the bottom leave the last ruled line blank. At the top, center the title on the first ruled line, leave the second line blank, and begin the theme on the third line. On succeeding pages, continue the theme on the first ruled line.

For typewritten themes use typewriting paper. Observe a one and one-half inch margin on the left, a one-inch margin on the right and at the bottom, and a two-inch margin above the title. Begin the theme four spaces below the title. On succeeding pages observe a one and one-half inch margin at the top.

Never write or type in the left margin, not even to number parts of an outline.

8A 2. Title. The title of a handwritten theme should be centered on the first line of the ruled theme paper. The first word of the title and all important words should be capitalized; articles, conjunctions, and prepositions are ordinarily not capitalized unless they come first:

The Function of the National Bank
Five Hundred Years of Peace
The Passing of the Chestnut and the Elm

When typewritten, the title is centered on the page two inches from the top, and *all* words are fully capitalized:

THE LOST OWL
A NEW VOGUE IN SLANG

Do not use periods after titles. Question marks, on the other hand, must be used if the title is a question, and exclamation points if the title is exclamatory.

Titles should not be repeated on following pages.

8A 3. Page Numbering. Number the pages with Arabic numbers (1, 2, 3, etc.). The first page need not be numbered. Succeeding ones should be numbered in the middle of the top margin without punctuation of any sort.

8A 4. Paragraph Indentions. In handwritten themes, start on the third line with a one-inch paragraph indention; in typewriting, begin four spaces below the title with a five-space paragraph indention. Observe these same paragraph indentions throughout your theme.

Allow proper spacing between sentences (two spaces in typing after the period). Otherwise do not leave gaps in your writing. Do not begin new lines with punctuation marks that relate to material in the preceding line.

8B. Proofreading Your Manuscript

After you have completed your copy, reread it once more to detect errors in copying and to determine whether you can observe any other faults. Oftentimes when you see a theme completed, especially if it is typewritten, you can view it more objectively, more impartially. If this reading helps you to detect new faults, you may correct them neatly on the page unless they are too numerous or too large for a simple revision. If the faults are simple and few, draw a single bold line through each faulty word or phrase and, using a caret, insert the right word or phrase above the discarded one. Do not use parentheses or brackets around a word or phrase that you wish to remove, since these marks are not meant for such a purpose. Use only the neat single line drawn boldly through the word or phrase or sentence. If these newly detected faults are so numerous as to make a messy page, or if some large alteration is necessary, recopy the page or pages needing revision.

8C. Endorsement and Submission of the Theme

Your manuscript may be submitted flat or folded longitudinally as your instructor may direct. If you have more than one sheet, use paper clips to attach them together. Do not bend or dog-ear the corners of the pages. Unless your instructor directs otherwise, sign your name in the upper right-hand corner of the first sheet, followed by your class and section number and the due date of the completed exercise (the date on which it is supposed to be submitted), as follows:

John R. Jamison
English 105c
September 25, 195–

On the second and following pages the name alone is sufficient; even it need not be used if the pages are securely clipped together. Submit your paper at the beginning of the class hour at which it is due.

9. REVISION OF THE CORRECTED PAPER

After your instructor has returned your paper, carefully study any advice he may have given you for its revision. As in your previous revision, if the errors are few and do not call for reorganization, they may be neatly corrected on the page. If, however, the errors are extensive, it will be advisable to rewrite the theme. In any event, revise first on the corrected page itself by drawing a single line through each discarded word or phrase and inserting a new expression, when needed, neatly above the line with a caret at the point of insertion. Then, if necessary, rewrite. Resubmit both the revised and rewritten copies to the instructor at the next class hour or at whatever time he designates for the return of revised themes.

This revision is very important. Though it may not change your mark for the particular theme involved, a carefully studied revision means progress toward your goal of effective writing. Therefore you must not guess at the meaning of your instructor's marks and symbols on your paper. These symbols are usually of two sorts. Either they are generally accepted abbreviations indicating faults (such as *coh.* for coherence, *inc.* for incomplete sentence), or they are numbers referring to the sections of the text. These section numbers are arranged in tabular form on the inside covers of this book.

When, for example, your instructor marks *p.* (or another agreed-upon symbol indicating an error in punctuation) in the margin, do not simply assume that a comma or some other mark of punctuation is needed. Look up the chapter on punctuation and find out precisely what punctuation is needed and why. If after an honest study of the problem you cannot discover the principle that applies to the fault, put a question mark in pencil after the instructor's criticism and ask him as soon as possible to explain it to you. Do not resort to him, however, until you have tried your best to find the answer in the text.

Keep a list of the errors or faults marked by your instructor in your themes. Such a list will show you at a glance your most common faults and also, as it grows shorter with succeeding themes, will encourage you with visible evidence of your improvement. Keep a separate list of the words which you misspell.

EXERCISE

The student themes that follow vary from good to bad. At least a few are carefully organized and well written. Some are fairly good, others mediocre, and some very poor. Using the questions in "A Test for Themes" (pp. 49–50) as a guide, analyze each of these themes and try to determine its value.

PING-PONG AND TENNIS

There is a wide difference between the sharp "click-click" of a ping-pong ball striking the paddle and table top and the snapping "twang" of a tennis ball striking the gut of a tennis racquet; but the difference between the exertion and the brain work required in the two games is almost negligible.

I have played tennis at times until I have become so tired that the quarter-mile between the court and my home has seemed as endless as infinity. I played tennis at times until I became so tired that I could not sleep, but lay awake half the night, or dozed off to awaken suddenly with a feeling that I was dashing desperately across the court in pursuit of a hotly hit fore-arm drive. But I have also played games of ping-pong when my shirt has been drenched with perspiration, my head has ached, and eyes have stung. I played games of ping-pong until I became so tired that I could not close my eyes without seeing ping-pong balls loom out of the darkness and flash past. Ping-pong is no rocking-chair game any more than golf is too tame for anyone under sixty-five.

Tennis requires that the players dash about the court with their utmost speed in an attempt to get in a position from which they can reach the ball. It requires that the players at times strike the ball with every ounce of force which they can summon, that they strive to the limit of their endurance and even a little beyond. It places almost every possible strain upon the body.

It is true that ping-pong does not require that you dash ten or fifteen yards at top speed in every rally, but on the other hand, you do at times have to move around the edges of the table at a speed somewhat in excess of that attained by the worm in its nocturnal ramblings. And in ping-pong there is no letup between serves. The point is won or lost and the ball served again. There is no pause while you walk back to the base line, pick up the balls, tie a shoelace, and examine your racquet. Instead, the ball when knocked out of court is picked up from the floor and—click, click—served again; no letup, no pause, no hesitation, nothing but unceasing action from the first point to the last.

Ping-pong requires faster brain-work than tennis. In tennis you generally have time to take at least three steps before you hit the ball. During these three steps you have plenty of time to decide where to hit the ball in order to do the most damage to your opponent's game. But in ping-pong you hardly have time to shoot a glance at your opponent to see at which side of the table he is standing. The ball crosses the net, bounces, is hit back, bounces, is hit again—all without a pause and with scarcely a glance away from the table. In fact at times the clicks seem almost to overlap. The mental fatigue in ping-pong is about five times as great as in a tennis game of the same duration.

And doubles—they are something else again. In tennis, doubles are considerably easier than singles. Each partner covers half the court, and any time he gets a chance to hit the ball he does. But ping-pong is different. How different you cannot fully appreciate until you have seen a real fast game of doubles. Because in ping-pong each partner covers the whole table on alternate shots. When the ball comes over the net and bounces, one of the two partners hits it. The next time it comes over, the other partner hits it, and so on in alternation. And the man who has just hit the ball must attempt to make himself resemble the flame of an extinguished candle in order that his partner may be unobstructed when he reaches for the ball. So you see that with one man slipping out of the way, and with his partner dashing back into position again on one side of the table, and with the opponents of these two players doing the same thing on the other, the whole thing resembles a football field immediately after the referee has blown his whistle. Ping-pong may be a parlor game, but I should hesitate before recommending it to someone who had to stop playing tennis because of a weak heart.

A CITY OF VILLAGE CHARM

Manchester symbolizes to me a way of life, a truly American way of living. Throughout its veins pulses the blood of our nation, the stalwart vigorousness of sincere folk who live life to its fullest. The tradesmen sweeping their sidewalks in the early morning, the boys with faces pressed against the window of the "Plumbing and Supply," which sells the makings of model airplanes, a chattering squirrel bobbing across the doctor's lawn—all these are a part.

On Thursday and Saturday nights our village overflows with people; people from the mills, people from home, the office, women in cotton dresses—some dressed for a movie, heavy boned farmers in huge, clumping boots, hunters in plaid shirts, inspecting with a critical eye the shotguns and new stock of orange and blue hunting caps displayed by "Wards'." Down by the "Hayes Stables," a relic of a half century ago, a clerk is demonstrating the advantages of a three-wheeled tractor. A small "pick up" whizzes by with a week's supply of eggs. Tonight it will carry home bags of grain, along with a contented poultryman. Perhaps he played a few games of Bingo at the American Legion Home, swapping yarns and renewing acquaintances. Perhaps went to "Bergrenn's" with his family to taste the new concoction of bananas, ice cream, pineapple, cherries, and maple syrup.

The bank's clock booms seven as a group of Scouts pass on their way to a meeting. Every other driver waves to the traffic officer who stands in the spotlight, exchanging greetings while he does his job. The Salvation Army Band can be heard playing "Rock of Ages" from its usual spot by the curb. On the side streets soft light from living room windows floods sectors of lawn. Men relax with the paper and a pipe, and women with their sewing—in the security which they have built.

They symbolize a way of life which has always been an American ideal, which is its own reason for being, and which I hope reverently to lead.

HISTORY IN HIGH SCHOOL AND COLLEGE

A former user of my high-school history book wrote inside the front cover:

> If all the world were flooded
> And I were doomed to die,
> I'd stand upon this history book
> Because it is so dry.

I could see his point. Nothing could be more uninspiring than learning a conglomeration of dates, names, and dull, dead facts. Studying a war meant memorizing the date of its beginning and ending, the names of generals and rulers, and the important battles. There was no discussion of the motives underlying the stated reasons for the war; no account was given of the struggle and heartbreak it brought the people. Peacetime was even less interesting. Someone painted a picture, another invented a machine; we remembered their names and birth dates long enough to pass a test, then promptly forgot them. Elections did not represent the growth of a nation, the advance of civilization, but only another list of names and dates. I had respect for my teachers and supposed they knew best; but sometimes when they asked something like "What was the maiden name of General Blank's second wife?" a small voice whispered rebelliously, "Who cares?" Our history courses cluttered our minds with useless details and all but extinguished our interest in the past.

When I learned that history would be a required subject in my freshman year at college, my feeling was not one of elation. However, the course is not like the one in high school. It is the story of the progress of civilization, of the why behind historical events, rather than an itemized account of the events themselves. We learn to appreciate the struggles past generations have gone through to create the world as we know it. The aim is to realize how human, how like ourselves they were. The individual pieces learned in the past fall into place and are held together in an understandable whole by our new conception of their importance in the advance of our culture. In high school we learned the date of Socrates' death and of the fall of Rome; now we discover the characteristics of a civilization that could put to death one of its greatest men, and see how the actions of various peoples and sects led to the destruction of an empire. The past lives again, connected to the present by the knowledge that the ancient world made us what we are today.

THE SCIENTIFIC OUTLOOK

I have trouble with all my science courses because I cannot avoid looking at them from an aesthetic point of view. I spent Saturday, for example, in a parasitology laboratory. If you know anything at all about parasitology, and I am inclined to think that few people do, you will know that it is one of the less aesthetic sciences. It deals, roughly, with the intimate details of dysentery, diarrhea, malaria, and other human parasitic diseases. And yet, several times during the course of the morning, I found myself oh-ing and ah-ing over some of the more malignant parasites of man. They are so cute. Take *Opisthorcus tonkae*, for example. The name itself is fascinating enough, but the animal is even more so. In a stained preparation it is a pinkish, oval thing with a variety of dark and light specks, lines, and splotches that, with the aid of a laboratory instructor and a descriptive chart, become internal organs. From an aesthetic point of view, however, they form an extremely pleasing design. And while I sit lost in contemplation of straight lines and curves, old roses and light pinks, my classmates are identifying these lines as sex organs and alimentary canals.

Then, too, my sense of the ridiculous gets the better of my scientific outlook. For instance, there is a parasite called *Hymenolepis megalops*. The classification sheet tells me that it (you can scarcely say he or she of a parasite) is a tapeworm of chickens and other animals, and I suppose it causes the chicken some uncomfortable moments. To me, however, it is the funniest looking thing I have ever seen. It has a large square head with four large suckers, one in each corner, resembling giant eyes. Its long and wormlike body is considerably narrower than its head, and consists of bell-shaped segments, each one fitting neatly into the one before it. The whole thing is stained a bright pink. On first seeing this amazing creature I couldn't stifle a little squeak of delight. "How perfectly silly! What a funny, stupid-looking thing," I said aloud. In the silence of the room my voice seemed to awaken echoes, and the instructor looked at me strangely.

I react the same way in all my science courses. In chemistry laboratory I have an overwhelming desire to drink the varicolored liquids in the reagent bottles. I am particularly tempted by the exquisite blue of copper sulphate. The solution looks clear and cool and clean, and it sets me to dreaming of strange, far-off lands, and queer fairy people, and all the unreal things I read about as a child. I feel that I would like to drink it or drown in it. To date, however, I have been realistic enough to resist. Ferric chloride affects me in another way. I would like to bathe in it. It has a warm, golden-orange color and it makes me think of autumn, and wood fires, and a new wool suit. In bacteriology laboratory I have been heard to say, "Look, how nice and red," when blood was first drawn from a poor, prostrate rabbit, and a positive presumptive test fills me with delight because the tiny inverted fermentation tubes look cute when they are half filled with gas.

My attitude is definitely affecting my grades. I can't remember classification, reactions, underlying principles, or general theory. I remember only that in stained preparation such-and-such an organism was green and pink with a fascinating embroidery of black lines; that a blue liquid and a brown liquid gave quantities of star-shaped white crystals; and that sometimes when I added alpha naphthol to a broth culture I got a cherry red color and sometimes I didn't. As you can see, these facts, though interesting and important to me, are scarcely any help on an examination.

CAMBRIDGE FROM THE ATMOSPHERE

Have you ever seen Cambridge from the top of Tunnel Hill at night? I have seen it many times. The one time I remember best was a cool evening in September. It was late in the afternoon when I decided to drive to the top of the hill. As I reached the top, I found myself in the middle of one of the most beautiful sunsets I have ever seen. I could barely see the sun as it set behind the hills in the west. All that was visible were the rays which shown through the trees. It was a very beautiful sight as the sun rays seemed to illuminate all the different colors visible in an autumn tree. A few minutes later there was no sun. Slowly the bright city fell into darkness. Lights all over town began to flicker on. Most of them were in the homes. Then there was the theaters, restaurants, and factory lights. I could see the marquee of the Colonial Theater in the distance.

Then I saw what is, perhaps, the most important factor of a city. The people. As they walked beneath me like giant flees I couldn't help wondering about them. What were they doing or thinking? What are their problems? What do they expect to do in the future. I couldn't help wondering about them.

I could see long lines of cars with their lights on. The center of town is where I saw the most of them. When I looked toward the right, I could see the old National Road with its' heavey traffic heading home after a busy weakend.

Then I turned toward the left. There, near at hand, were the several factories in the industrial section. I saw two giant smoke stacks, and as I watched them, they began to toot. I looked at my watch, and much to my amazement, it was already twelve midnight.

When I looked over the city again it seemed almost deserted. Many of the cars had parked for the night, the people had left the streets and entered their homes, and the once gay town began to turn into a morgue.

I started for home thinking that this was the end of a perfect autumn evening. Then when I thought of what I saw, I said to myself "Yes, this is Cambridge."

MULBERRY GARDEN

I like to think of my childhood. If I were to write an autobiography, I think I should spend at least three-fourths of the book on my youth. I should have chapters on chapters telling about Bobby's and my adventures in her large back yard.

All I can think of now when I say back yard, is a spacious garden playground, aproned with grass that was thick and shiny green. There were rows of red tulips there, and purple iris. Beside them was a patch brick path. The part we liked most was at the far end of the yard that belonged to the fat crab apple trees polka-dotted with red. From one of the trees hung a swing. We always raced for it, for there it was cool, and the low shade made us dreamy. When we grew tired of swinging, we sat quietly watching the busy ants race over the tiny dry hills of dirt. By watching their never-ending labors, we learned to respect them and avoided crushing them with our clumsy feet. Occasionally, of course, we grew impatient with the ants that climbed and tickled our legs. We did not look when we slapped them.

We often had tea parties under the mulberry tree. After we had carried down the small yellow table from the play room out into the sun, we placed four low chairs at each side of the table. We sat Winnie the Pooh, a brown bear, at one side, his button nose resting just above the table, the sun sparkling into his glass eyes; and Anna Bella, our most graceful doll, sat across from him. Bobby and I sat in between the two. We looked lovingly at our guests, first at the brown short bear, small and unassuming, and then at Anna Bella with her golden hair and shiny cheeks resplendent in the morning air. We loved them both, the shaggy bear and the lovely doll. Every now and then we patted down the bear's fur or smoothed out the doll's dress. We drank our chocolate as if it were tea, taking small sips at a time, keeping always the little finger curled high in the air.

When we played too long beneath the umbrella tops of the mulberry tree, our dresses became stained with indelible purple blotches. Bobby and I could not resist the delicacies of those small purple berries, no matter how great the penalty. Feeling the warm juicy pulp slide down our throats made us associate the taste with purple. For it was purple hands that pushed purple berries into a purple mouth. The flavor itself was purple.

We looked forward to Fall. Bobby's father always gave us rides in the wheelbarrow after he made a high seat of dry crumply leaves. It was a quiet ride from one end of the yard to the other, with only the low grumble of the wheel and the dry sound of the seat upon which we sat. To enjoy the ride, all our senses had to be awake. Every part of the garden had a special odor, of apples, and grass, and leaves. All the freshness and sweetness of the air we breathed was a part of us. Even as young as we were we could feel the sadness in the air of fading summer days. We did not mourn for long. The clear October air put new energy into our bodies. We climbed trees and talked to the remaining flowers; we rolled in the leaves and jumped from high places.

Now just as if someone has pulled a long black shade over that part of life, childhood has passed. How strange it is to revisit the place where we played! Now nothing remains but a memory, sweeter, sometimes I think, than any fleeting time of that childhood.

"PORTRAIT OF MY DAUGHTER" BY DOMINICO VALINOTTI

"I wonder what the artist looks like."

When I voiced this comment, several people stared at me in wonderment, as if I was some sort of an amazing specimen. I realize now that that was not the proper type of remark to make at the International Art Exhibition. One should critically survey the collection of paintings, then exclaim over the perfection of the composition and color harmony. This criticism should be of such intelligent quality that anyone who might overhear would admire the keen perception of the critic. However, when I saw the painting entitled "Portrait of My Daughter" by Dominico Valinotti I was so astounded that I expressed the first thought that came into my mind. I had always pictured an artist as being—well, a rather thin, unkempt individual with ragged clothing and untidy black hair; there is a forced soulful expression on his otherwise expressionless face; his eyes have a dreamy look, without the slightest spark of intelligence. But because in this portrait the daughter of the painter is nothing more than a common, ordinary-looking child, very plain and simple, I began to realize that my conception of an artist must be wrong. "Why, the father of that girl must be a very human person," I thought. I was filled with admiration for the unknown man, because I could see in his nature a desire to portray the world as it is, even though it be grim and cold, rather than falsely represent it in lovely, flattering colors. That fact, perhaps, made the attraction of Mr. Valinotti's painting greater than any other which I saw at the International. There was no evidence of intricate lines or beautiful coloring. Surrounded by masterpieces of subtle beauty, it was a rather drab-looking specimen. Yet it presented to me, by means of its few simple lines, a character sketch so realistic that it left a vivid impression on my mind of the remarkable talent of the artist.

As she is portrayed, the daughter of the artist is a very unlovely child of about twelve years of age. She is standing in an ungraceful position, arms hanging listlessly by her side, feet slightly apart and pointed outward. She is wearing a white cotton dress and a tan coat. The coat is trimmed with a frayed-looking beaver collar, and there is a tiny red flower in the buttonhole. Her legs, which remind one of wooden sticks, are encased in white cotton stockings, which, miraculously, are not wrinkled. Her straight, taffy-colored hair is arranged in a neat, yet unbecoming manner. The glasses which she wears are too large for her face and give her a rather owl-like appearance. I think they would be better referred to as "spectacles." Her mouth and nose, which are rather pretty and delicate, are not emphasized. Her face shows no signs of intelligence. Wonderment is expressed in her large grey eyes, as if she doesn't understand just what it is all about. She doesn't impress one as being a timid youngster, and yet, she is decidedly not at ease. I don't believe she would be popular with her schoolmates, for she shows no qualities which might endear her to another child. The room in which she is standing is a somber, uninteresting one, the only spot of color being a tiny figured curtain over the door-window. When I came upon this picture after having seen the other beautifully colored ones around it, I felt as if a bucket of cold water had suddenly been thrown over me. I shivered, and my eyes sought the little curtain for warmth, but it was so small that it only emphasized the drabness of the room. Quite a remarkable painting.

I admire the artist for his courage in painting such a picture. I admire him for his ability in making so vivid a character sketch. I admire him for his achievement of so unlovely a masterpiece. I admire him for his bravery in labeling it "Portrait of My Daughter."

WORKING IN AN IRON FOUNDRY

With the glow of white hot metal in my face and perspiration streaming down my body the ladleman shouted runout as the molten iron came spouting forth from the mold which he was pouring, forming a sea of flowing liquid at the bottom of the pit seventy-five feet below in which he was pouring the mold, while men played water hoses on the leak trying to freeze the iron so that it could be plugged up with fire clay. This was but one of the experiences that I went through while working for a year in the Torrel-Birmingham Iron Foundry in Ansonia, Conn., prior to coming to school. Above the roar of eight cranes, having a total lifting capacity of over two hundred tons, could be heard the sharp crackling of the electric furnace starting to melt down another heat of alloy iron for use in molds to be used in the defense program. Similar to the blast furnace are the four cupola furnaces, which together with the electric furnace have a total melting capacity of over one hundred and fifty tons a day. Of the many things to watch, the most interesting is the boiling of steel in order to lower its carbon content. During the time it is boiling, a series of laboratory tests are run to analyze the metal for carbon, sulphur, silicon and manganese in order to get the highest possible strength from the metal. When satisfactory results are received, a whistle is blown by the head melter to inform all concerned that the metal is ready to leave the furnace. A crane then picks up a huge preheated ladle and lowers it into a pit adjacent to the furnace. With everything prepared the whole furnace is slowly lifted up by a huge set of gears, which are concealed beneath the furnace, and the molten iron leaves the furnace at a temp of about 2600° F. Streaming into the ladle, it showers the area with sparks that present a spectacle similar to a fireworks display. Some of the products that are made from this metal are rubber mills, used chiefly by Firestone and Goodyear, large grinders and hydraulic presses, huge stone crushers, three thousand ton extrusion presses to be used in stamping out airplane parts, torpedo tube punches, gun molds, sugar mills so large that they would occupy a whole length of the library reserve room and perhaps three quarters of its width. Recently, there was cast and machined the largest paper mill in the world at this thriving industrial centre, which has the largest tonnage output capacity for any foundry in New England. Having become so interested in foundry work, I have decided that I should like to enter the field of metallurgy, for which this work has given me a great deal of practical experience.

MY EDUCATION IN TRAVELING

They say that traveling about the world, is the best way to complete your understanding of geographical and historical facts. Perhaps no one is able to agree with this, as much as an ex-serviceman can. In the next few paragraphs I would like to relate some of the places I saw, and what I got out of them in terms of an education.

In my four years in the Air Force, I covered approximately fifty five thousand miles. This included flights to Alaska, Japan, Korea, and thirty nine of the United States.

Alaska, the land of the Midnight Sun, was my home base for two years. There we saw a rugged Artic climate with all the unbelievable weirdness of twenty two hours of daylight in the summer, and nineteen hours of darkness during the winter months. It was here that I saw the magnificent Northern Lights with all their fiery beauty. Another sensation was being able to see the Siberean Coast while flying over Little Diomede Island on a clear day.

A flight to Japan, brought on a great change of pace in both atmosphere, and climate.

Here was a country that only seven years before, was terrorizing and shocking the United States in its conflict with us. Never before has a nation made such a rapid change from an ancient, superstitious way of life to one of modern civilization. Tokyo today is similar to a large American city.

The Koreans, unfortunately, being in a war zone, are still very primative in their ways of life. I saw a country that was beginning to grow in structure and culture, torn down to ruins. The city of Seoul was completely devastated, but one could still see that it was once a very beautiful capital, and built partly to resemble our own Washington D.C.

Our trips through the United States helped me to understand and agree with those who say that this nation is one of the most scenic and picturesque in the World. From Maine to California every state has an industry or culture, that it can be proud of.

These are a few of the things I saw and learned while in the service. They have helped me to develop a better viewpoint on world affairs, as well as a knowledge of the beauty that is in the world. This experience was priceless.

THE DUMP AT NIGHT

Black clouds which, since sunset, had come up from the west, covered the sky; and the sky and the hills were of one blackness. The white dust of the road beneath my feet was my only visual hold on my surroundings. But I knew the place very well. I knew that before me the road pitched steeply into a damp hollow to pass through a garbage dump whence it rose and wound around the hill which stood opposite.

I stood still and set myself to catch the slightest sound. From a distance came the shrill, persistent noise of a cicada. Nearby there was a brushing of bushes and the rustle of an animal's body passing over leaves. The whiteness of the road and the hardness of it beneath my feet, the cicada, an occasional rabbit or squirrel, and the freshness of the autumn air, flavored by the grapes and apples which grew on the hills and the garbage which lay in the valley, were all I was directly aware of.

Stick and flashlight in hand, I began the short, rapid descent to the dump. My footsteps in the dust seemed unnaturally loud in the stillness; so I slackened my pace and stepped more quietly. Soon I had reached the bottom and was walking on hard gravel through the middle of the garbage. The flavor of apples and grapes had vanished from the air.

A black object on the road two or three feet in front of me moved. In a flash, I remembered advice recently given: "Use the light constantly in going through the dump—it's lousy with skunks at this time of year;" and in the same flash, I turned the light on a skunk. He was moving slowly away, a clumsy, coarse black-and-white-haired animal with a surprisingly long, mobile neck and head in which were little eyes that flashed in the light. I felt that he was unaware of my presence; so I stood there intrepidly and waited for him to get out of my way.

When he had gone on for some distance in his leisurely fashion, I played the light over the dump. The first thing I noticed was the flashing of the bright tin of junked cans; the second, skunks—six or seven skunks peacefully eating garbage. The quiet working of their teeth was the only sound in the place and it seemed dreadfully close and intimate. I was actually surrounded by skunks, and the thought of what I had just been through in the dark made me rather uncomfortable. As they continued their meal with unconcern and detachment, however, I took heart and advanced.

But there was one who gave me pause. To leave the dump, I had to go within two feet of him and I was very much afraid it might make him nervous. I kept the light on him, hoping it might cause him to move. But he ate on obliviously. His tail stood straight in the air and it looked ominous. With great patience, I waited three or four minutes for the little animal to finish his meal and pass on. Then, as time pressed, I decided to take a chance. Cautiously I advanced step by step. When I came abreast of him, he heard me and raised his head. His eyes flashed. I ran. Whether or not he was very much frightened, I never knew.

Chapter 2

STRUCTURE OF SENTENCES

10. THE SENTENCE: A DEFINITION

The sentence is a unit of expression of thought or emotion, grammatically independent of all other constructions. Though a grammatically independent unit, it almost always has logical relationship with other sentences in its context. Yet the fact remains that it is indeed a unit as well as a part of a whole, and must stand firmly on its own feet.

10A. Complete Sentence

The important basic form of the sentence is the structurally *complete sentence.* A complete sentence is a group of words containing a subject (something spoken of) and a predicate (a word or words making a statement), and so phrased as to be grammatically independent. Such sentences are our chief concern in the study of sentence structure.

10B. Virtual Sentence

But certain words and word groups that properly qualify as sentences do not meet the terms of the definition of a structurally complete sentence. Thus mere sounds spoken with the right intonation may convey a complete meaning in the situation in which they are used: "Tut, tut!" "Humph!" "Tsk, tsk." Or single words may suffice: "Yes." "Oh!" "Alas!" "Ouch!" "When?" Or groups of words not containing a subject and predicate may be complete in meaning in their context: "To be sure." "Many thanks." "Coming with us?" "Such a sight!" We make frequent use of such sentences; they are indispensable and entirely correct in conversation, and now and then a few of them serve effectively as transitions even in formal writing or speaking: "Now for the next point." "And now to summarize." Some of these sentences may be regarded as elliptical—that is, as having an implied subject or predicate or both. For example, "Coming with us?" is clearly equivalent to "Are you coming with us?" Often, however, these sentences are complete as they stand, and mean no more nor no less than they say: "Ouch!" "Alas!" All sentences of the types discussed in this paragraph may be called *virtual sentences* since they are complete in meaning, even though they lack the structural form of the grammatically complete sentence. These sentences are frequently needed in informal writing and speaking, but, since they are informal in manner, should be sparingly used in formal writing.

10C. Incomplete Sentence

Virtual sentences are to be distinguished from the *incomplete sentence,* a structure lacking one or both of the essential parts of the structurally complete sentence, and not complete in meaning. Though the incomplete sentence of this sort is occasionally used effectively in literary works, it has no place in student writing. (For a discussion of the incomplete sentence, see Section 12A.)

10D. Writing Good Sentences

Since the sentence is the medium most used in conveying coherent thought, it is extremely important to know how to write good sentences. In writing good sentences, you will find helpful a knowledge of several skills. You should understand what a sentence is, what its component parts are, and how they are put together. You should study the form of sentences, their patterns as they relate to your various thoughts. You should study the organization of sentences into larger units of thought, such as the paragraph and the whole composition. You should study the words themselves of which sentences are composed. And you should study the proper punctuation of sentences. Ideally all these studies should be concurrent, and to some extent they are. All are interrelated, and, in examining one, you learn something about all the others; moreover, your themes and all your expression will give you training in these skills before you definitely study them.

10E. "Rules" of Sentence Structure

In beginning the study of the sentence, we are first concerned with its structure, often spoken of as its grammar. A study of the structure of the sentence involves a study of the forms of words, their classifications, and their relationship to each other in sentences. These relationships are determined by usage. The so-called "rules" of grammar, so far as they have validity, were not established by grammarians, but are simply the record of the speech habits of the people using the language. The "rules" vary according to the ways people speak and write. What has been said earlier (see Section 2B) about the main levels of English (standard and nonstandard) and the varieties of these levels applies here with special force. Thus when you write formal English in a course thesis, you will be writing a language whose sentences follow rather precise rules of sentence construction, always, of course, subject to change with the passing of time. When you write or speak informal English, you will be using a language more flexible and unstudied than formal English. One of your tasks in learning how to write and speak effectively will be to distinguish between these two important kinds of standard English, which are equally good for their own purposes, and then to distinguish between the standard ways of expression and those of nonstandard English, which you must learn to avoid.

The nature of the writing or speaking that you do will determine the nature of the grammar that you use. If your subject matter calls for formal expression, your sentences will be formal in structure and tone; if your subject matter is informal, your sentences will tend to be informal in structure and tone. You will have no use for nonstandard English unless you are writing a narrative involving a character who uses slang, dialect terms, or grammar not acceptable in standard English.

10F. The Sentence and the Parts of Speech

Each sentence is made up of words—one, or few, or many; and every word in a sentence has its function. When we look up words in the dictionary, we find that every word is classified, according to its function in a sentence, as a noun, pronoun, verb, adjective, adverb, preposition, conjunction, or interjection. These terms, designating the primary structural parts of a sentence, are commonly known as the *parts of speech.* They may be simply defined, with examples, as follows:

A noun is a name of a person, place, object, or idea: *man, country, apple, truth.*

A pronoun is a word used in place of a noun: *he, she, this, some.*

A verb makes a statement that someone or something acts, is acted upon, or is in a state of being or becoming, in past, present, or future time: *runs, was hit, exists, becomes.*

An adjective modifies, that is, describes or limits the meaning of, a noun or a pronoun: *red* apple, *thoughtful* boy, *twenty* horses.

An adverb modifies, that is, describes or limits the meaning of, a verb, an adjective, or another adverb: run *swiftly, very* dark, *too* brightly.

A preposition indicates direction, position, time, result, or other abstract relationships and, placed before a noun or substantive (any word or group of words standing for a noun), serves to link it to some other word: *to, for, after, between.*

A conjunction joins a word to another word, a phrase (see Section 11B) to another phrase, or a clause (see Section 11C) to another clause: John *and* James. Over the hills *and* far away. You work *while* he sleeps.

An interjection is an exclamation, usually expressing emotion: *Oh! Alas!*

Words are useful only as parts of speech, functioning with other words to express thought. Every word functions as a part of speech, and many words may serve as two or more parts of speech, as, for example, the word *right,* which may be used as a noun (his *right*), a verb (He *rights* a wrong), an adjective (the *right* answer), and an adverb (Turn *right*). To know how a sentence is put together, you must know the parts of speech that compose it. Each part of speech has its own special characteristics and sentence functions, and we shall soon study these. But now let us look at the basic structure of the sentence itself.

11. BASIC STRUCTURE OF THE COMPLETE SENTENCE

11A. Subject and Predicate

Every complete sentence contains a subject and a predicate. The subject is either a noun or pronoun or a group of words functioning as a noun (known as a substantive), and represents the person or thing or idea discussed. The predicate is the part of the sentence in which something is said or asked about the subject.

Thus in simplest form a sentence might read *Children play.* Here the noun *children* is the subject, and the verb *play* is the predicate.

In the sentence *He ran,* the pronoun *he* is the subject. In *Learning to swim is easy,* the phrase *learning to swim* is the subject. In *That he lost is evident,* the clause *that he lost* is the subject of *is*; and within the clause, *he* is the subject of *lost.*

Sometimes the verb may consist of two or three or even four words:

He *will call.*
He *will be calling.*
He *should have been called.*

When *not* or its contraction is combined with a verb, it is regarded as an adverb rather than as part of the verb.

She *will* not *go.*
He *does*n't *care.*

11A1. Subject and Expletive. In a sentence such as *There is a surprise for you,* the word *there* is not the subject but is what is known as an expletive introducing the true subject, *surprise.* The verb in such a sentence is singular or plural depending upon whether the true subject is singular or plural.

There *is* one more candidate.
There *are* three reasons for his departure.

11A2. Modifiers and Complements. In even the simplest sentence there are likely to be qualifying words known as modifiers. Thus in the sentence *Two little children played happily,* there are two adjectives (*two* and *little*) modifying the subject (*children*), and an adverb (*happily*) modifying the verb (*played*). The subject with all its modifiers is known as the complete subject. Stripped of its modifiers it is known as the simple or true subject.

Further, the predicate may be composed not just of a single verb, but of a verb and a word or words known as a complement (that is, that which *completes* the predicate). Complements may be of various kinds:

DIRECT OBJECT:	He hit *me.*
INDIRECT OBJECT:	Give *Mary* the necklace.
SUBJECTIVE COMPLEMENT or PREDICATE NOUN:	Fred is a *hero.*
SUBJECTIVE COMPLEMENT or PREDICATE ADJECTIVE:	Tom is *angry.*
OBJECTIVE COMPLEMENT:	He called Fred a *hero.*
OBJECTIVE COMPLEMENT:	He made Tom *angry.*

The predicate in such sentences consists of the verb and any necessary complements. The predicate with all its modifiers and complements is known as the complete predicate.

11A3. Position of the Subject. Normally the subject and its modifiers come first in the sentence, followed by the predicate. But in interrogative sentences (questions) the subject is often preceded by part of the predicate (*Are you going? Has the doctor arrived?*), and in many imperative sentences (commands) the subject *you* is not expressed but understood (*Come with me. Do something.*). Occasionally the normal word order is inverted for variety or emphasis (*Home is the hunter. Gone are the days of chivalry.*).

11A4. Compound Subject and Predicate. Either the subject or the predicate or both may be compound:

COMPOUND SUBJECT: *Dickens* and *Thackeray* were contemporaries.

COMPOUND PREDICATE: He *sighed* and *squirmed* and *fidgeted.*
COMPOUND SUBJECT AND PREDICATE: *Bob* and *Steve laughed* and *shouted.*

EXERCISE

In the following sentences underscore each subject with a wavy line and each predicate with a straight line. Remember that the complement of a verb is part of the predicate.

1. John dislikes me.
2. He invited Mary to the dance.
3. Following the rules is important.
4. They will finish tomorrow.
5. That our team will win is unlikely.
6. The little boy could not find his mother.
7. There is unrest everywhere.
8. Give me credit.
9. There are peaches enough for everyone.
10. Are they coming?
11. I laughed and cried.
12. Happy is the man with a clear conscience.
13. The club elected Barbara secretary.
14. Ruth and June are twins.
15. He won't quit and admit defeat.

11B. The Phrase and Sentence Structure

A group of related words not containing a subject and predicate is known as a phrase. Phrases serve the function of a single part of speech—noun or adjective or adverb. They may be named according to both (*a*) the part of speech they stand for and (*b*) their grammatical structure. Thus a phrase may be called (*a*) a noun phrase, an adjective phrase, or an adverb phrase; and it may also be called (*b*) a prepositional phrase or a verbal (participial, gerund, infinitive) phrase.

11B1. Phrases Named After Parts of Speech.

NOUN PHRASES: *Learning to swim* is easy. [Phrase serves as subject of the verb *is.*]

She enjoys *setting the table.* [Phrase serves as object of the verb *enjoys.*]

He seems *to be a failure.* [Infinitive phrase functioning as a noun—here, a subjective complement.]

In a sentence such as *It is easy to skip rope,* the word *it* is not the subject but is what is known as an expletive introducing the true subject, the noun phrase *to skip rope.* The sentence might read, *To skip rope is easy.*

ADJECTIVE PHRASES: The man *at the door* is a stranger. [Phrase modifies the noun *man.*]

Exhausted by his efforts, he collapsed. [Phrase modifies the pronoun *he.*]

She has a report *to make.* [Phrase modifies the noun *report.*]

ADVERB PHRASES: Mary arrived *in the evening.* [Phrase modifies the verb *arrived.*]

I am happy *to meet you.* [Phrase modifies the adjective *happy.*]

11B2. Phrases Named According to Grammatical Structure.

PREPOSITIONAL PHRASES: *From noon to midnight* is too long. [Noun phrase used as subject.]

The girl *from Boston* is pretty. [Adjective phrase modifying the noun *girl.*]

He lives *in the suburbs.* [Adverb phrase modifying the verb *lives.*]

VERBAL PHRASES. Verbal phrases are based upon one of the three derivatives of the verb known as verbals: participle, gerund, infinitive (see Section 15H).

PARTICIPIAL PHRASES. Participial phrases are always used as adjectives:

The man *calling the roll* is the coach. [Phrase modifies the noun *man.*]

Drawing a deep breath, he dives in. [Phrase modifies the pronoun *he.*]

The guest *brought by Sue* was unwelcome. [Phrase modifies the noun *guest.*]

GERUND PHRASES. The gerund is always a noun, but gerund phrases may be used as nouns, adjectives, or adverbs.

Caution *in driving a car* is essential for safety. [*In driving a car* is an adjective phrase modifying *caution.*]
Catching lightning bugs is fun for children. [Subject of the verb *is.*]
Children enjoy *catching lightning bugs.* [Object of the verb *enjoy.*]
He lives *by using his wits.* [Adverb phrase modifying *lives.*]

INFINITIVE PHRASES. Infinitive phrases may be used as nouns, as adjectives, or as adverbs:

To worry about examinations is natural. [Noun phrase serving as subject of the verb *is.*]
He tried *to run away.* [Noun phrase serving as object of the verb *tried.*]
His idea is *to confuse his opponent.* [Noun phrase used as subjective complement.]
I have a favor *to ask Tom.* [Adjective phrase modifying the noun *favor.*]
We came *to have a talk with you.* [Adverb phrase modifying the verb *came.*]
He is likely *to be sorry.* [Adverb phrase modifying the adjective *likely.*]

EXERCISE

Identify each italicized phrase in the following sentences as (*a*) a noun, adjective, or adverb phrase and (*b*) a prepositional, participial, gerund, or infinitive phrase. Be prepared to justify your identifications.

1. The boy *in the blue suit* dislikes *playing the piano.*
2. *Burdened by his conscience*, the man *wanted for murder* considered *giving himself up.*
3. *Studying the past* is fascinating *to me.*
4. *Racing against time*, he arrived *at midnight.*
5. The stranger *introduced by my host* wanted *to discuss politics.*
6. The old man *from the country* stared *in disbelief.*
7. He tried *to be unconcerned* but abandoned the effort *at last.*
8. I was sorry *to be absent* when you came *to talk with me.*
9. *Running to her mother*, the little girl began *to cry.*
10. He found *counting the pigeons* difficult *to accomplish.*

11B 3. Absolute Phrases. A phrase that has no grammatical relationship to the rest of the sentence is called an absolute phrase. It usually consists of a noun or a pronoun modified by a participle: for example, "*The spring being rainy,* gardens were planted late." Such an absolute phrase is also called a nominative absolute.

11C. The Clause and Sentence Structure

A group of related words containing a subject and a predicate, but not a complete sentence in itself, is known as a clause. If a clause is grammatically independent, that is, if it could stand alone if detached from the rest of the sentence, it is called a main or independent clause; if it is not grammatically independent, it is called a subordinate or dependent clause. A subordinate clause is usually, but not always, attached to a main clause by a word indicating its dependence. Just like phrases, subordinate clauses serve the function of a single part of speech—noun or adjective or adverb—and are named accordingly.

11C1. Noun Clauses.

That I broke my arm is true. [Subject of the verb *is.*]
They charged *that he had robbed the bank.* [Object of the verb *charged.*]
He said *he would go.* [Object of the verb *said*; subordinating conjunction *that* understood.]
Give it to *whoever owns it.* [Object of the preposition *to.*]
Happiness is *what everyone hopes for.* [Clause serves as predicate noun, or subjective complement.]
You may call me *what you wish.* [Clause serves as predicate noun, or objective complement.]

In such sentences as *It is probable that he will refuse* and *It is a fact that we were defeated,* the word *it* is not the subject but is an expletive introducing the true subject, a noun clause. These sentences might read, *That he will refuse is probable* and *That we were defeated is a fact.*

11C2. Adjective Clauses.

Boston is a city *that fascinates me.* [Modifies the noun *city.*]
He *who hesitates* is lost. [Modifies the pronoun *he.*]
He is the boy *you want.* [Modifies the noun *boy*; relative pronoun *whom* understood.]

The runner *whose shoe came off* finished last. [Modifies the noun *runner*.]

I know the office *where he works*. [Modifies the noun *office*.]

Adjective clauses, which are also called relative clauses, are usually connected to the word modified by a relative pronoun such as *who, whose, which, that* or by a relative adverb such as *when, where, why*. The relative pronoun *whose* is also called a relative adjective, since it not only has a substantive as an antecedent but also modifies a substantive in the subordinate clause. (Thus, in the sentence *The runner whose shoe came off finished last,* the word *whose* refers to *runner* in its pronoun function and modifies *shoe* in its adjective function.) A relative adverb has a substantive as an antecedent and also modifies a verb in the subordinate clause. (Thus, in the sentence *I know the office where he works,* the word *where* has *office* as its antecedent and modifies *works* in its adverbial function. The clause introduced by a relative adverb is adjectival.)

11C3. Adverb Clauses.

He will come *when you call*. [Modifies the verb *will come*.]

I am happy *that you are here*. [Modifies the adjective *happy*.]

I am sorry *you are ill*. [Modifies the adjective *sorry*; subordinating conjunction *that* understood.]

Winston is hitting better *than he did last year*. [Modifies the adverb *better*, which in turn modifies the verb *is hitting*.]

Though he was late, he came at last. [Modifies the verb *came*.]

Had he seen her, he would have told her. [Modifies the verb *would have told*; subordinating conjunction *if* understood: "If he had seen her . . ."]

EXERCISES

A. Identify each subordinate (italicized) clause in the following sentences as a noun, adjective, or adverb clause. Be prepared to justify your identifications.

1. Frank, *who is now working hard*, will probably do much better than he did before.
2. I did not know *whether we would hear from him in time*.

3. The man *I was seeking* had been transferred to an office *where no outsiders were admitted.*
4. *That football is a popular sport* can hardly be denied.
5. He reported *that the mail had not yet been delivered.*
6. *Had I known that she was lonely*, I should have telephoned.
7. It is not true *that Perkins is a coward.*
8. Try *as he would*, he could not budge the rock *that blocked his way.*
9. I shall give a copy to *whoever asks me for one.*
10. My home is *wherever I happen to be.*
11. Selfishness made him *what he is.*
12. *Since the weather was threatening*, we stayed at home.

B. The sentences in the two preceding exercises have been kept short and uncomplicated in order that identification of phrases and clauses would be easy. In most sentences the task is somewhat more elaborate, though still not actually difficult. One phrase may modify a word in another phrase or in a subordinate clause, and a subordinate clause may modify a word in another subordinate clause or in a phrase. Study, for example, the following sentence: "The wood in the old chairs that came from the house in Wisconsin that Grandfather Morris built in 1867 was imported." The prepositional phrase *in the old chairs* is an adjective phrase modifying the noun *wood*; the subordinate clause *that came from the house in Wisconsin that Grandfather Morris built in 1867* is an adjective clause modifying *chairs*; the prepositional phrase *from the house in Wisconsin* is an adverb phrase modifying the verb *came*; the prepositional phrase *in Wisconsin* is an adjective phrase modifying the noun *house*; the subordinate clause *that Grandfather Morris built in 1867* is an adjective clause also modifying the noun *house*; and the prepositional phrase *in 1867* is an adverb phrase modifying the verb *built.*

In the following sentences identify properly each phrase and each subordinate clause.

1. At eleven o'clock Brittin, who had overslept, came to see the teacher about the examination. [3 phrases, 1 subordinate clause]
2. Concealing his irritation, he promised that he would attend the party at the club after he returned from the meeting. [3 phrases, 2 subordinate clauses]
3. A man whose name I do not know came to my aid when I was stranded on the lonely road that leads to Blair Corners. [3 phrases, 3 subordinate clauses]

4. That you were frightened when you saw a face at the window is not sufficient explanation of your behavior. [2 phrases, 2 subordinate clauses]
5. Playing eighteen holes of golf requires more energy than I have after a hard day at the office. [4 phrases, 1 subordinate clause]
6. The doctor said that the wound which the bullet had inflicted would heal in a few weeks if I stayed in bed. [2 phrases, 3 subordinate clauses]

11D. Basic Pattern in Sentences

Sentences are either declarative, imperative, or interrogative. That is, they may make a statement (*Tom gave me a dollar*) or issue a command (*Give me a dollar*) or ask a question (*Will you give me a dollar?*).

Sentences are also classified as simple, compound, complex, and compound-complex.

11D1. Simple Sentence. A simple sentence contains one main clause and no subordinate clauses.

The dog barked.
The girl with the auburn hair walked past without glancing at the boys on the corner.

A sentence containing a compound subject or a compound predicate or both is still a simple sentence.

Henry and Bill arrived together.
The water leaped and splashed.
Mary and her sister ran to the window and waved gaily.

11D2. Compound Sentence. A compound sentence contains two or more main clauses and no subordinate clauses.

The wind blew and the trees swayed.
Sweeping across the lake, the wind blew hard against the flimsy cottages, and the mighty trees swayed in the blast.
The roof leaks, the wiring is primitive, and the heating system is about to break down.

11D3. Complex Sentence. A complex sentence contains one main clause and one or more subordinate clauses.

Shoot if you dare.
I shall join you when you arrive.

My little brother, who is not quite six years old, was overjoyed when I told him that he could go fishing with me if he promised to keep quiet.

The leading contestants for the title are Jerry Brock, who represents Madison High School, and Alton Williams, who won the mile race in the city track meet.

11D4. Compound-Complex Sentence. A compound-complex sentence contains two or more main clauses and at least one subordinate clause.

I own the book that you need, but I cannot find it.

If I am late, go without me, but be sure to take the golf clubs.

The fans groaned when Smith came to bat, but when he drove the ball over the fence they swarmed from the stands and carried him from the field.

EXERCISES

A. Classify the following sentences as simple, compound, complex, or compound-complex. Identify each subordinate clause as a noun, adjective, or adverb clause.

1. Sweeping wide to his left, the halfback outran one tackler, dodged another, and raced forty yards before being brought down from behind.
2. I am sorry, but I can do nothing for a boy who will not try.
3. The low rumble of thunder gradually grew louder, the wind stirred the branches of the great oak, and finally a steady rain beat a tattoo on the tent.
4. When it became clear that Jones could not win, he instructed his supporters to vote for Smith.
5. We talk wistfully of the good old days, but who would want to do without the conveniences made possible by modern technology?
6. Start when you are ready.
7. On the basis of the number of plays currently produced, William Shakespeare, dead these three hundred years, must be regarded as the world's most popular playwright.
8. An author who plans to write a historical novel must spend months or even years on research if he is to give an accurate picture of the period in which his story takes place.
9. Most people head for the country on summer week ends, but I prefer to stay in the city rather than join the throngs that clog every road leading to the seashore or the mountains.

10. The girl who had waited on the meek little man was surprised when she found a fifty-cent tip modestly concealed under a saucer.

B. Classify each sentence in the following passage as simple, compound, complex, or compound-complex. Identify each subordinate clause as a noun, adjective, or adverb clause.

When the speeches and the fireworks that mark July 4 are over, the first signs of autumn soon become evident. It is true that the warmest days of summer are yet to come, but there is a warning in the air. Darkness creeps on a little earlier each evening, the golden wheat has been cut and stacked and hauled away, and katydids begin their monotonous chant. What has happened to the bursting spring that swept in such a short time ago? Now the leaves that were so green have turned brown in the dry weather, and the tumbling brook has dwindled to a silver thread winding through dusty fields. Do you remember those plans of yours to spend long afternoons on the golf course, to float lazily in the cool pond under the willow, to lie on the diving board basking in the sun? Hurry if you wish to accomplish them. Before you know it, birds will gather in twittering clusters ready to head southward, school bells will ring, and the woods will be dotted with red and gold. Autumn is a lovely season, no doubt, and even winter has its pleasures. But no man can escape a feeling of melancholy at the death of summer.

12. COMMON FAULTS IN SENTENCE STRUCTURE

12A. Incomplete Sentence

As we have seen, virtual sentences are permissible and necessary in informal writing and speaking, and may be employed occasionally in formal discourse as transitions (see Section 10B). Thus a writer may elect to punctuate as sentences certain words or word groups that do not meet the definition of a complete sentence. But he should do so only when he is justified by the circumstances. Usually a "sentence" that lacks subject or predicate or is not grammatically independent is an incomplete sentence (also called *fragmentary sentence, sentence fragment,* a result of *period fault*)—one of the most common and most objectionable of writing errors. A student who is guilty of writing incomplete sentences is probably ignorant of the fundamental principles of composition.

The test of completeness is to make certain that the sentence has a clause containing both subject and predicate and that this clause is a main (independent) one rather than a subordinate (dependent) one that cannot stand by itself. Though no limit exists to the variety of errors that may be committed by careless or uninformed writers, actually most incomplete sentences found in student writing fall into comparatively few categories:

(1) a subordinate (dependent) clause;
(2) a participial or prepositional phrase, often followed by a subordinate clause;
(3) an appositive, often followed by a long phrase or a subordinate clause;
(4) a substantive followed by a long phrase or a subordinate clause.

Often an incomplete sentence of one of the first three types is clearly dependent upon a complete sentence that precedes or follows it, and to correct the error the writer need only link the two, forming a single sentence. Sometimes, however, it is preferable to keep the thought in the incomplete sentence separate and make the sentence grammatically independent.

12A 1. Subordinate Clause.

Because George Washington is revered today as the hero of the Revolutionary War and as one of the founders of our nation. We are astonished to learn of the bitter attacks launched against him by political enemies during his presidency.
[Correction: Join the passages by a comma after *nation.*]

Richards is developing into a skillful passer and a cool, resourceful quarterback. *Though he never played football until he came to college.*
[Correction: Join the passages by a comma after *quarterback*. Or better: "Though Richards never played football until he came to college, he is developing . . ."]

When the summer visitors have departed and the people who live on the island the year round have the beach to themselves.
[Correction: "After the summer visitors have departed, the people who live on the island the year round have the beach to themselves."]

12A 2. Participial or Prepositional Phrase.

Turning his back upon the view which he knew he would never see again. The sick man signaled the driver to proceed.
[Correction: Join the passages by a comma after *again.* Or: "The sick man turned his back upon the view which he knew he would never see again. He then signaled the driver to proceed."]

I always received my poorest grades in mathematics. *From the time when I first struggled with the multiplication table to the day I received my college diploma.*
[Correction: Join the passages by a comma after *mathematics.* Or better: "From the time when I first struggled with the multiplication table to the day I received my college diploma, I always received my poorest grades in mathematics."]

The speaker warned that war would bring disaster to the nation. *Weakened as it was by internal strife and without a single dependable ally.*
[Correction: Join the passages by a comma after *nation.* Or better: "The speaker warned that for a nation weakened by internal strife and without a single dependable ally, war would mean disaster."]

12A 3. Appositive.

It was a pleasure to take a course under Professor Markwood. *A man of deep scholarship but gifted also with an extraordinary ability to interest even the dullest student.*
[Correction: Join the passages by a comma after *Markwood.* Or: "It was a pleasure to take a course under Professor Markwood. A man of deep scholarship, *he was* gifted also with an extraordinary ability . . ."]

Here at last was Clovernook, the place where I had spent my childhood. *The only place in the world that I could still call home.*
[Correction: Join the passages by a comma after *childhood.* Or: "Here at last was Clovernook, the place where I had spent my childhood. *It was* the only place . . ."]

12A 4. Substantive Followed by Phrase or Clause.

The man in the flowered sport shirt hurrying to the dock and throwing the end of a rope to the frightened swimmer.
[Correction: Change the participles *hurrying* and *throwing* into finite forms: "The man . . . hurried to the dock and threw . . ."]

The boy in the blue serge suit with the tell-tale shine and the frayed cuffs. [Correction: Supply a predicate to go with the potential subject *boy*: "The boy in the blue serge suit with the telltale shine and the frayed cuffs *walked shyly to the front of the platform*."]

Fred Watson, friend of the people, who has done more to clean up our county than anyone else, and to whom every citizen should be grateful.
[Correction: Supply a predicate to go with the potential subject *Fred Watson*: "Fred Watson, friend of the people, who has done more to clean up our county than anyone else, *deserves the gratitude of every citizen*."]

It must be added that experienced writers sometimes use for stylistic effect sentences that are clearly incomplete. Such sentences are almost always designed to achieve a purpose that the writer believes he cannot achieve so well otherwise. For example, a series of incomplete sentences is useful in presenting a number of descriptive details or the scattered thoughts of a fictional character. But ordinarily avoid writing an incomplete sentence; and if you wish to employ one for a particular effect, call the teacher's attention to it in a footnote and be prepared to defend it.

EXERCISE

Revise the following passages so as to correct any incomplete sentences that occur in them. Give reasons for your revisions. Some of the passages are correct as they stand.

1. That letter, written in his own hand, definitely proving that he planned the crime long before he committed it.
2. Harbin showed rare resourcefulness in finding odd jobs to keep himself in spending money. Though I do not believe that before this year he ever did a day's work in his life.
3. After you leave the village, turn left and follow the dirt road until you come to some white farm buildings. There you will see one of the oldest grist mills in this part of the country.
4. The executor's troubles began when the heirs learned the contents of the will. A document that, though prepared with obvious forethought, did not prove satisfactory to any of the dead man's relatives.

5. Through the whole golf course winds a brook that is a constant menace to the players. Particularly to one like Jim, who hits a long ball but cannot control it.
6. During the years that he was studying law at night while working a full eight-hour shift at the steel mill. He learned to live without many things that most young men consider as their birthright.
7. When my cousin visited me last month I took him at his request to see Chinatown. A part of the city that I had not visited since childhood.
8. Abraham Lincoln, an uncouth prairie lawyer who showed no promise of the greatness that was to be his, and Mary Todd, a provincial belle who came from a prominent family and was extremely ambitious.
9. Forty years in the diplomatic service had made Bemis a skilled negotiator. A cautious and cynical old man, but one who served his country loyally and with distinction.
10. Property damage of several hundred thousand dollars caused by the disastrous fire and only partially covered by insurance.
11. Florence Nightingale performed a service to humanity by establishing the foundations of modern nursing practice. A woman of iron will who lived a long and useful life, she is known chiefly for her exploits during the Crimean War.
12. As children we were forbidden to go near the old Underwood house. Standing neglected amid pines and dying fruit trees and rank weeds, and with an evil reputation as the haunt of tramps and other undesirable characters.
13. In the desperate hope that he could undo by personal explanations the harm done by his opponent's bitter attacks and change imminent defeat into victory. The Governor embarked upon a last-minute speaking tour of the entire state, determined to fight to the end.
14. The water tumbling and leaping down a steep, rocky slope and creating a foam that can be seen from the other side of the lake.
15. The hospitality that he had received from the natives and the balmy climate and restful leisure that made the spot seem like the traditional Pacific paradise so often described by enthusiastic writers.

12B. *And-Who, And-Which* Fault

Another fault indicating that the writer is unsure of the structure of a sentence is the insertion of *and* or *but* before a subordinate clause beginning with *who* or *which.* The insertion of *and* or *but* is permissible only when the subordinate clause is parallel with a previous clause introduced by *which* or *who.*

FAULTY: I spent the afternoon searching through the thick brush for the old swimming hole, but which is now so altered as to be unrecognizable. (Omit *but.*)

FAULTY: The only person in sight was a thin, frightened old man, and who assured us that he was not the proprietor. (Omit *and.*)

CORRECT: This is a cave which actually is very small, but which seemed to me enormous when I explored it as a child.

CORRECT: Bricker is the man who drove the bus that sad day and who testified at the inquest.

EXERCISE

Most of the sentences below are examples of the *and-who, and-which* fault. A few are correct as they stand. Revise and rewrite the incorrect ones.

1. I had never been so bored in my life as I was last night at the movie, and which was the first Western film I had seen in years.
2. One of the most interesting figures in baseball history was Babe Ruth, and who was the only man to hit as many as sixty home runs in a single season.
3. History may be resolved into the biography of determined men and women who had strong convictions and who followed them resolutely.
4. Some fighter pilots flew as many as five daily missions, and which exceeded all earlier performances.
5. Economists used to talk and write about a strange abstract creature and who was known as the "economic man."
6. There is a relationship between the information which a person has and the reading which he has done.

12C. Comma Splice

The term "comma splice" is applied to the error of *joining* by a comma two independent clauses that should be *separated* by a stronger mark of punctuation—the period, the semicolon, or the dash. The term is suggested by the procedure of splicing two ropes or parts of a rope bv interweaving the strands. The same error is often called "the comma fault," but this term may be misleading because it refers to only one of the many potential errors in the use of the comma. The incorrect sentence formed by means of a comma splice or comma fault is sometimes called a run-on or run-together sentence.

In a sense the comma splice is the reverse of the incomplete sentence. One is the incorrect joining of two independent clauses; the other is the incorrect punctuation of an incomplete or fragmentary passage as a sentence. Both errors reveal that the student who makes them does not understand what is and what is not a complete sentence.

The comma splice may be corrected by (*a*) separation of the independent clauses by a stronger mark of punctuation, (*b*) insertion of a co-ordinating conjunction, or (*c*) reduction of one of the independent clauses to a subordinate clause or phrase. These methods of correction are not always equally desirable. Select the one that best conveys your meaning.

COMMA SPLICE: The paneled walls of his office give an impression of luxury, the truth is that he found wood to be less expensive than plaster.

CORRECTIONS: [Separation] The paneled walls of his office give an impression of luxury. The truth is that he found wood to be less expensive than plaster. [Or use the semicolon.]

[Co-ordination] The paneled walls of his office give an impression of luxury, but the truth is . . .

[Subordination] Though the paneled walls of his office give an impression of luxury, the truth is . . .

COMMA SPLICE: Last summer I had the pleasure of viewing the Grand Canyon, it is the most thrilling sight I have ever seen.

CORRECTIONS: [Separation] Last summer I had the pleasure of viewing the Grand Canyon. It is the most thrilling sight I have ever seen. [Or use the semicolon.]

[Subordination] Last summer I had the pleasure of viewing the Grand Canyon, the most thrilling sight I have ever seen.

The use of a conjunctive adverb between independent clauses joined by a comma does not correct a comma splice (see Sections

17D 2, 20C, 32B). Thus independent clauses joined by such conjunctive adverbs as *accordingly, also, besides, consequently, furthermore, hence, however, indeed, moreover, nevertheless, still, then, therefore,* and *thus* must be separated by a stronger mark than the comma—usually the semicolon.

COMMA SPLICE: I cannot be of much help to you in making an electric kiln, however, I am sure that there are pamphlets available giving specific instructions.

CORRECTION: I cannot be of much help to you in making an electric kiln; however, I am sure that there are pamphlets available . . . [Or better: I cannot be of much help to you in making an electric kiln; I am sure, however, that there are pamphlets available . . .]

Look out for comma splices in sentences in which an expression like "he said" joins two independent clauses without a coordinating conjunction.

COMMA SPLICE: "You are much too late," he said, "the bus left an hour ago."

CORRECTION: "You are much too late," he said. "The bus left an hour ago."

But note that there is no comma splice in the following sentence:

"If you do not hurry," he said, "you will miss the bus."

Independent clauses that are short and closely parallel may be separated only by commas. Here the choice between comma and stronger mark of punctuation must be a matter of judgment.

The children cried, the dogs barked.
I came, I saw, I conquered.

Among some modern writers there is a growing tendency to use the comma at points where textbooks, including this one, urge the use of a stronger mark of punctuation. But avoid the comma splice consistently in your own writing. By doing so you will prevent falling into the habit of using it unintentionally.

12D. Fused Sentence

When independent clauses that should be separated by a full stop are run together without even a comma to separate them, the result is an even more serious error than the comma splice. The passage resulting from such fusion may be called a fused sentence. The remedy for this serious fault is twofold: first, learn what a sentence is; then correct the fused sentence by using the same methods that are employed in correcting the comma splice.

FUSED: A good station wagon is almost an essential for a vacation trip for a family we owned one which was only two years old and in good condition.

CORRECTION: A good station wagon is almost essential for a vacation trip for a family. We owned one which was only two years old and in good condition. [A semicolon might be used instead of a period after *family.*]

EXERCISE

Revise the following passages so as to correct any comma splices or fused sentences that occur in them. Some of the passages are correct as they stand. In revising, try not only to achieve technical correctness but to produce effective sentences.

1. Those clouds rolling up do not necessarily mean that we are going to have rain at last, you remember the old adage that all signs fail in dry weather.
2. More and more women are entering the world of business, where in many occupations they have already all but displaced men.
3. I came to this city seven years ago, at that time the newspapers were just as full of agitation for smoke control as they are today, but nothing has been done to improve conditions.
4. We know that the human brain is a wonderful organ containing billions of nerve cells, however, we know very little about how it actually works.
5. "There is no point in our discussing it further," he said, "we have no room in this firm for a man who cannot be trusted."
6. Pasteur said that chance favors the prepared mind, even a superficial study of the history of science demonstrates the truth of his remark.
7. It is not right to make a child draw what you want him to draw instead he should be encouraged to draw what he pleases.

8. In the nineteen-thirties the number of the unemployed rose to a staggering total, accordingly extraordinary measures were taken to relieve suffering and to preserve the self-respect of the unemployed.
9. The door opened into a long hall, where the faded curtains at the windows stirred as the fresh air swept in for the first time in twenty years.
10. My heart sank when I reached for my wallet and found my pocket empty, too late I remembered that at the last moment I had decided to change to my brown suit.
11. As he lay in the summer sunshine the sound of a lawnmower came from somewhere out of sight beyond the trees, when the others arrived, eager to know how he had fared in the examination, they found him sleeping peacefully.
12. A series of excellent programs is arranged each year many leading artists are brought to the valley to take part in the productions.

12E. Adverbial Clause as Subject

A clause beginning with "because" is an adverbial clause, not a noun clause, and should not be used as subject.

FAULTY: Because the water is muddy does not mean that we have to abandon our fishing trip. [Adverbial clause wrongly used as subject.]

IMPROVED: We do not have to abandon our fishing trip just because the water is muddy.

FAULTY: Because you have a headache is no reason for spoiling the picnic for the rest of us. [Adverbial clause wrongly used as subject.]

IMPROVED: That you have a headache is no reason . . .
You should not spoil the picnic for the rest of us just because you have a headache.

12F. "Reason Is Because"

A statement beginning "The reason . . . is . . ." should logically be completed by a clause beginning with *that* (noun clause) rather than one beginning with *because* (adverbial clause).

FAULTY: The reason we are late is because we ran out of gasoline. [The reason this sentence is faulty is that "because" duplicates the idea already expressed in "reason."]

IMPROVED: The reason we are late is that we ran out of gasoline. [Noun clause, subjective complement of the verb *is*.]
We are late because we ran out of gasoline. [Adverbial clause properly used to modify the predicate *are late*.]

The use of a "because" clause as a noun clause is widespread in current speech and found often in current writing, particularly when "reason" and "because" are widely separated. But the usage is clearly redundant, and careful writers will avoid it.

EXERCISE

Correct the structural faults in the following sentences:

1. Because John misunderstood what I said about his conduct at the party caused a coolness between us.
2. Because I was such a brat that no baby-sitters would consent to stay with me forced my parents to take me with them wherever they went.
3. Schuyler at last admitted that the reason he was angry was not because he disliked the decision but because he had not been consulted.
4. The reason that the party faces defeat next year is because the governor and the legislature have failed to agree upon a tax program that will suit the voters.
5. Because Great Britain and France were reluctant to take a firm stand that might lead to war enabled Hitler and the Nazis to rearm Germany.
6. The reason for the collapse of the team is because several key players have been plagued by injuries.

Chapter 3

PARTS OF SPEECH AND SENTENCE STRUCTURE

For brief definitions of the parts of speech, see "The Sentence and the Parts of Speech," Section 10F.

13. THE NOUN AND SENTENCE STRUCTURE

13A. Definition and Classification

A noun (derived from Latin *nomen,* meaning *name*) is the name of a person, place, object, or idea. All names of things of all sorts are nouns. All nouns may be classified as either proper or common.

13A 1. Proper Nouns. Proper nouns are the specific names of persons, places, or things: *Shakespeare, Roosevelt, London, Friday, France, Connecticut, Lincoln Memorial, The New York Times, Goldilocks.* Proper nouns are always capitalized in English.

13A 2. Common Nouns. Common nouns are names that can be applied to any one of or all the members of a class of persons, places, or things: *man, men, city, apple, fruit, opinion, biscuit, radio, machine.* All common nouns may be divided into two classes, concrete and abstract. A limited group of common nouns are known as collective nouns.

13A 3. Concrete Nouns. Concrete nouns name things perceived by the senses: *man, men, city, apple, biscuit, radio, machine.*

13A 4. Abstract Nouns. Abstract nouns name qualities, ideas, concepts: *goodness, purity, humanity, opinion, truth, liberty,* *philosophy*. When personified, abstract nouns are often capitalized like proper nouns: *Fortune, Holiness, Pity*.

13A 5. Collective Nouns. Common nouns that name collections of persons, animals, or things are known as collective nouns: *army, people, class, gentry, multitude, herd, flock, team*.

13A 6. Expressions Serving as Nouns. Any word or written or spoken symbol of any sort, or a phrase, or a clause may serve as a noun in a sentence, and is often called a substantive:

X marks the spot where the conspirators met. [*X*, as subject of the verb *marks*, functions as a noun.]
Shoot is a transitive verb. [*Shoot* functions here as a noun-subject.]
The *beautiful* is not always true. [*Beautiful* is an adjective functioning as a noun-subject.]
To have the gift of good taste is a mixed blessing. [The infinitive phrase *to have the gift of good taste* serves as a noun-subject.]
That America is overpopulated was the main theme of his speech. [The clause *that America is overpopulated* serves as a noun-subject.]

13B. Gender

Nouns may be classified also according to gender as masculine, feminine, and neuter. Since in English this distinction is made on the basis of sex alone, there are no problems regarding the form of the word or agreement between adjective and noun such as exists in German, French, and Latin. All nouns designating male creatures are masculine; all designating females are feminine. All other nouns are of neuter gender, though a few of these by general consent are also spoken of as masculine or feminine, as indicated by the pronouns associated with them. Thus the following are often spoken of as feminine: *ship, car, moon,* and such abstractions as *truth, justice, liberty*.

The moon in her beauty tonight. . . .
Truth crushed to earth will rise again;
  The eternal years of God are hers.

In poetic statement, such words as *sun, death,* and *time* are often masculine.

A few nouns employ the endings *-ess, -ette, -trix* to indicate feminine gender: *heiress, actress, countess, empress, majorette, aviatrix.* But today we speak of a woman as a poet (not *poetess*), editor (not *editress*), author (not *authoress*).

13C. Inflection (Case and Number)

Nouns vary somewhat in form according to their use in a sentence. Such variation is called inflection. Noun inflection, a complicated feature of other languages, is fortunately very simple in English. Most of our nouns conform to one pattern, having two forms (cases) for the singular and two for the plural; in other words, we have a common form and a possessive form for the singular and a common form and a possessive form for the plural. The common forms may be used in every part of the sentence except where it is desirable to indicate possession with the case endings *-'s* or *-s'*.

	Singular	Plural
Common:	boy	boys
Possessive:	boy's	boys'

Note these exceptions: *man, woman, goose, mouse, ox, child* still retain early plural forms that trace back (with changes) to Old English: *men, women, geese, mice, oxen, children.* A few other nouns, also of Old English origin, lost their special plural endings in Old English times and have none today: *sheep, deer.* A number of nouns, derived from Greek, Latin, French, and other languages frequently retain their original plurals as in the following examples: *phenomenon, phenomena; thesis, theses; alumnus, alumni; criterion, criteria; curriculum, curricula; medium, media; madam, mesdames.* Some of these tend to conform to the common pattern (plural in *-s*), and a few have both forms. Always consult the dictionary when in doubt about any of these plurals.

13D. Function of Nouns

In a sentence a noun may serve as subject, subjective complement (or predicate nominative), direct object of a verb, object of a preposition, objective complement, indirect object of a verb, a word of direct address, a possessive, or an appositive. Some nouns may also be used as verbs (see Section 15B 3 b) or adverbs (see Section 17E 3).

13D 1. Subject. The subject of a verb is the person, thing, or idea about which something is asserted or affirmed:

John is a lawyer.
The *house* is octagonal.
Truth triumphs over persecution.

13D 2. Subjective Complement. The subjective complement is a noun (or any construction serving as a noun) or adjective that fills out or completes the meaning of a linking verb (forms of the verb *be, become, seem,* and other verbs of similar function: see Section 15B 2):

Beauty is *truth.*
He seems *honest.*

A noun serving as a subjective complement is often called a predicate noun.

Note: In writing definitions, avoid using clauses introduced by *when* or *where* as subjective complements:

FAULTY: Fratricide is when one kills one's brother.
CORRECT: Fratricide is the act of killing one's brother.

FAULTY: Home economics is where a girl learns the best ways of homemaking.
CORRECT: Home economics is the study of the problems of homemaking.

13D 3. Direct Object. The object of a verb, often called the direct object, is that which immediately receives the action, or is the result of the action, of a transitive verb. It may be a noun or any construction that stands for a noun:

The batter hit the *ball.*
The teacher dismissed the *class.*
The baker makes *bread.*

Occasionally verbs take a double object:

They asked the *farmer* the *way* to Lehighton.

(See also *retained object,* Section 15C 1).

13D 4. Object of Preposition. The object of a preposition is the noun (or any word or group of words standing for a noun) linked by the preposition to the word or phrase that it (together with the preposition) describes or limits.

The prince slid down the *mountain* of *glass.* [*Mountain* is the object of *down; glass* is the object of *of*.]

13D 5. Objective Complement. The objective complement fills out or completes the meaning of a noun or pronoun object:

They elected Garfield *President.*
They named [chose, appointed] Charles *secretary.*

13D 6. Indirect Object. The indirect object names the person or thing to or for whom an action is done:

He gave *John* a book.
He did *John* a favor.

The indirect object may be distinguished from the direct object in the following way: If the preposition *to* or *for* can be inserted before the supposed indirect object, or if the supposed indirect object can be made over into a prepositional phrase following the direct object, then we can be sure that it is an indirect object:

He gave to John a book.
He gave a book to John.

He did for John a favor.
He did a favor for John.

13D 7. Direct Address. A noun is used in direct address when one uses it parenthetically to single out or name the person spoken to:

Jerry, try to remember the salt.
If you would concentrate, *George,* you would not make so many errors.

13D 8. The Noun and Possession. For discussion of this important special function of nouns, see Section 36A.

13D9. Appositive. A noun is used as an appositive when it identifies or supplements the meaning of an immediately preceding noun:

Lincoln, the great *Emancipator*
William, the *cook*
Mr. Burroughs, my *employer*

EXERCISES

A. Study the following passage in the light of the definitions under 13A above.

1. Make a list of all the common nouns in the passage.
2. Divide this list of common nouns into concrete and abstract nouns.
3. List any proper nouns and collective nouns used by the author.

The English language is like a broad river on whose banks a few patient anglers are sitting, while, higher up, the stream is being polluted by a string of refuse-barges tipping out the muck of Fleet Street and the B.B.C. The English language has, in fact, so contracted to our own littleness that it is no longer possible to make a good book out of words alone. A writer must concentrate on his vocabulary, but he must also depend on the order, the timing and spacing of his words, and try to arrange them into a form which is seemingly artless, yet perfectly proportional. He must let his omissions suggest that which the language can no longer accomplish. Words today are like the shells and ropes of seaweed which a child brings home glistening from the beach, and which in an hour have lost their lustre. —CYRIL CONNOLLY, *The Unquiet Grave.*

B. The Function of Nouns. In writing this exercise, follow this procedure:

1. Leave alternate lines of your paper blank for the insertion of identifying numbers above each sentence.

2. Above each noun indicate its function by writing the number corresponding to the function as given in this list:

1. Subject
2. Subjective complement
3. Objective complement
4. Direct object of verb
5. Object of preposition
6. Indirect object of verb
7. Possessive
8. Direct address
9. Apposition

Example: The fruit[1] of toil[5] is the sweetest of pleasures[5].—VAUVENARGUES.

1. Work is a dangerous and destructive drug, and should be called by its right name—Fatigue.—ROBERTSON DAVIES.
2. A pacer's feet work in unison on each side, producing a side-wheeling motion.—GILBERT BAILEY.
3. Pink reacts like benzedrine on most males' jaded chivalry.—WILLIAM E. RICHARDSON.
4. The man who never alters his opinion is like standing water and breeds reptiles of the mind.—WILLIAM BLAKE.
5. I shall have six companions: My Sara, my babe, my own shaping and disquisitive mind, my books, my beloved friend, Thomas Poole, and lastly, Nature, looking at me with a thousand looks of beauty, and speaking to me in a thousand melodies of love.—SAMUEL TAYLOR COLERIDGE.
6. Some people make money their god.
7. They elected Frank captain.
8. Bishop Sherrill gave the troops his blessing.
9. Geoffrey Fisher, the Archbishop of Canterbury, wore gaiters at the convention.
10. It is well known that adolescent conflicts usually center around relationship with parents; love affairs; sexual impulses and how to manage them.—LYDIA G. DAWES.

14. THE PRONOUN AND SENTENCE STRUCTURE

14A. Definition and Classification

A pronoun is primarily, as the name implies, a word used in place of a noun or substantive which has been used already in the same or a preceding sentence or to which reference is understood. The noun or substantive to which the pronoun refers is known as the antecedent of the pronoun. There are several types of pronouns, which are named according to their nature and function as personal, reflexive, intensive, relative, interrogative, demonstrative, indefinite, and reciprocal pronouns.

14B. Personal Pronouns

Personal pronouns express personal relationships. They represent the speaker (First Person), the one spoken to (Second Person), and the person or thing spoken about (Third Person).

14B1. Inflection of Personal Pronouns. The personal pronouns are the only words that have retained a relatively complete inflection. Pronouns of the first and second persons are inflected as to number and case. Pronouns of the third person are inflected not only as to number and case but as to gender as well. There are three cases: the nominative, used for the subject and the subjective complement; the possessive, used as an adjective to indicate ownership; and the objective, used as the direct object or indirect object of a verb, or the object of a preposition.

PRONOUN AS SUBJECTIVE COMPLEMENT:	The last man to arrive was *he.*
PRONOUN AS POSSESSIVE ADJECTIVE:	John has *my* book.
PRONOUN AS OBJECT OF VERB:	Mary saw *him.*
PRONOUN AS INDIRECT OBJECT:	Give *him* the book.
PRONOUN AS OBJECT OF PREPOSITION:	Give the book to *him.*

The personal pronoun is inflected as follows:

FIRST PERSON

	Singular	*Plural*
NOMINATIVE:	I	we
POSSESSIVE:	my, mine	our, ours
OBJECTIVE:	me	us

SECOND PERSON

	Singular	*Plural*
NOMINATIVE:	you	you
POSSESSIVE:	your, yours	your, yours
OBJECTIVE:	you	you

THIRD PERSON

		Singular		*Plural*
	Masculine	*Feminine*	*Neuter*	*All genders*
NOMINATIVE:	he	she	it	they
POSSESSIVE:	his	her, hers	its	their, theirs
OBJECTIVE:	him	her	it	them

14B2. Possessives. The possessives *my, your, our, his, her, its* directly modify nouns and are often called possessive adjectives. *Mine, yours, hers, ours, theirs* are ordinarily used as subjective complements (The book is *mine*) but may serve as subjects (*Mine* is blue; *yours* is red).

Observe that the apostrophe is never used to mark the possessive of personal pronouns. (See Sections 14J 2 b, 36A.)

14C. Reflexive Pronouns

Reflexive pronouns regularly serve as the objects of verbs, though they sometimes occur as subjective complements. They are formed by compounding personal pronouns with *-self* and are used to indicate an identity of subject and object or of subject and complement.

OBJECT OF VERB: He congratulated *himself.*

SUBJECTIVE COMPLEMENT: Richard is *himself* again.

The reflexive pronouns are *myself, yourself, himself, herself, itself, oneself, ourselves, themselves.* Avoid using these reflexives as substitutes for personal pronouns.

AWKWARD: He gave the book to Jane and myself.

BETTER: He gave the book to Jane and me.

14D. Intensive Pronouns

The same compounds are used as intensive pronouns to emphasize a preceding noun or pronoun:

The president himself gave the commencement address.

14E. Relative Pronouns

The relative pronouns, *who, which, that,* and *what,* together with their compound forms, *whoever, whosoever, whichever, whichsoever, whatever, whatsoever,* are so named because they are commonly used to relate adjectival clauses to a noun or pronoun. They may also introduce noun clauses. A relative pronoun may be the subject or object of its clause or the object of a preposition or an adjective modifying a noun.

Like the personal pronouns, *who* and its compound forms *whoever* and *whosoever* are inflected, but only in three forms. *Who, whose,* and *whom* may be either singular or plural, according to the number of their antecedent. *Whoever* and *whosoever* take singular verbs.

NOMINATIVE:	who	whoever	whosoever
POSSESSIVE:	whose	whosever	whosesoever
OBJECTIVE:	whom	whomever	whomsoever

Which, whichever, that, what, whatever, and *whatsoever* are uninflected.

Relative clause serving as a noun clause, and subject of a verb:

> *Whoever lives with prejudice* becomes intellectually stale.—KATHLEEN GIBSON.

Relative clause as object of preposition:

> The grocer gave a new bat to *whoever collected most stamps.*

Relative clause as object of verb:

> They did not know *what he wanted.*

Relative clauses as adjective clause modifying noun:

> This is the book *which you requested.*
> The boy *whose calf took the prize* lives in Lebanon.
> The man *who bought old iron* now owns half the town.

Note that the use of *who* and *whom* is commonly restricted to human beings; *whose* and *that* may be used for human beings, animals, and things; *which* is used for animals and things.

14F. Interrogative Pronouns

Who, which, and *what* are also used in asking questions and in this use are called interrogative pronouns:

Who AS SUBJECT:	Who is coming with me?
Whose AS ADJECTIVE:	Whose book did you borrow?
Whom AS OBJECT OF VERB:	Whom did you see in Dresden?
What AS SUBJECT:	What is the answer to this question?

14G. Demonstrative Pronouns

The demonstrative pronouns, *this, that,* specifically point to a person, thing, or idea. *This* and *that* preserve only one inflectional form, the plural: *these, those.* Demonstrative pronouns have no possessive form.

> Those apples are sweet; *these* are sour.

In the preceding sentence, *those* is a demonstrative adjective, modifying apples; *these* is a demonstrative pronoun serving as subject of the second clause.

14H. Indefinite Pronouns

(1) Indefinite pronouns are used to convey a general impression, when we wish to avoid being specific. The most commonly used indefinite pronouns are *one, one another, anyone, each other, everyone, either, neither, none, everybody, everything, nobody, nothing, anything,* and certain adjectives, such as *all, each, few, many, several, such,* and *some,* which may be used as pronouns.

(2) *Each other* and *one another* are used to express a mutual relationship and are therefore sometimes called reciprocal pronouns. They are used only in the objective case. In exact formal usage, *each other* implies a relationship between two persons only:

> The captain and the colonel disliked each other intensely.

One another is used in larger relationships of three or more:

> The men were successful because they had learned how to co-operate with one another.

But this distinction is rapidly disappearing.

14J. Case

Since the form of a noun does not change except to indicate number and possession, the case forms of nouns cause little trouble in modern English (see Section 13C). But the personal pronouns (*I, you, he, she, it, we, they*) and the relative and interrogative pronouns *who, whoever, whosoever* have distinctive case forms that must be carefully distinguished.

14J 1. Nominative Case.

a) In formal English the pronoun subject of a verb is always in the nominative case. There are four cautions to remember here:

(1) The nominative case is used after the conjunctions *than* and *as* when these words are preceded by a predicate adjective.

He is older than I. He is as wise as I. [In both sentences *I* is the subject of the verb *am,* implied but not expressed.]

COLLOQUIAL: He is far wiser than me. He is as wise as me.
FORMAL: He is far wiser than I. He is as wise as I. [*I* is required as subject of the implied verb *am.*]

(2) The objective case is used after *than* or *as* when *than* or *as* follows a transitive verb (see Section 15B1) and its direct object.

I like him better than her. I like him as well as her. [*Her* is the object of the verb *like,* implied but not expressed.]

(3) The pronoun subject of a verb must be in the nominative case even when parenthetical phrases or clauses come between the pronoun and the verb. Thus in the sentence "Who do you believe will be the next governor?" the clause *do you believe* is parenthetical. The basic question is: "Who will be the next governor?" *Who* is in the nominative case, subject of *will be.*

WRONG: Whom do you think will be invited to meet him?
RIGHT: Who do you think will be invited to meet him? [*Who* is the subject of *will be invited; do you think* is parenthetical.]

(4) The pronoun subject of a clause that is itself the object of a verb or preposition is always nominative.

WRONG: Please treat courteously whomever answers your call.
RIGHT: Please treat courteously whoever answers your call. [*Whoever* is the subject of *answers,* not the object of *treat.* The whole clause *whoever answers your call* is the substantive object of *treat.*]

WRONG: The prize will be awarded to whomever wins most points.
RIGHT: The prize will be awarded to whoever wins most points. [*Whoever* is the subject of *wins,* not the object of *to.* The whole clause *whoever wins most points* is the substantive object of *to.*]

b) In formal English the pronoun used as a subjective complement after a linking verb (*be, become, seem,* etc.) is always nominative.

WRONG: Whom does he think we are?
RIGHT: Who does he think we are? [*Who* is the subjective complement of *are.* The sentence might be reconstructed thus to show the grammatical relationship: He does think we are who.]

COLLOQUIAL: It's her (him, them, us).
FORMAL: It is she (he, they, we).

INFORMAL (approved as commonly used by many educated people):
It is me (It's me).
FORMAL: It is I.

14J 2. Possessive Case.

a) The pronoun used to introduce a gerund is ordinarily in the possessive case. A gerund is a verbal noun ending in *-ing* (see Section 15F 2 e). The same verbal form may serve as an adjective, in which function it is called a participle.

If you wish to emphasize the act represented in the verbal, it takes on the nature of a noun (gerund), and the pronoun introducing it is in the possessive case; if you wish to emphasize the actor (the one doing the action), the verbal may be regarded as an adjective (participle) modifying the pronoun preceding it, and the pronoun will be in the objective case.

A gerund, with emphasis on the action, introduced by a possessive pronoun:

I object to his playing the fool. [I object to his action; *his* is possessive.]

A participle, with emphasis on the actor instead of the act:

I object to him playing the fool.

b) The possessive pronouns *yours, his, hers, its, theirs, ours,* and the relative possessive *whose* never use apostrophes.

These books are ours (not *our's*).
Its (not *it's*) colors are red and white.

Note that *it's* always means *it is* or *it has* and can never be used correctly as possessive *its.* The writer who is uncertain which form to use has only to ask himself whether substitution of *it is* or *it has* makes sense. If so, *it's* is correct. If not, *its* is correct.

A similar but less common error results from confusion between the possessives *your* and *their* and *you're* (*you are*) and *they're* (*they are*).

Your mail has come. Their mail is late.
You're always late. They're always late.

Again, if substitution of *you are* (*they are*) makes sense, *you're* (*they're*) is correct; if not, *your* (*their*) is correct.

14J 3. Objective Case.

a) A pronoun used as the direct or the indirect object of a verb is always in the objective case.

NONSTANDARD: I saw you and she at the party last night.

STANDARD: I saw you and her at the party last night [*You* and *her* are both objects of *saw*; though *you* does not change form for the objective, *she*, like *he* and *they*, must take the objective form after a verb or preposition. Since using the objective case directly after the verb is almost instinctive with anyone familiar with the language, one way of making sure of the right case in these compound objects is to test it by reversing the two objects: I saw her and you.]

NONSTANDARD: He asked Ruth and I whether we had our geometry assignment.

STANDARD: He asked Ruth and me whether we had our geometry assignment. [*Ruth* as a noun object cannot change form; but the accompanying pronoun *me* must be objective. Once more, apply the test of reversing the objects: He asked me and Ruth.]

COLLOQUIAL: Who do you think we saw riding up Main Street in a Cadillac? [Though formal grammar requires the objective case here, *who* assumes the nominative form partly because it has the position belonging to the subject in normal word order (subject, verb, and object). This use of *who* is permissible in conversation and reports of conversation.]

FORMAL: Whom do you think we saw riding up Main Street in a Cadillac? [*Whom* is the object of the verb *saw; do you think* is a parenthetical clause.]

NONSTANDARD: Did you tell Robert and he when you were going?

STANDARD: Did you tell Robert and him where you were going? [*Robert* and *him* are the compound indirect object of *tell; him* must be objective in form.]

b) In formal writing a pronoun used as the object of a preposition is in the objective case. Always look for the object of a preposition that ends a sentence or is detached from its object.

COLLOQUIAL: Who did you ask for?
FORMAL: Whom did you ask for? [*Whom* is the object of the preposition *for*. But the usage seems stilted.]

COLLOQUIAL: Who were you talking to when I saw you last night?
FORMAL: Whom were you talking to when I saw you last night? [*Whom* is detached from its preposition *to*.]

NONSTANDARD: Between you and I, I cannot understand modern art.
STANDARD: Between you and me, I cannot understand modern art. [Apply the test of reversing the pronouns: Between *me* and *you*, not *I* and *you*.]

NONSTANDARD: Some of we fellows formed a fraternity.
STANDARD: Some of us fellows formed a fraternity. [*Us* is object of the preposition *of; fellows* is an appositive.]

c) The pronoun used as the subject of an infinitive or as the predicate complement of an infinitive is in the objective case. We may speak of an infinitive as having a subject and a predicate complement when the construction in which the infinitive stands substitutes for a clause. Thus in the sentence "We know him to be an honest man," the construction *him to be an honest man* replaces or is equivalent to a clause: We know that he is an honest man. Hence by analogy we speak of *him* as the subject of the infinitive, and *an honest man* as the predicate complement after a linking verb (such verbs as *be, become, seem*).

STANDARD: I consider him to be a natural leader. [*Him*, the subject of the infinitive *to be*, is in the objective case.]

STANDARD: We believed the culprit to be him. [*Him*, the predicate complement, is in the objective case.]

14K. Number and Person

14K 1. Agreement of Pronoun and Verb. In formal English a pronoun and verb agree in number and person. Do not let modifiers coming between the pronoun and the verb cause you to forget the number of the pronoun.

This rule is of special importance in the use of the indefinite pronouns *any, anyone, anybody, each, each one, either, neither, everyone, everybody, none, no one, nobody. None* (a contraction of the singular pronoun *no one*) and *any* are today considered either singular or plural according to the meaning conveyed by the verb.

COLLOQUIAL: Each of the boys were on their marks.
FORMAL: Each of the boys was on his mark. [*Each* is singular and has a singular verb, and *his* agrees with its antecedent *each.*]

COLLOQUIAL: Neither of them were ready when he came home.
FORMAL: Neither of them was ready when he came home. [*Neither,* a singular pronoun, takes a singular verb.]

14K 2. Agreement with Nearer Subject. If two pronoun subjects differ in person or number, the verb should agree with the nearer. But such sentences are likely to be so awkward as to make revision preferable.

CORRECT: Either he or I am mistaken.
IMPROVED: Either he is mistaken or I am.
One of us is mistaken.

CORRECT: Either they or he is going.
IMPROVED: Either they are going or he is.

14K 3. Agreement of Relative Pronoun and Verb. A relative pronoun that has a plural antecedent is itself a plural and takes a plural verb.

One of the men who have charge of the celebration is seriously ill. [Since the antecedent is the plural *men,* not the singular *one, who* takes a plural verb.]

Watkins is only one of many who are in favor of delay. [Since the antecedent of *who* is the plural *many,* not the singular *Watkins, who* takes a plural verb.]

But note that in the following sentence the singular *one* is the antecedent of *who,* which therefore takes a singular verb:

Watkins is the only one of the candidates who is in favor of lower taxes.

The writer need only identify the antecedent of the relative pronoun in order to be sure whether the number of the pronoun and hence of the verb should be singular or plural. (See also Agreement of Subject and Verb, Section 15G.)

14K4. Agreement of Pronoun and Antecedent. A pronoun agrees in number and person with its antecedent.

The pronouns that must be specially watched are the indefinite pronouns (see above) and the possessives (*his, their*) referring to them as antecedents. Observe also that the demonstratives *these* and *those* are sometimes misused with the nouns *kind* and *sort*. *None* is either singular or plural according to the meaning conveyed by the verb.

COLLOQUIAL: Everybody should do their best to win.
FORMAL: Everybody should do his best to win.

COLLOQUIAL: Every man in the company waved their arms and cheered.
FORMAL: Every man in the company waved his arms and cheered.
FORMAL AND BETTER: All the men in the company waved their arms and cheered.

INFORMAL: None should neglect their work. [*None* signifies the whole group.]
FORMAL: None should neglect his work. [*None* emphasizes each considered separately.]

INFORMAL: What a pleasant party! They all seemed to like each other.
FORMAL: What a pleasant party! All the guests seemed to like one another.

14K5. Agreement of Pronoun and Antecedent in Separate Clauses. Errors in number more commonly occur when pronoun and antecedent are in separate clauses and hence the relationship between them is less immediately apparent. One should always look for the antecedent in such sentences and make the pronoun agree with it in number.

INCORRECT: The foreign film that one sees at a small art theatre may seem extraordinarily fine, but of course they represent only the very best of the foreign output. [Correction: Change *they represent* to *it represents* to agree with the singular *film*. Or change *film* to *films* and retain *they represent*.]

COLLOQUIAL: Everyone was excited about the victory, and they marched around the campus demanding a holiday. [Obviously *he* cannot be substituted for *they* in the second clause of this sentence. Hence this sentence is acceptable in conversation, and sentences of like nature are also found in informal writing in general.]

FORMAL: All the students were excited about the victory, and they marched around the campus demanding a holiday.

14K 6. General Use of Masculine Pronoun. A masculine pronoun is normally used in reference to an antecedent that includes persons of both sexes.

Each student must get permission from his parents. [It is unnecessary to write *his or her* parents.]

Either the indefinite pronoun *one* (*oneself*) or the masculine pronoun *he* (*himself*) may be used in reference to an antecedent *one*. The masculine pronoun is more commonly used.

One should save one's money.
One who neglects the daily assignments will soon find himself in trouble.

14K 7. A Pronoun and Its Collective Noun Antecedent. A pronoun having a collective noun as antecedent should be singular or plural according to whether the writer is thinking of the collective noun as a unit or as a group of individual and perhaps conflicting elements (see Section 15G 3.)

The Supreme Court adjourned its session at noon.
The crowd thundered its approval.
The football squad refused to let their many injuries be used as an excuse for the defeat.
The party that had been in power for twenty years lost the election because they could not agree upon a candidate acceptable to all factions.

So long as writers are consistent and make their pronouns correspond in number to the intended meaning of the noun, no problem exists; but a problem arises when, as in a discussion of sports, writers shift from one number to the other in referring to the same antecedent. The English meet this problem sanely by pluralizing such nouns: "Exeter are playing at Windsor this week. They have a good team this year, and the game will be close."

American usage is frankly inconsistent. We usually say: "Dartmouth is playing in the Stadium this week. They have a good team as usual, and the game will be close." In informal American English this inconsistency seems incurable; but in formal English, try for consistency: make your nouns and verbs and their pronouns correspond in number, as in the following example:

> The team is at its best now. [Not: *at their best.*] Each player is [*All the players are*] in excellent condition.

14L. Reference of Pronouns

14L1. Ambiguous Reference. A pronoun should have only one possible antecedent. Do not make the reader pause to decide which of two possible antecedents is the right one.

AMBIGUOUS: Jill was steering the boat when she tipped over. [Does *she* refer to Jill or the boat?]
CLEAR: Jill was steering the boat when it tipped over.

AMBIGUOUS: He told him that he must clear his absence with his instructor.
CLEAR: The dean told him to clear his absence with his instructor.

AMBIGUOUS: Peter asked John if he could help him with his algebra.
CLEAR: Peter asked John to help him with his algebra. [Or, if the other meaning is intended: Peter offered to help John with his algebra.]

14L2. Vague Reference. An antecedent should not be vague or remote. If other nouns that might cause confusion have been used between the antecedent and the pronoun, repeat the antecedent.

FAULTY: The founders had established the college in a prosperous valley. The whole area was rich in tradition, every knoll and stream having its legend. It was the pride of the region. [What is the antecedent of *it*?]
CLEAR: The founders had established the college in a prosperous valley. The whole area was rich in tradition, every knoll and stream having its legend. The college was the pride of the region.
IMPROVED: The founders had established the college, the pride of the region, in a prosperous valley, rich in tradition.

VAGUE: He wanted to be an air-force pilot; it was a career that had always excited his imagination. [A pilot is not a career; *it* cannot refer to pilot.]

CLEAR: He wanted to be an air-force pilot; flying was a career that had always excited his imagination.

14L 3. Reference to a Sentence or Clause. If in formal writing you use the pronouns *it, this, that,* and *which* to refer to the meaning of a sentence or clause, make sure that the reference is clear and specific. These pronouns are often used in this function in informal and, to a lesser degree, formal writing, but frequently they produce vagueness or confusion in meaning. Such writing can be improved by making the references more specific or by substituting nouns for the pronouns of vague reference.

CONFUSING: The registrar granted my request for a better room, which pleased me very much. [Does *which* refer to room or to the idea of the clause?]

CLEAR BUT CLUMSY: The registrar granted my request for a better room, a fact which pleased me.

CLEAR: I was much pleased when the registrar granted my request for a better room.

CLEAR BUT COLLOQUIAL: The next morning John forgot his raincoat, which was exactly what I thought he would do.

CLEAR: The next morning John forgot his raincoat, as I thought he would.

OR: The next morning, as usual, John forgot his raincoat.

VAGUE: The drum majorettes marched at the head of the procession, and it was a gay and pretty spectacle.

CLEAR: The drum majorettes marching at the head of the procession made a gay and pretty spectacle.

OR: The parade, with the drum majorettes at its head, was a gay and pretty spectacle.

FAULTY: While driving home, Jack ran into a deer. Though he was uninjured, this wrecked his car.

BETTER: While driving home, Jack ran into a deer. Though he was uninjured, the accident wrecked his car.

CLEAR: The sphere in which as individual human beings

we live really impinges very little upon the sphere of Mr. Millikan's symbolic and ingenious atoms. This is most fortunate, for no civilization can possibly transform itself as rapidly as science changes its fundamental conceptions.—CHRISTIAN GAUSS, *Primer of Tomorrow.*
[The reference of *this* to the thought of the preceding sentence is clear and unmistakable.]

CLEAR: No brute ever does a cruel thing. That is the monopoly of those with the Moral Sense.—MARK TWAIN.

14L 4. Vague Use of *They, It*. Do not use *they* or *it* without an antecedent.

VAGUE USE OF *they*: They say that the satellite states of Russia are about to revolt.

FORMAL AND MORE ACCURATE: Mr. X, the news commentator, thinks that the satellite states of Russia may revolt.

VAGUE: They observe few holidays at this college.

EXACT: This college observes few holidays.

VAGUE USE OF *it*: It says in the paper that a record low score is expected in the British Open.

FORMAL AND SPECIFIC: According to *The New York Times*, a record low score is expected in the British Open Championship.

14L 5. Shifts in Person and Number. Avoid shifts in person and number. If using *you,* do not shift to the third person *one.* If using the third person, do not shift to the first. In formal English keep to the third person point of view.

CONFUSED PERSONS: In the humble simplicity of the peasants in *The Informer* one could visualize all suffering humanity. You could see the oppressing of the poor and mourn for their fearful animal lives. One saw the Informer as the Judas of all times who would sell his soul for thirty pieces of silver.

CORRECTION: Substitute *one* for *you* in the second sentence above.

FAULTY: If people really learned from experience, we should find life much easier. [Shift from third person to first.]

IMPROVED: If people really learned from experience, they would find life much easier.

If we learned from experience, we should find life much easier.

FAULTY: One quickly discovers that in learning to drive you must develop self-confidence. [Shift from third person to second.]

IMPROVED: One quickly discovers that in learning to drive one [he] must develop self-confidence.

OR: You quickly discover that in learning to drive you must develop self-confidence. [But this use of the impersonal *you* is inappropriate in formal writing.]

FAULTY: You would think that one's own brother would be loyal, but we can never be sure of anything when money is involved. [Shifts from second person to third to first and shift in number.]

IMPROVED: One would think that one's own brother would be loyal, but one can never be sure of anything when money is involved.

Note that *one* is usually followed by *his* in the possessive. Thus we ordinarily say, "One should do his (not *one's*) duty." But when ambiguity might result (as in the preceding example), it is necessary to use *one's*.

SHIFT IN NUMBER: Everyone nowadays wears slacks; they wear them on almost all occasions.

REVISED: Everyone nowadays wears slacks on almost all occasions.

SHIFT IN NUMBER: Today one doesn't go to the movies any more. They just watch television.

REVISED: Today one doesn't go to the movies; he just watches television.

EXERCISES

A. Types of Pronouns and Their Functions. Identify the types of pronouns used in the following sentences and indicate whether they serve as subject, subjective complement, direct object of verb, object of preposition, indirect object of verb, possessive adjective, or as intensives or reflexives.

1. A work that aspires, however humbly, to the condition of art should carry its justification in every line.—JOSEPH CONRAD.
2. Aesthetics rests on nothing solid. It is a castle in the air.—ANATOLE FRANCE.
3. The beautiful is what your servant instinctively thinks is frightful.—E. AND J. DE GONCOURT.
4. The artist should put his work in order, and not the world which surrounds him.—ANDRÉ GIDE.
5. Art is the desire of a man to express himself, to record the reactions of his personality to the world he lives in.—AMY LOWELL.
6. Everyone could understand that a generation which travels sixty miles an hour must be five times as civilized as one which only traveled twelve.—WILLIAM RALPH INGE.
7. The friendships which last are those wherein each friend respects the other's dignity to the point of not really wanting anything from him.—CYRIL CONNOLLY.
8. An old fiction tells us that crocodiles shed tears over those whom they devour.

B. Case. The following sentences contain errors in case. Correct each error and state the reason for each correction.

1. The Hopis pay their homage to Katcinas, whom, they say, wants merriment and feasting.
2. Everyone makes mistakes, especially me; I could not wait to come to college before making mine.
3. When I asked Jack who I was going out with, he became curiously secretive.
4. The dishes are done, without any damage, by my brother and I, and everyone starts getting dressed to go to church.
5. Whenever I became aggressive, it was my younger sister who I always picked on, for I knew that I could easily overpower her.
6. He has now grown older and lost much of his respect for his parents, who he formerly admired.
7. While he was tortured by pangs of conscience, it was Emma who he thought of.
8. He had a resentment toward those who he called his father's enemies, they who were responsible for his family's misfortunes.
9. What was the reason for him dreaming of dying in the infirmary and fearing it so much when he was a child?
10. His tolerance is boundless, as is shown by his attitude toward his simple admirer, who his friend detests.

11. Her beauty and character went hand in hand and had a great influence on everyone who she came in contact with.
12. I never thought of him buying the house; I merely expected him to like it.
13. They had wanted to sail with my Uncle Walter and I, but he would have no part of it.

C. Number: Agreement of Pronoun and Verb. In the following sentences choose the right verb for the pronoun subject. In some sentences both verbs may be acceptable. Be prepared to defend your choice.

1. He looked to see whether any of the teachers (was, were) in sight.
2. None of the horses (was, were) destroyed when the barn burned.
3. Either my teacher or I (am, is) grossly mistaken about the quality of my writing.
4. It was not until I had made sure that none of the jewelry (was, were) missing that I began to wonder whether any of the workmen (was, were) involved in the attempted robbery.
5. Either of those paths (is, are) sure to lead us to camp.
6. Each of the three rookies (shows, show) promise.
7. (Are, is) any of you going to the game?
8. If everybody (is, are) willing to help, we should finish the work by noon.
9. None (is, are) righteous, no, not one.
10. None of the candidates (is, are) first-rate.

D. Number: Agreement of Pronoun and Antecedent. In the following sentences many of the pronouns do not agree with their antecedents. Rewrite the sentences correctly, and explain the reasons for the corrections.

1. The eighteen-year-olds are familiar with the platforms of the candidates because of the many times they come in contact with it in their school work.
2. Girls, more than boys, are pampered, humored, and protected in the comfort of the family circle. At college she must learn not to expect sympathetic understanding of her moods.
3. One would notice these things only if they looked closely at Aldo.
4. The time may come when everyone will use helicopters for any purpose for which they use automobiles today.
5. This church has continued and will continue to conduct their services in the manner first introduced at the establishment of the Greek Orthodox church.

6. More or less an isolationist, I believed that everyone in other countries should be like me and not worry about anyone's affairs but their own.
7. Something must be done to remedy this situation before someone is overcome with fatigue while awaiting their so-called dinner.
8. Rutherford showed that alpha particles from radium could be made to collide with alpha particles of other elements, such as that of hydrogen.
9. The early annals of history show many instances in which the blind were inhumanely treated, abused, or subjected to base uses. Up to the advent of the Christian era, the most he had learned to expect from his fellow men was pity.
10. He tends to be a person who is always looking for someone to put his head on their shoulder and bewail his troubles to.
11. A sponge is an inert organism. Its presence is indicated by the currents they produce in surrounding waters.
12. The cravat of today is of no practical value. We put them on in machinelike fashion when we dress in the morning as if it is of no importance.
13. The importance of hiring agents can now be visualized. He must be familiar with the local merchants, and he must constantly attempt to win new customers.
14. Everyone was thrilled by the oration, and at the close of the meeting they thronged to the platform to shake the hand of the speaker.
15. Her blue eyes diverted everyone's attention so that they never noticed the square, determined jaw.
16. When a person has reached the age of twenty-one or twenty-two, in most cases they are mature enough to put a car to good use and not let it interfere with their studies.
17. When this yard receives an order for a certain design, all the parts are cut to the proper shape and size, and then they assemble the framework of the craft to assure proper fits and joints.
18. The cost of operating the Exchange is borne by the Hartford Electric Light Company, and each member company pays their share of the expenses to the Hartford company.

E. Reference of *It, He, They, This, That, Which.* In the following sentences, the pronouns *it, he, they, this, that, which* are used to refer to clauses or ideas rather than to specific antecedents. Their meaning is often fairly clear, but better expressions of the thought are possible. Rewrite each sentence, eliminating the vague or general reference. Try to avoid awkwardness and ineffective repetition.

1. I completed the paper in the same manner that I did the first thousand words. Before I did this, I corrected the part that had been turned back to me.
2. Britain planned to supplement the water route to India by a system of motor roads with Haifa as the western terminus, and by a railway system. In addition to this, Britain was seeking transcontinental sovereignty of the air.
3. Creative energies should be released, and routine and unmotivated drill replaced by methods which call forth interest. This is done in the progressive school.
4. From the beginning, children are spoon-fed facts and made to learn material which does not appeal to them because it is presented in such a dull way. Progressive education seeks to eliminate this.
5. We returned home disgusted and put the car in the garage, hoping that my father would not take it out for the next few days, which he did not.
6. Eight years after Pascal's death appeared what purported to be the *Pensées*. The Jansenists published them and much squabbling went on during it.
7. The Pascals moved to Rouen during critical times. In 1639 they had a plague followed by a period of agricultural and industrial depression.
8. The *Pensées* are a jumbled mass of notes jotted down in a space of four years when Pascal's feebleness had begun to get the upper hand. This alone is enough to create wonder at his sheer intellectual power.
9. The Puritans were highly ridiculed—pictured as low-born persons and sour-faced hypocrites. This was very false, however, as Puritanism was not a mere class movement.
10. The curriculum of the early schools, including both grammar and high school, was classified and restricted in nature. We are trying to break away from this even today, favoring a curriculum designed to develop a well-rounded person.
11. In the fifteenth century the first formal persecutions were carried out against the witches. To excite popular hatred and to keep it fiercely alive, fear was mingled with it.
12. More skill is required to drive a finishing nail, since missing or glancing blows may result in damaging the wood, which will be exposed to view as poor craftsmanship.

F. Shifts in Person and Number. The following sentences show inconsistency in the use of person and number. Rewrite them to achieve consistency.

1. Yesterday I visited Princeton to see our team play. After entering the park you are in deep right field and have to walk to the opposite side to the visitors' stands.
2. In square-dancing one must have co-ordination and be able to dance with four persons instead of one. Another problem for beginners is understanding the directions of the caller. After you have completed a dance you are satisfied because you have gone through a number of steps and finished them correctly.
3. The more common types are the regular cross-country shoe and the track shoe with spikes. Wear the spikes on soft or wet ground and use the others on woods and hard-surfaced courses. The clothing of the runner should be not only light but warm.
4. When you are tired and hot it doesn't take long to locate refreshment, and we were back aboard in less than half an hour.
5. A golfer must be careful not to strike the ball so hard as to lose his balance. In other words you must not "press" your shot.
6. The first step in painting screens is that they must be well dusted. Next you make any repairs needed like retacking the molding. Then they are ready to be painted.
7. A leader in college activities must be circumspect. You cannot say just anything that occurs to you.
8. Every mature person has learned the truth that you get out of life just what we put into it.
9. One cannot hope to be popular if you spend all your time studying.
10. If you had tried in all the shoe stores in New York City, one could not have found a more courteous clerk than this young man.
11. If one finds that his best efforts are not appreciated, we soon grow discouraged.

G. Review Exercise. Choose the correct verb and pronoun forms in the following sentences. Explain the reasons for your choices:

1. If one will only take the trouble to get up early enough to see the dawn, (he, they) will find the experience rewarding.
2. The farmer, plagued by a shortage of help, frustrated by a drought that has lasted most of the summer, and now nearly wiped out by an invasion of army worms, can hardly be blamed when (he calls, they call) for help from the government.
3. Woman may indeed be said to have gained much by obtaining the right to have a career, but (she has, they have) also lost certain privileges enjoyed by (her grandmother, their grandmothers).
4. The Student Council pledged (its, their) full support in behalf of the Community Fund.

5. This battered old hobbyhorse is one of the few toys that (remain, remains) from my childhood.
6. Every patient who leaves the hospital must first make sure that (his, her, his or her) bill has been settled.
7. The youngest child and family favorite (has, have) cast a cloud of uncertainty over our vacation plans by coming down with the measles.
8. None of your purchases may be returned to the store unless (it is, they are) accompanied by a sales slip.
9. Robert is the only one of my brothers who (has, have) not served in the armed forces.
10. Such students may not be candidates for selection as "the senior most likely to succeed" and may not be elected to Phi Beta Kappa, but neither can (his, their) college days be regarded as fruitless.
11. The coach was in a black mood because the first-string quarterback was one of the players who had received (his, their) draft (notice, notices).
12. The committee wrangled all evening and then adjourned in disgust after concluding that (its, their) differences over the zoning plan were irreconcilable.
13. Marston is one of those people who (is, are) always writing angry letters to the newspaper.
14. Anyone who cannot remain placid in spite of minor annoyances such as finding (his, their) favorite necktie missing should not room with Bob.
15. It becomes more clear every day that unless man can somehow restrict to peaceful uses the explosive force that science can now release, (he, they) will not survive.

H. Review Exercise. Choose the correct pronoun forms in the following sentences. Be prepared to justify each choice.

1. The man (who, whom) you saw at the back door had come to read the meter.
2. The finalists—Winston and (I, me)—were told to report at the courts at noon.
3. Mr. Jackson asked whether it was Tom or (I, me) who had thrown the chalk.
4. Though (its, it's) been years since I saw the painting, I am sure that (its, it's) lost none of (its, it's) charm.
5. Run quickly and summon (whoever, whomever) is in charge.
6. The woman (who, whom) he thought was a clerk turned out to be an irate customer.

7. No matter (who, whom) you choose, you will not be satisfied.
8. If you think (your, you're) headed east, (your, you're) mistaken.
9. No one can be happier about the result than (I, me).
10. The Chamber of Commerce has offered a prize to (whoever, whomever) submits the best essay.
11. Fred may be as tall as (I, me), but I am sure I weigh more than (he, him).
12. The boy (who, whom) I saw at the movies with Mary is the one (who, whom) several months ago was arrested for reckless driving.
13. (It's, its) too bad that (your, you're) going to miss the game.
14. These children are the ones (who, whom) he said would attend the township school.
15. Though we were equally guilty, the principal scolded Bruce more than (I, me).
16. This is the one man (who, whom) I know to be my friend.
17. There is a girl (who, whom) I think used to go to high school with my sister.
18. Turn over the records to (whoever, whomever) the members have chosen as secretary.
19. The manager ordered the chief offenders—Dirk and (I, me)—to leave the theatre.
20. (Whoever, whomever) you are, and (whoever, whomever) you seek, do not bother me again.
21. Was it (he, him) (who, whom) you struck?
22. These are the people (who, whom) the disaster made homeless and (who, whom) the police said needed emergency aid.
23. (Its, it's) tragic that the child (who, whom) I remember so fondly is now the man (who, whom) I must prosecute for theft.
24. The mayor promised police protection to (whoever, whomever) offered to help the city in (its, it's) war with the underworld.
25. Tom knows a repairman (who, whom) he believes is more skillful than (I, me).

15. THE VERB AND SENTENCE STRUCTURE

The word *verb* is derived from Latin *verbum,* meaning *word,* or *the word;* and the verb is indeed the word, the most important of all the parts of speech. The motor word of expression, it has often been compared to an engine pulling a train of cars (the nouns and other parts of speech) filled with good things but useless until delivered by the action of the verb to their receiver. The verb is the necessary word in communication; thought is completed only by means of the verb, present or implied.

15A. Definition

The verb may be defined as a word that makes a statement. It states that someone or something acts or is affected by an action, or that someone or something is in a state of being or process of becoming.

15B. Classes of Verbs and Their Characteristics

The verb has several aspects that help us express shades and degrees of thought. Thus verbs may be regarded as transitive or intransitive, as active or passive in voice, as strong or weak or irregular in conjugation, and as having mood, tense, person, and number. Let us look at these aspects one by one.

15B1. Transitive and Intransitive Verbs. All verbs may be considered as either transitive or intransitive. Some verbs may be both. *Transitive* is derived from Latin *trans* (across) and *ire* (to go); hence transitive means a going across, a transfer of action from one thing to another.

a) Transitive verbs represent the transfer of action from a subject (the person or thing acting or acted upon) to an object, the receiver or the agent of the action. In other words, a transitive verb either takes a direct object or shows that the subject was acted upon by some agent. Transitive verbs have the special aspect of voice. If the subject acts upon the object, we say that the verb is in the active voice:

He hits the ball.

Here the subject (*he*) acts upon (*hits*) the object and receiver of the action (*ball*). If the subject is acted upon, we say that the verb is in the passive voice:

The ball was hit by him.

Here the subject (*ball*) was acted upon (*was hit*) by the agent of the action (*him*). Notice that the object of the verb in the active voice (*ball*) becomes the subject in the passive voice; and the subject (*he*) of the active verb becomes the object of the preposition *by* following the passive verb.

b) Intransitive verbs frequently express action, but their action does not pass over to any receiver; in other words, the intransitive verb does not take a direct object: *I go, I walk, I run, I feel, I grow.* Some verbs, including those just listed, though primarily intransitive, can be transitive in certain uses:

INTRANSITIVE: I walked for several hours.
TRANSITIVE: I walked the dog for an hour. [*Dog* is the direct object of *walked.*]

INTRANSITIVE: He runs in three events.
TRANSITIVE: He runs a magazine shop. [*Shop* is the direct object of *runs.*]

INTRANSITIVE: She looked angrily at him.
TRANSITIVE: She looked her hatred at him.

INTRANSITIVE: I feel good.
TRANSITIVE: I feel my way through the dark room.

15B2. Linking Verbs.

a) The verbs *be, appear,* and *seem* always remain intransitive and never take an object. The verb *become* in most of its uses belongs in the same category. These four are the most constantly used linking verbs. A linking (or copulative) verb joins the subject to a subjective complement, that is, to a descriptive or limiting adjective or an identifying noun or noun clause in the predicate:

The man is strong. [*Is* links the subject *man* and its descriptive adjective *strong.*]
We are seven. [*Are* links the subject *we* and the limiting adjective *seven.*]
Old King Cole was a merry old soul. [*Was* links the subject and the identifying noun *soul.*]
This is what I believe. [*Is* links the subject *this* and the noun clause *what I believe.*]
He appears (seems, becomes) happy. [*Appears* (*seems, becomes*) links the subject *he* and the descriptive adjective *happy.*]

b) Other linking verbs are the sense verbs, *feel, look, smell, sound,* and *taste,* and such other verbs as *grow, prove, remain,* *shine,* and *turn.* These verbs may all take objects in transitive uses; when used as linking verbs, however, they cannot take objects, and they are followed by subjective complements (predicate adjectives or predicate nouns), not by adverbs. One way of determining whether or not a verb is a linking verb is to substitute *is, becomes, seems,* or *appears* for it. If the meaning of the sentence remains essentially the same, then the original verb was a linking verb.

> The rose smells sweet. [The rose *is* sweet. *Smells* is a linking verb joining *rose* and the adjective describing *rose.*]
> The dean looks angry. [The dean *appears* angry. *Looks* is a linking verb joining the subject and *angry.*]
> The night grows dark. [The night *becomes* dark.]
> The task proved difficult. [The task *was* difficult.]
> His attitude remained unchanged. [His attitude *was* unchanged.]
> The sun shines bright. [The sun *is* bright.]
> The milk turns sour. [The milk *is* or *becomes* sour.]

c) Avoid using adverbs in place of adjectives after linking verbs when the sense clearly calls for an adjective.

FAULTY: I feel sadly.
STANDARD: I feel sad.

FAULTY: I feel badly.
STANDARD: I feel bad (or *ill*).

One may say either "I feel good" or "I feel well." Here the word *well* is an adjective, not an adverb.

15B 3. Strong, Weak, and Irregular Verbs. Verbs can also be divided into three classes according to form: strong verbs, weak verbs, and irregular verbs. Very similar in most of their features, strong and weak verbs are distinguished from each other in the ways they form the past tense and the past participle. If we know the *principal parts* of any strong or weak verb, namely, the present infinitive, the past tense, and the past participle, we can construct all its forms with the aid of certain auxiliary (helping or aiding) verbs. The present infinitive is the basic verb form (for example, *walk, run*) and is usually preceded by *to,* known as the sign of the infinitive (see Section 15H 1).

a) Strong Verbs. (1) The strong verbs seem to have been the original verbs in the language, the weak verbs being a later formation. The strong verbs are so named because they undergo vowel change to form the past tense and past participle and because they are the primary verbs: most of the familiar acts which we perform are described in terms of strong verbs (*drink, eat, run, drive, ride, sit, lie,* etc.) or verbs that once were strong (*laugh, walk, sleep, go, help*).

The strong verb forms its past tense by changing the vowel of the present infinitive form: *ride* (present infinitive), *rode* (past tense). Though the past participle is often identical with the past tense form, it may also show vowel change and frequently but not always, add a suffix, *-en,* or *-n: ridden* (the vowel is shortened as indicated by the spelling and pronunciation, and *en* is added). Some verbs omit the suffix: *drink* (present infinitive), *drank* (past tense), *drunk* (past participle).

Though Old English had as many as 333 of these verbs, today fewer than a third remain as strong verbs in form (Professor Baugh finds only 68 strong verbs, 13 mixed verbs), and another 81 have been made over into weak verbs. The strong verbs that remain differ very much in pattern, because there were originally six different classes. Today despite many changes toward simpler patterns, some of the old features remain, enough to confuse a beginner in the language. Fortunately, most of us know these typical forms by heart; but if you are in doubt about any form, you should always consult a good dictionary. By knowing the principal parts of any verb and the auxiliary verbs used with them, you can construct all the different forms that a verb may take.

(2) Here are representative examples of the principal parts of frequently used strong verbs.

PRESENT INFINITIVE	PAST TENSE	PAST PARTICIPLE
bear	bore	borne, born[1]
begin	began	begun
break	broke	broken
come	came	come

[1] *Born* as a participle is used only passively in the sense of *was given birth.*

PRESENT INFINITIVE	PAST TENSE	PAST PARTICIPLE
choose	chose	chosen
drink	drank	drunk
eat	ate	eaten
fall	fell	fallen
fight	fought	fought
find	found	found
fly	flew	flown
freeze	froze	frozen
get	got	got, gotten
give	gave	given
grow	grew	grown
know	knew	known
lie	lay	lain
ride	rode	ridden
rise	rose	risen
run	ran	run
see	saw	seen
sing	sang	sung
sit	sat	sat
speak	spoke	spoken
stand	stood	stood
strike	struck	struck, stricken
take	took	taken
win	won	won
write	wrote	written

(3) *Lie* and *lay, sit* and *set, rise* and *raise.* Some students have trouble with the correct use of the principal parts of the verbs *lie* and *lay, sit* and *set, rise* and *raise,* especially in conversation. Remember that *lie* is a strong, intransitive verb and means *to recline* and never takes an object. *Lay* is a weak, transitive verb and means *to put* or *place* and does take an object. Study the following patterns until you have them well in mind:

PRESENT:	I lie down to sleep.	I lay (put) the book down.
PAST:	I lay down to sleep.	I laid the book down.
PRESENT PERFECT:	I have lain down.	I have laid the book down.
PAST PERFECT:	I had lain down.	I had laid the book down.

Sit is a strong, intransitive verb and does not take an object in formal English; *set* is regularly a weak, transitive verb and usually takes an object. Study these patterns:

PRESENT:	I sit down.	I set (place) the bucket down.
PAST:	I sat down.	I set the bucket down.
PRESENT PERFECT:	I have sat down.	I have set the bucket down.
PAST PERFECT:	I had sat down.	I had set the bucket down.

Note that once one *sets* the bucket down, it *sits* there.

But *set* has certain idiomatic intransitive uses that are accepted as correct in both informal and formal usage. Thus I *set* a hen (place her on a nest of eggs) and she *sets* (we should expect *sits,* but the once colloquial *sets* has become the generally accepted form). The sun, of course, *sets* (that is, places itself). Cement *sets.* Jelly *sets.* We *set* out on a journey. Except for uses like these, the formula holds: once a thing is *set* (placed), it *sits.*

Rise is a strong, intransitive verb, meaning *to get up* from sitting, lying, or kneeling. It never takes an object. *Raise* is a weak, transitive verb, meaning *to lift* someone or something *up, to move* someone or something *higher, to build, to grow.* It regularly takes an object.

PRESENT:	I rise early.	I raise my hand.
PAST:	I rose early.	I raised my hand.
PRESENT PERFECT:	I have risen early.	I have raised my hand.
PAST PERFECT:	I had risen early.	I had raised my hand.

b) Weak Verbs. (1) Weak verbs, whose number is almost unlimited, seem for the most part not to have been verbs in origin, but nouns, adjectives, and other parts of speech made over into verbs by the addition of personal endings (now used only in the present tense, third person), and the addition of the suffix *-ed, -d,* or *-t* to form the past tense and the past participle. This early practice of forming new verbs from nouns and other parts of speech continues unchecked today; a few recent new verbs (added in the last few decades) are the following (to emphasize their verbal use, the past tense form is listed): *parked, radioed, typed* (in the sense of writing), *broadcasted* (also *broadcast*), *televised, hybridized, channelized, mechanized, anesthetized, cold-packed.* All these verbs are derived from nouns or other parts of speech. Whenever people need a verb to express a new phase of experience, they commonly add the weak verb endings to a noun naming or suggesting it, and thus form a new verb. This practice has many advantages; but in writing formal English you will do well not to coin new verbs. Always make sure, when in doubt, that the verbs you use are approved as standard English by referring to your dictionary.

(2) Here are examples of the principal parts of frequently used weak verbs:

PRESENT INFINITIVE	PAST TENSE	PAST PARTICIPLE
ask	asked	asked
buy	bought	bought
bring	brought	brought
dream	dreamed, dreamt	dreamed, dreamt
dress	dressed	dressed
feel	felt	felt
hate	hated	hated
have	had	had
hear	heard	heard
lead	led	led
learn	learned	learned
leave	left	left
lose	lost	lost
love	loved	loved
make	made	made
mean	meant	meant
read	read (pronounced *red*)	read (pronounced *red*)
say	said	said
sell	sold	sold
sleep	slept	slept
spend	spent	spent
teach	taught	taught
think	thought	thought
try	tried	tried
use	used	used
work	worked	worked

c) Irregular Verbs. (1) A handful of irregular verbs, which were probably regular in prehistoric times, use different forms or even different words to form the past tense. Some lack one or more of the principal parts. These verbs are the following (since some have no infinitive form, the present tense first person singular is given here):

PRESENT TENSE *First person Singular Indicative*	PRESENT INFINITIVE	PAST TENSE	PAST PARTICIPLE
am	be	was	been
can	—	could	—
do	do	did	done
go	go	went	gone
may	—	might	—
must	—	—	—
ought	—	ought	—
shall	—	should	—
will	—	would	—

The present tense forms of all these verbs may also be used to convey a future meaning. The past forms *could, might, should,* and *would* are frequently used with future meaning. Thus "I *might* go" is colloquially used in place of "I *may* go."

(2) Some of these verbs, together with the weak verb *have,* serve as *auxiliary* verbs; that is, they help in the formation of mood and tense aspects of other verbs. Thus the present tense forms of *be* are used to help form the progressive present (*I am sending*) and the present passive voice (*I am sent*) of other verbs; the past participle *been* is used to help form the passive present perfect tense (*I have been sent*). The verb *have* is used to form the perfect tenses: *I have told, I have been told, I shall have told, I shall have been told, I should have told, I had told, I had been telling. Will* and *would, shall* and *should, may, can,* and *must* are used to express future tense meanings and subjunctive and other modal aspects. *Do* and *did* are used for emphasis with other words in the present and past only: *I do believe; I did believe.*

15C. Voice

15C1. Definition. Voice indicates the relationship of the subject of a transitive verb to its action. This relationship is shown by two distinct formal systems used in conjugating transitive verbs, known as the active voice and the passive voice. The active voice commonly represents the subject as acting on an object, which is thus the receiver of the action: *He opened the door.* The passive voice represents the subject as being acted upon by an agent, either expressed (in a prepositional phrase) or implied: *The door was opened by him. The door was opened.*

Since the object of the active voice becomes the subject receiving the action in the passive voice, most passive verbs do not have objects. But occasionally the object of a transitive verb is retained as an object when the verb is made passive: *Each of the boys was given a prize.* This type of object is called a *retained object.* Note that the usual passive construction here would be: *A prize was given to each of the boys.*

Transitive verbs are conjugated in both voices through all the moods and tenses. Intransitive verbs have no voice and hence only one system of conjugation.

15C 2. Active Voice and Style. We do the greater part of our speaking and writing in the active voice. As the form of direct, vigorous statement, it is the chief medium of good writing. As a rule, use the active voice always unless you gain some special advantage by using the passive. Writing in the active voice lives; in the passive voice it is without animation.

15C 3. Passive Voice and Style.

a) The passive voice is helpful (though not always needed) in writing in which it is desirable to stress an action rather than the person performing it. Thus Julian Huxley writes:

> When muscles *are employed* in swimming, their force *must be applied* to the water through the intermediacy of some surface—the body *may be wriggled* or its motions [*may be*] *communicated* to an enlargement at the tail, or limbs [*may be*] *developed* as oars or paddles. [The italics and missing parts of the verbs are supplied by the editors.]

All expository writing employs the passive to some extent, particularly in areas such as science where the writer wishes to be objective and impersonal. On the other hand, reference to any text will show that even in scientific writing the passive is never used exclusively, and that in giving directions in laboratory exercises, most writers use mainly the active voice.

b) Weak Passive. Since vigorous writing calls for the active voice, it follows that any passive expression that might be more effective in the active voice should be revised and made active. Do not write "It is reported that . . ." or "It is believed that . . ." if you can write instead "The commissioner says . . ." or "The committee reports . . ."

PASSIVE AND INEFFECTIVE: An attempt should be made to learn the social graces, particularly dancing, if it is desired to attain success.

ACTIVE AND DIRECT: One must learn the social graces, particularly dancing, if he wishes to attain success.

WEAK: The spotted deer with their white flags were seen leaping the stone wall.

ACTIVE: We saw the spotted deer with their white flags leaping the stone wall.

15C4. Shift in Voice. Avoid unwarranted shifts from the active to the passive voice. It may be desirable at times to make such shifts in order to focus attention on one subject; but ordinarily try to keep your verbs active.

SHIFT IN VOICE: After the meeting was called to order by the chairman, the secretary read the minutes.

ACTIVE: After the chairman called the meeting to order, the secretary read the minutes.

SHIFT IN VOICE: When we opened the window, the mysterious noise could be heard clearly.

ACTIVE: When we opened the window, we could hear the mysterious noise clearly.

The sentences just cited as having shifts in voice are not seriously lacking in effectiveness. A shift in voice is a more serious fault, however, when it involves an unnatural use of the passive or a clumsy and purposeless shift in subject.

FAULTY: It was not until the janitor unlocked the door next morning that the vandalism was discovered by him.

IMPROVED: It was not until the janitor unlocked the door next morning that he discovered the vandalism.

FAULTY: John built a primitive oven, Karl gathered firewood, and the table was set by the girls.

IMPROVED: John built a primitive oven, Karl gathered firewood, and the girls set the table.

FAULTY: He discovered the joys of stamp-collecting, and all his spare time was devoted to his new hobby.

IMPROVED: He discovered the joys of stamp-collecting and devoted all his spare time to his new hobby.

FAULTY: Barton hurried down the road toward the river. His flashlight was used occasionally, flooding the trees and bushes with pools of light.

IMPROVED: Barton hurried down the road toward the river. He used his flashlight occasionally, flooding the trees and bushes with pools of light.

Permissible shift in voice, keeping attention focused on a subject:

When the athletes came out of the Arena, they were hoisted to the shoulders of the mob and paraded through the city streets.

EXERCISES

A. Transitive and Intransitive Verbs. Identify the type of each verb in the following sentences by writing capital *T* above each transitive verb and capital *I* above each intransitive verb.

1. Even the weariest river winds somewhere safe to sea.—SWINBURNE.
2. Robinson Crusoe lived many years on an island with no companions save his dog, a parrot, and finally his man Friday.
3. Worth makes the man, and want of it the fellow.—POPE.
4. At eight o'clock he stokes the furnace, winds the clock, and totters off to bed.
5. The new artist is always reviled in every country where and when he appears.—JOSEPH PENNELL.
6. Night came and covered the market-place with gloom.
7. He looked at the picture for a moment and was shocked.
8. The sun rose bright and warm and gave promise of a clear day.
9. They knocked at the door and listened. Inside, they heard a noise like the rustling of a mouse.

10. Lay not up for yourselves treasures upon earth, where moth and rust doth corrupt, and where thieves break through and steal.—MATTHEW 6:19.
(For the verb *lay up*, see Section 19C.)

B. Linking Verbs. The sentences below contain transitive and intransitive verbs. Some of the intransitive verbs serve as linking verbs. Identify each type by writing *L* above the linking verbs, *I* above the other intransitive verbs, and *T* above the transitive verbs.

1. The teacher proved his point with a reference to the right answer in the text.
2. My new acquaintance proved very boring in the hour's ride to Hartford.
3. The valley looked green and fertile.
4. He looked bitterly at her.
5. He looked his dislike with narrowed eyes.
6. His brain turned with dizziness as he looked far below.
7. His thoughts turned cynical and his face became moody.
8. As he turned the grindstone, he seemed very cheerful.
9. He grew more and more taciturn as she became more loquacious.
10. He grows cotton, sugar cane, sweet potatoes—anything that will grow well in this climate.

C. Principal Parts of *Sit* and *Set*, *Lie* and *Lay*, and *Rise* and *Raise*. Insert the right forms of the verbs that appear in parenthesis:

1. (sit, set) He _____ the jug on the hearth and _____ down by the fire.
2. (sit, set) She always _____ the table with her best silver when the minister came.
3. (sit, set) He _____ out for the village of Arden, which _____ on the hilltop near Arles.
4. (lie, lay) The dog _____ down wherever he likes to _____.
5. (lie, lay) He _____ down last night, and he still _____ there.
6. (lie, lay) Before he _____ down last night, he _____ his letters on the table.
7. (lie, lay) He has _____ the book down, and has _____ down on the couch.
8. (rise, raise) He _____ before dawn and started the job of _____ the roof of the shed.
9. (rise, raise) I _____ from my chair and _____ my hand in protest.
10. (rise, raise) After _____ corn one year, he _____ cotton the next.

D. Principal Parts of *Lie* and *Lay*. Correct errors in verb forms in the following sentences and give reasons for your corrections:

1. Regaining consciousness almost immediately, I looked round for my friends and found one standing dazed by the tree where he had been thrown and the other laying in front of the car.
2. My interest in flying remained keen. I used to lay on my army sack dreaming of a future as a pilot.
3. The so-called café was floorless except for a few timbers emerging from the sand, indicating that at one time there might have been a few boards laying around; there was also a little sawdust laying on the ground.
4. Seeing how white I was, she quickly ordered me to the nearby cot, and I laid there while she made the test.
5. I reluctantly jumped into the pool and tried the experiment of laying on my back in the water.
6. It would have been better if I could have laid down, but I had to serve supper.

E. The Weak Passive and Shifts in Voice. Some of the following sentences represent satisfactory uses of the passive voice; most, however, are ineffective. In writing this exercise, place the letter *S* after the number of each sentence that you consider satisfactory. Rewrite the others in the active voice.

1. My conception of high school was not unlike that of thousands of other pseudo-students; four years were spent waiting for the piece of paper that would pronounce me a graduate.
2. With just a few movements the gum was placed in her mouth, and chewed rapidly. Attempts were made to imitate the other girl who had the amused attention of the passengers.
3. In Greek thought, two *daimones* were assumed to attend everyone; some believed that there was one *daimon* only from whom emanated both good and evil at different times.
4. At the beginning of last semester I decided to take a practical course, one in which working with the hands rather than the brain was the first requisite. Agricultural engineering was decided upon.
5. My first reaction to study after high school was almost negative. In the army much time was spent in school, but I never gave promise as a leader in education.
6. In some seas large numbers of islands have been formed by the gradual subsidence of the land.
7. We subjected five general problems on memory to experimentation and conclusions were drawn.

8. The food is hurriedly eaten, and like a streak of lightning the student races across the campus.
9. The club members are in close contact with each other, and as a result close bonds between friends are developed.
10. In northern waters examples of jellyfish over seven feet wide have been found.
11. Copper tubing is very generally used for fuel and oil lines. The tubing is produced in the soft annealed condition and is seamless drawn.
12. All the ingredients are mixed until the composition is homogeneous. When the temperature is five to six degrees above the hardening point of the wax, pour the mixture into molds. Perfume is then added both for smell and taste.
13. He sat leisurely in a swivel armchair which was tipped against the wall. His right foot was twined around the right leg of the chair.
14. Between his thumb and forefinger he held two coins with which he continually played. The sound click, click, click was made by flipping one coin over the other.
15. The day had been Wednesday; two grilled mutton chops were revealed when Lord Edward lifted the silver cover.—ALDOUS HUXLEY.
16. Bascomb hit a sharp grounder toward left field, but the shortstop lunged like an acrobat, and what looked like a sure hit was turned into a double play.
17. If you look in the closet under the stairs there should be found several umbrellas.
18. Mother summoned me into the house, and my playmates were ordered to go home.
19. He studied hard enough to avoid failure, but most of his energies were devoted to making the varsity football team.
20. The fireman dashed back into the house, and the unconscious child was carried to safety.
21. When the librarian was requested by me to make a little less noise herself, I received an icy stare.

15D. Tense

Tense (Old French *tens,* Latin *tempus,* meaning *time*) indicates the time of the action or state of being or becoming expressed in the verb. There are six variations in tense for English verbs: present, past, future, present perfect, past perfect, and future perfect. A distinction of time is also expressed by the progressive forms of the verb, which indicate aspects of continuous action.

15D 1. Present Tense.

a) The present tense is supposed to indicate action or a state of being or becoming that takes place in present time or that is going on at present. In its simplest form (*I am, he sings, he plays*), it indicates habitual action or being rather than simple present action. In its so-called progressive form, composed of forms of the verb *be* together with the present participle (*is singing, is playing*), it indicates action taking place and *continuing* at the moment. This progressive form is the distinctively present tense: thus when one asks, "What are you doing?" the answer is not, "I play," but, "I am playing." Whenever we wish to express action taking place and continuing in the present time we use the progressive form. Both the simple form and the progressive form are used also to express future meaning:

He speaks (will speak) in Boston next week.
He is speaking (will speak) in Boston next week.

b) Historical Present (Dramatic Present). The historical present expresses past time in terms of present tense forms. This form is much used in nonstandard English ("I says to him and he says to me") and also in critical writing, in summaries, and in the dramatic reporting of historical or imaginary past events.

LITERARY HISTORY:	Aubrey tells us that Suckling was only twenty-eight years old when he died.
SUMMARY:	Saul bends his head and lets his hand rest in kindness on the head of David, who is kneeling and longing for power to help Saul further.
CRITICAL COMMENT:	Shakespeare does not condemn romantic love when he mocks it.
HISTORY DRAMATICALLY REPORTED:	About eight o'clock on the Saturday morning she purchases a large sheath-knife in the Palais Royal; then straightway, in the Place des Victoires, takes a hackney coach. "To the Rue de

l'Ecole de Médecine No. 44." It is the residence of the Citoyen Marat!—CARLYLE, *The French Revolution.*

15D 2. Past Tense. The past tense expresses action or a state of being that took place some time in the past: He worked, he rose. Indefinite past time is expressed by the past forms of the verb (in the examples given, no one knows from the verb form just what time the action occurred). Definite past time must be expressed by added modifiers or by time elements in a preceding sentence:

> He arrived at five o'clock. Shortly afterward, he insisted on having dinner.

The adverbial phrases *at five o'clock* and *shortly afterward* help to establish the time of the verbs *arrived* and *insisted.*

The progressive past tense expresses action or a state of being that was continuous for a period of time in the past:

> He was writing a letter. He was being very cautious.

15D 3. Future Tense.

a) The future tense indicates action or being in the future or time to come. There are several ways of expressing the future in English. Today, informal English uses the auxiliary verb *will* with the infinitive (as in *will go*) as the main way of indicating future time through all the persons, singular and plural: *I will go, you will go, he will go, we will go, you will go, they will go.*

In formal English some writers now use *will* almost exclusively for the future, but many others prefer to follow the formal rules for *shall* and *will* established by grammarians in the eighteenth century and taught as the only correct forms for formal English until very recently. These rules may be briefly summarized:

(1) To express the simple future, *shall* is used in the first person, and *will* in the second and third, both singular and plural: *I shall, you will, he will; we shall, you will, they will.*

(2) To express determination or command, *will* is used in the first person, and *shall* in the second and third: *I will, you shall, he shall; we will, you shall, they shall.*

(3) In asking questions, one uses the auxiliary expected in the answer: *Shall you go? I shall.* [Mere futurity.] *Will you endure this insult? I will not.* [Determination.]

Should and *would,* the past forms of *shall* and *will,* are treated in the same way as *shall* and *will.*

These rules have merit in that they make possible certain shades of meaning; but as observed above, *will* seems gradually to be displacing *shall* in almost all uses. *Shall* still persists, however, almost to the exclusion of *will,* in questions in the first person: *Shall I go? Shall we leave?*

b) Other means of expressing the future are these:

(1) The simple present form:

The Senators play (will play) in New York tomorrow.

(2) The progressive present form:

The Senators are playing in New York tomorrow.

(3) The use of the present or present progressive form of verbs indicating desire, intention, possibility, or obligation:

I wish to go to Boston tomorrow. I intend to go.
I should go. I am going to go. I am about to go.
I am to go. I may go.

(See also Auxiliary Verbs, Section 15B 3 c 2.)

15D 4. Present Perfect Tense. There are three perfect tenses, that is, tenses of perfected or completed action, namely, the present perfect, the past perfect, and the future perfect tenses.

The present perfect tense expresses action or a state of being as completed at the time the statement is made; often the completed action is regarded as continuing in the present.

I have known all along. [I still know.]
He has told me.
I have been fortunate. [Often equivalent to: I am still fortunate.]

15D 5. Past Perfect Tense. The past perfect tense expresses an action or state of being completed earlier than a past time mentioned or implied elsewhere in the sentence:

He had gone before I arrived. [The time of his departure, expressed in the past perfect tense, *had gone*, preceded that of my arrival, expressed in the past tense, *arrived*.]

He had gone before breakfast. [Here his departure, expressed in the past perfect tense, *had gone*, preceded the time of the adverbial phrase, *before breakfast*.]

15D 6. Future Perfect Tense. The future perfect tense expresses a future action or state of being that will have been completed by a certain time:

I shall have gone before he arrives.
He will have gone by midnight.

15D 7. Tense Relationships. a) Sequence of Tenses. Most students have no difficulty in using the right tense in simple sentences, but some are now and then confused as to the sequence of tenses—that is, the proper time relationship of the verbs to one another in complex sentences and successive sentences. The following recommendations and examples may help to overcome this difficulty.

In complex sentences the tense of the verb in the subordinate clause depends in part on the meaning desired and in part on the tense of the verb in the main clause.

(*a*) If the tense of the verb in the main clause is present, future, present perfect, or future perfect, the tense of the verb in the subordinate clause may be whatever the sense demands.

I work (shall work, have worked, shall have worked) because I like the job.
I shall work because I shall like the job.
I have worked because I have liked the job.

(*b*) If the tense of the verb in the main clause is past or past perfect, the tense of the verb in the subordinate clause will ordinarily be past or past perfect.

I worked because I liked the job.
I had worked because I liked (had liked) the job.

(*c*) To show that one action in the past is earlier than another past action, use the past perfect to express the earlier action.

The president reported that the committee had finished its work.

One exception to this rule may be stated as a fourth rule:

(*d*) Subordinated statements of permanent or general truths or beliefs are usually (not always) in the present tense, even when the main clause is in the past tense:

He said that John is sincere and loyal.
Gandhi believed that war is evil.
He told me that he raises cattle for a living.

But the past tense is often used even with statements like these.

b) Shifts in Tense. Be consistent in your use of tense. Do not shift from past to present or from present to past unless the sense requires it. Study the following paragraph and observe the logical sequence of tenses:

Setting up a Shakespearean festival in a non-theatrical Canadian community 100 miles from Toronto and even further from Montreal, Buffalo, and Detroit *involves* more problems than any we *could* reasonably *foresee.* Even Mr. Patterson, who *invented* the idea out of the wild blue yonder, never *realized* exactly what he *was getting* into. It *involves* the manufacture of strange and innumerable costumes, shoes, and props in workshops not accustomed to the mad ideas of the theatre; and it also *involves* extraneous housing and transportation problems that a large city could supply without much fuss.—BROOKS ATKINSON, "Canada's Stratford," *The New York Times.*

Notice that Mr. Atkinson maintains the present tense for each of the separate problems involved in establishing a theatre in Stratford. He uses the past to comment on the original conception of the plan.

FAULTY: He raced for the shelter of the forest, but just as he reaches the trees a shot rings out.

IMPROVED: He raced for the shelter of the forest, but just as he reached the trees a shot rang out.

EXERCISE

Sequence of Tenses and Shifts in Tense. The sentences following contain violations of the sequence of tenses and various shifts in tense. Rewrite them to secure logical relationships.

1. In "The New Dress" we found a woman withdrawing from society because she has an extreme inferiority complex. It is a story which takes place purely within the mind of Mabel. For this reason we get only a one-sided view of her character, but we could see how her mind worked and how she tortured herself by the feeling of inadequacy.
2. The birds visited the bird bath every day all summer. They splash and drink and sit in the lower limbs of the pine and arranged their feathers one final time before they take off for the south.
3. Perhaps the meat cutter was reminded of his father who stayed in the old country, or the mailman thinks of an old friend of whom he loses track.
4. In Greek mythology a wood nymph's life was bound up with that of her tree. She dies when it is cut down.
5. The Druids were an ancient Celtic religious order. They would be a combination of wonder-worker, historian, and judge. They often appear in the myths as wizards and diviners.
6. Wind and waves will gouge the bedrock, forming caves and columns. The softer strata tumble into the sea as sand.
7. I was overjoyed at the news and came to the conclusion that God heard my prayers and answered them.
8. Going to lunch, the new student enjoys meeting all his friends in line, and in the two hours which have elapsed there, he was able to discuss all his schedule for the coming week.
9. He acted as if nothing happened.
10. When I danced with my hostess, I felt free to leave.
11. Forty-two of the one hundred and sixty-two we started the hike with were still left. There will be fewer before we finish. Someone tried to sing, but his swollen, parched throat manages only a rasping hiss. We are in a horrible dream.

15E. Mood

All verbs have mood. Mood is the mode or manner of expression. English has three moods, the indicative, the imperative, and the subjunctive.

15E 1. Indicative Mood. The indicative mood primarily states a fact, or what is supposed to be a fact, or asks a question: *He is hungry. Is he hungry?* Most of our thought (for example, nearly all the discussion in this chapter) is expressed in the indicative mood. Since the subjunctive has lost most of its distinctive forms, the indicative mood may also be considered as taking over many of the subjunctive functions and expressing other aspects of thought, such as suppositions, conditions, and concession.

Only the indicative mood has a complete verbal inflection (commonly called conjugation) through all the six tenses in both active and passive voices (see Sections 15F 1 (1), 15F 2 a).

15E 2. Imperative Mood. The imperative mood expresses a command or request.

> Shoulder arms!
> Shut the door.
> Close your books.
> Put on your headlights.

The subject of statements in the imperative mood, always in the second person (*you,* singular or plural), is ordinarily omitted, but may be used for emphasis: *You move along now!*

The imperative mood is much used in laboratory manuals in giving directions on how to perform experiments.

Entire consistency in keeping to the use of one mood is neither expected nor desirable, but avoid clearly unwarranted shifts from the indicative to the imperative (or from the imperative to the indicative) when the sense suggests the consistent use of one mood.

FAULTY: The ingredients must be mixed thoroughly. Then place the pan over a low flame. [Shift from indicative to imperative.]

IMPROVED: Mix the ingredients thoroughly. Then place the pan over a low flame.

FAULTY: Lie flat in the water, with the face submerged. The arms should be outstretched, with hands clasped.

IMPROVED: Lie flat in the water, with the face submerged. Hold the arms outstretched, with hands clasped.

The imperative mood, which is informal in tone, should be used with caution in formal writing.

EXERCISE

Eliminate the shifts in mood in the following sentences by making them uniformly imperative.

1. First there should be a coat of flat white, and then apply the final coat.
2. Leave a forwarding address with the postman, but he should be told not to forward newspapers and magazines.
3. A good citizen gives generously of his time to community enterprises, but remember that one's first duty is to his family.
4. Take my picture if you must, but first I must be allowed to put on a necktie.
5. Sign your driver's license on the proper line. Then it should be folded and put in its envelope.

15E 3. Subjunctive Mood.

a) The subjunctive mood expresses possibility, desire, recommendation, concession, or condition rather than fact. This mood, which in the early state of the language had a fairly full conjugation through the past and present tense, has lost nearly all its distinctive forms with the passage of time, so that now only a very few remain. Even those few have almost disappeared from popular speech, but they are still maintained to some degree in informal and formal English. The only important uses of these subjunctive forms are found in rather formal statements of conditions contrary to fact and of concessions, introduced by such conjunctions as *if, though, supposing that, provided that,* and in clauses introduced by *that* expressing wishes, recommendations, demands, or necessity.

b) The most important subjunctive verb forms are those of the verb *be* (used as a main or an auxiliary verb), almost always preceded by *if* or *though.* See the conjugation of the subjunctive forms of *be,* Section 15F 1 (2).

Representative uses of the verb *be* in the subjunctive mood:

If I be too bold, please forgive me. [But *am*, the indicative, has almost entirely replaced *be* in the first person.]

If it be imperative, we shall draft all the young men. [Indicative *is* is more commonly used.]

If I were you, I'd learn how to fly a helicopter. [Condition contrary to fact; this use of the subjunctive seems firmly rooted. Though *if I was you* is often heard, *if I were you* is preferred by educated people. Note that *were,* though past in form, has present meaning.]

If the truth were known, people would not elect him.

The council recommends that all tents be open for inspection at nine o'clock.

c) In other verbs the only subjunctive inflectional form that is still used (only in very formal English) is the present third person singular, which differs from the indicative in that it does not end in *-s*:

CONCESSIONS: Though he deny the charge, I shall still believe it.
Though he concede our victory, we should be cautious.

Observe that these concessive statements differ in sense from simple indicative statements: for example, *though he concede our victory* is a supposition—*supposing that he were to concede our victory;* but *though he concedes* (indicative) *our victory* may be read as an established fact—*he concedes our victory, but we must be cautious.*

STATEMENTS OF RECOMMENDATION, WISH, DEMAND, OR NECESSITY:

The committee urges that the firm buy the mill immediately.
We request that he serve as chairman.
They insist that he be summoned as a witness.
It is necessary that he go now.

d) Other minor uses (statements of concession, wishes, entreaty) may be seen in such expressions as these:

Come what may, I shall go with you.
Say what you will, I shall not believe it.
Be that as it may, I shall keep my promise.
Lord have mercy on his soul.
Blest be the tie that binds our hearts.
Long live the king!

These, however, are not so much active, living uses of the subjunctive as they are stock phrases, a few fossil forms persisting out of the past. We do not vary them to any great degree or form new expressions on their model.

As has been suggested earlier, since the subjunctive has lost most of its inflectional forms we may regard the indicative as in the process of taking over its functions.

EXERCISE

Subjunctive Mood. The following sentences exhibit the increasing tendency to use the indicative rather than the subjunctive mood in places where the subjunctive is formally preferable. Revise indicative forms into subjunctives when subjunctives are proper.

1. The students would find it too much bother and too expensive to drive between classes even if there was ample parking space outside every classroom.
2. If he was an independent, he would be free to go and do as he pleased, except that there is nowhere to go and nothing to do.
3. Even if he was unkind to you, and you say he was not, you should not be harsh toward him.
4. Even if liberty is won by one generation, it may be lost by another.
5. If he was you, we could count on his showing good sense in this emergency.
6. If one was sure of the result, one could act with some wisdom.
7. I move that Mr. Blood shall be named moderator.
8. If he was president, we could count on an able administration.
9. I urge that his remarks ought to be stricken from the record.

15F. Conjugation

15F1. Conjugation of *Be*. Basic in the conjugation of all verbs is a knowledge of the conjugation of the verb *be,* which is given below, inflected through the six tenses. Since *be* is an intransitive verb expressing a state of being, it has no voice. Notice as you study this verb how it employs three separate words or roots to form its various parts, namely *be, is* (*am* and *are* are related to *is* in origin), and *was.* Notice also how it makes use of the auxiliary verbs *will, shall,* and *have* (also a weak verb in its own right) to form its tenses. Thus the future is formed by using the auxiliary *shall* or *will* with the infinitive form of *be*: I *shall* or *will be*; the present perfect is formed by using the present tense of *have* with the past participle of *be,* namely, *been: I have been;* the past perfect is formed by using the past tense of *have,* namely *had,* with the past participle: *I had been;* the future perfect is formed by using the future tense of *have* (*shall* or *will have*) with the past participle: *I shall have been.*

(1) Indicative Mood:

PRESENT

Singular	*Plural*
I am	we are
you are	you are
he is	they are

PAST

I was	we were
you were	you were
he was	they were

FUTURE

I shall or will be	we shall or will be
you will be	you will be
he will be	they will be

PRESENT PERFECT

I have been	we have been
you have been	you have been
he has been	they have been

PAST PERFECT

I had been	we had been
you had been	you had been
he had been	they had been

FUTURE PERFECT

I shall or will have been	we shall or will have been
you will have been	you will have been
he will have been	they will have been

The commonly used progressive forms of this verb are:

PRESENT: I am being, you are being, he is being, we are being, you are being, they are being.

PAST: I was being, you were being, he was being, we were being, you were being, they were being.

The progressive forms for the other tenses of *be,* which may also be made by adding the present participle *being* to the simple tense forms, are not commonly used.

(2) Subjunctive Mood:

PRESENT:	I (you, he, we, you, they) *be.*
PAST (with present meaning):	I (you, he, we, you, they) *were.*

Observe that the so-called past tense here is past only in form; in meaning it is regularly present. Thus the sentence "If I *were* you, I should go" is equivalent to "I *am* not you, but I should go."

(3) Imperative Mood:

PRESENT: *be*

(4) Infinitive:

PRESENT:	*to be*
PAST:	*to have been*

(5) Participle:

PRESENT:	*being*
PAST:	*been*
PRESENT PERFECT:	*having been*

15F2. Conjugation of Strong and Weak Verbs. Here are the conjugations of a representative strong verb, *strike,* and a representative weak verb, *send.* All other strong and weak verbs follow these patterns, with due allowance of course for the different ways in which they form the past tense and the past participle. Note that in the present tense and present perfect tense, only the third person singular changes form: *he strikes, he sends, he has struck, he has sent.* Otherwise, all other forms in all tenses correspond entirely to the principal parts.

a) Indicative Mood, Active Voice.

PRESENT

Singular	*Plural*	*Singular*	*Plural*
I strike	we strike	I send	we send
you strike	you strike	you send	you send
he strikes	they strike	he sends	they send

PAST

Singular	*Plural*	*Singular*	*Plural*
I struck	we struck	I sent	we sent
you struck	you struck	you sent	you sent
he struck	they struck	he sent	they sent
	FUTURE		
I shall or will strike	we shall or will strike	I shall or will send	we shall or will send
you will strike	you will strike	you will send	you will send
he will strike	they will strike	he will send	they will send
	PRESENT PERFECT		
I have struck	we have struck	I have sent	we have sent
you have struck	you have struck	you have sent	you have sent
he has struck	they have struck	he has sent	they have sent
	PAST PERFECT		
I had struck	we had struck	I had sent	we had sent
you had struck	you had struck	you had sent	you had sent
he had struck	they had struck	he had sent	they had sent
	FUTURE PERFECT		
I shall or will have struck	we shall or will have struck	I shall or will have sent	we shall or will have sent
you will have struck	you will have struck	you will have sent	you will have sent
he will have struck	they will have struck	he will have sent	they will have sent

The progressive forms of these verbs are made by adding the present participles (*striking, sending*) to the simple forms of the verb *be,* given above:

PRESENT:	I am striking, etc.
PAST:	I was striking, etc.
FUTURE:	I shall or will be striking, etc.
PRESENT PERFECT:	I have been striking, etc.
PAST PERFECT:	I had been striking, etc.
FUTURE PERFECT:	I shall or will have been striking, etc.

b) Indicative Mood, Passive Voice. The passive voice is formed by adding the past participle of any strong or weak verb to the various tense forms of the verb *be.* Here are the first person forms in the various tenses for *strike* and *send* (the second person and the third person also follow the pattern described)

PRESENT:	I am struck	I am sent
PAST:	I was struck	I was sent
FUTURE:	I shall or will be struck	I shall or will be sent
PRESENT PERFECT:	I have been struck	I have been sent
PAST PERFECT:	I had been struck	I had been sent
FUTURE PERFECT:	I shall or will have been struck	I shall or will have been sent

The passive progressive forms in the first person are these:

PRESENT:	I am being struck	I am being sent
PAST:	I was being struck	I was being sent

c) Subjunctive Mood. (1) Active Voice. The only active subjunctive form distinct from the indicative is found in the present tense, third person singular, which loses its *s* ending as a subjunctive: *(if) he strike, (if) he send.*

(2) Passive Voice. The only passive subjunctive forms distinct from the indicative are those of the present and past tenses, which are formed by adding the past participle to the subjunctive forms of *be:*

PRESENT:	(if) I (you, he, etc.) be struck, be sent
PAST (with present meaning):	(if) I (you, he, etc.) were struck, were sent

d) Imperative Mood. (1) Active Voice: strike, send.
(2) Passive Voice: be struck, be sent.

e) Verbals. (1) Infinitive:

ACTIVE

PRESENT:	to strike, to send
PRESENT PERFECT:	to have struck, to have sent

PASSIVE

PRESENT:	to be struck, to be sent
PRESENT PERFECT:	to have been struck, to have been sent

(2) Participle:

ACTIVE

PRESENT:	striking, sending
PAST:	struck, sent
PRESENT PERFECT:	having struck, having sent

PASSIVE

PRESENT:	being struck, being sent
PAST:	been struck, been sent
PRESENT PERFECT:	having been struck, having been sent

(3) Gerund:

ACTIVE

PRESENT:	striking, sending
PRESENT PERFECT:	having struck, having sent

PASSIVE

PRESENT:	being struck, being sent
PRESENT PERFECT:	having been struck, having been sent

15G. Agreement of Subject and Verb

A verb regularly agrees in person and number with its subject. Singular verbs have singular subjects; plural verbs have plural subjects.

It is to be noted that there is an increasing tendency, particularly in informal writing and speaking, to let the sense of an expression determine the number of the verb; but the general principle that the verb agrees in person and number with its subject holds for most formal and informal discourse.

15G 1. True Subject.

a) Learn to look for the specific subject: do not let modifying or parenthetical phrases mislead you; watch particularly phrases introduced by *along with, as well as, besides, in addition to, together with.*

WRONG: Monte Irvin, together with Whitey Lockman and Hank Thompson, join the home run circle for this afternoon. [*Together with Whitey Lockman and Hank Thompson* is a prepositional phrase. *Monte Irvin*, the singular subject, requires a singular verb.]

RIGHT: Monte Irvin, together with Whitey Lockman and Hank Thompson, joins the home run circle for this afternoon.

RIGHT: [With compound subject] Monte Irvin, Whitey Lockman, and Hank Thompson join the home run circle for this afternoon.

WRONG: This victory, as well as the last two, were won at the expense of a new flock of cripples.
RIGHT: This victory, as well as the last two, was won at the expense of a new flock of cripples.
RIGHT: This victory and the last two were won, etc.
OR: The last three victories were won, etc.

b) Do not let an intervening clause mislead you or cause you to forget the true subject.

WRONG: A teacher who has to maintain discipline in a crowded schoolroom holding forty mischievous children are going to have little time for instruction. [The plural *children* of course has no bearing upon the number of the verb, which must be the singular *is* to agree with the singular subject *teacher*.]

c) The number of a verb is determined by its subject, not by the subjective complement.

WRONG: The only weak spot in the line are the guards. [The verb should agree in number with *spot*, not with *guards*.]
RIGHT: The only weak spot in the line is the guards.
RIGHT: The weak spots in the line are the left guard and the left tackle. [Here the verb agrees with both the subject and the compound subjective complement; but the plural subject determines the number of the verb.]

WRONG: The autumnal trees, spreading a rich carpet of crimson and gold over the undulating folds of Blue Knob, is a sight to behold. [The verb should agree in number with *trees*, not with *sight*. Substitute *are* for *is*.]

WRONG: The equipment needed for the players are a shuttlecock, two rackets, and a net. [*Equipment,* though a collective noun, regularly takes a singular verb. But revision of the whole sentence is preferable here to a substitution of *is* for *are*.]

15G 2. Compound Subject. Compound subjects regularly take plural verbs; but a compound subject that indicates a single person, object, or idea requires a singular verb.

Learn to distinguish between a compound subject (two or more nouns or substantives joined by *and,* indicating two or more separate persons, objects, or ideas) and the compound subject which indicates a single person, object, or idea:

RIGHT: Music and dramatics are his chief interests.

RIGHT: The president and chief stockholder in the company is Mr. McCandless. [The two nouns refer to the same person. The article *the* is regularly omitted before the second noun in constructions of this sort.]

RIGHT: The president and the secretary have arrived.

RIGHT: This patriot and statesman has now become governor.

RIGHT: Every Tom, Dick, and Harry knows as much as I do about the situation. [Tom, Dick, and Harry, though more than one person, are here considered as a unit through the use of the indefinite adjective *every*.]

15G 3. Collective Noun. Collective nouns take singular verbs if the group named is regarded as a unit. They take plural verbs if the group are considered as individuals. It is essential for the writer to be consistent once he has chosen which number to use.

RIGHT: The class is dismissed.

RIGHT: The class are working on several projects.

RIGHT: The faculty is unanimous in its attitude toward absences.

RIGHT: The faculty are divided in opinion on absences.

RIGHT: The gang were rounded up one by one. [Often it is more natural to avoid treating a collective noun as a plural by rephrasing the sentence: "The members of the gang were rounded up one by one."]

Here also may be considered such words as *number, half, part:*

RIGHT: A number of students were thumbing the pages of the reference books and taking notes. [The indefinite article *a* used with *number* indicates *several*, and hence requires a plural verb.]

RIGHT: The number of available men is small. [*The* indicates a limited concept, hence is followed by the singular.]

RIGHT: Half of the meat was gone by noon. [Emphasis on quantity.]

RIGHT: Half of the men were sick. [Emphasis on number.]

RIGHT: Two thirds of the money is spent.

RIGHT: Two thirds of the apartments are rented.

15G 4. Subjects Introduced by *Or, Nor,* Etc. Subjects introduced by *or, nor, either . . . or, neither . . . nor* are considered as separate, not compound, subjects. If both subjects are singular, they take a singular verb in formal English. "Either Jane or Mary is going" means that just one of the girls is going, not both.

RIGHT: Either Robert or John *is* going to help us.

If both subjects are plural, they take a plural verb:

Neither the Smiths nor the Browns *are* going to the game.

If one subject is singular and the other plural, the verb agrees with the nearer subject:

Either Robert or his cousins *are* going to run the ice cream concession.
Neither Weston nor the Smiths *have* chosen a candidate.
Neither the Smiths nor Weston *has* chosen a candidate.

These sentences seem somewhat awkward, but are often no worse than the possible recastings necessary to avoid the problem. Compare, for example, the following revisions with the sentences above:

Robert is going to run the ice cream concession or his cousins are.
Weston has not chosen his candidate, nor have the Smiths.
Weston has not chosen his candidate; the Smiths also have still to choose one.
BETTER: Weston and the Smiths have not chosen a candidate.

15G 5. Subjects with Plural Form. A number of nouns have only plural form, and a few others have irregular plurals that are sometimes mistaken for singulars.

a) Plural forms ending in *-ics*: Commonly *economics, aesthetics, mathematics,* and *physics* take singular verbs; *acoustics, athletics, ethics, politics,* and *tactics* take either singular or plural verbs, depending on their meaning. Thus all these nouns used simply as naming or defining their specific fields take singular verbs:

Ethics is a branch of philosophy.
Athletics is a required course in this college.
Politics is more than political science.

But if any noun is used as denoting "activities, practices, or phenomena" (see *-ics* in *Webster's New Collegiate Dictionary*), it takes a plural verb:

His *ethics are* dubious.
Athletics are important for sound health.
Politics govern all his actions.

b) Certain plural forms of classical borrowing: *Data, phenomena,* and *strata* regularly take plural verbs, though there is a popular tendency of late to treat *data* as a singular noun. *Series* and *species* may be either singular or plural, depending on the meaning.

The data are (not *is*) compiled and waiting for analysis.
The phenomena of the seasons are (not *is*) a source of constant wonder.
Passenger pigeons once darkened our skies; the species *is* now extinct.
Several species of tropical fish *were* in the aquarium.

c) Other plural forms: In formal usage, *glasses, pants, riches, scissors,* and *trousers* take plural verbs. *Summons* (plural *summonses*) always takes a singular verb. *News* is usually singular in American usage. *Means, measles, mumps, pains* (in the sense of taking care) are singular or plural according to sense and usage.

RIGHT: The means *is* clearly indicated; the result will justify it.
RIGHT: His means *are* limited.
INFORMAL: Mumps *are* on the increase in the state.
FORMAL: Mumps *is* a serious disease for adults.
INFORMAL: Measles *are* spreading throughout the school.
FORMAL: Measles *is* a highly contagious disease.

In using these words in any one context in formal or informal English, try for consistency. Choose one form and keep to it.

d) Nouns of measure: Plural nouns or noun phrases that may be taken as indicating units of time, quantity, or other forms of measure regularly take singular verbs.

Two bushels of wheat *is* enough for the planting.
Six years *is* a long time in a dog's life.

15G 6. Relative Pronoun and Verb. A verb whose subject is a relative pronoun has the same person and number as the antecedent of the pronoun.

RIGHT: I, *who am* not satisfied with our plan, wish to propose several changes. [*Am* agrees with the antecedent of *who*, namely *I*.]
RIGHT: He is the one man who *is* best fitted for the task.

ILLOGICAL: He is one of the ablest students that *has* ever come to this college.

RIGHT: He is one of the ablest students that *have* ever come to this college. [The antecedent of *that* is *students*; hence a plural verb is required.]

ILLOGICAL: He is one of the most gifted speakers who *has* appeared in our assembly hall.

RIGHT: He is one of the most gifted speakers who *have* appeared in our assembly hall. [Of the most gifted speakers who *have* appeared, he is one.]

The problem of distinguishing between singular and plural in such sentences as the last two is difficult for many writers, and examples of illogical usage may be found now and then in good writing. Though the fault is not serious, since the meaning is at least implied, logic and complete clarity require the plural in formal usage.

15G7. Subjects Following Verbs. a) In inverted sentence order, the number of the verb agrees with the noun or nouns following it:

Following this introductory chapter are ten others dealing with various aspects of economics. [*Ten others* is the inverted subject of *are.*]
Then, if ever, come perfect days. [*Days* is the subject of *come.*]
With the dog days begins (not *begin*) the hottest part of summer.
Here comes the bride, with the groom beside her.
Here come the bride and groom.

b) *There is, there are,* and expletive *it.* The expletives *there* and *it* must not be confused with the subject. An expletive merely fills out a structure. In structures beginning *there is* (*are*), and *it is* (when *it* has no antecedent and is not the impersonal *it* of such sentences as "*It* rains"), the expletives fill the place of the delayed noun or substantive. The subject of *there is* (*are, was, were,* etc.) regularly follows the verb and determines the number of the verb.

There are many who regret his folly. [*Many* is the subject of *are.*]
There is nothing to report.
There are a house and a garage on the lot.
There are a road leading to the right and another road to the left over a river. [*A road . . . and another road* are the compound subject of *are.*]

On the other hand, singular *is* is often found in informal writing in such sentences as the last two just quoted.

The expletive *it* is always followed by a singular verb.

> It is disillusionment, not fading strength, that makes people grow old.
> Yesterday it was the chestnuts that were being blighted; today it is the elms and the oaks.

15G 8. Agreement of Pronoun and Verb. See Sections 14K 1, 2, 3.

EXERCISES

A. Agreement of Subject and Verb. Choose the correct verb forms in the following sentences. In a few sentences either form may be correct. Explain the reasons for your choices.

1. The principal headache for golfers on Oakwood course (is, are) the lightning-fast greens.
2. The Turnpike Commission (is, are) in disagreement concerning the speed limit to be set.
3. The hammer and saw (is, are) in the basement.
4. There (is, are) mice in the pantry again.
5. The manufacturer of automobiles capable of speeds upwards of eighty miles an hour (is, are) unable to disclaim all responsibility for the death rate on our highways.
6. Eighty per cent of our students (come, comes) from public schools.
7. My pride and joy (is, are) my new television set.
8. The manager along with the first-base coach (was, were) banished from the field by the umpires.
9. The Senate (has, have) voted to pass the bill over the President's veto.
10. Mathematics and one science that enables the student to familiarize himself with laboratory procedure (is, are) required in the freshman year.
11. The chief support of the fifteenth-century chapel (is, are) those delicate-looking buttresses.
12. Either the girl in pink or the one with the flowers in her arms (is, are) in charge of the tea this afternoon.
13. Though economics (is, are) his major, one might say that athletics (is, are) what he thinks about most.
14. There (is, are) already hints of autumn in the air.

15. He seems to think that a number of important points (has, have) been ignored.
16. The shortstop and leading hitter on the team (is, are) threatening to carry off the league batting title.
17. Either the doctor or the nurses (has, have) made a mistake.
18. The time when the accident rate from reckless driving seems to be highest (is, are) the hours just after midnight.
19. Three score years and ten (is, are) the life span allotted to mankind in the Bible.
20. The performance was so wretched that I could only conclude that the quartet (was, were) still at odds with each other as to interpretation.
21. The heat wave, together with the storms that will inevitably follow it, (is, are) expected to take the usual heavy toll of life.
22. Neither of the streams that supply water for these irrigation projects (is, are) very large.
23. The folly of wishing away the months or sometimes years that separate one from longed-for goals (become, becomes) more evident as one grows older.
24. The town council (was, were) denounced by the angry mayor for what he termed irresponsible conduct.
25. Either the lower meadows or the tract that borders the lakes (is, are) going to have to be sold if I am to pay my taxes.
26. The contortions that poor Garber went through as he tried to keep his face straight (was, were) something to remember.

B. Agreement of Subject and Verb. Determine whether the following sentences are correct or incorrect. Rewrite the sentences which you think incorrect and give the reasons for your corrections.

1. Communication between the Eastern and Western sections of the United States were inadequate at the turn of the century.
2. This vast multitude of stars are wandering about in space.—SIR JAMES JEANS.
3. The coach is charged with seeing that each of the men develop the greatest amount of skill and endurance possible.
4. It is a truism to say that the work of our lives end with death.
5. The blue serge dress with its round white collar and neat pin represent her idea of life.
6. The secretary and treasurer of the glee club has just resigned, and the club meets tonight for a new election.
7. Chromium-tube leather chairs and a black chrome-trimmed table was the only furniture in the little room.

8. A bedridden, kindly old rancher or an invalid storekeeper make the ideal villain for a detective story.
9. The little deeds that he performs gives me the impression that he is a very thoughtful person.
10. The minister preached on the theme that the wages of sin is death.
11. In this hospital the weird psychiatric phenomena of battle dreams was studied.
12. The water range of the tides are about two feet, and the crest of the high tides lag slightly behind the progress of the moon.
13. Arizona's only Pueblo tribe of Indians, the Hopis, are living under the guidance of the same god they worshiped long before Columbus discovered America.
14. Sometimes a detective or a store clerk see someone take an article and place it on his person.
15. The committee on ways and means have debated the problems of the budget at length, but still are not ready to report.
16. One popular hypothesis is that the terrific extremes of temperature that follow the path of the sun on the moon has completely solidified or vaporized the moon's atmosphere.
17. In the grade schools there seems to be many highly intelligent children who are not motivated for school work.
18. Alec Guinness is one of the greatest artists who has ever acted on the silver screen.
19. Under these conditions, in which freedom of expression in one's essays were almost nonexistent, I wrote only on compulsion.
20. Two copies of class lists of students enrolled in each class has been sent to each instructor.
21. According to the real estate agent, there is a garage and a storage house on the property.
22. The Green, with its stately old churches and their relationship to the early colonial history of the area, add to the color of the city.
23. This responsibility, combined with his literary career and other activities, were a great strain on his health, and he was obliged to seek rest in Italy.
24. Constant advice from friendly teachers and ever kind parents were unavailing to make me improve my slack attitude toward my studies.
25. Some say that the complex social life of these institutions are a detriment to education.

15H. Verbals and Sentence Structure

A verbal is a word form derived from a verb, but, unlike a verb, it cannot make a statement. In its verbal aspect it may take objects and modifiers; and as a noun or an adjective it may be used in all the functions served by nouns and adjectives. There are three types of verbals, the infinitive, the participle, and the gerund.

15H 1. Infinitive.

a) Definition. The infinitive is the infinite—that is, the unlimited—form of the verb. The verb as it normally functions in a sentence is *finite*; that is, it is limited in meaning by mode, tense, person, and number to a special statement or predication of action or being or becoming. An infinitive is not thus restricted: it is general in its meaning, not limited in its isolated form to any specific use. Literally, the infinitive is the unrestricted verbal alone; the preposition *to* which is frequently used with the infinitive is not part of it, but only its sign and connecting link to other structures. *To* and the infinitive together really make an infinitive phrase, but for convenience the construction is also called an infinitive, as in this discussion.

Infinitives have two tense forms:

PRESENT: to go
PERFECT: to have gone

Infinitives of transitive verbs have voice:

PRESENT, ACTIVE VOICE: to hit
PASSIVE VOICE: to be hit
PERFECT, ACTIVE VOICE: to have hit
PASSIVE VOICE: to have been hit

b) Functions of the Infinitive. The infinitive, though not restricted in its basic nature, can serve various uses in a sentence. (1) Its most important use is to be observed in verb phrases; with auxiliary (helping) verbs it serves as the main part of the verb phrase, the part that carries the basic meaning: I can *go*. In this sentence *go,* the present infinitive, is added to the auxiliary *can* to form the verb phrase *can go.* It is clear that *go* is the verb form of primary importance here, carrying the main thread of meaning. *Can* as an auxiliary helps to establish a special shade of meaning for the main verbal element.

(2) The infinitive can serve also in the following uses:

(*a*) As a phrase completing the meaning of certain verbs:

He is *to go.*
He happened *to fall.*
They used *to meet.*

(*b*) As a noun phrase, subject of a clause:

To succeed financially is his ambition. [Here *to succeed* is the subject of *is.* The infinitive *to succeed* has an adverb modifying its verbal aspect.]

(*c*) As a noun, direct object of a verb:

I should like *to know* the truth. [Here *to know* is the direct object of the verb phrase *should like* (*like* itself is an infinitive); that *to know* has the value of a noun here may be proved by substituting a noun for it: I should like *a knowledge of* the truth. Observe also that *to know* has a direct object of its own, namely, *truth.*]

(*d*) As a noun, subjective complement:

His policy is *to wait.* [*To wait,* equivalent to *waiting,* has the force of an adjective limiting the meaning of *his policy.*]

(*e*) As a noun, appositive:

His highest hope, *to serve* his country, was granted him. [*To serve* is an appositive of *hope.*]

(*f*) As a noun, object of the prepositions *about, but, except:*

He had no choice but (*or* except) *to go.* [Here *but* (or *except*) serves as a preposition introducing *to go,* which functions as a noun, equivalent to the verbal noun *going.*]
He is about *to leave.*

(*g*) As an adjective modifying a noun:

His ability *to play* was limited. [*To play* is equivalent to a verbal adjective: his *playing* ability.]

(*h*) As an adverb modifying an adjective:

He is very eager *to please.* [*To please* is equivalent to an adverbial phrase modifying *eager*: he is eager in respect to pleasing.]

(*i*) As an adverb modifying a verb:

He went to Spain *to study* its people. [*To study* modifies *went* as an adverb of purpose; *people* is the direct object of *study.*]

c) Tense of the Infinitive. (1) An infinitive in the present time (the present infinitive) represents action or state of being, occurring usually at the same time as that of its controlling verb. The time relationship can be illustrated by turning the infinitive into a clause representing the same time as that of the main clause, as in the following sentences:

It makes him happy to see her. [He sees her and it makes him happy.]
It will make him happy to see her. [He will see her and it will make him happy.]
It made him happy to see her. [He saw her and it made him happy.]
It has made him happy to see her. [He has seen her and it has made him happy.]
It will have made him happy to see her. [He will have seen her and it will have made him happy.]

(2) An infinitive in the perfect tense (the perfect infinitive) represents action that has taken place before the action of its controlling verb:

He is believed to have been an informer. [He was formerly an informer, before the time represented in the main verb, *is believed.*]
I am glad to have met you. [The speaker has met the person some time earlier than the moment of his speaking. In the sentence "I am glad to meet you," the actions agree in time.]

Avoid using the perfect infinitive when the sense clearly calls for the present infinitive:

WRONG: We shall be happy to have seen you.
RIGHT: We shall be happy to see you.

WRONG: I should not have tried to have answered the question.
RIGHT: I should not have tried to answer the question.

WRONG: I wish to be among the first to have congratulated you.
RIGHT: I wish to be among the first to congratulate you.

d) The Split Infinitive. The infinitive is said to be "split" when adverbs or adverbial phrases are inserted between *to,* the sign of the infinitive, and the infinitive itself. It is advisable to avoid splitting infinitives if it is possible to do so without awkwardness. But it is better to split an infinitive than to write an awkward construction. Often the problem can be avoided by recasting the sentence.

COLLOQUIAL: She decided *to just not go.*
FORMAL: She decided not *to go.*
FORMAL: She decided *that she would not go.*

MISPLACED ADVERB: He was able *to almost elude* his pursuers.
BETTER: He was almost able *to elude* his pursuers.

PERMISSIBLE: He planned *to rapidly improve* production and build new kilns. [As the adverb *rapidly* stands, it modifies both *improve* and *build.* If *rapidly* is placed after *planned,* it may be misread as modifying *planned* only; if placed after *production,* it no longer modifies *build*; if placed after *kilns,* it no longer modifies *improve.*]

Sometimes the adverb can be omitted advantageously.

WORDY: Nelson expected every man to faithfully do his duty.
BETTER: Nelson expected every man to do his duty.
PASSABLE: Nelson expected that every man would do his duty.

See H. W. Fowler's excellent article "Split Infinitive," in the *Dictionary of Modern English Usage,* for a more detailed discussion.

e) The Dangling Infinitive. See Section 15H 4 c.

EXERCISES

A. The Function of the Infinitive. Explain the grammatical function of each infinitive in the following sentences:

1. To achieve a high scholastic standing is perhaps my chief aim in coming to college.
2. He wrote yesterday that he would be able to come.

3. He wanted to know my plans.
4. The best plan of attack is to surprise the enemy.
5. Hamlet said that to die was the same as to sleep—"to sleep, perchance to dream."
6. When his supplies were gone, General Wainwright had no alternative but to surrender at Corregidor.
7. His ability to defend his position was limited by shortage of supplies.
8. Intrepid Americans have explored Antarctica to map the region in our country's interest.
9. It is better to have loved and lost than never to have loved at all.
10. I should like to be informed of your plans and when you intend to come.

B. Errors in Tense. The sentences below contain examples of faults in the tense of the infinitive. Revise each sentence and explain the reasons for the changes that you make.

1. Father said that he would have liked to have seen you before he left home.
2. To have built a furnace fire, first you must clean the furnace thoroughly.
3. He had hoped to have caught the train easily, but he missed it.
4. Vitamin B was fed to a diet-deficient rat, and as a result he is said to recover muscle control within twenty-four hours.
5. She planned to have been ready before he called to take her to the dance.
6. One must spend long hours on the technique of wood engraving to have mastered the art.
7. Mary said that she would have liked to have come with us.
8. I intended to have gone camping with you.
9. I should have liked to have seen his face when he opened the package.
10. We expected you to have brought your sister with you.

C. The Split Infinitive. The sentences below contain split infinitives. Rewrite these sentences with the aim of eliminating the split constructions and improving their expression. Are there any that you cannot successfully change?

1. It is our problem to not only cure the disease but also to get rid of its underlying causes so that it will not crop up again in the future.
2. My mind was flexible when it came to deciding the way in which I was to some day astound the public with my achievements.

3. Lipstick gives an attractive appearance to the mouth and can be employed to seemingly change its shape.
4. His experience in the war taught him to more than ever trust his own opinion and to be wary of that of others.
5. In wartime women proved themselves not only able to efficiently take men's places in factories, but sometimes able to even surpass the records set by men.
6. Uranium rays were found to easily penetrate photographic plates.
7. The story is written from the viewpoint of a person who can see what is happening, but it is written so as to not completely tell the reader what these happenings represent.
8. The best way to solve the problem of correct exposure is to carefully read the slip of paper which comes with every roll of film.
9. Take care to quietly close the door as you go out.
10. His success stemmed from his ability to in some way or other anticipate his opponent's every move.

15H 2. Participle.

a) Definition. A participle is a verbal form commonly ending in *-ing, -ed, -d, -t, -en,* or *-n* which may serve two purposes: (1) it may help to complete a verb; (2) it may modify a noun or substantive. As a verbal it may have the complements and modifiers of a verb, but it cannot make an assertion by itself as a verb does. A participle with its complements and modifiers is known as a *participial phrase.*

Both the participle and the gerund speed up discourse. Sentence after sentence of clauses would, in course of time, become cumbrous and heavy. Slipping in (notice the participle!) unobtrusively, verbals carry the weight of a clause and help to throw main ideas into bold relief by subordinating (notice the gerund!) less important ones.

The participle has three forms, present, past, and perfect, and participles derived from transitive verbs have two voices, active and passive.

b) Present Participle. (1) The present participle in the active voice is formed by adding the suffix *-ing* to the present infinitive of the verb: *walking, riding, giving.* The present participle in the passive voice is formed by adding the past participle to the present participle *being: being given, being seen.*

The present participle agrees in time with the verb of the clause to which it is joined or related in thought:

Seeing the pigeons, he thought of St. Mark's. [The two times agree: He saw the pigeons and he thought of St. Mark's.]

Being hidden in the shrubbery, he overheard their conversation. [The time of the action represented in the present passive participle, *being hidden*, agrees with that of the verb *overheard*.]

(2) Functions of the present participle.

(*a*) The present participle as a verb-maker: The present participle is used to complete all the progressive verb phrases in all tenses: I am *asking,* I shall be *asking,* I was *asking,* etc. The present participle of the verb *be* is used to help form the passive progressive verb: I am being asked, I was being asked, etc.

(*b*) The present participle as a verbal adjective: As an adjective, a participle describes or limits the noun or substantive it modifies in terms of the action of the verb from which it is derived. Participles fill all the functions of adjectives and at the same time, as remarked above, retain their verbal powers.

Raising his axe, he split the block neatly down its center. [*Raising*, a present participle, serves as an adjective modifying *he*; as a verbal it also takes a direct object, *axe*.]

Quickly giving her a sharp glance, the instructor continued his discussion. [*Giving*, the present participle, serves as an adjective modifying *instructor; her* is the indirect object and *glance* the direct object of *giving; quickly* is an adverb modifying *giving*.]

The formula being given, the solution of the problem was easy. [The present passive participle, *being given*, serves as an adjective modifying *formula. The formula being given* is an absolute construction (see Section 11B3).]

c) The Past Participle. (1) The past participle usually ends in *-en, -n* (*ridden, born*) or *-ed, -d,* or *-t* (*loved, said, sent*). It is ordinarily passive in meaning (a sight rarely *seen*; that is, a sight that *is seen* rarely).

(2) The functions of the past participle:

(*a*) The past participle as a verb-maker: The primary function of the past participle is to help form verbs. It is used with the verb *have* to form the perfect tenses: He has (had, will have) *seen.* It is used with forms of the verb *be* to form the passive verb: He is (will be, was, has *been,* had *been*) *seen.*

(*b*) The past participle as adjective: Many past participles are used frequently as adjectives: *beaten, broken, drawn, driven, forsaken, gone, known, proved, shown, stolen, sunken, swollen, tired, worn.* Some words that were originally past participles, such as *cloven, drunken, graven, molten, rotten, shorn, sodden, sunken, waxen,* are not used any longer except as adjectives.

His broken arm healed rapidly. [*Broken,* a past participle, serves as a descriptive adjective modifying *arm*; or it may serve as a subjective complement or predicate adjective: His arm was *broken.* Observe that in this use it completes the passive past tense.]

d) The Perfect Participle. The perfect participle has both active and passive forms. The perfect active participle is formed by adding the past participle to the present participle *having: having seen, having sung.* The perfect passive participle is formed by adding the past participle to the perfect participle, *having been: having been seen, having been sung.*

The action represented by the perfect participle indicates time prior to that of the verb of the clause to which it is joined.

Having played as pitcher, outfielder, and first baseman, the new manager is one of the most experienced men on the team. [The time represented by the participle is prior to that represented in the verb of the clause. The perfect participle *having played* serves as an adjective modifying *manager.* Note that the present participle would be incorrect in this particular sentence: Playing as pitcher, outfielder, and first baseman, the new manager is one of the most experienced men on the team.]

e) The Dangling Participle. (See Section 15H 4 a.)

15H 3. Gerund.

a) Definition. A gerund is a verbal form commonly ending in *-ing* which serves as a noun. Gerunds may function in sentences as other nouns do, but at the same time they retain their verbal nature in that they can take complements or be modified by adverbs. A gerund with its complements and modifiers is known as a gerund phrase.

b) Functions of the Gerund.

(1) Gerund as subject:

Working is better than idling. [Both *working* and *idling* are subjects; *idling* is the subject of the unexpressed verb *is*.]

(2) Gerund with subjective complement as subject:

Being funny is an occupation for him. [*Being* is a gerund; *funny* is the subjective complement of *being*.]

(3) Gerund with adverb modifier:

Working hard is better than idling. [*Hard* is an adverb of degree modifying *working*.]

(4) Gerund with adverbial modifier as object of verb:

He enjoys working hard.

(5) Gerund and its direct object as subject:

Building a house is expensive today. [*House* is the direct object of *building*.]

(6) Gerund with a possessive noun:

I have not heard Wilson's playing. [Observe that if the sentence read, "I have not heard Wilson playing," *playing* would be a verbal adjective (participle) modifying *Wilson* instead of a verbal noun, modified by the possessive noun *Wilson's*.]

(7) Gerund with a possessive pronoun. (See Section 14J 2.)

(8) Gerund as object of a preposition:

After playing *Finlandia*, the orchestra paused for intermission. [*Playing* is object of the preposition *after*.]

His little terrier greeted him by rushing toward him, turning over, and wagging his tail vigorously. [*Rushing, turning over*, and *wagging* are three gerunds, forming a compound object of the preposition *by*.]

c) The Dangling Gerund. See Section 15H 4 b.

EXERCISE

Identify the participles and gerunds in each sentence and explain their functions.

1. Walking is better exercise than riding.
2. After eating lunch, Edward had returned to his gardening.
3. *Henry V* is a play of large scope, crowded with characters.
4. Picking up speed rapidly, the express was soon racing down the valley.
5. The New World seen through the eyes of strangers is a familiar literary theme, challenging to many authors.
6. Having finished breakfast, Mrs. Smith got into her automobile to go to the meeting; but after making several attempts to start the cold engine, she gave up and called for her son.
7. All people have the habit of forgetting rapidly things which they once considered important.
8. I prefer John's driving to Robert's, but Robert's driving is improving.
9. Racing cars was Rover's only bad habit.
10. Racing cars should be well designed.
11. The Arctic has been described as silent and waste, and covered with ice floes.
12. The ship was confronted with a long reef blocking the entrance to the harbor.

15H 4. Misuse of Verbals: Dangling Modifiers. A verbal is misused when it dangles—that is, when it should modify one word but instead seems to modify another (sometimes with ridiculous results). Misused verbals of this sort (dangling participle, gerund, and infinitive phrases) are generally known as *dangling modifiers.* Other (nonverbal) constructions (elliptical clauses, appositives, and prepositional phrases) also dangle at times, and since the faults involved are similar, they may be considered here.

NOTE: Not all dangling modifiers are serious faults. Some badly, even grotesquely, impair meaning; others are relatively harmless. But if you unguardedly write the latter type, you may easily fall into the mistake of writing the former. Make sure that your sentences do not have dangling modifiers.

a) Dangling Participial Phrases.

DANGLER: Walking down the street, her red hat drew admiring glances. [*Walking* seems to modify *hat.*]

One may correct a dangling participial phrase (1) by using as subject of the following main clause the noun or pronoun really modified by the participle or (2) by turning the participial phrase into a clause.

IMPROVED: Walking down the street, she was aware that her red hat was drawing admiring glances.
As she walked down the street, her red hat drew admiring glances.

Unskillful writers sometimes place a dangling participial phrase at the end of a sentence. Such a construction is usually awkward and lacks emphasis even if the dangler is corrected.

DANGLER: The runner was ruled safe at third, thereby provoking a chorus of jeers from the stands. [*Provoking* seems to modify *runner.*]
CORRECT: The umpire ruled the runner safe at third, thereby provoking . . .
BETTER: By ruling the runner safe at third, the umpire provoked a chorus of jeers from the stands.

b) Dangling Gerund Phrases.

DANGLER: On arriving at the station, the bulletin board informed us that the train would be an hour late. [*Arriving* seems to modify *bulletin board.*]

Methods of correction are the same as those used in correcting dangling participial phrases.

IMPROVED: On arriving at the station, we learned from the bulletin board that . . .
When we arrived at the station, the bulletin board informed us that . . . (or, . . . we learned from the bulletin board that . . .).

c) Dangling Infinitive Phrases.

DANGLER: To thrive, you must water these plants daily. [*To thrive* seems to modify *you.*]

Methods of correction are the same as those used in correcting dangling participial and gerund phrases.

IMPROVED: To thrive, these plants must be watered daily.
If these plants are to thrive, you must water them daily.

d) Dangling Elliptical Clauses.

DANGLER: When only a boy, a horse kicked him. [*When only a boy* seems to modify *horse.*]

Methods of correction are the same as those used in correcting dangling phrases.

IMPROVED: When only a boy, he was kicked by a horse.
When he was only a boy, a horse kicked him (or, . . . he was kicked by a horse).

e) Miscellaneous Dangling Phrases. Any phrase is a dangling modifier if like other danglers it seems to modify the wrong noun or pronoun.

DANGLER: An abject coward, the first shot will send him flying. [The appositive phrase *an abject coward* seems to modify *shot.*]

DANGLER: In infancy his parents brought him to this country. [The prepositional phrase *in infancy* seems to modify *parents.*]

Methods of correction are the same as those used in correcting other dangling phrases.

IMPROVED: An abject coward, he will fly at the first shot.
Because he is an abject coward, the first shot will send him flying (or, . . . he will fly at the first shot).

IMPROVED: In infancy he was brought to this country by his parents.
When he was an infant, his parents brought him to this country.

Or in this sentence the insertion of a possessive pronoun would make the meaning clear.

In his infancy his parents brought him to this country.

f) The following kinds of phrases that may look like dangling modifiers are not genuine danglers:

(1) Absolute phrases (which are always grammatically independent of the rest of the sentence):

The enemy having surrendered, the battle was over.

(2) Participial, gerund, or infinitive phrases that are idiomatic and do not suggest a particular action:

Generally speaking, truth will out.
In swimming, proper breathing is important.
To be brief, the trip was a failure.

EXERCISE

Revise the following sentences in a way to eliminate dangling modifiers. Some of the sentences are correct as they stand.

1. By building a small dam right here, a pond of considerable size will result.
2. Waiting impatiently on the porch, stealthy footsteps inside indicated to the visitor that someone was at home.
3. While finishing preparations for a month's vacation in Canada, the draft board sent me a notice to report for physical examination.
4. Staring glumly out of the window, the leaden skies and soggy fairways convinced us that there could be no golf that day.
5. To become a successful politician, a keen knowledge of human nature is necessary.
6. As a child he was almost drowned, thus causing him to have a fear of the water.
7. After opening the package the meaning of the mysterious message became clear.
8. At the age of two an accident took the lives of both his parents.
9. Though nearly exhausted by the time we reached the lower end of the lake, our pledge to the others kept us moving forward.
10. Delighted by having won the race, the information that he had broken the track record was an added thrill.
11. While learning to drive, a learner's permit is necessary.
12. A new battery having been installed, we were ready to resume our journey.
13. Lying on the floor, partially hidden by the draperies, we found the ring that we believed had been stolen.
14. Hurrying to mail the letter in time for the last collection, a sudden doubt as to the wisdom of her procedure made her stop short.
15. A strict disciplinarian, no student ever whispered in his classroom.
16. When asked without warning to present my side of the case, my knees trembled and my voice stuck in my throat.
17. Speaking of coincidences, did I ever tell you about the strange experience I had at camp last summer?
18. In fishing, expensive equipment does not always guarantee success.
19. To enjoy the scenery, the secondary roads should be traveled rather than the trunk highways.

20. Though pursued by a series of misfortunes, victory was ours at last.
21. Bending over to remove the chewing gum from my shoe while no one was looking, the sound of tearing cloth gave me a shock.
22. Tempted by the cookies piled invitingly on the plate, his shyness seemed to disappear.
23. A hard worker, no task was too difficult for him to undertake.
24. Exhausting our oil reserves at a ruinous rate, gobbling up our timber, watching our topsoil wash off into the sea, certain disaster lies ahead of us.
25. While going through forgotten records last summer, an amusing item of family history came to my attention.

16. THE ADJECTIVE AND SENTENCE STRUCTURE

16A. Definition

An adjective is the part of speech that modifies only a noun or substantive. To *modify* is to describe the qualities of any person, object, idea, or action, or to limit its meaning. An adjective thus describes or limits the meaning of the noun, pronoun, or other substantive which it modifies.

16B. Basic Kinds of Adjectives

All adjectives may be divided into two related classes as to meaning: descriptive and limiting adjectives. Most adjectives are primarily descriptive: they name a quality or characteristic of the noun they modify (*standing* grain, *red* house, *still* waters, *pleasant* thought). A smaller but very important group are primarily limiting adjectives: they point out, make definite, or otherwise indicate number or quantity. This group comprises several different types of adjectives:

(1) the definite article *the* and the indefinite articles *a, an*;
(2) the demonstrative adjectives *this* and *that*, with their plurals *these* and *those*;
(3) the possessive adjectives *my, his, her, its, our, your, their*;
(4) the possessive relative adjective *whose*;
(5) the numerical adjectives *one, two, three*, etc., and *first, second*, etc.
(6) the indefinite adjectives *all, both, each, every, some, any, no.*

The possessive adjectives, the possessive relative adjectives, and the indefinite adjectives *all, both, each, any,* and *some* are also used as pronouns.

16C. Classification of Adjectives as to Use in Sentences

Adjectives may be classified by their use in sentences as *attributive adjectives, predicate adjectives* (also called *subjective complements*), and *objective complements.*

16C 1. Attributive Adjective. An *attributive adjective* commonly precedes the noun it describes, but it may follow: *bay* horse; *red* house; *hazardous* decision; the scout camp, *vacant* and *cheerless; vacant* and *cheerless,* the scout camp.

16C 2. Predicate Adjective (Subjective Complement). A *predicate adjective* (or *subjective complement,* a term which embracingly describes nouns, pronouns, and adjectives in the predicate) is an adjective that completes the meaning of a linking verb (any form of *be, become, appear, seem,* etc.—see Section 15B 2), and hence describes or limits the noun used as subject:

> The house is *red.*
> The scout camp seemed *vacant* and *cheerless.*
> The day became *dark.*

16C 3. Adjective as Objective Complement. An adjective is an *objective complement* when it follows and completes (complements) the meaning of a noun or pronoun in the objective case:

> Your indolence makes me *sick.* [*Sick* is an objective complement describing the objective pronoun *me.*]
> Fear struck the visitor *numb.*
> Grief made her *hysterical.*

16D. Verbal, Phrasal, and Clausal Adjectives

Since all words that modify nouns in any of the ways indicated above are by that fact adjectival, it follows that participles (verbals commonly ending in *-ing, -ed, -t, -en*) so used are *verbal* (or participial) *adjectives* (see Section 15H 2); that prepositional phrases modifying nouns are *adjectival phrases* (that is, phrasal adjectives); and that relative clauses, which modify nouns or substantives only, are adjectival clauses (or clausal adjectives).

Verbal adjective (participle) modifying a noun:

The *burning* bonfire.

Verbal adjective as predicate adjective:

The fire was *burning*.

Adjectival prepositional phrase:

The house *by the lake*.

Relative, and hence adjectival, clause:

Cairn terriers, *which are related to the Skye breed*, are tireless hunters.

16E. Noun Adjectives

Nouns may be used as adjectives if no adequate adjective exists for the same meaning. Thus, since no equally satisfactory adjectives exist for the ideas, we may use nouns as adjectives in such phrases as these: *airplane* workers, the *Iron* City, *city* traffic, *economics* classes, *football* field, *building* inspector.

But when satisfactory adjectives exist, we use them, at least in formal discourse, instead of nouns, as in the following: *medical* journal (not *medicine* journal), *horticultural* studies (not *horticulture* studies); or we may use a phrasal construction: *professor of electrical engineering* (not *electrical engineering professor*).

16F. Comparison of Adjectives

If we exclude the pronominal adjectives (the demonstrative adjectives *this* and *that* with their plurals *these* and *those*) on the ground that they are basically pronouns rather than adjectives, we may say that English adjectives do not change form except for comparison. Unlike Latin, French, German, and other Indo-European languages in which adjectives have inflectional endings to agree in gender, number, and case with the nouns they modify, English has no inflectional forms for the adjective save for the suffixes *-er, -est* used to indicate degrees of comparison.

16F 1. Degrees of Comparison. Adjectives have three degrees of comparison, *positive, comparative,* and *superlative.* The positive degree is the simple form of the adjective, which merely describes a quality of a person, object, or idea, with no suggestion of comparison of a like quality in another person, object, or idea: a *brave* man. The comparative degree indicates that some quality is more intense (greater or less, better or worse) in one person, object, or idea than another. It is formed by adding the suffix *-er* to the simple form of the adjective: the *braver* man. The superlative degree indicates that some quality is most intense in the person, object, or idea described, and is formed by adding the suffix *-est* to the simple form of the adjective: the *bravest* man.

Words of one or two syllables form comparisons with these suffixes as follows:

POSITIVE DEGREE	COMPARATIVE DEGREE	SUPERLATIVE DEGREE
tall	taller	tallest
pretty	prettier	prettiest
stately	statelier	stateliest

But words of three or more syllables usually substitute the adverbs *more* and *most* or *less* and *least* (for diminishing comparison) for the *-er, -est* endings, the adverbs being placed before the simple form of the adjective:

POSITIVE DEGREE	COMPARATIVE DEGREE	SUPERLATIVE DEGREE
beautiful	more beautiful	most beautiful
sensible	more sensible	most sensible
hospitable	less hospitable	least hospitable

Though we rarely use *-er, -est* with words of three or more syllables in formal English, we may with judgment use *more* and *most* with words of one and two syllables. *Euphony,* or the way the word sounds, and emphasis determine whether one uses *-er, -est* or *more, most* in various situations.

16F 2. Irregular Comparison. A small number of much-used words either are irregular in form or have other words supplied to form the comparative and superlative degrees:

POSITIVE DEGREE	COMPARATIVE DEGREE	SUPERLATIVE DEGREE
good	better	best
much, many, some	more	most
bad, evil, ill	worse	worst
little	less, lesser	least
late	later	latest, last
well	better	best
far	farther, further	farthest, furthest
old	older, elder	oldest, eldest

NOTE: *Elder* and *eldest* are restricted in use to nouns of relationship: *the elder sister, the eldest* (*brother*, etc., understood).

16F3. Comparison and Adjectives of Absolute Meaning. A special group of adjectives that name absolute qualities of nouns are logically not subject to comparison. Thus if a ball is really *round,* another ball cannot be *rounder,* nor a third *roundest.* Actual roundness is absolute. Other adjectives with absolute meaning are these: *absolute, complete, daily, dead, empty, everlasting, first, infinite, last, matchless, mortal, perfect, single, square, straight, unique, universal.*

But language often ignores logic. Nearly all these adjectives are used in the comparative and superlative degrees, despite logic, in informal English, and now and then many of them occur in such uses in formal writing. Certain of these words, namely, such words as *perfect, straight, round, square,* really have two meanings. In their absolute sense they are not comparable, but in their relative sense (as in a *more complete study*) they are naturally comparable.

On the other hand, there is little to be gained by being illogical in the use of most of these words. In formal English, then, though we may correctly say *almost unique, nearly round, more nearly round, nearly* or *almost perfect* to qualify the absolute meaning, in general it is better not to say *more perfect, more* or *most unique, deadest,* etc.

16F4. Faults in Comparison of Adjectives. For faults in the use of comparatives, see Section 18.

16G. Agreement of the Demonstrative Adjective with Its Noun

The demonstrative adjectives *this* and *that* are the only adjectives to have plural forms. The relation of the possessive adjectives to their nouns has already been considered (see Pronouns). When one uses a demonstrative adjective, he should logically select the form that agrees with the number of the noun modified or pointed out by the demonstrative. True, one sometimes hears in careless conversation such sentences as the following:

Those kind of people bore me.
These kind of apples are sour.

But good English, both formal and informal, requires that the number of the demonstrative adjective must agree with its noun:

That kind of person bores me.
This kind of apple is sour.

16H. Predicate Adjectives and the Linking Verb

The linking verbs *be* (with its various forms, *is, was, will be,* etc.), *become, seem, appear,* etc., regularly take an adjective, not an adverb, to complete their meaning in the predicate:

The garden is *full* of weeds.
His eyes became *stern.*
She seemed *happy* yesterday.
The prospects of victory appear *good.*

16H 1. Sensory Verbs. The sensory verbs *feel, look, sound, smell,* and *taste,* and other verbs such as *grow, prove,* and *turn* also take adjectives, not adverbs, to complete their meaning when they are used as linking verbs.

He feels sick (not *sickly*).
He looks prosperous (not *prosperously*).
Her voice sounds sharp (not *sharply*).
The air smells fragrant (not *fragrantly*).
This pie tastes delicious (not *deliciously*).
He grew bitter (not *bitterly*).
They proved steadfast (not *steadfastly*).

Note that we say, "He looks well," not, "He looks good." *Well* thus used is an adjective after *looks,* not an adverb. The only reason that we do not say, "He looks *good,*" is that *well* is the accepted adjective for the expression. On the other hand, "It looks good" is approved English. "He feels good" is correct usage when we refer to a state of mental or spiritual satisfaction. "He feels well" is correct when we wish to indicate a state of physical health.

16H 2. Test for Linking Verbs. In general, whenever the linking verb *be* (in any of its forms) can be substituted for any verb without seriously altering the sense, that verb serves as a linking verb. Accordingly, an adjective, not an adverb, is used to complete the predicate. Thus *is* or *was* could be substituted for any of the verbs in the examples just given without seriously changing their meaning:

The pie *tastes* delicious: The pie *is* delicious.
Her voice *sounds* sharp: Her voice *is* sharp.

Some of these verbs, however, may take either an adjective or an adverb to complete their meaning:

His look grew *sullen* (adjective).
The plant grew *quickly* (adverb).
The milk turned *sour* (adjective).
The man turned *quickly* (adverb).

But observe that most of these verbs also have transitive uses:

He tasted the pie.
He smelled bacon frying.
He sounded the horn.
He felt the child's head.

16J. Excessive Use of Adjectives

Though the right adjectives help to express meaning, too many adjectives will obscure it. Go through your sentences and strike out all adjectives that are purely decorative and not essential to your meaning. The following sentences show how adjectives can mar style and expand meaning to an airy thinness:

The awkward, clumsy, stumbling speaker spent more than thirty tedious, time-consuming, boring minutes on his worthless and trivial address.

Beautiful, elegant, accomplished as she was, how shall I describe her lissom, delicate, and debonair ways?

Sentences thus laden take much time in saying little. Here are quicker versions:

The speaker stumbled through thirty tedious minutes.

Her ways were delicate and debonair.

Do not be afraid to cut away all adjectives, and other words as well, that give only an indefinite impression. In particular avoid using trite or hackneyed adjectives, especially the much abused counter words *nice, pleasant, beautiful, pretty, wonderful* (see Section 64B).

EXERCISES

A. The Types of Adjectives and Their Functions. Classify the adjectives in the following sentences as to basic kinds and as to their sentence functions.

1. Mechanics, clean as hospital orderlies, were busy with the final mysterious rites of their trade.—ERNESTA BARLOW.
2. The seven principal stars in the constellation of the Great Bear are also known as the Dipper or Charles's Wain.
3. The crowd was so dense that it was hardly possible to move; such throngs always made him nervous and irritable.
4. Red, blue, yellow, green—no color was missed in that startling display.
5. The damp mist washed his face and clung to his hair, and hung in minute drops on the woolen fibers of his sweater.
6. He wore bow ties and sharp jazzy suits; his lips were blue and he had gaudy small swerving eyes; altogether he looked like a mean mouse.—TRUMAN CAPOTE.

B. Agreement of the Demonstrative Adjective with Its Noun. The sentences below violate the rule requiring agreement in number between a noun and its demonstrative adjective. Rewrite these sentences correctly and explain the changes you make.

1. He criticized those kind of people who restrain their children and cause most of our social ills.
2. People throw empty bottles and waste paper around the roadside picnic areas. These kind of people make a place unattractive for others who might like to stop.
3. Many volunteer for blood donations. One must admire these sort of people.
4. These kind of characters are very convincing to us, and the comedy they enact is backed by a strong social thesis.
5. Soap opera on television pictures mothers so sentimentally that one wonders who can bear to watch these sort of shows.

C. Predicate Adjectives and the Linking Verbs. Choose the right word and explain the reason for your choice.

1. (happy, happily)	She looked very ________.
2. (good, well)	He feels ________.
3. (sweet, sweetly)	Victory tastes ________.
4. (good, well)	His chances of success look ________.
5. (quick, quickly)	His debts grew ________.
6. (shrill, shrilly)	The whistle sounded ________.

17. THE ADVERB AND SENTENCE STRUCTURE

17A. Definition

An adverb is the part of speech that ordinarily modifies a verb, an adjective, or another adverb. It may also modify a phrase, a clause, or a sentence. Just as the adjective limits or describes its noun or pronoun, the adverb describes or limits the action of the verb or the quality of the adjective, adverb, or construction modified.

An adverb modifying a verb:

He spoke *eloquently*.

An adverb modifying an adjective:

The speaker was *very* eloquent.

An adverb modifying another adverb:

He spoke *very* eloquently.

An adverb modifying a phrase:

His greed was *almost* beyond imagination. [*Almost* modifies the prepositional phrase *beyond imagination.*]

An adverb modifying a noun clause:

Exactly what he said will remain a mystery. [*Exactly* modifies the noun clause *what he said.*]

An adverb modifying a sentence:

He disliked the inconveniences of traveling. *Moreover*, his knowledge of German was very slight. [*Moreover*, a conjunctive adverb, modifies the meaning of its sentence rather than any word in the sentence.]

17B. Form of Adverbs

Like adjectives, adverbs have no inflection except for the *-er, -est* endings of comparison; many adverbs do not even have these (see Section 17F). Most adverbs are formed by adding the suffix *-ly* to the adjective: adjective, *brave*; adverb, *bravely*. These adverbs in *-ly* must not be confused with the small group of adjectives ending in *-ly,* for example, *brotherly, fatherly, friendly, lonely, lovely, manly, surly, ugly*. Such adjectives are usually made into adverbs by means of prepositional phrases, the whole phrase serving as an adverb: *in a brotherly way, with a surly glance.*

17B 1. "Flat" Adverbs. Certain words not ending in *-ly* may serve as either adverbs or adjectives, depending on their use in sentences. Representative of these words, known commonly as flat adverbs, are the following: *well, fast, early, much, little, straight, far, soon, first, last.*

Duncan sleeps well.
He drove fast.
He walks straight (not *straightly*).
First (not *firstly*), there was a heavy wind.
Last (not *lastly*) came the elephants.

The use of the word in the sentence determines whether it is an adverb or an adjective. Consider the difference in these three sentences:

He rose early. [*Early* is an adverb modifying the intransitive verb *rose.*]

The early settlers traded with the Indians. [*Early* is an adjective modifying *settlers.*]

The train was early. [*Early* is a subjective complement (predicate adjective) after *was.*]

17B 2. Adverbs of Dual Form. With the flat adverbs may be associated such words as *close, near, right, late, loud, hard, slow,* which are used as adverbs both in their simple form and with the suffix *-ly*. Several of these words change meaning with the addition of *-ly*. Study the following acceptable usages:

He sat close (not *closely*) beside her. She looked at him closely (narrowly).

Do it right (not *rightly*). He rightly surmised the truth.

The car came near. It nearly (almost) stopped.

He rose late (not *lately*). I saw him lately.

He spoke loud enough for all to hear. He spoke loudly.

He hit the ball hard (not *hardly*). I hardly (barely) knew him.

INFORMAL: Drive slow. He drove slow all the way.

FORMAL: Drive slowly. He drove slowly all the way.

17C. Adverbs Classified as to Meaning

There are several kinds of adverbs. Most may be classified by their meaning as adverbs of manner, time, place, and degree. They answer the questions: How? When? Where? To what extent?

17C 1. Adverbs of Manner. Adverbs of manner describe how the action of the verb takes place. Most of these adverbs end in *-ly*.

The boxer fought *bravely.*

The clock ticked *slowly.*

He played *violently.*

17C 2. Adverbs of Time. Adverbs of time indicate when the action of the verb takes place or has taken place. The most commonly used adverbs of time are *now, then, soon, today, yesterday, tomorrow, immediately, presently, already, at once, yet, afterwards, recently.* Nouns (*today,* etc.) may also function as adverbs of time. Any word, phrase, or clause that answers the question "When?" and modifies a verb is an adverb of time:

Please write me a letter *soon.*
John works *nights.*
I have *already* mailed my letter.
He went to Chicago *Friday.* [*Friday* is an adverb of time; *to Chicago* is an adverbial phrase of place.]
He came home *yesterday.* [*Yesterday* is an adverb of time; *home,* basically a noun, is an adverb of place.]
I shall buy a new car *next year.*

17C3. Adverbs of Place. Adverbs of place indicate direction or where the action of the verb takes place.

The train moved *onward.*
Orpheus looked *back toward Eurydice.* [*Back* is a simple adverb of place; *toward Eurydice* is a prepositional phrase serving as an adverb of place.]
Few people ever come *there.*

Other much used adverbs of place are *here, north* (*south,* etc.), *out, abroad, away, below, above, far, farther, further, anywhere, somewhere.* Any word, phrase, or clause that answers the question "Where?" and modifies a verb is an adverb of place.

17C4. Adverbs of Degree. Adverbs of degree indicate the extent or degree of any quality when they modify adjectives or adverbs, or the degree of action of a verb.

Adverb of degree modifying an adverb:

He was *very* much excited. [*Much* is also an adverb of degree modifying the participle *excited.*]

Adverb of degree modifying a verb:

He could *hardly* swallow.

Other frequently used adverbs of degree are: *almost, rather, partly, partially, much, somewhat, about, utterly, entirely, completely, nearly, all, less, least.*

Though *very* can modify an adjective or an adverb (*very* bitter, *very* truly), in formal English it is usually followed by *much* when used with a participle: *very much* excited (not: *very* excited); *very much* pleased (not: *very* pleased). But when the participle is so frequently used as an adjective that we no longer think of it as a participle, *much* is omitted: *very* tired (not: *very much* tired).

17D. Adverbs Classified as to Special Functions

Adverbs may be classified as to special functions in discourse as adverbial conjunctions, conjunctive adverbs, correlative adverbs, and interrogative adverbs.

17D 1. Adverbial Conjunctions. Adverbial clauses are commonly introduced by subordinating conjunctions, such as *because, when, where, since, though.* Such conjunctions are often spoken of as adverbial conjunctions. (See Subordinating Conjunctions, Section 20E.)

17D 2. Conjunctive Adverbs. A very important special class of adverbs is that of the conjunctive adverbs, including such directive words and expressions as *first* (*second* or *secondly,* etc.), *last, indeed, moreover, accordingly, however, therefore, surely, certainly, still, nevertheless, hence, furthermore, in other words, in fact, as a matter of fact.* Conjunctive adverbs indicate a shift or transition in thought between clause and clause, between sentence and sentence, between paragraph and paragraph, and between divisions of thought. These adverbs modify whole clauses or divisions of thought rather than any single element in a sentence; hence they may be regarded as parenthetical or absolute in nature. When used to link co-ordinate clauses, as in the sentence just before this one, they are preceded by a semicolon. (See Sections 20C, 32B.)

17D 3. Correlative Adverbs. Correlative adverbs (also known as correlating conjunctions: see Section 20D), such as *as . . . as, not so . . . as, the . . . the,* function in pairs to show relationship between clauses. The correlative in the main clause serves as a simple adverb; the correlative introducing the subordinate clause serves as an adverbial conjunction.

He is as tall as I am. [The second clause is elliptical; completed, the sentence would read: *He is as tall as I am tall.* The first correlative adverb *as* serves also as a simple adverb of degree modifying the predicate adjective *tall*; the second *as* serves as an adverbial conjunction, modifying the adjective *tall* implied in the second clause and linking the clause to *as tall* in the main clause.]

The sooner the better. [In elliptical sentences of this sort, *the* is not a definite article, but an adverb of degree. Such a sentence expanded might read: *By what degree you come sooner, by that degree it will be better*. The first *the* may thus be considered as having the function of a relative adverbial conjunction; the second, in the main clause, is an adverb of degree.]

17D 4. Interrogative Adverbs. The interrogative adverbs *when, where, how, why, whence, whither* are used to introduce questions:

When are you going to town?
How are you?
He asked me why I did not come earlier. [This sentence presents a question in indirect discourse; in direct discourse, the question would be: "Why didn't you come earlier?"]

17E. Adverbs and Other Parts of Speech

As observed earlier, the same word that serves as an adverb may also serve as other parts of speech, as, for example, *north, south* (which may also be nouns or adjectives), *early, late, slow* (which may also be adjectives). More particularly, words distinctly adverbial in nature may occasionally serve as other parts of speech, and other parts of speech may serve as adverbs.

17E 1. Adverbs Used as Nouns.

He drove in here at seven. [*Here*, ordinarily an adverb of place, functions here (adverb) as a substantive, an object of the preposition *in*.]

The girl watched the in-and-out of the shuttle weaving the silk. [*In-and-out* is a compounded adverb (she watched the shuttle move *in* and move *out*) serving here as a substantive, the direct object of *watched*. *In* and *out* were, of course, originally prepositions.]

17E 2. Prepositional Adverbs. Many prepositions (especially those of direction) serve as adverbs without expressed objects:

The death fires danced *between*.
The children ran *around* wildly.
He put *off* going to the doctor.

Especially interesting are the uses of *up, down, off,* and *out. Up* is used colloquially with a large number of verbs, losing its adverbial sense and becoming part of the verb. (See Section 19C.)

17E 3. Nouns Used as Adverbs. Nouns are frequently used as adverbs.

She is ten years old. [That is, she is old to the extent of ten years: *ten years*, a noun phrase, serves as an adverb of degree modifying the predicate adjective *old*.]

I plan to go home Wednesday. [I plan to go to my home on Wednesday: *home*, basically a noun, is an adverb of place modifying the infinitive *go. Wednesday*, a noun, serves as an adverb of time also modifying *go*.]

He works nights. [He works of the night or by the night: *nights* is an adverb of time.]

You should have come a day earlier. [You should have come earlier by a day: *earlier* is an adverb of time modifying *come; a day*, a noun phrase, serves also as an adverb of time modifying *earlier*.]

17F. Comparison of Adverbs

Like adjectives, adverbs are compared in three degrees, positive, comparative, and superlative.

17F 1. Degrees of Comparison. Most adverbs use *more* and *most* to form the comparative and superlative degrees, and *less* and *least* in diminishing comparison.

POSITIVE DEGREE	COMPARATIVE DEGREE	SUPERLATIVE DEGREE
courteously	more courteously	most courteously
eagerly	more eagerly	most eagerly
willingly	less willingly	least willingly

A small number use the suffixes *-er, -est,* and are indistinguishable in form from their corresponding adjectives. We know them as adverbs only when we see them modifying a verb, an adjective, or another adverb:

POSITIVE DEGREE	COMPARATIVE DEGREE	SUPERLATIVE DEGREE
fast	faster	fastest
hard	harder	hardest

Other examples: *cheap, deep, dear, early, high, long, loud, quick, soon, slow.* In formal usage, *cheap, deep, dear, high, quick,* and *slow* ordinarily add *-ly* and use *more* and *most, less* and *least.*

17F 2. Irregular Comparison. Like adjectives, some adverbs are irregular in comparison. It will be noted that these adverbs do not differ in form from their corresponding adjectives (see Section 16F 2).

POSITIVE DEGREE	COMPARATIVE DEGREE	SUPERLATIVE DEGREE
far	farther, further	farthest, furthest
ill	worse	worst
well	better	best
late	later	latest, last
little	less	least
much	more	most

Bad is not used as an adverb in formal English, but occurs in conversation:

COLLOQUIAL: Does it hurt *bad*?
FORMAL: Does it hurt *much*?

Good is also not used as an adverb in formal English, but the use occurs in nonstandard English:

NONSTANDARD: Hit him *good*!
STANDARD: Hit him *hard*!

17G. Faults in Comparison of Adverbs

For faults in the use of comparatives, see Section 18.

17H. Common Misuses of Adverbs

17H 1. Confusion of Adverb and Predicate Adjective. Do not confuse adverbs with predicate adjectives. Predicate adjectives follow linking (copulative) verbs and describe or limit the subject noun. Adverbs modify verbs directly, describing or limiting the action or assertion of the verb.

INCORRECT: He ate rapid. [*Rapid*, an adjective, cannot modify a verb.]
CORRECT: He ate rapidly. [*Rapidly*, an adverb of manner, modifies *ate*.]

CORRECT: The man looks hungry. [*Hungry* is a predicate adjective after the linking verb *looks*. It describes *man*: the *hungry* man.]
CORRECT: The man looks hungrily at the cake. [*Hungrily* is an adverb of manner, modifying *looks*, an intransitive verb in this use, not a *linking verb*.]

17H 2. Misplacing of Adverb. Make sure that your adverbs are placed effectively in the sentence.

a) Ordinarily adverbs are placed with or near to words they modify, but they may be used at various places in the sentence for emphasis so long as their modification is clear and the effect not awkward.

CORRECT: Angrily he tore the letter open.
CORRECT: He angrily tore the letter open.
CORRECT BUT LESS EMPHATIC: He tore the letter open angrily.
CORRECT: Gracefully the ship slid down the greased ways into the dark water.
CORRECT: The ship slid gracefully down the greased ways into the dark water.
INEFFECTIVE: The ship slid down the greased ways into the dark water gracefully. [*Gracefully* is remote from the verb, and the effect is unsatisfactory.]

b) Place your adverbs so that they express your meaning exactly. Such words as *only, almost, just, even* are often misplaced and should be used with care. Though the context may make the meaning clear, any passage is improved if its words are logically arranged.

NOT EXACT: He *only* made one request.
EXACT: He made *only* one request.
CLUMSY: He had climbed to the top of the tower *almost*, before he looked down.
EXACT: He had climbed *almost* to the top of the tower before he looked down.

17H 3. Squinting Modifier. Avoid using words or phrases in ambiguous relationships. At times a word or phrase may be placed so that it seems to modify both the part of the sentence preceding it and the part following it. Such a modifier, usually adverbial, is said to "squint," that is, to look both ways, whereas it should be arranged so that it will be associated only with the part to which it actually relates. To get rid of a squinting modifier, rewrite the sentence in such a way as to make the modification clear.

SQUINTING MODIFIER: The girl with whom I was dancing *timidly* inquired whether anything was wrong.

REVISED: The girl with whom I was dancing inquired *timidly* whether anything was wrong.

SQUINTING MODIFIER: The teacher asked the boy *with a faint smile* to repeat the question.

REVISED: *With a faint smile* the teacher asked the boy to repeat the question.

17H 4. Double Negative. Avoid using double negatives. The adverb *not* should not be used in the same grammatical construction with other negatives, such as *no* (adj.), *nothing, scarcely, hardly*. One is almost never in doubt about the meaning of a double negative, for in language two negatives do not make an affirmative. But the double negative is a redundant expression, an expression that marks the user as illiterate or careless.

NOTE: The adverb *not* may be intensified by the addition of other adverbs or adverb phrases, such as *no, decidedly not, not at all, not for a moment;* but these are added independent words, not part of the grammatical construction in which the adverb *not* is found: No, you cannot go, decidedly not. I will not permit it, not for a moment.

NONSTANDARD: He don't hardly know the price.
INFORMAL: He doesn't know the price.
FORMAL: He does not know the price.

NONSTANDARD: We don't have no apples.
STANDARD: We don't (do not) have any apples.

REDUNDANT: How can anyone know but that he may not be a candidate again?

IMPROVED: How can anyone know but that he may be a candidate again?

IMPROVED: How can anyone know that he may not be a candidate again?

The expressions *cannot help but, cannot doubt but* are widely used in conversation and may be found occasionally in informal and even in formal writing. But both are clearly redundant and the careful writer should avoid them. See Glossary of Usage, Section 72.

EXERCISES

A. Types of Adverbs and Their Functions. Identify the types of adverbs (manner, time, place, degree) in the sentences below and indicate their functions.

1. The old man ambled slowly up the road, stopping now and then to look meditatively out over the fields.
2. Reluctantly she got up and went forward to greet the visitor.
3. The cat purred contentedly, rubbing his silky head gently against her legs.
4. He rode the skis hard into the midst of the cut-off. He shifted expertly into a graceful Christiania and swirled easily around the first turn.
5. He dropped down a steep knoll and then suddenly cut into the most dangerous turn in the course. He braced himself. He was going too fast.
6. A philosophy based on science, however, leads us to think positively in the right direction for the improvement of human society.
7. This is notably an age of close international relationships. Therefore one would suppose that our students should be well trained in foreign affairs.
8. Recently the state of New York officially adopted a system of hand-signaling for motorists that agreed closely with that in use in most other states.
9. First, there is an adequate labor supply; second, there are distinctly advantageous living conditions for the workers; third, the states themselves offer very attractive inducements to the manufacturers.
10. The tackle hit the halfback hard in a final lunge and brought him down six inches from the goal line.

B. Misuses of Adverbs. Most of the following sentences contain a variety of faults in the use of the adverb. Some incorrectly use adjectives where adverbs are needed. Others misplace adverbs or employ double negatives. Some are correct as they stand. Revise each faulty sentence and state the reasons for your revisions.

1. He played hard and studied hard: this was his formula for success.
2. After several attempts he felt bitter and decided that it wasn't hardly worth trying.
3. He did not care how poor it was done provided the job passed inspection.
4. He looked eager at me and asked whether I had seen a stray dachshund.
5. If you try hard, you should be able to finish the task easy by five o'clock.
6. Unless Malaya secures a reasonable income from its natural rubber, it cannot move ahead in its program for a better economy very fast.
7. They could not help but approve of a scheme so acceptable to the general public naturally.
8. One rainy night I had an accident and smashed up his new car very bad.
9. I only wanted the stencil, but she insisted on selling me the whole kit.
10. The fire fighters had limited the fire to the north bank almost when it leaped the dried streambed suddenly.
11. In old days the prisoners in solitary confinement made friends of rats and mice even.
12. The clerk asked the woman with a sullen look whether he could do anything for her.
13. You don't know but that you may not be in the same predicament yourself some day.
14. He only wanted to pay me fifty cents an hour, but I felt that so small a sum was not hardly worth my time.
15. The mysterious stranger who had concealed his face furtively moved towards the exit.
16. He cannot help but go when he hears that Elinor is coming.
17. One passenger whom I remember vividly described the accident for the police.
18. After the last game of the year the coach said that I played very good.
19. He runs swift when he has to, but he doesn't have hardly any competition.

18. COMPARISON OF ADJECTIVES AND ADVERBS AND SENTENCE STRUCTURE: FAULTS IN COMPARISON

18A. Incomplete or Unclear Comparison

Comparisons must be logically complete and clear to the reader. In conversation it is possible for the tone of voice and the context of a statement to make the sense of a comparison clear, as when, given the choice of two books, we say, "I like this book better." But in written English, unless a preceding statement makes the comparison entirely clear, it is better to complete the statement: "I like this book better than that one." Unless the comparison is clear in its context or fully stated, ambiguity may result:

AMBIGUOUS: I believe in him more than Wilson.
CLEAR: I believe in him more than Wilson does.
CLEAR: I believe in him more than in Wilson.

NOTE: Some comparisons (known as absolute comparisons) are permissibly incomplete, as for example, *higher income group, lower classes, least flycatcher, darkest hour.* It is also permissible in conversation to use such incomplete comparisons as these: "There's a better way to live." "It's hotter today." But these comparisons, though clear enough in conversation, must in writing either be preceded by some statement clarifying the comparison or be complete in themselves:

CLEAR AS A RESULT OF CONTEXT: I don't like digging ditches. There's a better way of making a living.
CLEAR THROUGH COMPLETED COMPARISON: There's a better way of making a living than digging ditches.
CLEAR AS A RESULT OF CONTEXT: It was rather warm yesterday. It's hotter today.
CLEAR THROUGH COMPLETED COMPARISON: It's hotter today than yesterday.

18B. Exclusion of Person or Thing Compared

The phrasing of a comparison must not exclude the person or thing compared. Consider the following sentence: *The tiger is more ferocious than any beast in the jungle.* Logically, if the tiger is more ferocious than any beast in the jungle, he is more ferocious than himself, since he is one of the beasts in the jungle. To avoid this absurdity, use *any other* in place of *any*: *The tiger is more ferocious than any other beast in the jungle.* A like error occurs when *any* is used with the superlative:

Solomon was the wisest of any in his time.

CORRECT: Solomon was the wisest of all in his time.
MORE CONCISE: Solomon was the wisest man of his time.

18C. Faulty Use of Superlative

The superlative form of the adjective can be used only when the comparison involves three or more persons or objects:

ILLOGICAL: Alfred is the strongest of the two brothers.
LOGICAL: Alfred is stronger than his brother.

ILLOGICAL: This is the best of the two axes.
LOGICAL: This is the better of the two axes.
BETTER: This is the better axe.

18D. Comparison of Things of Different Classes

Things compared must be of the same order or class. In the sentences below the writers meant to compare things of the same class but failed to do so:

The genius of Shakespeare is much greater than Byron.
The profit of baseball is greater than any other sport.

What these writers meant to say was the following:

The genius of Shakespeare is much greater than that of Byron.
OR: Shakespeare's genius is much greater than Byron's. [*Genius* must be compared with *genius*, not *genius* with an author.]
The profit of baseball is greater than that of any other sport.

OR: Baseball is more profitable than any other sport. [*Profit* must be compared with *profit,* one sport with another.]

18E. Double Comparisons

In expressions involving a double comparison, both elements of the comparison must be properly linked to the idea, person, or thing with which they are compared. Do not omit the conjunction *as,* which links the first element to the object of comparison.

FAULTY: I can cook as well, if not better, than my mother. [The first element of the comparison, *I can cook as well*, has no link with the person of the comparison, *mother*.]

CORRECT, BUT CLUMSY: I can cook as well as, if not better than, my mother.

IMPROVED: I can cook as well as my mother, if not better.

BETTER: I can cook at least as well as my mother.

EXERCISE

Faults in Comparison. The sentences following contain various faults in comparison. Correct each and explain the reasons for your corrections.

1. Two bulldozers were at work tearing and gouging the rocky earth. The second and largest was digging a deep hole.
2. The first half of the hike was not too trying because it was the easiest part.
3. There are now appearing in student papers newer and more unusual errors or defects in composition.
4. Their quarrels were not serious, not any more so than other couples made up of a capricious girl and a sensitive young man.
5. This story is constructed around two episodes. I have chosen the last because I feel that it is the most important.
6. At the end of my junior year I had the best averages in my subjects than in any other year in high school.
7. The new coach has succeeded in arousing more team spirit.
8. Harvard is older than any college or university in the United States.
9. No bird song seems to me sweeter than a woodthrush.
10. To me, French is just as difficult, if not more difficult, than Latin.
11. Women's fashions of fifty years ago, strange as they seem to us now, were no more absurd than modern women.

19. THE PREPOSITION AND SENTENCE STRUCTURE

19A. Definition

A preposition is a word which indicates direction, position, time, result, or other abstract relationship and which, placed before a noun or any substantive, serves to link it to some other word. The noun or substantive following the preposition is the *object* of the preposition and is in the objective case, and the preposition with its object is called a *prepositional phrase,* as, for example, *to town, at home.*

19A 1. Prepositional Phrases. Prepositional phrases are usually either adjectival or adverbial. They are adjectival when they modify nouns or substantives: the house *across the road,* the man *in the bank,* the land *beyond the horizon,* red sails *in the sunset.* They are adverbial when they modify verbs: He hid *behind the fence.* (Adverb of place.) He stayed *at his task.* (Adverb of place.) The train arrived *at eight o'clock.* (Adverb of time.)

19A 2. Most Commonly Used Prepositions.

about	beside, besides	from	out of
above	between	in	over
according to	but (meaning *except*)	into	regarding
across		in consequence of	since
after	by	in front of	through
against	by means of	in place of	till
among	concerning	in spite of	to
around	despite	like	toward, towards
at	down	of	under
before	during	off	until
behind	except	on	up
below	for	out	with, without
beneath			

Some of these, such as *by means of, in place of,* are known as phrasal prepositions. Some, such as *after, before, for, since,* and *but,* serve also as conjunctions; some serve as both adverbs and prepositions: *about, above, around, before, below, by, down, out, under, up, since, without,* etc.; and some of these serve in a special way to form new verbs.

19B. Idiomatic Use of Prepositions

All prepositions have more than one meaning, as you will see by consulting a good dictionary; some have many meanings. This variety in sense helps to make our language flexible, but at the same time it imposes considerable difficulty on new learners of the language and now and then perplexes even those born to its use. Not only do the separate prepositions vary in their meanings, but many enter into certain fixed forms of expression which we call *idioms* (see Idiom, Section 60). Thus we agree *with* a person, but agree *to* a plan; we differ *with* him, but our ideas differ *from* his or are *different from* (not *different than*) his; we accuse people *of* crime, not *with* crime; we entertain *at* dinner, not *to* dinner; we live *in* a city, not *at* a city. The list of variations ends only with the end of the list of prepositions. Many of these idiomatic uses we know through long familiarity with them. The correct usage for those we may be uncertain about is often to be found in the dictionary under the key word of the expression, if not under the preposition itself. Form the habit of consulting the dictionary when in doubt about any idiomatic use of prepositions as well as other words.

19C. The Preposition as Verb-Maker

Some prepositions have a special idiomatic use in that they are added to simple verb forms to give those verbs new meaning. For these words the preposition, though separately written, becomes a distinct part of the verb. The original meaning of the preposition is either absorbed into the new meaning of the verb or lost. For example, when we *get up* (colloquial) a party, or *make up* an examination, *up* has little or nothing of its original sense in the new verb phrase. *Up* is one of the most prolific of these verb-makers. We *wake up, get up, rouse up, sit up, think up, run up, move up, count up, add up, play up, dream up, grow up*—the list could be extended.

Certain verbs are much more active than others in composing these new formations: *get* enters into various combinations with many of the prepositions listed above (*get out, get around, get by,* etc.); *go, make, put* are other verbs that lend themselves to such forms. Many of these verb forms are colloquial and some are slang, but many others are acceptable in both formal and informal English as simple equivalents of more learned verbs. Thus to *get up* in the morning, though a homely term, is fully acceptable in a formal context, just as *go to bed* is better than the slightly gilded verb *retire.* But these prepositions are often redundant (see Section 19F). In formal writing always ask yourself whether the preposition can be omitted without harming the sense.

19D. Relation of the Preposition and Its Object

The object of a preposition is always in the objective case in formal English.

NONSTANDARD: Between you and *I*, they charged us too much.
STANDARD: Between you and *me*, they charged us too much.

NONSTANDARD: To you and *I* it seems silly to argue on so small a point.
STANDARD: To you and *me* it seems silly to argue on so small a point.

It is clear that in these examples and many like them, the pronoun *you,* which cannot change form, causes the confusion. Always look to see whether *you* is preceded by a preposition; if so, any pronoun linked with it by *and* must be in the objective case. Errors such as these cannot be permitted in formal or informal English. On the other hand, custom sanctions the violation of the rule with the pronoun *who*:

INFORMAL: Who are you going with?
FORMAL: Whom are you going with?
FORMAL: With whom are you going?

19E. Preposition at End of Sentence

A preposition may be used at the end of a sentence or a clause in all levels of expression. Good writers do not hesitate to use prepositions at the end of a sentence if they seem natural there and would be awkward or stilted elsewhere. Many of the prepositions thus used are properly parts of the verbs or function as adverbs. In giving directions, we find such usage necessary: Put the cleaner *on*; then wipe it *off*. In formal English, however, for the sake of variety, try to avoid ending a series of sentences with prepositions except in those rare situations where such emphasis is called for.

AWKWARD: *For* what sort of people do they take us?
IMPROVED: What sort of people do they take us *for*?

CORRECT: Now the honey bees begin
To garner golden honey *in*.

CORRECT: When the engine failed, the crew bailed *out*. The pilot stayed *on*.
UNSATISFACTORY: After two days they were picked up by a freighter passing *by*.
BETTER: After two days they were picked up by a passing freighter. [Avoid, if easily possible, the unpleasant repetition of any preposition.]

COLLOQUIAL: A preposition is sometimes a good word to end a sentence with.
FORMAL: A sentence may be ended with a preposition.

19F. Superfluous Prepositions

Avoid using unneeded prepositions. Careless writers and speakers often use more prepositions than are necessary in expressing their thought. In formal writing avoid redundant prepositions, such as *off of, in back of, inside of, onto,* and the unnecessary addition of *up* to verbs:

CARELESS: The child was thrown off of the horse.
BETTER: The child was thrown off the horse.

WORDY, THOUGH MUCH USED: The tennis court was in back of the house.
BETTER: The tennis court was behind the house. (On the other hand, *back of* is acceptable: Back of the house stood a pine tree.)

CARELESS: He ran out onto the court.
BETTER: He ran out on the court.

ACCEPTABLE: Let us go on to the next problem. [*On* is an adverb modifying *go.*]

CARELESS: Let me taste of your cake. [This fault arises from a confusion of the verb *taste* with the noun: Give me a taste (noun) of your cake.]
BETTER: Let me taste your cake. [But *of* may be used with such verbs in intransitive meanings: The church smelled of incense.]

CARELESS: He felt of the bruise on the boy's arm.
BETTER: He felt the bruise on the boy's arm.

WORDY: He added up the receipts and found that they totaled up to a thousand dollars.
BETTER: He added the receipts and found that they totaled a thousand dollars.

19G. Omitted Prepositions

Avoid omitting prepositions essential to your meaning, especially in formal writing. In conversation and informal writing we frequently omit prepositions which need to be supplied in formal writing.

INFORMAL: Afternoons at Lexington we play golf and evenings we play bridge.
FORMAL: In the afternoons at Lexington we play golf and in the evenings we play bridge.
INFORMAL: The night of the performance there was a violent storm.
FORMAL: On the night of the performance there was a violent storm.

Occasionally it is desirable to use a construction in which two prepositions have one object, as in the following sentence: *He had a deep respect for and belief in his chosen candidate.* Try to avoid such awkward constructions if possible; but if you use them, always use the preposition called for by each part of the construction. For example, do not write: *He had a deep respect and belief in his chosen candidate.*

WRONG: He had a lively interest and curiosity about psychoanalysis.
BETTER: He had a lively interest in and curiosity about psychoanalysis.
MUCH BETTER: He had a lively interest in psychoanalysis.

EXERCISES

A. The Functions of Prepositions. Identify the prepositional phrases in the following sentences and state whether they are adjectival or adverbial.

1. What bothered me in London was—all the clever people going wrong with such clever reasons for so doing which I couldn't confute.—EDWARD FITZGERALD.
2. Before her extended
   Dreary and vast and silent the desert of life.
   —LONGFELLOW.
3. The art of communicating ideas by signs made with the fingers is called dactylology.
4. The dandelion root, like chicory, has been used as a substitute for coffee.
5. Dabchicks, grebes, and water ouzels are notable for their skill in diving.
6. An erg is the amount of work done by a dyne working through the distance of one centimeter.
7. Shall I skulk and dodge and duck with my unreasonable apologies and vain modesty?—EMERSON.
8. Richardson calculates that since 1870 the export of animals from Victoria alone has taken out of its soil two million tons of superphosphates.—JULIAN HUXLEY.
9. In reply to the U. S. proposal the French came up with a plan for a European army in which nationals would be mixed at the company level.—*The New York Times.*
10. She walked with measured steps, draped in striped fringed cloths, treading the earth proudly, with a slight jingle and flash of barbarous ornaments.—JOSEPH CONRAD.

B. Prepositions as Verb-Makers. Compose a list of ten sentences using *up* as part of the main verb of each sentence, as in this example: Ten men make *up* the list of those chosen to go on the expedition.

C. Other Idiomatic Uses of Prepositions. Indicate whether the uses and the positions of the prepositions in the following sentences are acceptable, and if so, in what varieties of English (formal, informal, colloquial).

1. To whom are you sending the book?
2. I don't know the man of whom you are speaking.
3. I am going to give my son a good talking to.

4. His views in politics differ sharply from mine.
5. He accused her with dancing with others all evening.
6. When we saw him doing seventy in his sport car, we wondered what he was up to.
7. What do you want with jams and jellies for?
8. Nobody knows what he was arrested for.
9. The death of Parnell seemed to have a direct bearing on Stephen's disgust of politics.
10. One Saturday morning in the spring is set aside to the task of putting up the screens.
11. I wish I knew to whom this letter is to be sent to.
12. He had a great love and devotion to his country.
13. The parakeet hopped off of his perch.
14. The milk tasted of formaldehyde.
15. He tasted the salt breeze on his lips.
16. The day of the wedding the bridegroom disappeared.
17. He spent the morning in thinking up answers that would make her sit up and take notice.
18. We got up a party and went up to Sardi's, where John cut up many capers for the rest of the evening.

20. THE CONJUNCTION AND SENTENCE STRUCTURE

20A. Definition

A conjunction is the part of speech that joins a word to another word, a phrase to another phrase, a clause to another clause. There are four types of conjunctions, namely, co-ordinating conjunctions, conjunctive adverbs, correlative adverbs, and subordinating conjunctions.

20B. Co-ordinating Conjunctions

Co-ordinating conjunctions join words, phrases, or clauses that are independent of one another, giving them a grammatical equality. There are five of these: *and, but, or, nor, for.* Co-ordinating conjunctions are sometimes used in pairs to indicate equal relationship, and thus used are spoken of as *correlatives* or correlating conjunctions. These correlatives are: *both . . . and, either . . . or, neither . . . nor, not only . . . but also.*

In joining clauses these conjunctions may be punctuated variously, depending on the length and the sense of the constructions which they unite. Ordinarily they are preceded by commas unless a more deliberate pause is desirable, in which case a semicolon is commonly used. With short clauses where the sense is clear, the comma may be omitted (see Section 31A).

20C. Conjunctive Adverbs

Conjunctive adverbs help to effect a transition or passage from one thought to another, linking independent clause to independent clause, sentence to sentence, sentence group to sentence group, and paragraph to paragraph. They are like co-ordinating conjunctions in that they are frequently used to link independent clauses (but not words and phrases). The main conjunctive adverbs are *however, moreover, therefore, accordingly, nevertheless, consequently, furthermore, first* (*secondly,* etc.), *last, hence,* and *thus.* To these may be added such transitional phrases as *on the other hand, in fact, for example, of course, in other words, in the first place.* When these conjunctive adverbs join independent clauses, they are, if used at the beginning of a clause, preceded by semicolons and sometimes followed by commas:

> Several witches were burned in an effort to stop the plague; however, people still died in masses.
>
> It has long been recognized that our earth is not the center of the universe; moreover, the solar system of which the earth is a part is lost among many giant galaxies.

But more commonly, for the sake of emphasizing the words beginning the clauses, conjunctive adverbs are inserted inside the clause and set off by commas:

> Our mechanical comforts of today are much greater than those of our grandfathers; our food, however, is less nutritious, and our housing more cramped and jerry-built.

Such a sentence may be punctuated as two sentences for emphasis:

> Our mechanical comforts of today are much greater than those of our grandfathers. Our food, however, is less nutritious, and our housing more cramped and jerry-built.

NOTE: Though *however* is usually a conjunctive adverb, it sometimes serves as an adverbial conjunction: However hard I tried, I never made an *A* in geology.

The two conjunctive adverbs *yet* and *so* (in the sense of *consequently*) are sometimes classed as co-ordinating conjunctions and punctuated like them, especially in narrative. But in most good informal and formal writing *so* is very sparingly used.

20D. Correlative Adverbs

The correlative adverbs, *as . . . as, not so . . . as, the . . . the,* serve as conjunctions in pairs to show relationships between clauses. For discussion of these, see Section 17D 3.

20E. Subordinating Conjunctions

Subordinating conjunctions introduce subordinate clauses, that is, clauses that depend in grammar and meaning on the main clause. They may introduce noun clauses (*that, why, where,* and the relative pronouns *which, who,* and *what*) or adjectival clauses (the relative pronouns *who, which,* and *that,* and *when* and *where* used as relatives). But most are adverbial, and it is to these that we refer in the following paragraph.

In their meanings these subordinating (adverbial) conjunctions indicate various relationships, and the clauses they introduce can be named from their meanings. These are the main types of subordinate (adverbial) clauses, classified as to meaning, and the principal subordinating conjunctions which help to indicate their nature:

CAUSE:	because, since, inasmuch as, as
COMPARISON:	than, as, as . . . as, so . . . as, as if, as well as
CONDITION:	if, whether, whether . . . or, in case that
DEGREE:	unless, as far as, as much as, much as
MANNER:	as if, as though, how, however
PLACE:	where, wherever, whence, whither
PURPOSE:	that, in order that, so that, lest
RESULT:	that, so that
TIME:	after, as soon as, before, since, when, while

20F. Faults in the Use of Conjunctions

20F 1. Excessive Use of *And* and So. Avoid excessive use of *and* and *so* in linking successive independent clauses. Though *and* may be used to join sentence elements equal in rank, avoid the overuse of *and* and *so* in both conversation and writing. In conversation some students join almost every sentence by *and, so, and so,* or *and then,* to the exclusion of all other conjunctions with their shades of exact meaning:

We planned yesterday to go to the Bowl, *and so* this morning we started out at ten, *and* we got there in two hours, *so* we had plenty of time for a hot meal, *and* we got into our seats at the twenty-yard line ten minutes before the kickoff.

REVISED: We had planned yesterday to go to the Bowl. This morning we started out at ten and got there in two hours, in plenty of time for a hot meal before the game. We were in our seats at the twenty-yard line ten minutes before the kickoff.

EXCESSIVE USE OF *and*: I was a child then, *and* we did not hear much music; *and* we stood around the village green or sat on the wooden benches *and* listened to the band play Sousa's famous marches.

REVISED: When I was a child, we did not hear much music. Standing around on the village green or sitting on the wooden benches, we listened to the band playing Sousa's stirring marches.

The *and* and *so* habit is bad and becomes worse when it is punctuated with vocal pauses after the *and*'s (*and-uh*). Try to arrest this habit in conversation and writing as well, by using complete stops and occasional subordinations.

To break the *so* habit, never use *so* in the sense of *consequently*.

For formal and informal writing, *and* or *but* may be used occasionally to introduce sentences.

> I would make boys all learn English; and then I would let the clever ones learn Latin as an honor and Greek as a treat. But the only thing I would whip them for is not knowing English.
>
> —WINSTON CHURCHILL.

They should not be used thus, however, if their omission or the use of some other connective would produce a better effect, and they should not be used frequently. The temptation to use *and, but,* and *for* to link sentences thus is natural, but should be withstood. The following passage by a great and justly admired scholar and critic illustrates this tendency to an excessive use of co-ordinating conjunctions at the beginning of sentences:

> In the first place Coleridge (at least during the years of the Note Book) read with an eye which habitually pierced to the secret spring of poetry beneath the crust of fact. And this means that items or details the most unlikely might, through some poetic potentiality discovered or divined, find lodgment in his memory. In the second place, Coleridge not only read books with minute attention, *but he also habitually passed from any given book he read to the books to which that book referred.* And that, in turn, makes it possible to follow him into the most remote and unsuspected fields. And his gleanings from those fields, transformed but recognizable, will meet us again and again as we proceed. For to follow Coleridge through his reading is to retrace the obliterated vestiges of creation.—JOHN L. LOWES, *The Road to Xanadu.*

Such co-ordinate linkings—*And this . . . , And that . . . , And . . . , For . . .* are not incorrect English; they may even be justified by the sense of the passage and by the fact that the passage was part of a lecture. On the other hand, such practice becomes tedious if continued. Use these conjunctions sparingly as links between sentences.

20F 2. Excessive Use of *But, However,* Etc. Avoid the use of *but, however,* and *on the other hand* in a series of succeeding sentences. To use these conjunctions is to reverse the trend of your thought; and a succession of such about-faces is likely to make the reader dizzy. Though it is desirable at times to set up a series of positive and negative ideas, ordinarily it is better to present positive ideas in one group of sentences and opposing ideas in a second group, the order of the groups depending on the emphasis desired.

FAULTY: In the Coliseum he tried to visualize lions, gladiators, crowds, and emperors. *But* it was so small! What would they do with the Yale Bowl? *But* here were the chariot races and the combats. The space, *however*, seemed too limited to contain them. *On the other hand*, the records of history were surely not all fable. *But* on the whole he was not disappointed. The hot Italian sun struck him full in the face and he sprawled out luxuriously.

IMPROVED: In the Coliseum he tried to visualize lions, gladiators, combats, chariot races, crowds, and emperors. But it was so small! The space seemed too limited to contain them. What would they have done with the Yale Bowl? On the other hand, the records of history were surely not all fable. He liked what he saw. The hot Italian sun struck him in the face and he sprawled out luxuriously.

20F 3. Use of Vague or Inexact Conjunctions. Avoid in formal writing the use of vague or inexact conjunctions. Choose those that best fit the meaning you wish to express. You will probably have little trouble in using most conjunctions correctly; a few, however, need careful attention—chiefly *because, for, since, so* (wrongly used for *so that*), *while,* and colloquial *like.*

a) Avoid using *because* for *for, for* for *because,* or *since* for *because* if vagueness or inexactness would result from such uses. *Because* gives the direct cause or reason for an action; *for* primarily gives an added observation, rather than a direct reason or cause. This distinction is breaking down in informal English, but it is usually observed in formal writing. *Since* may indicate either a causal or a time relationship and hence should be used with care to avoid confusion.

INEXACT: She was worried because she kept looking out the window to see whether any one was coming. [*Because she kept looking out*, etc., does not give the cause for her *worry*.]

IMPROVED: She was worried, for she kept looking out the window to see whether any one was coming.

INEXACT: He was not at the party, because I saw him downtown.
BETTER: He was not at the party, for I saw him downtown.

INEXACT: He failed his examination, for he was not prepared for it.
CLEAR: He failed his examination because he was not prepared for it.

UNCLEAR: She had been running the store since her husband was away. [Which of the two meanings is intended?]

CLEAR: She had been running the store since the day her husband left.
CLEAR: She had been running the store because her husband was away.

b) Avoid using *like* as a conjunction in formal and informal English. Though this use of *like* occurs frequently in conversation, it is still not accepted in standard writing. Use *as* or *as if* instead.

COLLOQUIAL: It looks like it will rain. [*Like* is used as a conjunction.]
FORMAL: It looks as if it will rain.
INFORMAL: It looks like rain. [*Like* is used as a preposition.]

COLLOQUIAL: It seemed like the horses were racing out of the screen.
FORMAL: It seemed as if the horses were racing out of the screen.

c) In formal English avoid using *while* when you mean *though* or *and* or *but. While* ordinarily suggests a time relationship. Though it can be used either as a concessive or as a co-ordinating conjunction, be sure that your use of it is not ambiguous.

INEXACT: He uses a brassie for tee shots, *while* I use a driver. [Do the actions take place at the same time?]
EXACT: He uses a brassie for tee shots, *but* I use a driver.

NOT CLEAR: *While* the traffic was very heavy, he decided to drive to Newburgh.
CLEAR: Though the traffic was very heavy, he decided to drive to Newburgh.

Avoid using *so* in formal English when you mean *so that.*

COLLOQUIAL: He parked his car carefully, so he could get away at once after the reception.
FORMAL AND INFORMAL: He parked his car carefully, so that he could get away at once after the reception.

20F 4. Excessive Use of Conjunctive Adverbs. Avoid excessive use of conjunctive adverbs and other directive words and phrases. In speeches and in complex expository writing it is often helpful to be reminded of each step in a process by conjunctive adverbs, such as *first, second,* etc., and of shifts in thought by such adverbs as *however* and *moreover.* But these can become tedious if used too frequently. Use them only if they seem necessary for clarity.

Shakespeare is to be well represented in the summer theater this year. For example, Antioch College offers an eleven-week festival devoted to his plays. Moreover, in San Diego forty-five performances of *Othello, The Merchant of Venice,* and *Twelfth Night* will be given. Furthermore, equally attractive programs are being offered in Camden, Maine, Ashland, Oregon, and Stratford, Ontario. [The transitional words and phrases *for example, moreover*, and *furthermore* are unnecessary here and make the sentences heavy.]

EXERCISES

A. Study the use of conjunctions in "Petroleum: A Legacy of Ancient Seas" (pp. 35–38) and then answer the following questions:

1. Make a list of six examples of independent clauses in this article joined by co-ordinating conjunctions.
2. List six examples of subordinate clauses joined to main clauses by subordinating conjunctions.
3. How often and where is *and* or *but* used as a sentence beginning?
4. How often and where are conjunctive adverbs used?

B. Faults in the Use of Conjunctions. The sentences below illustrate excessive, vague, or otherwise faulty use of conjunctions. Revise each sentence and explain the reasons for your revisions.

1. And he rationalized himself into thinking that he could take just one drink. And before he realized what had happened he had stepped off the wagon into the horrible, nightmarish muck below.
2. I managed to get an introduction to her, but I was practically speechless when she spoke to me, but I did succeed in finding out where she lived.
3. In 1841 Dickens underwent a surgical operation, but this did not interfere with his career, for soon after he visited America. But his trip was not a happy one, for he did not understand American ways, and they rather shocked him.
4. Our junior counselors proved to be most friendly, and they placed themselves at our disposal, for we were somewhat confused with the great flood of new things which came our way.
5. It was a wonderful evening, and we marched home from the Armory with our minds crowded with wonderful thoughts of that evening—of the past week—and now as I reminisce, I think of those seven days, and my heart is warm and happy, for they can never be replaced in my estimation by anything.

6. I had decided on making forestry my profession while I was a freshman in high school.
7. He was evidently not interested in the salesman's talk, because he showed several signs of impatience.
8. When the Union army met the Confederate army at Gettysburg, it seemed like the battle would end in a draw.
9. Our registration took place on Monday and Tuesday, so we were able to start classes on Wednesday.
10. This room has only three windows, while that one has four.
11. He drove his car up close to the guardrail, so he could get a better view of the mountains.

Chapter 4

FORM OF THE SENTENCE

So far, we have been concerned primarily with the structure or the composition of the sentence—that is, what a sentence is, its parts, and their relationships. Now we shall consider the form that sentences take, the various ways in which the elements of structure are used to achieve effective expression. This is the art of rhetoric. We shall still be interested in structure, for form assumes structure. But form implies yet more: it has been asserted that in an ideal sense there is one best way for the expression of every thought. In other words, form is meaning rightly shaped.

Writing effective sentences is more than a matter of determining what shall be the basic structure of each sentence. If you examine a piece of effective prose, you will usually find that some sentences are short, some long; that some begin with the subject, some with a subordinate element; that some are uncomplicated in structure, some extremely complicated; that in some the main thought is expressed early and followed by qualifying clauses, whereas in others the completion of the main thought is delayed until the end of the sentence; that some sentences are neatly balanced, clause against clause. Such variety is partly the natural result of differences in pattern stemming from the material and purpose of the sentence, and partly the result of conscious artifice. You should learn the principal devices that skillful writers find useful in constructing good sentences, and should strive consciously to give to each sentence the form in which the expression of the particular thought concerned will be most effective. At first this process will of necessity be artificial to a considerable degree; in time it will require less attention; but it will never become instinctive. The sentences of even the most practiced writers do not spring from the mind fully formed; all have been planned, and some have been pruned and rephrased and rearranged time after time with a view to their precise effect upon the reader.

21. LOOSE SENTENCE

A loose sentence is one in which the main statement is made early and is then followed by subordinate material. It may be of any length. It is the pattern in which we express ourselves most naturally and easily, and student writing and even professional writing normally contain a large proportion of loose sentences. There are, however, two cautions to be observed with regard to this pattern: (1) Like any other, it becomes monotonous if overused, and since it is the most natural and easy pattern it is the most frequent cause of sentence monotony in student writing. (2) A lazy writer will often be satisfied with loose sentences rather than make the effort required to construct a sentence on a different pattern that might be far more appropriate and emphatic.

Examples of natural and effective loose sentences:

> This is my friend Bert Thurston, who has just joined the Navy.

> Mary slipped at the last moment and tumbled off the board with a splash and a cry that made the dozing sunbathers start from slumber and look about them in a questioning daze.

> I am writing this in a beach cottage on a Florida key. It is raining to beat the cars. The rollers from a westerly storm are creaming along the shore, making a steady boiling noise instead of the usual intermittent slap. The Chamber of Commerce has drawn the friendly blind against this ugliness and is busy getting out some advance notices of the style parade which is to be held next Wednesday at the pavilion. The paper says cooler tomorrow.—E. B. WHITE, *One Man's Meat.*

22. PERIODIC SENTENCE

A periodic sentence is one in which completion of the main statement is delayed until the end or near the end of the sentence.

In comparison with the loose sentence it creates suspense and gives emphasis to the main point. On the other hand, it is more formal and more artificial, and a reader becomes aware of sentence monotony more quickly in a sequence of periodic sentences than in a sequence of loose sentences.

Examples of effective periodic sentences:

There in the doorway, puzzled by the excitement, clutching a battered doll, stood the missing child.

A man who insists upon a comfortable nap when he comes home from work, who likes to eat his meals in restful quiet, and who requires eight hours of unbroken sleep each night should never become a father.

Just as the professor became aware of my look of fatuously exaggerated attentiveness and, sensing it to be a feeble attempt at deception, cleared his throat preparatory to calling upon me, the bell rang.

Are their humility, which seems imposed by moral principles, their shyness in relation to the extra-collegiate world, derived from the ages when learning was the possession of pious brotherhoods and shut away between the walls of foundations?—EDMUND WILSON.

Living now in the very center of the greatest producing state of the Union, with the rich anthracite coal fields to the east and the great petroleum areas to the west, and not far away the limitless soft coal mines with their coke ovens, their natural gas wells, and their iron ore, all of it feeding the Pittsburgh mills, I saw in process an evolution of which I had never dreamed.—FRED LEWIS PATTEE.

To arrest, for the space of a breath, the hands busy about the work of the earth, and compel men entranced by the sight of distant goals to glance for a moment at the surrounding vision of form and color, of sunshine and shadows; to make them pause for a look, for a sigh, for a smile—such is the aim, difficult and evanescent, and reserved only for a very few to achieve.—JOSEPH CONRAD.

There, on that October evening—there, in that exuberant vista of gilding and crimson velvet set amidst all those opposing mirrors and upholding caryatids, with fumes of tobacco ever rising to the painted and pagan ceiling and with the hum of presumably cynical conversation broken into so sharply by the clatter of dominoes shuffled on marble tables, I drew a deep breath, and "This indeed," said I to myself, "is life."—MAX BEERBOHM, *Seven Men.*

You will find that in most good writing there is a mixture of loose and periodic sentences, and that usually the loose greatly outnumber the periodic. The illustrative paragraphs in Chapter 6 provide useful material for an examination of the sentence patterns of established authors.

23. SUBORDINATION

23A. Effective Subordination

No doubt you have already perceived that effective subordination is an essential element in the building of good sentences. The child writes short, abrupt sentences or links series of short independent clauses by means of the co-ordinating conjunctions *and* and *but*; the skillful writer usually puts only his most important ideas into independent clauses and reduces the others to clauses, phrases, or single words that modify elements in the main clauses.

FAULTY: Many people do not bother to vote. Yet they complain about inefficiency and corruption in government. Such people have no right to complain.

IMPROVED: People who do not bother to vote have no right to complain about governmental inefficiency and corruption.

FAULTY: The uproar in the auditorium was deafening for a time. The chairman kept pounding his gavel. The room grew quiet slowly. The chairman asked the speaker to resume.

IMPROVED: Though for a time the uproar in the auditorium was deafening, the chairman finally succeeded in restoring order and asked the speaker to resume.

FAULTY: The earthquake was a severe one. Fortunately it occurred in a sparsely settled area. There was comparatively little loss of life.

IMPROVED: Because the earthquake, though severe, occurred in a sparsely settled area, there was comparatively little loss of life.

Note that just as a sequence of short, choppy sentences suggests an immature writer and quickly grows tiresome, so a long sentence is likely to be ineffective if it consists of a string of independent clauses or if the writer tries to crowd too much into it. The remedy is to subordinate properly and to break up the sentence if necessary.

FAULTY: Harry joined us just before dark, and I was much relieved to see him, for I had not relished the idea of spending the night with only Joe as a companion, and I suspect that Joe felt exactly as I did, but he said nothing.

IMPROVED: When Harry joined us just before dark I was much relieved, for I had not relished the idea of spending the night with only Joe as a companion. Though Joe said nothing, I suspect that he felt exactly as I did.

FAULTY: The general store in the village near the farm where I spent last summer with my Danforth cousins was the center of local life, for the villagers not only bought most of their necessities there, from shoes and axes and dishes to salt and ink and patent medicines, but gathered to discuss the weather and local politics and especially the peculiarities of city visitors, this last being a topic of never-ending interest.

IMPROVED: The general store in the village near the farm where I spent last summer with my Danforth cousins was the center of local life. There the villagers bought most of their necessities, from shoes and axes and dishes to salt and ink and patent medicines. There they gathered to discuss the weather and local politics and especially the peculiarities of city visitors, a topic of never-ending interest.

23B. Faulty Subordination

Subordination may sometimes be illogical or awkward. For example, you should not relegate the most important thought of a sentence to a subordinate clause or phrase and give a less important thought undeserved prominence in the main clause.

FAULTY: As the doomed man teetered precariously on the ledge and finally plummeted to the street, the crowd watched in horror.

IMPROVED: As the crowd watched in horror, the doomed man teetered precariously on the ledge and finally plummeted to the street.

FAULTY: He studied hard and made his first respectable grade in the subject in the final examination, managing to pass the course by a whisker.

IMPROVED: By studying hard and making his first respectable grade in the subject in the final examination, he managed to pass the course by a whisker.

FAULTY: Though he won the championship, he had had a restless night and was below his usual form.

IMPROVED: Though he had had a restless night and was below his usual form, he won the championship.

A sequence of subordinate clauses with each succeeding clause dependent upon the one before it is always awkward. An extreme example of such subordination is the familiar nursery tale about "the dog that worried the cat that killed the rat that ate the malt that lay in the house that Jack built."

AWKWARD: At the play I sat next to a man who told me that he knew the author, who had been his classmate when both attended a little college that has produced several writers who have become famous.

IMPROVED: At the play I sat next to a friend of the author. They had been classmates at a little college that has produced several famous writers.

AWKWARD: Professor Bromley assured us that he would give us an examination that would contain questions that would enable him to identify those students who had not done the outside reading that he had assigned.

IMPROVED: Professor Bromley promised us an examination that would determine whether we had done the assigned outside reading.

AWKWARD: Our new partner provided the practical knowledge that had been sadly deficient when Frank and I had embarked upon the venture that was now on the verge of failure.

IMPROVED: The practical knowledge possessed by our new partner remedied the deficiency that had brought Frank and me to the verge of failure.

EXERCISE

The following passages are unskillful and ineffective for various reasons. Without making major changes in phrasing, revise each passage in such a way as to make it more effective.

1. The druggist has on his shelves many ointments that are said to relieve the misery of sunburn, though the best remedy is to avoid getting burned in the first place.

2. I never studied chemistry in high school. I expected to have difficulty with the subject in college. I was pleasantly surprised. Some of my classmates had studied chemistry in high school. The method of teaching in college was different. They said that they might even have been better off if they had had no previous training.
3. Benjamin Franklin was a printer by profession, but he had many other interests, for he was also a writer and a scientist and an inventor and a statesman, and he retired from business when he was only fifty-four, and he achieved his greatest success thereafter.
4. The discovery of America opened up avenues that led European adventurers to new areas that possessed natural resources that exceeded the fondest expectations of those few enlightened men who had long dreamed that a vast new world lay beyond the western seas that for centuries had been the boundary of the world that civilized men knew.
5. Every person of middle age should begin at once to plan for his retirement, because even though his retirement date seems comfortably distant it will come sooner than he thinks, and he should make sure well in advance not only that he will have enough to live on but also that he will have interesting hobbies to keep him occupied, for many persons become despondent after retirement because life suddenly seems so empty and purposeless.
6. All the fishermen were sound asleep and dreaming of a day of sport filled with the quiet joys of angling when the flash flood swept the little cabin off its foundations.
7. The distinguished scientist paused at the door of the empty lecture hall where he had been introduced to the science in which he had earned a reputation that had made him the most famous native of the little town that had once regarded him as an eccentric who would come to no good.
8. Long before Bernard Shaw capitalized on the idea, various writers had enunciated the once-shocking theory that the human male, instead of being the dominant, aggressive pursuer, is really the destined victim of the female, who is not the timorous, helpless creature that by tradition she was supposed to be but a ruthless and cunning huntress who stalks her prey as a cat stalks a mouse and in so doing carries out the purpose for which she was created by nature, but Shaw was the first to draw widespread attention to the theory by giving expression to it in an entertaining manner.
9. My father remembers when the woods near our home were full of chestnut trees. He used to gather whole bagfuls of delicious chest-

nuts every autumn. A disease called chestnut blight destroyed all the trees. Experts have succeeded in developing a type of tree that resists the blight. Certain imported chestnut trees also are able to resist the blight. Some day boys may again be able to gather chestnuts in the woods. That day is still far off.

10. I found my freshman course in English very difficult, for I had not written many themes in high school, and at college I had to write a theme every week, but I worked very hard at my writing, and eventually I found that following a few simple rules enabled me to improve my work greatly, but I fear I shall never be an outstanding student in English, for I am sadly lacking in originality.

24. PARALLELISM

One valuable device in the effort to attain maximum effectiveness in sentence structure is parallelism. Giving parallel form to sentence elements that are parallel in thought is not only a logical procedure but one that makes for sharpness and emphasis of expression. There may be parallelism between words, between phrases, between clauses: noun matched with noun, adjective with adjective, participial phrase with participial phrase, relative clause with relative clause, and so on. Sometimes the parallelism may be so natural as to require no effort of the writer and go almost unnoticed by the reader; sometimes it is elaborate and striking. The following sentences contain characteristic examples of parallel structure.

He was tired but happy. [Parallel subjective complements.]

Bob is a hard hitter, a sure fielder, and a swift runner. [Parallel subjective complements.]

It is too late for breakfast, too early for lunch. [Parallel phrases used as subjective complements.]

He climbed the stairs, took off his clothes, and fell into bed. [Parallel verbs.]

Rushing to the platform and seizing the microphone, he demanded an immediate vote. [Parallel participial phrases.]

Read not to contradict and confute; nor to believe and take for granted; nor to find talk and discourse; but to weigh and consider.—FRANCIS BACON. [Parallel infinitive phrases used adverbially to modify the verb *read*.]

We need candidates who are independent, who are not afraid to speak out, and who place national welfare above party loyalty. [Parallel relative clauses.]

To be a Majesty, to be a cousin of Sovereigns, to marry a Bourbon for diplomatic ends, to correspond with the Queen of England, to be very stiff and very punctual, to found a dynasty, to bore ambassadresses into fits, to live, on the highest pinnacle, an exemplary life devoted to the public service—such were his objects, and such, in fact, were his achievements.—LYTTON STRACHEY, *Queen Victoria.* [Parallel infinitive phrases, in apposition with the pronoun *such.*]

The dean, obviously at the end of his patience, reports that Earl is deliberately ignoring his studies, that he will not listen to advice from any quarter, and that the only thing to do is to give in and permit him to quit school. [Parallel noun clauses, objects of the verb *reports.*]

Our petitions have been slighted; our remonstrances have produced additional violence and insult; our supplications have been disregarded; and we have been spurned, with contempt, from the foot of the throne.—PATRICK HENRY. [Parallel main clauses.]

Sentence elements linked by correlative conjunctions (*either . . . or, neither . . . nor, both . . . and, not only . . . but* [*also*], *whether . . . or*) illustrate parallelism. The elements that follow such pairs of correlatives must be identical grammatically.

The chairman was both awkward in manner and hesitant in speech.

You will find us either in the classroom or in Professor Brock's office. [Note that it would be wrong to write, "You will either find us in the classroom or in . . ."]

Not only was she late, but she seemed to enjoy our irritation.

She was not only late but also scornful of our rebuke. [Note that it would be wrong to write, "She was not only late but was also scornful . . ."]

She could not decide whether the report was true or Janet was deceiving her.

In a sentence involving parallel structure it may be necessary for the sake of clarity to repeat the word that introduces the first parallel element—usually an article, a preposition, a conjunction, an auxiliary verb, or the *to* of an infinitive.

CONFUSING: Tell them to bring the papers involved in the investigation and report for instructions.

CLEAR: Tell them to bring the papers involved in the investigation and *to* report for instructions.

CONFUSING: I am prepared to take the bad with good.
CLEAR: I am prepared to take the bad with *the* good.

CONFUSING: He reported that Charles would bring Jane and Mary, who had to work until noon, would come later.
CLEAR: He reported that Charles would bring Jane and *that* Mary, who had to work until noon, would come later.

CONFUSING: Watson had promised to telephone when Bob arrived and expressed confidence that it would be before midnight.
CLEAR: Watson had promised to telephone when Bob arrived and *had* expressed confidence that it would be before midnight.

CONFUSING: Old Barrows scolded me for misbehavior in study hall and lateness.
CLEAR: Old Barrows scolded me for misbehavior in study hall and *for* lateness.

Misleading parallelism: Because a reader assumes that sentence elements parallel in structure will be parallel in thought and function, it is misleading to give such structure to elements that are not actually parallel.

MISLEADING: They looked in the closet, in the desk drawers, in the file cabinet, and in the meantime Mary telephoned for the police.
CLEAR: While they looked in the closet, in the desk drawers, and in the file cabinet, Mary telephoned for the police.

MISLEADING: I have achieved security by thrift, by industry, by patience, and by George I am going to hang on to it.
CLEAR: I have achieved security by thrift, by industry, by patience, and I intend to hang on to it.

25. BALANCE

Balance is an elaborate form of parallelism. A balanced sentence is one in which there is close similarity in length and structure between major portions of the sentence, usually clauses.

Poising one major element of the sentence against another is particularly effective in showing contrast.

> Eloquence without sincerity seldom gains victory; sincerity without eloquence seldom gains a hearing.
>
> Render unto Caesar the things that are Caesar's; and unto God the things that are God's.—Matthew 22:21.
>
> My heart had palpitated at the thoughts of a boarding-school ball, or a gala-day at Midsummer or Christmas; but the world I had found out in Cooke's edition of the British Novelists was to me a dance through life, a perpetual gala-day.—WILLIAM HAZLITT.
>
> To teach English to a class that has had several years of Latin and Greek is one thing; to teach English to technical students who have had no language training at all is quite another matter.—FRED LEWIS PATTEE.
>
> Its lofty mountains begin to lift themselves into the light of heaven; its broad and fertile plains stretch out in beauty to the eye of civilized man; and at the mighty bidding of the voice of political liberty the waters of darkness retire.—DANIEL WEBSTER.

Often there is balance between two sentences, or between parts of two sentences.

> Barton always guarantees immediate delivery and inevitably causes disappointment. Boone makes no promises whatever and occasionally delights us with his promptness.
>
> For as the heaven is high above the earth, so great is his mercy toward them that fear him. As far as the east is from the west, so far hath he removed our transgressions from us.—Psalms 103:11–12.
>
> At the feet of the tallest and plushiest offices lie the crummiest slums. The genteel mysteries housed in the Riverside Church are only a few blocks from the voodoo charms of Harlem.—E. B. WHITE.
>
> The fortunes of the master and the servant, intimately interacting, rose together. The Baron's secret skill had given Leopold his unexceptionable kingdom; and Leopold, in his turn, as time went on, was able to furnish the Baron with more and more keys to more and more back doors.—LYTTON STRACHEY.
>
> Measured against eternity, measured against hope and desire, measured against even the scholars' own aspiration and pretense, most scholarly researches do indeed look trivial, futile, and ridiculous. But measured against history, even the slightest of them does not look so bad.—BERNARD DE VOTO.

CAUTION: Excessive use of balance will result in a studied and obviously artificial style.

EXERCISES

A. Point out examples of parallelism and balance in the following paragraph:

Habit is thus the enormous fly-wheel of society, its most precious conservative agent. It alone is what keeps us all within the bounds of ordinance, and saves the children of fortune from the envious uprisings of the poor. It alone prevents the hardest and most repulsive walks of life from being deserted by those brought up to tread therein. It keeps the fisherman and deck-hand at sea through the winter; it holds the miner in his darkness, and nails the countryman to his log-cabin and his lonely farm through all the months of snow; it protects us from invasion by the natives of the desert and the frozen zone. It dooms us all to fight out the battle of life upon the line of our nurture or our early choice, and to make the best of a pursuit that disagrees, because there is no other for which we are fitted, and it is too late to begin again.—WILLIAM JAMES.

B. Point out examples of parallelism and balance in the paragraphs in Sections 50B and 51B.

26. EMPHASIS

The word *emphasis* means not only stress but also effectiveness of expression. If a sentence expresses with clarity and vigor the meaning in the mind of the writer, it has emphasis.

The primary step in achieving emphasis is to write simply and concisely (see Section 27, Economy). No sentence that is wordy or sprawling will be emphatic. Sayings that have become proverbs are almost invariably terse and neat:

A stitch in time saves nine.
He who hesitates is lost.
Too many cooks spoil the broth.
Spare the rod and spoil the child.

But few thoughts are capable of such concise expression, and ordinarily the writer must consider in addition to simplicity and directness the most desirable arrangement of each part of the sentence in relation to other parts. The periodic sentence, effective subordination, parallel structure, and balance are important means of securing emphasis, already discussed. Others are (*a*) placing the most important parts of the sentence in the positions of greatest importance and (*b*) repeating key words for effect.

26A. Emphasis Through Position

Normally the most emphatic position in the sentence is the end. This is the reason that the periodic sentence is more emphatic than the loose sentence: in the periodic sentence the reader has to await completion of the main thought until the end, or near the end. The next most emphatic position is the beginning. Thus it follows that the most effective sentences begin and end strongly, with the least important elements coming in between. Maximum emphasis, of course, is not always possible or even desirable. The attempt to achieve it in every sentence would result in obvious artificiality; moreover, the style would quickly become monotonous. But see to it that your sentences do not seriously lack emphasis, and make every key sentence as emphatic as possible.

One means of gaining emphasis through position is to invert the normal word order of a sentence and thus startle the reader and focus his attention upon the sentence element that is out of its expected place. Such an element is usually placed first. The following sentences illustrate this device.

> Blessed is he that walketh not in the counsel of the ungodly.—Psalms 1:1. [The subjective complement, which normally follows the verb, here precedes it.]
>
> Greater love hath no man than this, that a man lay down his life for his friends.—John 15:13. [The direct object, which normally follows the verb, here precedes it. Note also that the sentence is periodic.]
>
> Without fear lives the man whose trust is in God. [The prepositional phrase modifying *lives* comes before the verb rather than after it.]
>
> Yield he would not, even though death threatened. [Part of the verb is placed before the subject.]

Another useful device—and one that is so natural and logical as hardly to require pointing out—is to arrange elements of a series in order of climax, with the most significant or striking element last. Even when the elements of a series seem of about equal importance, it is usually possible to determine which should receive the greatest emphasis.

> She is eighteen, good-natured, and beautiful.
> His behavior drew jeers from the fans, a warning from the umpire, and the promise of a punch in the nose from the batter.
> Through the excited crowd ran a new, a fantastic, a heartstopping rumor.
> My little nephew teased the cat, frightened the canary, and upset the goldfish bowl.

26B. Emphasis Through Repetition

Repetition of key words is an obvious means of gaining emphasis. This device, of course, must be used cautiously. It is well said that the difference between skillful and unskillful repetition is the difference between style and the absence of style. Student writing is likely to contain too much repetition rather than too little (see Section 27C). The writer of the following passage kept repeating because he was unable or too lazy to avoid doing so:

> My home town is one of the pleasantest towns I have ever seen. This town is a small town, looking much like other towns of its size, but few towns enjoy so many natural advantages.

Here of course the path to improvement lies through drastic reduction of repetition. But repetition, effectively used, can provide desirable emphasis. Though it is a device more characteristic of formal writing than of informal writing, you should be alert to its potential advantages.

In paragraphs and longer pieces of writing, repetition of sentence patterns is a common means of securing coherence and emphasis (see Section 50B); in the individual sentence, repetition is usually confined to key words.

> Dead is the monarch, dead the servant who cringed before him, dead the city in which they dwelt.
> In the lead was Hughie—Hughie, who never before had even finished a race; Hughie, who had come along just for the ride; Hughie the hopeless.
> Liberty, I am told, is a divine thing. Liberty when it becomes the "Liberty to die by starvation" is not so divine!—THOMAS CARLYLE.

EXERCISE

Repetition is a familiar device in the oratory of all languages and epochs. So is parallelism, particularly the balanced sentence. Point out all examples that you can find in the following familiar speeches from Shakespeare's *Julius Caesar:*

Brutus: . . . Not that I loved Caesar less, but that I loved Rome more. Had you rather Caesar were living, and die all slaves, than that Caesar were dead, to live all free men? As Caesar loved me, I weep for him; as he was fortunate, I rejoice at it; as he was valiant, I honour him; but, as he was ambitious, I slew him: there is tears for his love; joy for his fortune; honour for his valour; and death for his ambition. Who is here so base that he would be a bondman? If any, speak; for him have I offended. Who is here so rude that would not be a Roman? If any, speak; for him have I offended. Who is here so vile that will not love his country? If any, speak; for him have I offended . . .

Antony: . . .

I come to bury Caesar, not to praise him.
The evil that men do lives after them;
The good is oft interred with their bones;
So let it be with Caesar. The noble Brutus
Hath told you, Caesar was ambitious:
If it were so, it was a grievous fault;
And grievously hath Caesar answer'd it.
Here, under leave of Brutus and the rest—
For Brutus is an honourable man;
So are they all, all honourable men—
Come I to speak in Caesar's funeral.
He was my friend, faithful and just to me:
But Brutus says he was ambitious;
And Brutus is an honourable man.
He hath brought many captives home to Rome,
Whose ransoms did the general coffers fill:
Did this in Caesar seem ambitious?
When that the poor have cried, Caesar hath wept:
Ambition should be made of sterner stuff.
Yet Brutus says he was ambitious;
And Brutus is an honourable man.
You all did see that on the Lupercal
I thrice presented him a kingly crown,

Which he did thrice refuse: was this ambition?
Yet Brutus says he was ambitious;
And, sure, he is an honourable man.
I speak not to disprove what Brutus spoke,
But here I am to speak what I do know.
You all did love him once—not without cause:
What cause withholds you, then, to mourn for him? . . .
But yesterday the word of Caesar might
Have stood against the world: now lies he there,
And none so poor to do him reverence.
O masters, if I were dispos'd to stir
Your hearts and minds to mutiny and rage,
I should do Brutus wrong, and Cassius wrong,
Who, you all know, are honourable men:
I will not do them wrong; I rather choose
To wrong the dead, to wrong myself and you,
Than I will wrong such honourable men . . .

27. ECONOMY (CONCISENESS)

(See also Wordiness, Section 71.)

The writer who uses too many words reduces in direct ratio the effectiveness of his style. Though one must not blindly sacrifice for conciseness other desirable qualities, sentences that are compact and terse are usually superior to sentences that express the same thought in twice as many words. This holds true especially for the types of writing that a student is usually called upon to do, and even in the most imaginative and poetic prose the skillful writer distinguishes carefully between luxuriant language used for effect and the mere wordiness that stems from lack of control and judgment.

Next to glaring errors in such fundamental matters as grammar, sentence structure, and spelling, wordiness is probably the most common weakness of student writing. Squeeze unnecessary words from your style like water from a sponge: even the most experienced writers find it essential to examine a first draft intently in order to detect and eliminate wordiness. Practically all student writing is likely to benefit, some of it enormously, from pruning of deadwood, from tightening, from simplification.

One reason for the prevalence of wordiness in freshman themes is the unfortunately widespread delusion that college teachers want "fine writing" and reward it with high grades. The truth is that such "fine writing," or "university English," is the despair of most teachers. Sentences must be clear, direct, and emphatic; and you should pause and consider before yielding to any flourish of language that endangers your achievement of these qualities.

27A. Grammatical Simplification

Sometimes wordiness can be reduced and expression strengthened by the replacement of a sentence by a clause, a clause by a phrase, a phrase by a word: that is, by effective subordination (see Section 23A). Revision of the following passage of "primer English" will illustrate the process:

> I have a dog. He is a white dog. His name is Jack. He is always barking.

Here four choppy sentences can be readily combined into one. "He is a white dog" can be reduced to the single adjective *white*. "His name is Jack" can be reduced to the adjective phrase *named Jack*. And "He is always barking" can be reduced to the relative (subordinate) clause *who is always barking*. Thus the sentence will read, "I have a white dog named Jack, who is always barking." Not only have four choppy sentences become a single smooth one, but seventeen words have been reduced to eleven.

The need for such reduction is rarely so obvious, the solution rarely so easy; but if you examine your own sentences with this point in mind, you may be astonished at the improvements you can accomplish.

WORDY: The man who is carrying the umbrella and who looks so worried is a salesman for a firm that publishes books.

IMPROVED: The worried-looking man with the umbrella is a salesman for a publishing firm.

WORDY: The runner from Yale who is now leading the race looks to me like the man who will win.

IMPROVED: The Yale runner now in the lead looks to me like the winner.

27B. Substitution of the Simple for the Elaborate

Unless there is a loss in accuracy or force, it is wise to use simple words and phrases rather than grand ones. Flowery language used for its own sake is almost always objectionable. Colorful writing has a purpose just as plain writing does, but anything that strikes the reader as pretentious and out of place should be avoided.

FAULTY: The dazzling brilliance of the heavens at the dawn of her natal day augured promisingly for the gala festivities scheduled at the family homestead as sunlight faded into dusk.

IMPROVED: The clear skies of her birthday morning promised good weather for the party at her home in the evening.

FAULTY: The responsibilities that crowd remorselessly upon the shoulders of the chief executive of this mighty nation stretching from Canada to the Gulf must delay many a time his entrance into the realm of Morpheus.

IMPROVED: The responsibilities of the president of the United States must cause him many sleepless nights.

27C. Elimination of Undesirable Repetition

Though skillful repetition may contribute to emphasis (see Section 26B), repetition is often unnecessary and clumsy. In a theme, a writer who has little to say on his topic may intentionally or unintentionally keep repeating his few thoughts over and over. In a sentence or paragraph, an unskillful writer may repeat when doing so is unnecessary and positively harmful.

One frequent fault in student writing is the excessive repetition of a prominent word that the writer finds himself unable to dodge. In an essay on fraternities, the word "fraternities" will and should occur a number of times; in an essay on Shakespeare, the word "Shakespeare" will and should occur a number of times; but the repetition in the following passages is excessive and easily avoidable:

FAULTY: Fraternities have won a permanent place on this campus. Fraternities offer numerous advantages, and those freshmen who join fraternities find the fraternity house a home away from home such as nonfraternity men never know.

IMPROVED: Fraternities have won a permanent place on this campus. They offer numerous advantages, and those freshmen who join a fraternity have a home away from home such as others never know.

FAULTY: William Shakespeare was a native of Stratford-on-Avon, and though Shakespeare left Stratford for London as a young man, his works are filled with what Shakespearean scholars believe to be memories from Shakespeare's Stratford boyhood.

IMPROVED: William Shakespeare was a native of Stratford-on-Avon, and though he went to London as a young man, his works are filled with what scholars believe to be memories of his Stratford boyhood.

As these revisions suggest, proper use of pronouns is usually the simplest and most natural means of avoiding the repetition of nouns, though sometimes an offending word can simply be omitted. Moreover, intelligent substitution of pronoun for noun will often contribute not only to conciseness but to coherence. Writing is always *composition,* and composition is the art of forming a whole by placing together and smoothly uniting different elements: too often in student papers the second sentence is composed as if the writer had forgotten what he had put in the first. Many a theme opens with a passage like the following:

> Freshman regulations serve no good end and should be abolished. Freshman regulations are a great annoyance to the students who must obey them, and even the students who enforce the regulations find them a nuisance.

Here are no errors in grammar or sentence structure; yet how much neater and sharper is the following revision, effected largely by sensible use of pronouns:

> Freshman regulations serve no good end and should be abolished. They are an annoyance to the students who obey them and to those who enforce them.

On the other hand, a certain amount of repetition of key words is natural. If excessive repetition of such a word cannot be eliminated by proper use of pronouns and by judicious omissions, it is better to endure the repetition than to eliminate it by means of unnatural synonyms and circumlocutions. In the revision of the sentence about Shakespeare on page 226, two recurrences of the proper name have been avoided by the substitution of pronouns, and the adjective "Shakespearean" has been dropped; but repetition of the name would be preferable to such a phrase as "the bard of Avon" or "the immortal poet." Such circumlocutions are a favorite device in sports journalism.

FAULTY: Gerowsky had a banner day in the field and at bat, and Jackson pitched consistently to win an easy victory. The jackrabbit shortstop turned three apparent hits into double plays, and the opposing pitchers could not keep him off the bases. The lanky portsider ably supported the stellar play of the powerful Pole by keeping eight hits well scattered and fanning nine men.

IMPROVED: Gerowsky had a banner day in the field and at bat, and Jackson pitched consistently to win an easy victory. Gerowsky turned three apparent hits into double plays, and the opposing pitchers could not keep him off the bases. Jackson did his part by keeping eight hits well scattered and fanning nine men.

Certain types of repetition are confusing as well as awkward: for example, repetition of a word too soon after its first use, repetition of a word in a different sense, use of two words different in meaning but identical in sound, and superfluous repetition of the subordinating conjunction *that.*

FAULTY: He failed to report that he had failed his swimming test.
IMPROVED: He did not report that he had failed his swimming test.

FAULTY: It will be of interest to observe whether the new policy will result in lower interest rates.
IMPROVED: I am eager to see whether the new policy will result in lower interest rates.

FAULTY: It is hard to say whether this fine weather will continue.
IMPROVED: We cannot be sure that this fine weather will continue.

FAULTY: The Student Council charged that if the faculty had not interfered that the disturbance would not have amounted to anything.
IMPROVED: The Student Council charged that if the faculty had not interfered the disturbance would not have amounted to anything.

27D. Tautology

Tautology is needless repetition of an idea in different words. Its prevalence in student writing stems in large part from the fact that often the student is struggling to discuss a topic on which he has little to say. When anyone writes "in this day and age" instead of "in this day" or "today," he is guilty of tautology. So is he when he writes "peer ahead into the future"; or "refer back"; or "resumed again"; or "a true fact."

The freshman's horror of appearing to pose as an expert leads him to say, "In my opinion I think . . . ," or even, "Of course I may be wrong, but in my opinion it seems to me . . ." Such repeated apologies do not win the confidence of the reader. Indeed, usually no apology whatever is necessary. When a writer is discussing a matter of opinion, we assume that what he says *is* his opinion.

27E. Expletives

Though the expletives *There is . . .*, *There are . . .*, *It is . . .*, and *It seems . . .* have a legitimate purpose, eliminating them will often result not only in greater conciseness but in stronger sentences.

WORDY: There is no need for me to have your help.
IMPROVED: I do not need your help.

WORDY: There were many good reasons why I could not vote for you.
IMPROVED: I had many good reasons for not voting for you.

WORDY: It is said that no man is a hero to his valet.
IMPROVED: No man is a hero to his valet.

WORDY: It seems inevitable that he will lose.
IMPROVED: He seems certain to lose.

27F. Intensives

Certain words, chiefly adverbs, intended to give emphasis and hence called *intensives,* may often be of little value or actually have a weakening effect. *Very* and *much* are the most frequent offenders; other intensives that sometimes reduce rather than increase emphasis are *certainly, extremely, surely, undoubtedly*. The following sentences are less emphatic with the intensives than without them.

I am [very] happy to meet you.
She is [much] delighted with her gift.
It is [certainly] a pleasure to be here today.
The governor is [surely] a brilliant executive.
The players were [extremely] depressed after the defeat.

27G. Adjective and Adverb

A style loaded with adjectives and adverbs is likely to be wordy and unemphatic. Such qualifying words are valuable in so far as they sharpen meaning and add color, but they should be used only if they contribute something. The following sentences are stronger without most of or all the bracketed modifiers.

The [bright] sunlight filtering through the thick [green] foliage cast dancing patterns upon the [cheerfully] rippling water of the [little] brook.

The [serious] student who desires [earnestly] to conquer calculus must [resolutely] resign himself to [many] days of [severe] concentration.

EXERCISE

Revise the following passage so as to reduce wordiness without altering meaning or impairing effectiveness. Be prepared to defend your alterations.

There is undoubtedly truth in the statement that in the course of the last hundred years that there have been very radical changes in the program of courses offered within the ivy-covered walls of the colleges of this country of ours. There was a time when the colleges devoted more time to the time-consuming study of the classic languages of ancient Greece and Rome than they devoted to the study of all other subjects. The college student of a hundred years ago certainly learned very much more of the history of Greece and Rome than he learned of the more recent history of his own great modern American democracy. The student was supposed to know how to write verses of an often very inferior kind in Greek and Latin rather than know how to use his own native English language with effectiveness in the routine affairs of common, ordinary life from day to day. In general it may probably be safely averred that the learned professors who were in charge of planning the curricula that were offered in the colleges in those far-off days certainly seem to have adhered in a very blind manner to old, antiquated procedures that were already grossly out of date in a practical society that was becoming practically entirely industrialized at an extremely rapid rate. The professors were rather inclined to look with a frown upon the study of the science and the technology that were destined to bring many new transformations in this practical modern world of the twentieth century. But on the other hand, however, it is also a true fact in a way that not all the changes and alterations that have been made have been in the way of improvements. I believe that in my opinion the professors of a hundred years ago certainly might very well contend with some degree of reason that the study of the history of the ancient world of Greece and Rome is perhaps somewhat more appropriate for the college student of even this practical modern world we live in than some of the rather absurd courses for which a student can obtain credit toward a college degree in some colleges in this day and age.

28. VARIETY

No matter how effective the individual sentences may be, a passage of any length will be monotonous and flat if the sentences lack variety. The experienced writer achieves at least adequate variety almost without conscious effort, simply by adjusting length and structure to the varied purposes of his sentences. But most students need to make some deliberate effort to obtain variety by what will be at first artificial methods. The more these methods are practiced, the less artificial they will become.

Sentences may be long or short; they may be loose or periodic; they may be simple, compound, complex, or compound-complex; they may be declarative, interrogative, exclamatory, or imperative. But no passage should contain many sentences of any one length or pattern unless for a definite purpose.

28A. Subordination

Effective subordination contributes vitally to sentence variety. For treatment of this topic see Section 23A.

28B. Sentence Element Before the Subject

Since by far the most familiar sentence pattern in English is that in which the subject comes at the beginning and is followed by verb and complement, a simple way to gain variety is to place a sentence element before the subject. The sentence may begin with a single adjective, adverb, participle, or infinitive; with a prepositional, participial, or infinitive phrase; with an absolute construction; with a subordinate adverbial clause.

ADJECTIVE:	Suspicious, he opened the door slowly.
ADVERB:	Indeed you may be right.
PARTICIPLE:	Frowning, he shook his head.
INFINITIVE:	To prosper, one must work hard.
PREPOSITIONAL PHRASE:	In the evening light the pool looked gray and forbidding.
INFINITIVE PHRASE:	To reach the highway you will have to retrace your steps.
ABSOLUTE CONTRUCTION:	The bell having rung, all conversation ceased.
ADVERBIAL CLAUSE:	Since the outcome is now certain, we may as well leave immediately.

An occasional sentence may begin with a co-ordinating conjunction. Such a sentence must of course have an appropriate logical connection with the one preceding it.

Just then the distant notes of a bugle announced that the relief forces were near. And it was none too soon.

Abandoning the doorbell, he pounded on the panels and shouted again and again. But there was no reply.

You may as well pull the blinds, lock the door, and go swimming with me. For no one will want a haircut this warm afternoon.

The normal subject-verb-complement order may be inverted so that the verb or the complement precedes the subject. Such inversion, which gives emphasis to the sentence element that comes first (see Section 26A), should be used sparingly and with judgment.

ADVERB AND VERB FIRST:	Then occurred the event that was to change his career.
ADVERB AND AUXILIARY VERB FIRST:	Never have the roads been so crowded.
DIRECT OBJECT FIRST:	This insult he could not ignore.
OBJECTIVE COMPLEMENT FIRST:	A quitter Jack called him.
SUBJECTIVE COMPLEMENT FIRST:	Few are those who practice what they preach.

In many exclamatory sentences the normal order is inverted.

> How beautiful was the lake that night!
> What fun we had with our little cousins!

In most questions the verb or part of the verb precedes the subject, and the question form not only contributes to sentence variety but may be rhetorically effective in other ways.

> Are we to endure such neglect forever?
> Is it not true that the gate receipts have become more important than the game?

28C. Interrupting Elements

Since in the normal sentence pattern the subject is followed by the verb and the verb by the complement, anything that intervenes between subject and verb or between verb and complement produces some degree of variety. Such interruption, however, should not occur if it produces awkwardness.

INTERRUPTION BETWEEN SUBJECT AND VERB:

> The boy from Stanford, undismayed by the coolness of his reception, repeated his request for a dance.
> Professor Grunther, who has served on the faculty for nearly forty years, will retire in June.

INTERRUPTION BETWEEN VERB AND COMPLEMENT:

> Matthews demanded, with even more sarcasm than usual, that the honorable gentleman disclose the source of his information.
> She stared, while her heart beat wildly, at the creeping shadow on the floor.

EXERCISE

Show by close analysis how the sentences in each of the following passages are varied in length and pattern.

1. With the single exception of Falstaff, all Shakespeare's characters are what we call marrying men. Mercutio, as he was own cousin to Benedick and Biron, would have come to the same end in the long run. Even Iago had a wife, and, what is far stranger, he was jealous. People like Jacques and the Fool in Lear, although we can hardly imagine they would ever marry, kept single out of a cynical humor or for a broken heart, and not, as

we do nowadays, from a spirit of incredulity and preference for the single state. For that matter, if you turn to George Sand's French version of *As You Like It* (and I think I can promise you will like it but little), you will find Jacques marries Celia just as Orlando marries Rosalind.

—R. L. STEVENSON, "Virginibus Puerisque."

2. Why do we, in fact, almost all of us, desire to increase our incomes? It may seem, at first sight, as though material goods were what we desire. But, in fact, we desire these mainly in order to impress our neighbours. When a man moves into a larger house in a more genteel quarter, he reflects that "better" people will call on his wife, and some unprosperous cronies of former days can he dropped. When he sends his son to a good school or an expensive university, he consoles himself for the heavy fees by thoughts of the social kudos to be gained. In every big city, whether of Europe or of America, houses in some districts are more expensive than equally good houses in other districts, merely because they are more fashionable. One of the most powerful of all our passions is the desire to be admired and respected. As things stand, admiration and respect are given to the man who seems to be rich. This is the chief reason why people wish to be rich. The actual goods purchased by their money play quite a secondary part. Take, for example, a millionaire who cannot tell one picture from another, but has acquired a gallery of old masters by the help of experts. The only pleasure he derives from his pictures is the thought that others know how much they have cost; he would derive more direct enjoyment from sentimental chromos out of Christmas numbers, but he would not obtain the same satisfaction for his vanity.—BERTRAND RUSSELL, *Sceptical Essays.*

3. When I think of what easy remnants essays may be made I wonder that every lukewarm pen does not engage its leisure in throwing them together. A man of moderate ingenuity has but to cast about in nearest circumstance to find matter for his thought. If his study window looks upon a garden, a score of subjects will rise from grass and flowering bush to crowd his ink-pot. He has but to hold himself in leisure, then dip and start. Perhaps upon the lawn a sundial meets his eye and, in speculation of the wise saw that is carved upon the bronze, his thoughts will run through all eternity to find the edge of time. *Horas non numero nisi serenas!* It was such a motto—I count but the sunny hours—that sent Hazlitt through a dozen pages of delightful meditation that sing like a drowsy tune of summer. The flowering of a jonquil or the drooping of a lilac guides us to the running of the year. By what magic does nature sort its colors from the sun and tip its brush with yellow for the daffodil? By what favor does the iris get its motley to racket through the month of June? Or if stars be out, we sit in wonder at the everlasting whipcord that sends us spinning through alternate day and

night. The flash of Orion on its breathless journey of a million years provides us argument for eternity.—CHARLES S. BROOKS, *Like Summer's Cloud.*

29. RHYTHM

Sentences that strike the reader with their beauty are likely to possess a rhythmical quality usually associated with poetry. Rhythm is infinitely variable. Parallelism and balance and judicious repetition contribute to it; choice of words is all-important in its achievement; but there is no pattern, no formula, for the rhythmical sentence. Modern English prose in general is less elaborately rhythmical than that of earlier periods, and the student in particular should be wary of striving for an artificial rhythm that might make his style pretentious rather than impressive.

The best examples of consciously achieved prose rhythm in English are probably to be found in the work of such seventeenth-century writers as Jeremy Taylor, John Donne, and the translators of the King James Version of the Bible (1611). Nineteenth-century authors such as DeQuincey, Carlyle, Ruskin, and Pater also employed it frequently, and it is clearly observable in the work of many conscious stylists of our own time. A reading of the following illustrative passages, some of which are too elaborately rhythmical to serve as models for today's freshman, will suggest something of the potential beauty of a rhythmical style, and close analysis will reveal some of the methods by which effective rhythm is achieved.

1. O eloquent, just, and mighty Death! whom none could advise, thou hast persuaded; what none hath dared, thou hast done; and whom all the world hath flattered, thou only hast cast out of the world and despised; thou hast drawn together all the far-stretched greatness, all the pride, cruelty, and ambition of man, and covered it all over with these two narrow words, *Hic jacet*!—SIR WALTER RALEIGH (1614).

2. Who bends not his ear to any bell which upon any occasion rings? but who can remove it from that bell which is passing a piece of himself out of this world? No man is an island, entire of itself; every man is a piece of the continent, a part of the main. If a clod be washed away by the sea,

Europe is the less, as well as if a promontory were, as well as if a manor of thy friend's or of thine own were. Any man's death diminishes me, because I am involved in mankind, and therefore never send to know for whom the bell tolls; it tolls for thee.—JOHN DONNE (1624).

3. But the iniquity of oblivion blindly scattereth her poppy, and deals with the memory of men without distinction to merit of perpetuity. Who can but pity the founder of the pyramids? Herostratus lives that burnt the temple of Diana, he is almost lost that built it; time hath spared the epitaph of Adrian's horse, confounded that of himself. In vain we compute our felicities by the advantage of our good names, since bad have equal durations; and Thersites is like to live as long as Agamemnon. Who knows whether the best of men be known? Or whether there be not more remarkable persons forgot, than any that stand remembered in the known account of time? Without the favor of the everlasting register, the first man had been as unknown as the last, and Methuselah's long life had been his only chronicle.—SIR THOMAS BROWNE (1658).

4. Thus far, for Florian, what all this had determined was a peculiarly strong sense of home—so forcible a motive with all of us—prompting to us our customary love of the earth, and the larger part of our fear of death, that revulsion we have from it, as from something strange, untried, unfriendly; though life-long imprisonment, they tell you, and final banishment from home is a thing bitterer still; the looking forward to it but a short space, a mere childish *gouter* and dessert of it, before the end, being so great a resource of effort to pilgrims and wayfarers, and the soldier in distant quarters, and lending, in lack of that, some power of solace to the thought of sleep in the home churchyard, at least—dead cheek by dead cheek, and with the rain soaking in upon one from above.—WALTER PATER (1895).

5. There was no human figure near him nor any sound borne to him over the air. But the tide was near the turn and already the day was on the wane. He turned landward and ran towards the shore and, running up the sloping beach, reckless of the sharp shingle, found a sandy nook amid a ring of tufted sand knolls and lay down there that the peace and silence of the evening might still the riot of his blood.

He felt above him the vast indifferent dome and the calm processes of the heavenly bodies; and the earth beneath him, the earth that had borne him, had taken him to her breast.

He closed his eyes in the languor of sleep. His eyelids trembled as if they felt the vast cyclic movement of the earth and her watchers, trembled as if they felt the strange light of some new world. His soul was swooning into some new world, fantastic, dim, uncertain as under sea, traversed by cloudy shapes and beings. A world, a glimmer, or a flower? Glimmering and trembling, trembling and unfolding, a breaking light, an opening flower, it spread in endless succession to itself, breaking in full crimson and unfolding and fading to palest rose, leaf by leaf and wave of light by wave of light, flooding all the heavens with its soft flushes, every flush deeper than other.

Evening had fallen when he woke and the sand and arid grasses of his bed glowed no longer. He rose slowly and, recalling the rapture of his sleep, sighed at its joy.—JAMES JOYCE, *A Portrait of the Artist as a Young Man* (1916).

6. But what after all is one night? A short space, especially when the darkness dims so soon, and so soon a bird sings, a cock crows, or a faint green quickens, like a turning leaf, in the hollow of the wave. Night, however, succeeds to night. The winter holds a pack of them in store and deals them equally, evenly, with indefatigable fingers. They lengthen; they darken. Some of them hold aloft clear planets, plates of brightness. The autumn trees, ravaged as they are, take on the flash of tattered flags kindling in the gloom of cool cathedral caves where gold letters on marble pages describe death in battle and how bones bleach and burn far away in Indian sands. The autumn trees gleam in the yellow moonlight, in the light of harvest moons, the light which mellows the energy of labour, and smooths the stubble, and brings the wave lapping blue to the shore.—VIRGINIA WOOLF, *To the Lighthouse* (1927).

7. But this was the reason why these things could never be forgotten—because we are so lost, so naked and so lonely in America. Immense and cruel skies bend over us, and all of us are driven on forever and we have no home. Therefore, it is not the slow, the punctual sanded drip of the unnumbered days that we remember best, the ash of time; nor is it the huge monotone of the lost years, the unswerving schedules of the lost life and the well-known faces, that we remember best. It is a face seen once and lost forever in a crowd, an eye that looked, a face that smiled and vanished on a passing train, it is a prescience of snow upon a certain night, the laughter of a woman in a summer street long years ago, it is the memory of a single moon seen at the pine's dark edge in old October—and all of our lives is written in the twisting of a leaf upon a bough, a door that opened, and a stone.

For America has a thousand lights and weathers and we walk the streets, we walk the streets forever, we walk the streets of life alone. . . .

Storm shook the house at night—the old house, his mother's house—where he had seen his brother die. The old doors swung and creaked in darkness, darkness pressed against the house, the darkness filled them, filled the house at night, it moved about them soft and secret, palpable, filled with a thousand secret presences of sorrowful time and memory, moving about them as he lay below his brother's room in darkness, while storm shook the house in late October, and something creaked and rattled in the wind's strong blast. It was October, and he had come home again: he could not believe that his father was dead. . . .

Trains cross the continent in a swirl of dust and thunder, the leaves fly down the tracks behind them: the great trains cleave through gulch and gulley, they rumble with spoked thunder on the bridges over the powerful brown wash of mighty rivers, they toil through hills, they skirt the rough brown stubble of shorn fields, they whip past empty stations in the little towns and their great stride pounds its even pulse across America. Field and hill and lift and gulch and hollow, mountain and plain and river, a wilderness with fallen trees across it, a thicket of bedded brown and twisted undergrowth, a plain, a desert, and a plantation, a mighty landscape with no fenced niceness, an immensity of fold and convolution that can never be remembered, that can never be forgotten, that has never been described—weary with harvest, potent with every fruit and ore, the immeasurable richness embrowned with autumn, rank, crude, unharnessed, careless of scars or beauty, everlasting and magnificent, a cry, a space, an ecstasy!—American earth in old October.—THOMAS WOLFE, *Of Time and the River* (1935).

8. In the time of your life, live—so that in that good time there shall be no ugliness or death for yourself or for any life your life touches. Seek goodness everywhere, and when it is found, bring it out of its hiding-place and let it be free and unashamed. Place in matter and in flesh the least of the values, for these are the things that hold death and must pass away. Discover in all things that which shines and is beyond corruption. Encourage virtue in whatever heart it may have been driven into secrecy and sorrow by the shame and terror of the world. Ignore the obvious, for it is unworthy of the clear eye and the kindly heart. Be the inferior of no man, nor of any man be the superior. Remember that every man is a variation of yourself. No man's guilt is not yours, nor is any man's innocence a thing apart. Despise evil and ungodliness, but not men of ungodliness or evil. These, understand. Have no shame in being kindly and gentle, but if the time comes in the time of your life to kill, kill and have no regret. In the time of your life live—so that in that wondrous time you shall not add to the misery and sorrow of the world but shall smile to the infinite delight and mystery of it.—WILLIAM SAROYAN, *The Time of Your Life* (1939).

9. . . . Even though large tracts of Europe and many old and famous States have fallen or may fall into the grip of the Gestapo and all the odious apparatus of Nazi rule, we shall not flag or fail. We shall go on to the end, we shall fight in France, we shall fight on the seas and oceans, we shall fight with growing confidence and growing strength in the air, we shall defend

our Island, whatever the cost may be, we shall fight on the beaches, we shall fight on the landing grounds, we shall fight in the fields and in the streets, we shall fight in the hills; we shall never surrender, and even if, which I do not for a moment believe, this Island or a large part of it were subjugated and starving, then our Empire beyond the seas, armed and guarded by the British fleet, would carry on the struggle, until, in God's good time, the New World, with all its power and might, steps forth to the rescue and the liberation of the old.—WINSTON CHURCHILL, *Blood, Sweat, and Tears* (1941).

Chapter 5

PUNCTUATION AND MECHANICS

30. PURPOSE OF PUNCTUATION

Punctuation exists for the sole purpose of clarifying written expression. It serves as a substitute for the many devices that a speaker consciously or unconsciously uses to obtain clarity—pauses long and short, the rise and fall of the voice, changes in pace and volume, changes in facial expression, gestures. If the meaning of a passage is immediately and unmistakably clear to the reader, there can be no quarrel with the punctuation. But the experience of countless writers has demonstrated that in certain recurring situations it is wise to set up certain signposts in the form of punctuation; furthermore, readers have come to assume that writers will follow conventions in punctuation and that the punctuation employed by one writer will not differ greatly from that employed by another. Hence there has evolved a series of conventions followed by most writers and assumed by most readers. The sections that follow are not therefore a series of rules arrived at by grammarians but merely a statement of the procedures in punctuation characteristic of contemporary written English.[1]

31. COMMA

A student who has mastered the use of the comma will have little difficulty with other marks of punctuation. The comma serves a variety of purposes, but in all its functions it is the punc-

[1] For a more detailed treatment of punctuation see George Summey, Jr., *American Punctuation* (New York: The Ronald Press Co., 1949).

tuation mark that is used to separate elements while producing the smallest possible break in thought. All its misuses occur in situations in which either a stronger mark or no mark at all is needed.

31A. Comma Between Independent Clauses Joined by Conjunctions

The comma is used normally between independent clauses joined by one of the co-ordinating conjunctions: *and, but, for, or, nor.*[2] At such a point the comma indicates immediately to the reader that one independent clause has ended and another is beginning.

> The long struggle was over, and darkness closed down upon the trodden mud and the leveled grain and the anguish of the wounded.
>
> The road wound here and there through the countryside, for the builders had simply followed the tracks worn by early settlers.
>
> Two heads may indeed be better than one, but too many cooks spoil the broth.

NOTE: The comma is *not* to be used between independent clauses not joined by a conjunction. Its use under such circumstances would produce a comma splice (see Sections 12C, 32B).

In some sentences of this sort the comma has an additional function—to prevent temporary misreading.

> Every member of the House was in favor of the basic principles of the measure, but Thompson and his supporters wished to have minor changes incorporated. [Here if it were not for the comma a reader might think at first that "everyone was in favor of the measure but Thompson and his supporters." The comma makes clear that *but* is here not a preposition with the meaning of *except* but a conjunction beginning another independent clause.]
>
> Mary picked up the baby, and little Fred toddled along at her side. [Here if it were not for the comma a reader might think at first that Mary had picked up the baby *and* little Fred. The comma makes clear that the *and* does not join two objects of a preposition but is a conjunction introducing another independent clause.]

[2] In modern writing there is a tendency to regard *yet* and *so* as co-ordinating conjunctions. Individual teachers should advise their students on this point; the writers of this book prefer to regard *yet* and *so* as conjunctive adverbs (see Section 32B).

Parents should studiously avoid trying to solve all problems that arise, for children must learn to think for themselves. [Here if it were not for the comma the reader might think at first that the writer means "all problems that arise for children." The comma makes clear that *for* is not a preposition but a conjunction beginning a new main clause.]

When both clauses are short and the meaning is unmistakable, you may elect to do without the comma.

Jack was nine and Bobby was six.
Words are good but deeds are better.

On the other hand, if one or both clauses are long and contain internal commas, you may elect to use a semicolon between clauses in place of the comma. This is done to indicate to the reader that at the point where the semicolon is used there is a more important break than at the points marked by commas.

General Arnold, who was put in command of West Point, was an officer of courage and ability; but feelings of resentment, added to a desire to rid himself of financial troubles, prompted him to attempt to betray his country.

Here use of the semicolon is advisable, but you should not form the impression that in every compound sentence in which there is already one comma you should use the semicolon before a coordinating conjunction. In the following sentence, for example, there is no need for a semicolon: "Mary Watson, who is coming this afternoon, is my cousin, but I have never met her." You must decide whether the situation calls for comma or semicolon. The pattern that best achieves clarity, proper emphasis, and ease of understanding for the reader is the pattern that you should adopt. (See Section 32C.)

31B. Comma in Series

The comma is used to separate sentence elements of equal importance in a series of three or more—words, phrases, or clauses.

At this point the states of Maryland, Virginia, and West Virginia come together.
Members of our armed forces serve on land, at sea, and in the air.

He bought ten acres of meadow land near town, divided it into lots, and made a handsome profit.

Ahead of them stretched the vast, hot, empty desert.

"We live in a society," thundered the speaker, "where more money is spent on gambling than on education, where people are more interested in baseball than in world affairs, and where success is measured chiefly in terms of dollars."

Practice varies in the use of a comma before the "and" introducing the final element in a series. Since the absence of a comma at that point sometimes causes confusion and the presence of a comma never does, it is wise to form the habit of using the comma.

The negotiations finally resulted in agreement about wages for overtime, abolition of company police and mutual understanding. [Here the absence of the comma before "and" causes momentary confusion.]

Coach Williams had previously held appointments at Dickinson, Washington and Jefferson and Hamilton. [The confusion here is removed by the placing of a comma before the final "and."]

Normally the comma is used between adjectives in a series ("Fred has grown to be a tall, handsome, sturdy boy"); but if an adjective is so closely related in thought to the noun modified that the two form a unit as if they were a compound, the comma should not be used.

The timid old lady stepped forward hesitantly. [Here "old lady" is regarded as a unit modified by "timid."]

The compact, plotted short story is far less common than it used to be. [Here "short story" is regarded as a unit modified by "compact" and "plotted."]

When in doubt whether to use the comma in such a situation, you can usually decide by reading the phrase aloud: if a pause between adjectives seems advisable, use the comma. In the sentences just given it is clear that a pause is needed after "compact" but would be inappropriate after "timid" or "plotted."

EXERCISE

Punctuate the following sentences correctly.

1. The dark gloomy day drew to a close and mist began to shroud the woods the meadows and the farm buildings.

2. A county fair is a fascinating place for children for there they find exciting rides horse races prize animals and countless other attractions.
3. This is your bed and that one is mine.
4. Going barefoot bringing home the cows hunting for hickory nuts and gathering berries are experiences familiar to country children.
5. Among the children in that little school were some who were intelligent but untrained some who were far superior to their companions in intelligence and training and some who were simply incapable of learning but the skillful conscientious teacher determined to do what she could for those in each group.

31C. Comma After Introductory Subordinate Elements

The comma is used normally after a subordinate clause preceding the main clause. But if the subordinate clause is short and closely related to the main clause, the comma may be omitted.

After she had washed the breakfast dishes and made the beds, she dressed to go shopping.
Though I am not actively interested in politics, I take care to vote at every election.
When the gong sounds it will be one o'clock.

Similarly, use of the comma is often called for after a phrase preceding the main clause, but here it is difficult to establish a rule that will cover all instances. Normally the comma is advisable if the introductory phrase is long or is an absolute, or contains a verbal (participle, gerund, or infinitive); and transitional phrases (*in fact, on the other hand*) or even single transitional words (*indeed, however*) are usually followed by a comma. But in this situation you will often have to decide for yourself whether a comma is needed, and when in doubt you will probably be safer in omitting it. The essential point is to forestall possible misreading. The sentences which follow show conventional practice.

After the long, weary climb up the slippery hill, we coasted down at lightning speed.
Having delivered his ultimatum, he turned on his heel and stormed away.
His heart pounding, he lunged for the tape.
To put it bluntly, I am disgusted with him.

As a matter of fact, he told me himself.
In the morning we shall make a fresh start.
After his arrival we sat down to dinner.

31D. Commas with Parenthetical Elements

31D1. Restrictive and Nonrestrictive Modifiers. One of the most frequent errors in punctuation involves the handling of restrictive and nonrestrictive modifiers. A restrictive clause or phrase is one that is essential to the meaning of the word it modifies, hence "restricts" the meaning of that word; such a phrase is *not* set off by a comma or commas. A nonrestrictive clause or phrase, conversely, is one that is not essential to the meaning of the word it modifies; such a clause or phrase, which adds information about the word modified but is not essential to its meaning, *is* set off by a comma or commas. The restrictive element is so closely related to the word modified that to set it off by commas would be undesirable; the parenthetical nature of the nonrestrictive element is clearly indicated by the use of commas.

In trying to decide whether a clause or phrase is restrictive or nonrestrictive you should ask yourself, "Is it necessary to the *identification* of the word modified?" If it is, you should *not* use commas; if it is not, you *should* use commas.

The man who is at the door is an old friend of yours. [Here the clause *who is at the door* identifies the particular man concerned. If it were omitted, the reader would have no idea what man is meant. Hence it is a restrictive modifier and is not set off by commas.]

Fred Jackson, who is at the door, was a college friend of my father. [Here the man spoken of is identified by name, and the clause *who is at the door*, though it tells where he is, is not necessary to the identification of Fred Jackson. Hence in this sentence the clause is nonrestrictive and is set off by commas.]

To go swimming when one has just finished eating is foolhardy. [The writer wished to say not that to go swimming at all is foolhardy but only that to do so just after eating is foolhardy. Hence the modifying clause is restrictive and is not set off by commas.]

At three o'clock, when the mail arrives, half the village gathers at the post office. [Three o'clock is a clearly identified hour without the addition of the clause *when the mail arrives*. Hence this clause is nonrestrictive and is set off by commas.]

He was given the room next to mine. [Without the modifying phrase the reader would not know what room is meant. Hence the phrase is restrictive and is not set off by a comma.]

The favorite rendezvous of the students is Sam's Sandwich Shop, not far from the campus. [Though the final phrase supplies additional information, it is not necessary to the identification of Sam's Sandwich Shop. Hence it is nonrestrictive and is set off by a comma.]

Sometimes a clause or phrase may be treated as restrictive or nonrestrictive depending upon the meaning of the sentence.

The coach explained the new signals to the players, who had not heard them before. [*All* the players had to have the signals explained.]

The coach explained the new signals to the players who had not heard them before. [Some of the players already knew the signals, and only those who did not had to have them explained.]

EXERCISE

Decide whether the modifying clauses and phrases in the following sentences are restrictive or nonrestrictive, and punctuate accordingly. Be prepared to defend each decision.

1. There are politicians who are interested in the welfare of the people and others who are interested only in themselves.
2. He does not like girls who chew gum but apparently is fond of Peggy who is always chattering.
3. Mr. Pennock insecure in the driver's seat was driven almost to distraction by the ceaseless prattle of his wife who sat in the rear with the children.
4. Bobby had been told always to count to ten before striking a blow, but he found this rule difficult to observe when his adversary started to pummel him.
5. He was terrified when the lights flickered out, but he managed to stay in the old house till dawn when his ordeal was to come to an end.
6. If he who hesitates is lost, then my friend Charley who can never make up his mind is certainly done for.
7. The officer flustered and angry could not make the least impression upon the soldiers.
8. My home town where several skirmishes were fought during the Revolutionary War has more spots of historic interest than most cities ten times its size.

9. The man who headed the charity drive drove us to his home where he showed us the plans and introduced us to his wife who invited us to dinner.
10. Television which is making sports promoters pass sleepless nights may turn out to be as great a boon to them as radio which created a vast new audience for sports events.

31D 2. Parenthetical Elements. Any parenthetical element that interrupts or stands out in such a way as to require punctuation for clarity should be set off by a comma or commas. Such elements of course are nonrestrictive. Examples are appositives, absolute phrases, transitional or qualifying elements, items in dates and addresses, certain single adverbs and mild interjections, contrasting elements, substantives used in direct address, conversational expressions such as "he said," a question that refers to an earlier statement in the same sentence, and any element that clearly interrupts the normal flow of the sentence.

a) Appositives. Most appositives are nonrestrictive and hence set off by commas.

George Washington, first president of the United States, was a Virginian.
My father, leader of the project, was the first to arrive.

Sometimes, however, the appositive is restrictive and hence is not set off by commas.

Scott's novel *The Heart of Midlothian* contains his most lifelike heroine. [Scott wrote more than one novel, and the title points out which one is meant.]
Alexander the Great. William the Conqueror. [An appositive that is part of a title is restrictive.]
The poet Rossetti was also a painter. [The appositive *Rossetti* is essential to indicate what poet is meant.]
The word *phenomena* is plural. [The appositive *phenomena* identifies the word meant.]

An adjective phrase that follows the noun modified is really an appositive. Like other appositives, it is usually set off by commas.

The corporal, tired and hungry, struggled back to camp.
The teacher, amused by this turn of events, permitted the discussion to continue.

b) Absolute Phrases.

The dishes having been washed, she hurried out to the movies.
The druggist, his day's work done, locked up and went home.
He had only to make two telephone calls and sign some letters, everything else having been attended to by his secretary.

c) Transitional or Qualifying Elements.

This morning, for example, he was very late.
The experience, to be sure, was new to him.
My friend, however, decided to accompany me.
That is, I never knew it until now.

d) Items in Dates and Addresses.

He lives at 133 Devon Drive, Philadelphia 32, Pennsylvania. [Postal zone numbers are not separated from the name of the city.]
His death occurred on Friday, March 19, 1942, in Salina, Kansas. [Some writers prefer to place the day of the month first and omit commas, thus: 19 March 1942.]

e) Certain Single Adverbs and Mild Interjections.

Yes, we shall be glad to come.
No, he never told me.
Well, he seemed to be in a hurry.
Oh, let it go.
Why, I really don't know.

If an interjection is strongly exclamatory it should be followed by an exclamation mark.

Oh! You startled me.
Alas! This is the end.

f) Contrasting Elements.

She is really forty, not thirty-five.
Jack, not Tom, was the aggressor.

g) Substantives Used in Direct Address.

Sit down, Mary, and listen to me.
Gentlemen, you are welcome.
Come here, you!

h) Conversational Expressions Such as "He Said."

"I go," he said, "but I shall return."
"It's a small world," Sally observed.

When another mark of punctuation is present, the comma is not needed.

"Not on your life!" he cried.
"Are you ready?" John asked.

i) Repeated Questions.

It's too late now, isn't it?

j) Interrupters.

David, the Bible tells us, killed Goliath with a pebble.
Gray hair, at least gray hair like Mrs. Brown's, is often becoming.

31E. Comma for Clarity. A comma should be used whenever necessary to prevent misunderstanding. Instances of this function of the comma are found in the preceding sections, but the following examples also make it clear:

After all, his troubles are his own fault.
Inside, the stove created an atmosphere of comfort.

31F. Superfluous Commas. The comma should not be used unless there is specific need for it. Fewer commas are found in most modern writing than in the writing of even a generation ago. You should follow the conventions described in the preceding sections, but when (as often happens with every writer) you cannot quite decide whether a comma is needed at a particular point you are probably safer in omitting it.

31G. Comma Splice. See Section 12C.

EXERCISE

Copy the following sentences, adding commas wherever they are needed. Be prepared to defend every comma added. Some of the sentences may need no additional punctuation.

1. It seems certain that Jackson devoted admirer of the poet must have written him many letters but only a few scraps of the correspondence remain.
2. Though the earlier part of the book is dull the second half which concerns the explorer's troubles with the natives is tense exciting reading.
3. Born in Schenectady New York on April 17 1905 he studied engineering at Cornell where his father had been a student before him.
4. The college library I am told contains four hundred thousand volumes but I understand that its holdings in biology chemistry and physics are only fair.
5. Her eyes wet with tears the girl in front of me turned to her companion and whispered "Let's get out of here."
6. As the members of the panel warmed to their subject the talk grew more and more spirited and finally the chairman poor fellow had to bang his gavel on the table and shout "Silence!"
7. My friend you will never find what you seek for many eager hunters have scoured every inch of the ground.
8. Her new winter coat was lying on the floor among debris that had not been disturbed for weeks.
9. The book that contains the character you have in mind is Jane Austen's *Pride and Prejudice* rewritten and published in 1813 when the author was thirty-eight.
10. To be sure that decision was not reached until two o'clock when the group was weary from writing draft after draft tearing each one up and starting all over again.
11. Before the farmer had always granted us favors like showing us a basketful of lively little kittens that had just arrived but this time he acted as though our visit was unwelcome.
12. In the event of an early adjournment meet me at Alice's home where we shall telephone to Frank Richard and Henry.
13. The moon had gone under a cloud the night wind began to stir the branches of the great oaks and we became aware of a variety of low sounds that had previously gone unnoticed but since it was just as easy to forge ahead as to turn back at this stage we tried to calm our nerves and plunged on through the dank forbidding forest.

14. Yes I agree with the points that you have made but permit me to remind you my dear sir that you have not touched upon the question of the protective tariff the most fundamental issue.
15. The gate for example hung on a single rusty creaking hinge and the pasture land once neat as a carpet was grown up in locust sumach and scrub pine.
16. Having discovered that the doctor not the doctor's brother was the murderer the detectives blustering to conceal their embarrassment hurried to the jail to release the innocent man.
17. In particular the student should be careful never to confuse the words *uninterested* and *disinterested* the two having quite different meanings.
18. Impressed by the height of the buildings the roar of the traffic and the throngs of pedestrians the young farm boy stood staring in the middle of the sidewalk unmindful of amused glances and occasional smothered chuckles.
19. To taste defeat when one has been confident of victory is bitter I admit but that is no excuse for acting like a spoiled child.
20. Undismayed by the storm we built a cheerful fire unrolled our blankets on the floor and prepared to spend the night in the cabin hoping that the snow would cease before morning but when we awoke to find drifts blocking the door and the wind blowing harder than ever we looked at each other in grim uneasy silence.

32. SEMICOLON

The primary use of the semicolon is to indicate a pause almost as complete as that of a period, but without beginning a new sentence. It may also be used, with caution, at points where the comma would normally be used but where for special reasons a stronger mark seems to be needed.

32A. Semicolon Between Independent Clauses

The semicolon is used between the clauses of a compound sentence that are not joined by a co-ordinating conjunction (see Comma Splice, Section 12C).

> Ernest hesitated before raising his hand to knock on the door; he regretted now that he had not worked out a plan of campaign for his interview with the principal.

Thirty years ago Melville was almost forgotten; today he is regarded as one of America's greatest authors.

His first time at bat he singled to left field; in the fourth inning he drove in two runs with a double off the rightfield wall; his last time up he struck out ingloriously on three straight pitches.

In this function the semicolon serves much the same purpose as the period; the main difference is that use of the semicolon keeps the clauses within the same sentence. The semicolon should be used only when the clauses are closely related, and particularly when they are also parallel in structure. It is impossible to formulate a rule that will fit all instances; the experienced writer usually has no difficulty deciding for himself. In modern writing the semicolon is used rather sparingly, especially in narrative and dialogue, but it frequently serves a purpose not served by the period.

32B. Semicolon Before Conjunctive Adverbs Introducing Independent Clauses

The semicolon is necessary even when a conjunctive adverb (such as *accordingly, also, besides, consequently, furthermore, hence, however, indeed, moreover, nevertheless, still, then, therefore,* and *thus*) joins independent clauses not connected by a co-ordinating conjunction. Use of the comma instead of the semicolon would produce a comma splice (see Section 12C). *So* and *yet* have come to be regarded as co-ordinating conjunctions by some authorities, but the writers of this book prefer to consider them conjunctive adverbs like those listed above.

They had received no message from their commander for three days; furthermore, their supplies were running low.

Jack had promised to join us at camp; however, on Friday we received a wire stating that he could not be there. [In such a sentence many writers prefer to place the conjunctive adverb parenthetically within the second clause: "on Friday, however, we received a wire stating that he could not be there."]

His brother had warned him that studies are not the only important element of a college career; so he went out for soccer and, when winter came, tried out as a reporter for the campus newspaper. [In this sentence and many others of its type, proper subordination would make for improvement: "Remembering his brother's warning that studies are not the only important element of a college career, he went out for soccer and, when winter came, tried out as a reporter for the campus newspaper."]

There is no rule for determining whether a conjunctive adverb connecting two independent clauses should be followed by a comma. *However* should invariably be, and certain other conjunctive adverbs (notably *besides, indeed,* and *moreover*) usually are. You have to determine whether you wish the reader to make the slight pause after the connective that a comma would call for. In modern writing the comma is missing at such a point more often than it is present.

32C. Semicolon for Clarity

The semicolon instead of the normal comma may be used for clarity even between independent clauses joined by a co-ordinating conjunction if the clauses are long and contain internal punctuation. The semicolon should be used only if its presence is of value to the reader.

Startled by the mysterious noise, which had seemed to come from somewhere inside the vast, lonely house, she hurried into the room where the baby slept, switched on the light, and crept to the side of the crib, which stood in the far corner; but her fears were quieted at the familiar sight of the golden curls and the battered doll clutched in the chubby little hands.

32D. Semicolon Between Co-ordinate Elements Containing Commas

The semicolon is often needed to separate co-ordinate elements that contain commas. To follow the normal practice of using commas to separate such elements may cause confusion.

The subjects which caused me most trouble in my freshman year were chemistry, which most of the other men had studied in high school; mathematics, always a nightmare for me; and, oddly enough, English, in which I had never received a grade lower than B.

> The old lawyer peered severely at her through his dusty spectacles, of the old-fashioned iron-rimmed kind; turned his back, as if oblivious of her presence, to stride abruptly to the window and stand for a full minute staring down into the street; and finally walked with bowed head back to his desk, the ghost of a smile on his usually grim face.

But you should not use the semicolon automatically every time an internal comma appears in one element of a series. Use the semicolon only when confusion may result otherwise. In the following sentences commas serve perfectly well the purpose of separating co-ordinate elements:

> The committee consisted of Frank Jones, Patty Wills, and my brother, who was named chairman.
>
> He said that he had always wanted to attend a reunion dinner, that he still intended to come, in spite of his injury, and that we had better stop for him if we valued our health.

EXERCISE

Copy the following sentences, adding commas and semicolons (or periods) wherever they are needed. Be prepared to defend every mark of punctuation added.

1. The romantic glow that hovers over childhood and youth usually fades in later years it is wisely said that every mature person carries within him a dead poet.
2. The so-called Civic Center contains the art gallery and museum one of the finest in the country a park of nearly three hundred acres beautifully kept and the fashionable apartment houses and hotels most of which have attractive lawns or gardens.
3. We may feel rebellious when the summer sun pours through the open windows and more fortunate mortals bronzed and hearty pack picnic hampers bathing suits sun oil and the baby into the family car and head for the beach but we stick grimly to our tasks.
4. Sugar provides energy and is important to the diet of every child nevertheless it is clear that little Linda is eating more candy than is good for her.
5. My roommate prides himself on reading every novel on the best-seller lists I contend that life is too short for such foolishness.

6. It is years since I have received a letter from Tom Bragg therefore I know almost nothing about his present circumstances.
7. Sports writers seem unable to agree upon the reasons for the poor showing of the team it seems obvious to me however that at least one is the low caliber of the pitching.
8. The giant hawk circled gracefully above the grain fields and the woodland the boy lying on his back beside the brook watched the bird with sleepy eyes.
9. The new janitor was unable to identify him so the professor paid for his absentmindedness by having to trudge home for his office key.
10. Miss Watkins looked wistfully across the roofs of the adjacent buildings where pigeons were making their customary throaty sounds and flapping lazy wings let her eyes rest upon hazy Mount Morrison unbelievably blue in the distance and thought of the vacation just ended and of the weary endless weeks that must drag by before the next one came.

33. PERIOD

The principal uses of the period are to mark the end of a sentence that is not an exclamation or a question and to indicate an abbreviation. It has also two minor uses.

33A. Period at End of Sentence

The period at the end of a declarative or imperative sentence is perhaps the most elementary and fundamental mark of punctuation.

33B. Period After Abbreviations

The period is used to indicate an abbreviation: Mr., Mrs., Dr., A.B., p.m., Pa., Vt., Ave., St., etc., e.g., bldg., oz., viz.

33C. Periods Indicating Omissions

Three spaced periods (an ellipsis) are used to indicate the omission of words from a quoted passage. If the omitted portion begins at the end of a sentence closing with a period, three spaced periods following the usual closing period are necessary.

> The next great influence into the spirit of the scholar is the mind of the past . . . Books are the best type of the influence of the past, and per-

haps we shall get at the truth . . . by considering their value alone. . . . The theory of books is noble.—EMERSON.

33D. Periods Indicating Break in Thought

Similarly, periods are occasionally used to indicate a break in thought or the abandonment of a topic.

But one thing I want to say . . . Oh, what's the use? As for the future, well . . .

33E. Superfluous Periods

The period should *not* be used after the title *Miss,* after the title of a book or essay, or after the signature of a letter. In modern writing it is not found with such abbreviations as AAA, REA, CIO, Station KDKA.

33F. Period Fault

See Incomplete Sentence, Section 12A.

34. QUESTION MARK

34A. Direct Question

The question mark is used to indicate a direct question.

Where are you?
He said, "Where are you going?"

An indirect question should not be followed by a question mark.

He asked where I was going.

34B. Question Mark Within Sentence

The question mark may be used within the sentence as shown in the following examples:

It was not until two o'clock—or was it almost three?—that I heard from him.

Have you no regard for the feelings of your parents? the disappointment of your fellow-students? the contempt of the very people who will profit by your betrayal?

34C. Question Mark in Parentheses

The question mark may be used within parentheses to indicate uncertainty.

Origen (185?–254?) was an early Christian writer and teacher.
At the time of Bede's birth in 673(?) Northumbria was the literary center of Western Europe.

34D. Superfluous Question Mark

In a sentence in which a question introduces a quoted question, only one question mark is used, not two.

Did she not say, "Will you let me know promptly?"

34E. Double Punctuation

No period or comma should be used along with a question mark.

"Who is it?" he whispered. "It's Ned," I replied.
He cried, "Won't you hurry?" [Incorrect: He cried, "Won't you hurry?".]

34F. Special Use of Period for Question Mark

In modern writing there is a tendency to use the period instead of the question mark after some sentences that are questions only in form.

Will you please let me have a reply at your very earliest convenience.

35. EXCLAMATION POINT

The exclamation point is used to express astonishment, elation, or other strong emotion, and to give emphasis.

Alas! What an ending!
Aha! That settles it!
Get out of here!
No, Sir! no, Sir! There will be no secession! Gentlemen are not serious when they talk of secession.—DANIEL WEBSTER.

Whether the exclamation point should be used with a particular interjection depends upon the degree of emphasis desired.

> Oh! You startled me.
> Oh, let it go.

No period or comma should be used along with an exclamation point.

> "Stand where you are!" cried the sentry.
> "It's only I, please," ventured the child.
> But again came a stern command, "Halt!"

Overuse of the exclamation point weakens, not strengthens, the style. This most emphatic mark of punctuation should be used only when emphasis is justified by the situation.

36. APOSTROPHE

The apostrophe is used to indicate the possessive case of nouns and indefinite pronouns, to indicate omissions, and to form the plural of certain classes of words.

36A. Possessives

If the word (singular or plural) does not end in *s*, the apostrophe and *s* are added.

> the teacher's desk
> the lawyer's advice
> Pope's poetry
> anyone's guess
> somebody's mistake
> women's rights
> children's books

If the singular ends in *s* or another sibilant (an *s* sound), the apostrophe and *s* are usually added; but if the second *s* causes difficulty of pronunciation, the apostrophe alone may be added. Proper names of two syllables or more ending in a sibilant (except *-ce*) add the apostrophe alone if the second *s* causes difficulty.

> Ross's bicycle
> Knox's hat
> Thomas's umbrella
> Horace's works
> Jesus' teachings
> Croesus' millions

If the plural ends in *s*, the apostrophe alone is added.

the Johnsons' automobile
the girls' dresses
[In names of organizations the apostrophe is frequently omitted: Teachers Insurance and Annuity Association; Veterans Administration.]

In nouns of joint possession the last noun alone takes the possessive form, but if individual possession is intended each noun takes the possessive form.

Sears and Roebuck's downtown store
Washington and Jefferson's football schedule
Henry and Susan's uncle [but: Henry's and Susan's injuries were quite different.]

In compounds the last word alone takes the possessive form.

son-in-law's request
William the Conqueror's victory

But when the possessive form of a compound is awkward, substitution of an *of*-phrase is advisable.

the house of the president of the college [not: the president of the college's house]

Normally an *of*-phrase is used with inanimate objects.

the owner of the store [not: the store's owner]

But common usage permits certain exceptions, particularly idiomatic phrases denoting time or measure (*an hour's wait, a week's vacation, a stone's throw*) or personification (*the law's delay, death's summons, for mercy's sake*).

CAUTION: The apostrophe is never used with the pronouns *his, hers, its, ours, yours, theirs, whose.*

This book is hers.
My father is taller than yours.
The dog wagging its tail is ours.
Whose coat is that?

Students frequently confuse the possessive *its* (*The day has reached its end*) with the contraction *it's* meaning *it is* (*It's a fine day*) or *it has* (*It's been a fine day*). This error is inexcusable, for a moment's thought will invariably make it impossible.

> It's a pity you did not arrive earlier. [Can *it is* be substituted for *it's*? Yes. Therefore the word is a contraction and requires an apostrophe.]
> The dog was glad to see its master. [Can *it is* or *it has* be substituted for *its*? Obviously not. Therefore the word is a pronoun and requires no apostrophe.]

A similar test will infallibly distinguish the pronoun *whose* (*Whose child is lost?*) from the contraction *who's* meaning *who is* (*Who's going to win?*).

36B. Omissions

The apostrophe is used to indicate the omission of letters or figures. It must be placed precisely at the point where the omission occurs.

can't	let's [let us]
doesn't	o'clock [of the clock]
haven't	spirit of '76
you're [you are]	class of '54

36C. Plural of Certain Classes of Words

For clarity, the apostrophe and *s* are used to form the plural of letters of the alphabet, figures, and words *considered as words.*

His record showed nothing but *A's.*
He seldom dots his *i's.*
Her *9's* are indistinguishable from her *7's.*
Too many *and's* suggest immaturity of style.
His speech was punctuated by irritating *uh's* and *well's.*

EXERCISES

A. Form the possessive of each of the following:

1. lady	6. John Adams	11. Mr. Williams
2. students	7. brother-in-law	12. ladies
3. Lois	8. Aristophanes	13. princess
4. deputy	9. Thomas	14. Alexander the Great
5. Moses	10. the Browns	15. cousins

B. Use apostrophes correctly in the following sentences:

1. Mr. Browns house was ruined by the flood, and all the Davidsons cattle were drowned.
2. Anyone whose minds already made up isnt going to be influenced by what Im about to say.
3. His *wells* are always pronounced *wull*, and his *fors* sound more like *fur*.
4. Mrs. Prentice never tires of talking about her son-in-laws peculiarities.
5. My two weeks vacation tired me more than a months hard work at the office.
6. If its true that youre dissatisfied with your present position, whose fault is it but yours?
7. The Siwash students who wear *Ss* on their sweaters seldom have *As* on their grade sheets.
8. At two oclock members of the Class of 37 will play a game of softball against this years seniors.
9. Talk as you will about the floods of 36, you cant persuade me that those weve had this year werent just as bad.
10. Its all well and good for the experts to talk about seeing that the baby gets its rest, but theyd better add a chapter of advice for sleepless parents.

37. COLON

The colon is used almost exclusively to introduce something that follows. Thus it differs fundamentally from the period and the semicolon. The similarity of names between colon and semicolon is misleading, for their functions are quite different.

37A. Colon After Formal Introductory Statement

The colon is used after a formal introductory statement which indicates that something is to follow. The dash may be used for the same purpose. In general, the colon is the more formal mark of punctuation and is almost invariably used when that which follows is a complete sentence or series of sentences.

The word following a colon usually begins with a small letter except when it is the first word of a quoted sentence or the first word in a series of sentences.

The governor acts always with a single goal in mind: the presidency. [Dash equally appropriate.]
She came to hate the endless chores that swallowed her time: washing dishes, making beds, scrubbing floors. [Dash equally appropriate.]
Four of our first five presidents were Virginians: Washington, Jefferson, Madison, Monroe. [Dash could be used, but colon is preferable.]
I have only this to say: whatever happens, I shall do my best.
He began as follows: "It is my high honor to welcome you to these Memorial Day exercises."

Use of the colon after *were* in the following sentence would be incorrect: "His reasons for changing his mind were the lateness of the hour, the condition of his clothes, and his uncertainty as to his reception." The colon is used only when the introductory words constitute a complete statement.

My favorite novelists are Meredith, Lawrence, Hemingway, and Faulkner.
These are my favorite novelists: Meredith, Lawrence, Hemingway, Faulkner.

37B. Colon Between Independent Clauses

The colon may be used to separate two independent clauses when the second clause is a commentary upon or explanation of the first.

His books about life on the prairies are anything but authentic: he has never been west of Pittsburgh.
Philip is not the type of boy who likes to pose as a sophisticate or a man of mystery: he is always just plain Philip.

37C. Colon Before Long Quotations

The colon rather than the comma is used between an introductory statement and a *long* quotation. There is a middle ground where the choice between colon and comma is up to the writer.

37D. Colon After Formal Salutation

The colon is used after the formal salutation of a letter. The comma may be used for this purpose in informal correspondence, but the colon is never incorrect.

37E. Special Uses of Colon

The colon is used between figures indicating hour and minute or biblical chapter and verse, and between the title and subtitle of a book.

> 11:30 A.M.
> John 3:16
> *Campus Echoes: An Anthology of College Verse*

38. DASH

The most important function of the dash is to indicate a sudden break or shift in thought. It may also be used for other purposes where a choice lies between dash and comma, or dash and colon, or dash and mark of parenthesis. Overuse of the dash weakens a style rather than strengthens it.

38A. Dash Indicating Break or Shift in Thought

The dash is used to indicate a sudden break or shift in thought.

> The next step is to—Good gracious! What was that?
> I assure you that I—but you wouldn't understand.
> Very well, if that's the way you want it—
> Sleep, sleep, sleep—that's all you seem to do.
> Chicken, ham, eggs, fruit, vegetables—there was no lack of food.

38B. Dash After Formal Introductory Statement

The dash may be used instead of the colon after a formal introductory statement which indicates that something is to follow.

> He has only one interest—music.
> I miss the sounds of the city—the roar of the elevated, the squeal of tires, the shouts of newsboys.

38C. Dashes with Parenthetical Elements

Dashes may be used instead of commas or parentheses to set off parenthetical elements requiring emphatic punctuation.

> The subjects that I liked—chemistry, physics, and mathematics—were the ones on which I worked hardest. [Commas round the paren-

thetical phrase would be confusing because of the other commas present. Parentheses would be too formal and heavy.]

You said—can you deny it?—that I was entirely to blame.

There was my good friend Bob—ah, the irony of it!—dancing with the girl to whom I planned to propose.

In this function dashes are like parentheses, but they are more informal and dramatic, and hence less appropriate in formal contexts.

39. PARENTHESES

Parentheses are used to set off interrupting or supplementary material. When used for this purpose they of course indicate a sharper interruption than that indicated by two commas. Parentheses also serve to enclose figures or letters of the alphabet used to enumerate items in a list.

The abandoned cemetery (melancholy and yet, it seemed to me, lovely in its loneliness) commanded a superb view of the distant mountains.

Though the author's fondness for coincidence is found throughout the novel (see especially Chapter LV), the plot is more firmly constructed than usual.

I prefer the gray suit because (1) it is made of material that will not wrinkle easily and (2) it is conservative in color and pattern.

In view of (*a*) the superiority of the North in industrial capacity, (*b*) the tight blockade of Southern ports, and (*c*) political quarrels and interference that reduced military effectiveness, the success of the South in continuing resistance for four years was astonishing.

A comma is never used before the first parenthesis. No mark of punctuation coming at the end of a parenthetical passage should be enclosed within the final parenthesis unless it belongs to the parenthetical passage.

Parentheses should not be used to indicate deletions. Passages to be deleted should be firmly crossed out.

40. BRACKETS

Brackets are used to enclose words interpolated by the writer in a quoted passage.

> "Our earliest information concerning this territory [the Netherlands] is derived from the Romans."—MOTLEY, *The Dutch Republic*.
>
> "The first attempt to wrest this territory from the French [the expedition led by Braddock in 1755] ended in humiliating failure."
>
> "My esteemed colleague [Senator Cook] has misinterpreted my remarks."

The insertion of the Latin word *sic* (meaning *thus*) in brackets after an error in a quoted passage indicates that the error occurs in the original.

> "However disagreable [*sic*] this solution may be, it is our only hope."

In bibliographical information brackets have the special use of indicating the date of publication of a book that has no date on the title page.

> A. F. Sieveking, *Gardens Ancient and Modern*, London [1899], p. 114.

Brackets may also be used, as in this handbook, to enclose editorial comment.

EXERCISE

Use colons, dashes, parentheses, brackets, and other marks of punctuation correctly in the following sentences.

1. In two respects our vacation was a disappointment the weather was too cool to permit swimming and our cousins from Illinois were unable to join us.
2. I really should not touch another waffle but of course if you insist.
3. The last time that I flew did you know that I have a pilot's license I had an alarming experience.
4. Three factions appeared moderates like my father radicals led by Homer Wilkinson and rigid conservatives pledged to oppose the legislation to the end.
5. The passage alluded to is as follows "Disputes on any points of issue on division of profits for example shall be setled *sic* by arbitration as provided hereafter."
6. Though sparsely populated Arizona is exceeded in size by only three states Texas California and New Mexico.
7. Do not forget what Macaulay said of Boswell as a biographer "He has outdistanced *all his competitors* the italics are mine so decidedly that it is not worth while to place them."

8. The unfortunate orator asserted that the retiring president had served for seven years actually it had been seventeen years and that he was an authority in the field of astronomy he meant agronomy.
9. The myriads of annoying insects the black flies were worst of all made us think longingly of the place we had been so eager to leave a week earlier home.
10. Choosing a mate is one of the most important acts in a person's career it may mean the difference between happiness and misery.

41. QUOTATION MARKS

The principal use of quotation marks is to set off direct quotations. Quotation marks are used also with certain titles and to set off words used in a special sense.

41A. Direct Quotations

Direct quotations are set off by double quotation marks. A quotation within a quotation is set off by single marks; one within that, by double marks again.

It was Shakespeare who wrote, "All that glisters is not gold."

"Endless drill in fundamentals," the coach began, "is the secret of success in football."

"It is clear," said the teacher, "that 'Fourscore and seven years ago' is a more effective opening phrase than 'Eighty-seven years ago.' "

"Our history professor," wrote Mary to her mother, "remarked brightly as he returned our test papers, 'Now you know what Tom Paine meant when he said, "These are the times that try men's souls." ' "

If a quoted passage consists of two or more sentences, quotation marks are used only at the beginning and the end of the passage, not round each sentence.

"The perfect historian," wrote Macaulay, "is he in whose work the character and spirit of an age is exhibited in miniature. He relates no fact, he attributes no expression to his characters which is not authenticated by sufficient testimony. But, by judicious selection, rejection, and arrangement, he gives to truth those attractions which have been usurped by fiction."

Quotation marks are not used to set off indirect quotations.

Fred asked why we had not come earlier.

The guide told us that the museum was about to close.

41B. Punctuation at End of Quotation

At the end of a quotation, a period or comma is always placed inside the quotation marks, but a semicolon or colon is always placed outside. A question mark or exclamation point is placed inside the quotation marks if it applies to the quotation only, outside if it applies to the whole sentence.

> "Reading," said Bacon, "maketh a full man."
>
> General Braddock muttered after his defeat, "We shall better know how to deal with them another time"; he did not know that he was not to have a second chance.
>
> There are three leading candidates for the title of "most popular man in the class": Liggett, Simms, and Watson.
>
> The sentry shouted, "Halt!"
>
> The sentry shouted, "Who is there?"
>
> I was astonished to hear the little slip of a girl tell her friend that the gigantic wrestler was "cute"!
>
> Did you hear him say, "I won't do it"?

41C. Quotation Marks in Dialogue

In the reporting of dialogue, each change of speaker is marked by the beginning of a new paragraph.

> "Daddy," Julie pleaded. "Daddy, listen to me."
>
> "Don't bother me now, honey."
>
> "But Daddy," wailed the child. "It's awful important. Won't you please listen?"
>
> "Very well. What is it?"
>
> Julie's face was solemn. "It's Dinah," she announced. "She's had puppies. Six of them. And I want to keep them all."

41D. Quotations of More than One Paragraph

If a quoted passage consists of two or more paragraphs, quotation marks are used at the beginning of each paragraph but at the end of only the final paragraph.

41E. Quotation Marks with Titles

Though there is strong preference for the use of italics to indicate titles of books and periodicals (see Section 42A), quotation marks are used with the titles of chapters, articles, and other such subdivisions.

> The first chapter of Harold Nicolson's book on Tennyson is appropriately entitled "The Tennyson Legend."
>
> An interesting pictorial essay called "The American Revolution" appeared in the issue of *Life* for July 3, 1950.
>
> My favorite Masefield poem is "Sea-Fever," in the volume *Salt-Water Ballads*.

In current practice, however, even such titles as these are likely to be italicized instead of quoted except when they appear, as above, in close association with the larger work of which they form a part.

41F. Special Use of Quotation Marks

Quotation marks may be used sparingly to set off words used in a special sense.

> The chairman explained that His Excellency could not be present for certain "good" reasons; what the "real" reasons were the presiding officer said he would leave us to conjecture.—JAMES HARVEY ROBINSON, *The Mind in the Making*.

41G. Faulty Use of Quotation Marks

Quotation marks should not be used with titles of themes, to give emphasis, to indicate a humorous intention, or to apologize for slang.

EXERCISE

Insert quotation marks and indicate paragraph divisions in the following passages:

1. Mr. Gore was waiting for her at the apartment when she let herself in at the kitchen entrance. Well, Mary, he said. How are you? Fine, fine, said Mary. And how is yourself and the family? All blooming, he said. Sorry to rout you out like this. I'd no time to telegraph, even, till I arrived. Aah, she said, that's all right. That's all right. Will you have some tea now? It's rather late, he said, looking at his watch. It'll do you good, she said. Well—it would. If it's not too much bother? Not a bit of bother in the world, said Mary.—CHRISTOPHER LAFARGE, "Mary Mulcahy."

2. Them stairs, continued Mrs. Brady darkly, with my bad heart, will be the death of me. Whew! Well, dearie! What's the news? You got a paper, Miss Levin languidly reminded her. Yeah! agreed Mrs. Brady with sudden vehemence. I got a paper! She slapped it upon the counter. An' a lot of time I'll get to *read* my paper, won't I now? On a Saturday night! She moaned. Other nights is bad enough, dear knows—but *Saturday* nights! How I dread 'em! Every Saturday night I say to my daughter, I say, Geraldine, I can't, I say, I can't go through it again, an' that's all there is to it, I say. I'll *quit,* I say. An' I *will,* too! added Mrs. Brady firmly, if indefinitely. Miss Levin, in defense of Saturday nights, mumbled some vague something about tips. Tips! Mrs. Brady hissed it. She almost spat it. Plainly money was nothing, nothing at all, to this lady. I just wish, said Mrs. Brady and glared at Miss Levin, I just wish you had to spend one Saturday night, just one, in that dressing room!—KATHARINE BRUSH, "Night Club."

42. ITALICS

Italics are used to indicate titles and for other special purposes. In manuscript or typewritten material, words to be italicized are underlined.

42A. Italics for Titles

Titles of books, periodicals, pamphlets, plays, long poems, musical compositions, and all other publications issued separately are italicized. An initial *a, an,* or *the* is capitalized and italicized only if it is part of the title; ordinarily *the* is not considered part of the title of a magazine or newspaper.

> The author of *A Bell for Adano* is John Hersey.
>
> We subscribe to the *New York Times*, the *Pittsburgh Post-Gazette*, the *Atlantic Monthly, Coronet,* and *Life*. [Some writers prefer not to italicize the name of the city in the titles of newspapers: the New York *Times*.]

But the titles of books of the Bible and the Bible itself and other sacred works are not italicized.

The use of quotation marks to indicate titles is normally limited to titles of subdivisions (chapters, articles) of a separate publication and to titles of short stories and short poems. In current practice, however, even such titles are likely to be italicized instead of quoted except when they appear in close connection with the larger work of which they form a part. See Section 41E.

Names of ships and aircraft (for example, the *Queen Mary*) and titles of works of art (for example, Rembrandt's *Night Watch*) are sometimes italicized, but current usage is divided on this point. In informal writing, capitals alone are used.

42B. Italics for Foreign Words and Phrases

Foreign words and phrases not yet anglicized are written in italics. The process whereby such expressions become accepted as normal English is a gradual one, and whenever the student is in doubt he should consult a good dictionary. Examples of expressions usually written in italics are: *bon vivant, enfant terrible, faux pas, hors de combat, in medias res, nouveau riche, raison d'être, savoir vivre, sine qua non, Weltschmerz.* Examples of expressions of foreign origin that have become anglicized are: agenda, à la carte, à la mode, ante bellum, bon mot, café, chassis, coup d'état, coupé, entrepreneur, hors d'oeuvre, laissez faire, milieu, sauté, quasi, savant, status quo. The following Latin words and abbreviations are italicized: *ca., circa, et al., ibid., idem, infra, loc. cit., op. cit., passim, sic, supra, vide.* (See also Section 86E.)

42C. Italics for Emphasis

Italics are used to give emphasis to words or phrases that require it but should be used sparingly for this purpose. The more frequently they occur, the less emphasis they supply.

42D. Special Uses of Italics

Words, letters, and figures used as in the following sentences are italicized:

> No one should have difficulty distinguishing between *its* and *it's*.
> It is wrong to say that one should never begin a sentence with *and*.
> The *t* in *listen* is silent.
> The letter *e* is the most frequently used letter in the alphabet.
> This student's *7* is indistinguishable from his *9*.

But quotation marks are used to enclose a quoted word that is part of the context.

> To Sally, everything is "nice" that is not definitely distasteful.
> Many small children say "wa-wa" for "water."

43. HYPHEN

The hyphen is used to hold together the elements of certain compound words and to indicate the division of words into syllables (syllabication).

43A. Compounds

It is impossible to formulate a rule making clear which compounds should be written as separate words, which should be written as solid words, and which should contain hyphens. Many times the only safe guide is an unabridged dictionary, and occasionally even the compilers of dictionaries disagree. There is a tendency away from hyphenation, but hyphens are regularly used in the following classes of compounds:

(1) Compound modifiers composed of two or more words temporarily joined to form a single adjective used before a noun.

an eight-cylinder motor
a tear-stained face
a well-written theme
the sixteenth-century drama
a matter-of-fact tone
a chip-on-the-shoulder attitude

But a compound modifier consisting of an adverb in *-ly* and a following adjective or participle is usually not hyphenated.

a highly effective melodrama
a widely known speaker

(2) Compounds with the prefix *self-,* and compounds in which such prefixes as *anti-, ex-, post-, pre-, pro-,* and *vice-* are joined with proper adjectives and with certain other words.

self-important
self-reliance
anti-American
ex-husband
pre-Christian
vice-president

(3) Numbers from twenty-one (twenty-first) to ninety-nine (ninety-ninth).

(4) Fractional numbers, spelled out, unless numerator or denominator already contains a hyphen.

three-fourths
but
twenty-one hundredths

Some writers, however, prefer not to use hyphens in fractional numbers.

(5) Compounds in which it is necessary to separate a double vowel.

re-emphasis
co-operate
extra-academic
pre-existing

(6) Compounds which without the hyphen might be misunderstood.

re-cover (not "recover")
re-creation (not "recreation")

(7) Compounds describing family relationships.

father-in-law
daughter-in-law

43B. Syllabication

Hyphens are used to divide words into syllables for purposes of pronunciation or spelling (as in a dictionary) and to carry over part of a word from the end of a line to the beginning of the next line. Though the proper point at which to divide a word is often a matter of common sense, troublesome questions of division are best answered by reference to a dictionary. The rules that follow, though they do not cover every instance, are helpful.

(1) Words of one syllable should never be divided.

through
wealth
strength
strained

(2) A single letter at the beginning or end of a word should never be allowed to stand by itself.

WRONG: e-vent	man-y
a-gainst	ever-y

(3) Letters that form a single sound should never be divided (for example, *ai* as in *plain, ea* as in *mean, oi* as in *boil, eau* as in *trousseau, ph* as in *graphite, gh* as in *rough, th* as in *theory, gn* as in *sign, ng* as in *sing, sc* as in *science, sch* as in *school*).

(4) If pronunciation permits, a logical point for division is that at which a prefix or suffix joins the root syllable.

eat-able	be-fore
trans-act	en-act
read-er	anti-dote
sleep-ing	de-liver
wasp-ish	kind-ness

(5) A word already hyphenated because it is a compound (pre-Elizabethan, pro-British) should never be further divided by a second hyphen.

44. CAPITALS

The correct use of capitals is important, but in most modern writing capitalization is kept to a minimum. It is advisable to use capitals only when they are specifically called for by one of the conventions described below.

44A. Capital at Beginning of Sentence

The first word of a sentence (or a group of words used as a sentence) is capitalized.

> The meeting yesterday ended in confusion.
> Never again.

Though the first word of a quoted sentence should of course begin with a capital, no capital should be used when the quoted passage simply completes a sentence following an interruption like *he said* or when the quoted passage is simply incorporated as an element in a sentence.

"I alone am guilty," he said. "You are innocent."
"I alone," he said, "am guilty."
It was Macbeth who spoke of life as "a tale told by an idiot."

44B. Capital at Beginning of Line of Poetry

The first word in a line of poetry is capitalized, except in the poetry of some modern writers who choose to disregard capitals and punctuation marks.

The time draws near the birth of Christ:
  The moon is hid, the night is still;
  A single church below the hill
Is pealing, folded in the mist.

—TENNYSON

44C. Capitalization of Proper Nouns and Adjectives

Proper nouns, proper adjectives, and their abbreviations are capitalized. Common nouns are capitalized only if they stand for a name or are part of a name.

(1) Names of persons, places, nationalities:

William Shakespeare
Shakespearean
Philadelphia
Philadelphian
England
English
Englishman
New Mexico
Lake Ontario
Cape Breton

(2) Names of organizations and of historical events, epochs, or documents:

Sons of the American Revolution
the Westinghouse Airbrake Company
the Methodist Church
Roman Catholic
the Republican Party
World War II
the Renaissance
the Declaration of Independence

(3) Days of the week, holidays, months:

Tuesday | Easter | November

(4) Names of God and sacred personages, events, and writings, and pronouns referring to God:

the Son of God
the Savior, the Saviour
the Holy Trinity
the New Testament
Exodus
the Psalms
the Virgin
Easter
the Bible
Chronicles
the Apocrypha
in His name

(5) Titles of books, magazines, newspapers, articles, chapters, poems, themes. The first word and all other words except articles (*a, an, the*) and short prepositions and conjunctions are capitalized.

The Mill on the Floss
Travels with a Donkey
The Ring and the Book
Journal of Modern History

(6) Common nouns indicating relationship when used as a substitute for a name or as part of a name:

I went with Dad.
You ask Mother this time.
Uncle Jack.
Cousin Mary

But note the following:

This is my mother. | He is my uncle.

(7) Common nouns forming part of a specific name:

Harvard University [but: He is a graduate of a university.]
Blair High School [but: He studied hard in high school.]
Every student must take Mathematics 1. [but: He likes mathematics.]
This is Professor Jackson. [but: His father is a professor.]
the Missouri River [but: The river is deep.]
112 Maple Street [but: The street is lined with maples.]
the Bureau of Internal Revenue
the Department of Psychology
a member of Congress
the Senate of the United States

(8) *North, south, east, west,* and their derivatives are capitalized only when they designate a specific geographical region. Names of the seasons are not capitalized.

The South was victorious at Bull Run.
He comes from the East.
Chicago is the metropolis of the Middle West.
The population of the Southwest is growing rapidly.
His home is south of Boston.
The wind is blowing from the west.
He will enter college in the fall.
Last spring he was sent to California.

44D. Capitalization of *I* and O

The pronoun *I* and the interjection *O* are capitalized, but not the interjection *oh* except, of course, when it comes at the beginning of a sentence.

44E. Capital After Colon

Usually the word following a colon is capitalized only when it is the first word of a quoted sentence or the first word in a series of sentences.

EXERCISE

Use capitals properly in the following passages. Do not use capitals unnecessarily.

1. Our congress in washington, d. c., is composed of the senate and the house of representatives, whereas the british parliament is composed of a house of lords and a house of commons.
2. Last friday the sheriff of our county was brought to trial for perjury before a visiting judge, judge charles thomlinson, of nearby drake county.
3. The camp where the johnson children spent most of july and august is called camp shawnee. Located on a small river that empties into lake michigan just south of the canadian border, it is operated by the fortune manufacturing company for the families of its employees.
4. My friend bob, the son of a professor at one of the largest universities in the south, is majoring in mathematics and minoring in

chemistry. He was the only student to whom old professor scanlon gave a decent grade in chemistry 1 last year. At present he is living at 116 east brady street, out beyond grandview cemetery, but he will join me in holbrook hall on the campus after christmas.

5. Because my cousin, henry watson, was too sickly to attend grade school and high school regularly, he was educated largely at home by his father and mother. Before he was eight, aunt ellen had taught him long passages of the bible by heart, especially some of the psalms and whole chapters of the new testament, and he was reading *macbeth* and *the cloister and the hearth* while I was racing through *the rover boys in the rockies.* Even now he can still recite tennyson's "the charge of the light brigade" and page after page of milton's *paradise lost.*

6. After graduation from high school in merion, west virginia, last june, I spent a month at my uncle's ranch in the southwest, where I enjoyed myself so much that I decided to give up going to college. But when uncle jack reported my decision to mother, who is a graduate of wellesley college, she wrote me a long letter in which the last sentence read, "this is one matter, son, in which dad and I want you to follow our advice." So my address in september will be either hanover, new hampshire, or cambridge, massachusetts.

45. ABBREVIATIONS

Except in the most informal writing or in technical writing, abbreviations should be kept to a minimum. The brief list below includes practically all the abbreviations that a student may use without hesitation.

a) The titles *Mr., Mrs., Messrs., Dr.,* and *St.* (Saint) before proper names (Dr. Smith) but not when used alone (The doctor is not in). *Hon.* and *Rev.* are permissible only when followed by the given name or initials, or by *Mr.* in place of the given name or initials, in addition to the surname (Hon. James Hartley, Rev. Mr. Rider). In formal announcements and invitations, *Honorable* and *Reverend* should be spelled out and preceded by *the.*

b) Titles following proper names: Esq., Sr., Jr., M.D., Ph.D., Bart. (Baronet).

c) The conventional abbreviations: A.D. 1954, 75 B.C. (note arrangement), a.m. (or A.M.), p.m. (or P.M.).

For the use of special abbreviations in footnotes, see Section 86E.

46. NUMBERS

46A. Numbers as Words or Figures

Numbers that can be expressed in one or two words are usually written out except in tables and citations:

two hundred dollars
twenty-eight per cent
eighteen years old
three million people

Otherwise figures should be used:

His savings amounted to $319.56.
The population of the county seat is 13,416.
Of the total income, 28.9 per cent went for taxes.

46B. Figures in Dates, Hours, Etc.

Figures are always used for dates (except in formal social correspondence), hours (when followed by a.m. or p.m.), street numbers, telephone numbers, and page references.

June 3, 1953
7:15 p.m. (but seven o'clock)
214 Brook Street
MUseum 1-2367
pages 415–509

46C. Numbers at Beginning of Sentences

Numbers at the beginning of a sentence should be written out. If the writer prefers, he may recast the sentence and use figures.

Three hundred and ninety-seven citizens attended the meeting.
Attendance at the meeting was 397.

Because it is equally awkward to put the figure for a year at the beginning of a sentence and to write the number out, it is advisable to begin the sentence in a different fashion:

The year 1588 marked the destruction of the Spanish Armada.

46D. Numbers in Parentheses

Numbers that are written out are repeated in parentheses in only the most formal legal or business writing.

Please send me seven hundred (700) copies.

46E. Roman Numerals

Roman numerals are often used to number sections of an outline or long paper, chapters of a book, and the acts of a play. They are usually used for volume number of journal publications in bibliographies and footnotes. Lower-case Roman numerals are often used to number scenes of a play and the introductory pages of a book.

EXERCISES

Anyone interested in learning the principles and conventions of punctuation would do well to practice by studying passages from reputable contemporary authors, noting the reason for every mark of punctuation. The illustrative paragraphs in Chapter 6 will prove useful for this purpose.

An even more instructive exercise is to punctuate a passage from which all punctuation marks have been removed, and then if possible compare one's work with the original.

The first two passages that follow have been taken from the writings of well-known authors; the third has been specially prepared in order that a larger-than-normal number of punctuation problems might be worked into relatively small space. Copy each passage, supplying punctuation and effecting proper changes in mechanics. But make only those corrections that seem to you called for by the principles and conventions set forth in this book. The third passage requires division into paragraphs.

1. But it is at night and after dinner that the best hour comes there are no such pipes to be smoked as those that follow a good days march the flavor of the tobacco is a thing to be remembered it is so dry and aromatic so full and so fine if you wind up the evening with grog you will own there was never such grog at every sip a jocund tranquility spreads about your limbs and sits easily in your heart if you read a book and you will never do so save by fits and starts you find the language strangely racy and harmonious

words take a new meaning single sentences possess the ear for half an hour together and the writer endears himself to you at every page by the nicest coincidence of sentiment it seems as if it were a book you had written yourself in a dream to all we have read on such occasions we look back with special favor it was on the 10th of april 1798 says hazlitt with amorous precision that I sat down to a volume of the new heloise at the inn at llangollen over a bottle of sherry and a cold chicken I should wish to quote more for though we are mighty fine fellows nowadays we cannot write like hazlitt and talking of that a volume of hazlitts essays would be a capital pocket book on such a journey so would a volume of heines songs and for tristram shandy I can pledge a fair experience.—R. L. STEVENSON, "Walking Tours."

2. The last time I checked up on the locales of the thirty six radio daytime serials better known as soap operas that are broadcast from new york five days a week to a mass audience of twenty million listeners the score was small towns 24 big cities 12 I say score advisedly for the heavy predominance of small towns in soapland is a contrived and often emphasized victory for good clean little communities over cold cruel metropolitan centers thus daytime radio perpetuates the ancient american myth of the small town idealized in novels comedies and melodramas at the turn of the century and before supported by thornton wilder in our town and undisturbed by the scandalous revelations of such irreverent gossips as sherwood anderson and edgar lee masters soapland shares with the united states at least five actual cities new york chicago boston washington and los angeles but its small towns are as misty and unreal as brigadoon they have such names as hartville dickston simpsonville three oaks great falls beauregard elmwood oakdale rushville center and homeville our gal sunday is set in virginia but no states are mentioned for the towns in the other serials.—JAMES THURBER, "Soapland." [3]

3. The loneliness of strangers in a small town had drawn the two men together the thin stoop shouldered one it had turned out was from mobile alabama his name was henry watkins and he sold leather goods his new acquaintance who was stout and red faced had introduced himself as thurston grady traveling representative of the witherspoon steel and iron company of birmingham they had finished their roast beef and vegetables their pineapple and cheese salad their pie and their strong steaming coffee the dumpy sallow faced waitress her jaws chomping a wad of gum plodded in silence between dining room and kitchen removed the last of the dishes pocketed with a casual thank yuh the coins left for her and disappeared business pretty good in your line asked watkins pushing his chair back and

[3] From an article originally in *The New Yorker*. Copr. 1948 James Thurber.

preparing to make use of a toothpick which he took from his pocket oh just about what youd expect replied the other following suit fair one week and poor the next never really good what about you watkins shaking his head stared moodily at the floor slow very slow he complained the toothpick suspended in pudgy unsteady fingers and not likely to get better before I started this trip last monday the boss had me on the carpet henry he said you havent been worth your keep the last six months whats the matter nobody in the south buying leather goods any more or are you just sleeping too late and taking too many local gals to third rate movies thats all the thanks I get for working day and night one more going over from that guy and Ill he snapped the toothpick with helpless irritation thats always the way it is nodded grady sympathetically if you do well the firm takes it for granted but just slip a little man alive how quickly theyre on your neck well neither of us is going to make many sales in this town commented watkins continuing to stare out into the nearly deserted streets or have any fun for that matter he added thats for sure replied grady they take the sidewalks in sharp at nine p m he laughed feebly at the ancient joke watkins did not bother to reply he stood up yawned scratched himself comfortably and followed by grady sauntered into the lobby where the two men slumped into ancient imitation leather chairs before a large window for a time they leafed indolently through the reading matter that lay on the table between them a newspaper and stray copies of life the saturday evening post and the readers digest soon however they abandoned the effort required by that activity slumped deeper in their chairs and stared vacantly into the street a light rain was falling the fog in the street grew more dense lights winked on one by one a dog trotted round the corner looked expectantly to right and left its ears alert its tail wagging and then turned and trotted off in a business like fashion somewhere a whistle blew sharply and the bored men welcoming any distraction stood up and peered into the dusk waiting soon a siren began to wail and down the street roared a red truck a grinning young giant at the wheel raincoat clad figures clinging to the back and sides people emerged here and there from houses gathering in little knots their collars turned up against the rain a few small boys on bicycles pumping frantically hurried after the truck the sound of the siren diminishing until it faded out entirely well grunted watkins I guess thats as much as we can expect tonight yeah said grady and were lucky at that he yawned prodigiously its not the company buddy he grinned Ive had a hard day and expect a worse one tomorrow think Ill turn in good night then said watkins think Ill hold on a bit longer settling back in his chair he soon was lost in open mouthed sleep his head lolling to one side his dreams peopled by eager customers in a brand new territory where everybody wore out twelve pairs of shoes a year traveled incessantly carrying expensive leather suitcases and wore gloves even at meals.

Chapter 6

THE PARAGRAPH

47. DEFINITION AND SCOPE OF THE PARAGRAPH

The paragraph is a group of related sentences forming a unit of thought. Every piece of prose of any length is made up of a series of paragraphs.

The word "paragraph" is derived from two Greek words, *para,* meaning "beside," and *graphein,* meaning "to write," and it originally meant simply a mark or symbol, ¶, placed in the margin of a page to indicate a subdivision of writing. Gradually the word came to stand for the subdivision itself, and the older use died out though the symbol remains. Today a writer indicates the beginning of a new paragraph by starting on a new line and indenting the first word. Thus not only is the reader notified of a change of subject matter or direction, but also the break in continuity provides momentary rest for eye and mind.

Though the paragraph is a unit of thought, the limits of such a unit may vary widely. A writer may describe in a single paragraph the entire landscape viewed from a hill, or only the view in one direction, or only a certain wood or meadow; he may discuss the entire administration of Franklin D. Roosevelt, or only the struggle against the depression of the thirties, or only a single piece of legislation; he may give in condensed form the principles of the game of football, or confine himself to the dimensions of the field, or explain only the penalty for offside. Though in general it is wise to restrict narrowly the ground to be covered in a single paragraph, unity consists fundamentally in staying within what bounds the writer has set for himself.

The length of paragraphs varies according to circumstances. A writer who has only to make a simple point will write a short paragraph, and a writer who is wrestling with a complex thought will write a longer one. Moreover, the average length varies from one field of writing to another. Paragraphs in newspapers are regularly short, averaging perhaps forty-five or fifty words; the average length in magazines is greater, and in articles and books of a serious nature, much greater. Some beginning students start a new paragraph with every sentence or two; others lump all five or six hundred words of a theme into one unwieldy paragraph. Though these extremes are clearly to be avoided, it is difficult to establish fixed rules. It is safe to say, however, that in student writing the paragraphs should normally run between one and two hundred words, and that except in special circumstances a theme of five hundred words should contain at least two paragraphs and not more than five.

48. PARAGRAPHING OF DIALOGUE

A special convention governs the paragraphing of dialogue: each change of speaker is indicated by a new paragraph, for the clearer understanding of the reader. Explanatory insertions such as "he said" and "she replied" are included in the paragraph with the words of the speaker; longer explanatory passages between speeches may be included with a speech or paragraphed separately, according to the writer's preference. The following passage shows conventional procedure:

> The little boy edged closer to the oddly dressed man seated before the easel. "What are yuh paintin', Mister?" he asked.
>
> The painter sighed, laid down his brush with elaborate care, and turned to look at the freckled face. Then he smiled.
>
> "Well, what does it look like to you?"
>
> The boy hesitated. "Is it the sunset?"
>
> "Right the first time."
>
> "Gosh, it's pretty, isn't it?"
>
> "You mean the sunset?" laughed the painter. "Yes, it's beautiful."
>
> "No, no," stammered the boy. A flush crept over the tanned face. "I meant the picture."

EXERCISE

Copy the following passage, paragraphing it correctly:

"What was that?" snapped Blake. "What's the matter with you?" laughed Potter. "It's only an owl." "Oh. Sorry. It sounded like the wail of a lost soul." Potter eyed his companion curiously. "You're all on edge," he remarked. "What's it to you?" "Nothing. Only, since we're going to be pretty close to each other for a month or so, I thought maybe you'd want to tell me what's bothering you." He paused. "It might make things more pleasant—for both of us." Blake did not answer. The water lapped against the sandy shore, and again the cry of the owl drifted from the forest. Over the curve of the hill stole an edge of the moon. Blake stood up. "Maybe you're right," he muttered. He kept his eyes fixed on the widening strip of moonlight on the lake. "I begin to think that this trip was a mistake from the beginning. But that's hardly your fault." Potter smiled in the darkness but said nothing. "As a matter of fact," the other continued quietly, still not looking toward his companion, "I'm scared to death." "Nonsense! You don't mean that." Blake turned. His face was white. "You'll soon see that I'm telling the truth."

49. UNITY WITHIN THE PARAGRAPH

Achieving unity within the paragraph is largely a matter of common sense. If you keep clearly in mind the limits you have established, and never let your subject matter go beyond them, your paragraph is certain to have basic unity. The writer of the following paragraph failed to observe this simple rule:

My first day at college was a mad whirl. I stood in line for what seemed hours before I could even register. I stood in line again for the privilege of paying my tuition fee for the first semester. I stood in line to buy the books I would need for the courses on my schedule—English, history, math, and the rest. I never shall forget my struggle with that frustrating math. It cast a shadow over my entire freshman year. Some self-confident upperclassmen herded me into another line which I learned too late was to deliver me into the hands of students soliciting—or rather demanding—subscriptions for the college humorous magazine. From that time on I avoided any line I saw forming, only to learn later that I had missed getting my athletic card and a ticket to the freshman dance.

The sentences concerning the writer's difficulties with mathematics form an awkward digression from his topic. His troubles with that study might become the subject of a paragraph in a theme on the highlights of his first year in college, but they have no place in the paragraph describing his first day.

49A. Topic Sentence

In the illustrative paragraph just above, the opening sentence informs the reader of what is to follow. Such a sentence is called a *topic sentence*. The topic sentence is a useful device for both writer and reader: it helps to safeguard the writer against the introduction of irrelevant material, and it fixes the attention of the reader upon the theme of the paragraph. It is employed frequently in writing of all kinds, but is most common in exposition. Usually the topic sentence occurs at the beginning of the paragraph, as in the following examples.

1. Individuality is disappearing more and more. In great plants the machine tools are set by the engineers at the top. The man who guides a traveling crane or who controls the motors of a rolling mill is no more capable of repairing the mechanism in his charge than he is of taking the *Queen Mary* safely across the ocean. He may be astoundingly skilful in his manipulation of levers and switches, but other minds dominate the mechanism—design it, improve it, keep it in repair.—WALDEMAR KAEMPFFERT, *Science Today and Tomorrow.*

2. New York City was the powder keg of the colonies. As the headquarters of the British army in North America, and the central link in the colonial chain, it afforded a strong base from which to divide the colonies and beat down opposition to the Stamp Act with military force. But the British government had made no preparations to utilize the strategic position of the city. The guns of the fort were in disrepair, the carriages rotten; powder was scarce; the fort itself was commanded by neighboring buildings with little cover available for its defenders; and the garrison consisted of only 151 men and officers. Instead of presenting a threat to the Sons of Liberty, the British troops in New York seemed to be at the mercy of the patriots.—JOHN C. MILLER, *Origins of the American Revolution.*

The topic sentence does not necessarily come at the beginning. It may come at the end, as in Paragraph 3, or it may come somewhere within the paragraph, as in Paragraph 4, where the fifth sentence is the topic sentence.

3. You tell me that money cannot buy the things most precious. Your commonplace proves that you have never known the lack of it. When I think of all the sorrow and the barrenness that has been wrought in my life by want of a few more pounds per annum than I was able to earn, I stand aghast at money's significance. What kindly joys have I lost, those simple forms of happiness to which every heart has claim, because of poverty! Meetings with those I loved made impossible year after year, sadness, misunderstanding, nay, cruel alienation, arising from inability to do the things I wished, and which I might have done had a little money helped me; endless instances of homely pleasure and contentment curtailed or forbidden by narrow means. I have lost friends merely through the constraints of my position; friends I might have had have remained strangers to me; solitude of the bitter kind, the solitude which is enforced at times when mind or heart longs for companionship, often cursed my life solely because I was poor. I think it would scarce be an exaggeration to say that there is no moral good which has not to be paid for in coin of the realm.—GEORGE GISSING, *The Private Papers of Henry Ryecroft.*

4. Defoe narrates the day-by-day adventures of a castaway who passes half a lifetime on a desert island. Fielding spins a complicated plot about lusty young Tom Jones, whose difficulties resolve themselves in the final chapters like the parts of a mechanism falling into place. Jane Austen keeps the reader interested in the quiet life of a village where nothing more exciting than a dance or an elopement occurs. James Joyce relates at great length, in a style marked by unusual words and deliberate mystification, the adventures and thoughts of several people in Dublin through a single day. What we call the novel is thus an immensely varied literary form. It may be written by a participant in the story, or by several participants, or by an omniscient author who not only views the actions of the characters but knows their every thought. It may present the adventures of one person or follow the paths, now crossing and now diverging, of half a hundred people. It may preach a moral or merely entertain. It may be as short as *Ethan Frome* or as long as *War and Peace.*

Many well-unified paragraphs do not even contain a topic sentence. In such paragraphs, however, the topic is always clearly implied. Thus in Paragraph 5 the reader can hardly fail to perceive that the writer's topic is the power of habit; in Paragraph 6, the miracle of the machine age.

5. Riderless cavalry horses, at many a battle, have been seen to come together and go through their customary evolutions at the sound of the bugle-call. Most domestic beasts seem machines pure and simple, undoubt-

ingly, unhesitatingly doing from minute to minute the duties they have been taught, and giving no sign that the possibility of an alternative ever suggests itself to their mind. Men grown old in prison have asked to be readmitted after being once set free. In a railroad accident a menagerie-tiger, whose cage had been broken open, is said to have emerged, but presently crept back again, as if too much bewildered by his new responsibilities, so that he was without difficulty secured.—WILLIAM JAMES, *Psychology.*

6. Before the nineteenth century there were no ships in the world much over 2,000 tons burden; now there is nothing wonderful about a 50,000-ton liner. There are people who sneer at this kind of progress as being a progress in "mere size," but that sort of sneering merely marks the intellectual limitations of those who indulge in it. The great ship or the steel-frame building is not, as they imagine, a magnified version of the small ship or building of the past; it is a thing different in kind, more lightly and strongly built, of finer and stronger materials; instead of being a thing of precedent and rule-of-thumb, it is a thing of subtle and intricate calculation. In the old house or ship, matter was dominant—the material and its needs had to be slavishly obeyed; in the new, matter has been captured, changed, coerced. Think of the coal and iron and sand dragged out of the banks and pits, wrenched, wrought, molten, and cast, to be flung at last, a slender, glittering pinnacle of steel and glass, six hundred feet above the crowded city!—H. G. WELLS, *The Outline of History.*

49B. Clinching Sentence

Another step toward unity may be taken by the use of what may be called a *clinching sentence.* Such a sentence, usually coming at the end of the paragraph, reiterates or summarizes the main thought or makes a wider application of it or gives a striking illustration. Thus in Paragraph 7 the writer states in his final sentence that the story of Columbus, just told, is only one example of a type of experience common in history. In Paragraph 8 the final sentence sums up the paradox in the popular notion about Florence Nightingale's career and prepares the reader for the paragraphs that are to follow. In Paragraph 9 the final sentence reiterates the point stated in the first. In Paragraph 10 the final sentence serves the same purpose, with a touch of humor adding to the effect.

7. Probably the most astounding instance of accidental discovery in either ancient or modern history was the finding of the western hemisphere by

Columbus. He sailed away from Spain firm in the faith that by going west he would learn a shorter route to the East Indies; quite unexpectedly he encountered a whole new world. It is noteworthy that he was not aware of the significance of what he had found. Indeed, it has been said that he did not know where, in fact, he was going nor where he was when he arrived nor where he had been after his return, but nevertheless he had had the most extraordinary adventure of all time. He realized that he had had a remarkable experience, and by extending the knowledge of what he had done, he laid a course which others might follow. Such consequences have been common when accident has been favorable to one engaged in a search and the enterprise has proved fruitful.—WALTER B. CANNON, *The Way of an Investigator.*

8. The name of Florence Nightingale lives in the memory of the world by virtue of the lurid and heroic adventure of the Crimea. Had she died—as she nearly did—upon her return to England, her reputation would hardly have been different; her legend would have come down to us almost as we know it today—that gentle vision of female virtue which first took shape before the adoring eyes of the sick soldiers at Scutari. Yet, as a matter of fact, she lived for more than half a century after the Crimean War; and during the greater part of that long period all the energy and all the devotion of her extraordinary nature were working at their highest pitch. What she accomplished in those years of unknown labor could, indeed, hardly have been more glorious than her Crimean triumphs; but it was certainly more important. The true history was far stranger even than the myth. In Miss Nightingale's own eyes the adventure of the Crimea was a mere incident—scarcely more than a useful stepping-stone in her career. It was the fulcrum with which she hoped to move the world; but it was only the fulcrum. For more than a generation she was to sit in secret, working her lever: and her real life began at the very moment when, in the popular imagination, it had ended.—LYTTON STRACHEY, *Eminent Victorians.*

9. Before considering how to educate, it is well to be clear as to the sort of result which we wish to achieve. Dr. Arnold wanted "humbleness of mind," a quality not possessed by Aristotle's "magnanimous man." Nietzsche's ideal is not that of Christianity. No more is Kant's: for while Christ enjoins love, Kant teaches that no action of which love is the motive can be truly virtuous. And even people who agree as to the ingredients of a good character may differ as to their relative importance. One man will emphasize courage, another learning, another kindliness, and another rectitude. One man, like the elder Brutus, will put duty to the State above family affection; another, like Confucius, will put family affection first. All these divergences will produce differences as to education. We must have

some conception of the kind of person we wish to produce, before we can have any definite opinion as to the education which we consider best.—BERTRAND RUSSELL, *Education and the Good Life.*

10. The English have a great passion for doing things privately. "We are the secret people," as G. K. Chesterton sang. We love to get together behind closed doors. Thus is our gambling carried on, thus much of our scholarship, as well as much of our revelry. The novel accepted as most typically English, *Pickwick Papers,* is about a Pickwick Club. Not long ago some clever advertisers invented a fictional body called The Mustard Club, in order to appeal to the British club-spirit for the greater consumption of Mounseer Mustard-seed. The Englishman is not very partial to eating and drinking and celebrating in public places: he loves to join up with a society, take a room, and there unbend. Our democracy has its own exclusiveness. Hence all these proletarian gatherings of Buffaloes, Foresters, Ancient Brythons, and all the rest: hence these banquets at which the chairman wears the oddest insignia of office: hence the middle-class assemblages of people with special ties and slogans. The institution of a club enables you to keep the other fellow out. That is a practice which the British most heartily enjoy. To combine the popping of corks with the throwing of black-balls, what bliss!—IVOR BROWN AND GEORGE FEARON, *This Shakespeare Industry.*

49C. Tone

A subtler but often highly effective means of securing unity is by striking a tone that gives the paragraph emotional consistency apart from logical unity. This device, though it is not one of mechanics, and though it often derives from the writer's mood rather than being consciously adopted, is not beyond the reach of the college student. Paragraph 11 is permeated by a tone of nostalgia, of regret for the passing of childhood and longing for scenes and experiences and sensations that can never be recaptured. You should identify for yourself the tone of each of the other paragraphs that follow.

11. The more the ancient rural life receded into the background of men's lives, the more it roused their feelings of romance. The farm, the village ways, harsh enough in actuality, seemed, to the barefoot boys who had gone to New York or were making their fortunes in State Street, merry and jolly or softly sweet as Goldsmith's scenes of Auburn. They liked to remember their schooldays, the wadded hoods, the knitted caps and mittens,

the snowbound evenings under the lamp, the games, the slates and pencils, rosy apples in the dish, nutting-time, coasting-time. Sawing wood in the frosty air had surely seemed less dull than adding figures. This was the theme of a hundred poems and stories that multiplied with time, as the farm became a universal symbol—the farm, the weather-painted house and barn, the well-sweep, the orchard, the sandy field surrounded by the woods, the small blue lake at the foot of the hill. No New England boy or man could ever forget the country, the cider-making days of old, the heaps of golden apples under the trees, the cider-mill worked by the plodding horse and all agush with autumn juices. The new generation of city-dwellers longed to be reminded of these rural scenes, and the popularity of the "household poets" rose with the exodus from the "household" setting, the homestead and the farm. This was the secret of Whittier's fame. He was the emblem of Thanksgiving, when two or three New Englanders gathered together, or a household of scattered uncles and aunts and cousins, in far New York or on the Western plains. He brought back the painted autumn woodlands, the pumpkin pies of old, the succotash, the doughnuts and the chowder, the wild grapes, the tubs of maple sugar, the school-house, the old-fashioned winter that seemed so different from the modern winter because of the modern devices that had softened its rigors. The pioneers carried Whittier with them, as emigrant Scotsmen carried the poems of Burns. *Snow-Bound* was their image of Pallas, the safeguard of their memories. It was the touchstone of their past.—VAN WYCK BROOKS, *The Flowering of New England.*

12. Sophia went into the room, of which the white blind was drawn. She appreciated Mr. Boldero's consideration in leaving her. She was trembling. But when she saw, in the pale gloom, the face of an aged man peeping out from under a white sheet on a naked mattress, she started back, trembling no more—rather transfixed into an absolute rigidity. That was no conventional, expected shock that she had received. It was a genuine unforeseen shock, the most violent that she had ever had. In her mind she had not pictured Gerald as a very old man. She knew that he was old; she had said to herself that he must be very old, well over seventy. But she had not pictured him. This face on the bed was painfully, pitiably old. A withered face, with the shiny skin all drawn into wrinkles! The stretched skin under the jaw was like the skin of a plucked fowl. The cheek-bones stood up, and below them were deep hollows, almost like egg-cups. A short, scraggy white beard covered the lower part of the face. The hair was scanty, irregular, and quite white; a little white hair grew in the ears. The shut mouth obviously hid toothless gums, for the lips were sucked in. The eyelids were as if pasted down over the eyes, fitting them like kid. All the skin was extremely pallid; it seemed brittle. The body, whose outlines were clear under the

sheet, was very small, thin, shrunk, pitiable as the face. And on the face was a general expression of final fatigue, of tragic and acute exhaustion; such as made Sophia pleased that the fatigue and exhaustion had been assuaged in rest, while all the time she kept thinking to herself horribly: "Oh! how tired he must have been!"—ARNOLD BENNETT, *The Old Wives' Tale.*

13. The patriots proposed to overcome the handicap of high wages and scarcity of labor by putting the "idle and indolent" and women and children to work. Alexander Hamilton, in particular, impatiently awaited the day when thousands of American children would be happily trooping off to the factories. The high birth rate of the colonies offered hope that some day America would be able to compete with Great Britain if children were properly utilized. One colonist deemed it proper that they be employed "from the time they are able to move their hands or feet." High wages were denounced as the bane of the colonies: "It is certain," remarked an American, "that high wages more frequently make labouring people miserable; they too commonly employ their spare time and cash, in debauching their morals and ruining their health." Clearly, to save the American workingman from himself, it was necessary to beat down wages to a salutary level; and many of the advocates of manufacturing were ready to do this service for American labor.—JOHN C. MILLER, *Origins of the American Revolution.*

14. Main Street with its two-story brick shops, its story-and-a-half wooden residences, its muddy expanse from concrete walk to walk, its huddle of Fords and lumber-wagons, was too small to absorb her. The broad, straight, unenticing gashes of the streets let in the grasping prairie on every side. She realized the vastness and the emptiness of the land. The skeleton iron windmill on the farm a few blocks away, at the north end of Main Street, was like the ribs of a dead cow. She thought of the coming of the Northern winter, when the unprotected houses would crouch together in terror of storms galloping out of that wild waste. They were so small and weak, the little brown houses. They were shelters for sparrows, not homes for warm laughing people.—SINCLAIR LEWIS, *Main Street.*

15. All through the ghostly stillness of the land, the train made on forever its tremendous noise, fused of a thousand sounds, and they called back to him forgotten memories: old songs, old faces, old memories, and all strange, wordless, and unspoken things men know and live and feel, and never find a language for—the legend of dark time, the sad brevity of their days, the unknowable but haunting miracle of life itself. He heard again, as he had heard throughout his childhood, the pounding wheel, the tolling bell, the whistle-wail, and he remembered how these sounds, coming to him

from the river's edge in the little town of his boyhood, had always evoked for him their tongueless prophecy of wild and secret joy, their glorious promises of new lands, morning, and a shining city. But now the lonely cry of the great train was speaking to him with an equal strangeness of return. For he was going home again.—THOMAS WOLFE, *You Can't Go Home Again.*

16. This was the end of man, then, end of life, of fury, hope, and passion, glory, all the strange and bitter miracle of chance, of history, fate, and destiny which even a stonecutter's life could include. This was the end, then: —an old man, feeble, foul, complaining and disease-consumed who sat looking from the high porch of a hospital at the city of his youth. This was the sickening and abominable end of flesh, which infected time and all man's living memory of morning, youth, and magic with the death-putrescence of its cancerous taint, and made us doubt that we had ever lived, or had a father, known joy: this was the end, and the end was horrible in ugliness At the end it was not well.—THOMAS WOLFE, *Of Time and the River.*

50. COHERENCE WITHIN THE PARAGRAPH

It is not enough that a paragraph be confined to a single topic; the writer must secure close coherence within the paragraph. The means of doing so vary in importance and are extremely numerous. A few of the most obvious and useful means are set forth below, but with the reminder that the treatment is not exhaustive.

50A. Logical Order

It is clearly desirable to place the component parts of a paragraph in logical order. The simplest example is the order of time, which is followed almost invariably in narrative and is natural in any kind of writing involving successive steps.

Illustrations of the use of such chronological order in pure narrative are unnecessary; the following paragraph shows its use in the presentation of narrative materials with an expository purpose:

17. Pasteur was led by chance to his method of immunization. One day an old and forgotten bacterial culture was being used for inoculating fowls. The fowls became ill but did not die. This happening was illuminative. Possibly by first using cultures that had little virulence and then repeating

the injections with cultures of greater virulence, the animals could be made to develop resistance to infection gradually. His surmise proved correct. By this procedure, as readers of his dramatic biography will remember, he was able to immunize sheep against anthrax and human beings against rabies.—WALTER B. CANNON, *The Way of an Investigator.*

In description, any one of numerous plans may be used, provided logical order is achieved. Thus in Paragraph 18 the writer traces the sunlight as it steals downward; in Paragraph 19 we move upward with the climbers and then look with them successively to the north, west, south, and east; and in Paragraph 20 a homely comparison helps the reader to visualize the terrain of a battlefield.

18. Every Sabbath morning in the summer time, I thrust back the curtain, to watch the sunrise stealing down a steeple which stands opposite my chamber window. First, the weather-cock begins to flash; then, a fainter lustre gives the spire an airy aspect; next, it encroaches on the tower, and causes the index of the dial to glisten like gold as it points to the gilded figure of the hour. Now, the loftiest window gleams, and now the lower. The carved frame-work of the portal is marked strongly out. At length, the morning glory, in its descent from heaven, comes down the stone steps, one by one; and there stands the steeple, glowing with fresh radiance, while the shades of twilight still hide themselves among the nooks of the adjacent buildings. Methinks, though the same sun brightens it every fair morning, yet the steeple has a peculiar robe of brightness for the Sabbath.—NATHANIEL HAWTHORNE, *Twice-Told Tales.*

19. The stairs grew more narrow and musty as they went higher; but all the way at intervals there were deep slits in the walls, framing thin pictures of the outspread country below the tower. Still up they went past the bell-ropes, past the great bells themselves that hung like a cluster of mighty fruit, until finally they came out through a small turret to meet the March sky. The spire, that rose as high again as they had already come, occupied nearly all the space and left only a yard of leaded roof on which to walk; but even so, up here where the breeze blew strongly, they seemed to stand in the very course of the clouds with the world at their feet. Northward they looked across the brown mill-stream; across Guy's green orchard; across the flashing tributary beyond the meadows, to where the Shipcot road climbed the side of the wold. Westward they looked to Plasher's Mead and Miss Peasey flapping a tablecloth; to Guy's mazy garden and the gray wall under the limes; and farther to the tree-tops of Wychford Abbey; to the

twining waters of the valley and the rounded hills. Southward they looked to Wychford town in tier on tier of shining roofs; and above the translucent smoke to where the telegraph-poles of the long highway went rocketing into Gloucestershire. And lastly eastward they looked through a flight of snowy pigeons to the Rectory asleep in gardens that already were painted with the simple flowers of spring.—COMPTON MACKENZIE, *Guy and Pauline.*

20. Soon after this message was sent by Major Walter H. Taylor, General Longstreet rode up. General Lee pointed out to him the enemy's position, and while he was engaged with other military duties, Longstreet made a careful survey of the front with his field-glasses. The two were, at the time, on a long hill, Seminary Ridge, that fell away to the east and then rose again to the road that led from Gettysburg to Emmitsburg. East of this road was rolling land parallel to Seminary Ridge and about three miles in length. At its southern end was an eminence of some 600 feet known as Round Top. Northeast of this, at a little distance, was a second hill, slightly lower, styled Little Round Top. At the northern end of the ridge was a high cleared position, on part of which was the burial ground of the town, which gave its name to the hill and to the ridge—an ominous name, soon to be all too apt, Cemetery Hill, Cemetery Ridge. From where Lee and Longstreet stood, they could see that the high ground continued eastward and southward from Cemetery Hill, reaching another height called Culp's Hill. The whole of the opposite ridge was, therefore, a fishhook with the shank running from south to north and with the point to the southeast. Round Top was at the end of the shank of the hook, so to speak, where the line might be joined. Cemetery Ridge was the shank, Cemetery Hill the beginning of the bend, and Culp's Hill the point. Gettysburg was directly north of the bend. It was a most formidable position, distant an average of about 1400 yards from Seminary Ridge, which, in turn, afforded excellent ground for a defensive battle.—DOUGLAS SOUTHALL FREEMAN, *R. E. Lee: A Biography.*

A process is most successfully explained by a step-by-step analysis.

21. Heavy tumblers, glass ash trays, and thick glass cooking utensils are cast or pressed rather than blown. From a ribbon of glass issuing from the molten mass in the furnace, chunks of the proper size are cut off. These, looking like fiery meteors, go flying down chutes at dizzy speed to presses which stamp them to the desired shape in a mold. The finished pieces are then delivered to annealing furnaces through which all glassware must go if it is to be freed from the strains which are set up when it cools.—GEORGE RUSSELL HARRISON, *Atoms in Action.*

22. The actual process of riveting is simple enough—in description. Rivets are carried to the job by the rivet boy, a riveter's apprentice whose ambition it is to replace one of the members of the gang—which one, he leaves to luck. The rivets are dumped into a keg beside a small coke furnace. The furnace stands on a platform of loose boards roped to steel girders which may or may not have been riveted. If they have not been riveted there will be a certain amount of play in the temporary bolts. The furnace is tended by the heater or passer. He wears heavy clothes and gloves to protect him from the flying sparks and intense heat of his work, and he holds a pair of tongs about a foot-and-a-half long in his right hand. When a rivet is needed, he whirls the furnace blower until the coke is white hot, picks up a rivet with his tongs, and drives it into the coals. His skill as a heater appears in his knowledge of the exact time necessary to heat the steel. If he overheats it, it will flake, and the flakes will permit the rivet to turn in its hole. And a rivet which gives in its hole is condemned by the inspectors.—*Fortune*, "Skyscrapers: Builders and Their Tools."

Enumeration is another form of logical arrangement.

23. There are four historical layers underlying the minds of civilized men—the animal mind, the child mind, the savage mind, and the traditional civilized mind. We are all animals and never can cease to be; we were all children at our most impressionable age and can never get over the effects of that; our human ancestors have lived in savagery during practically the whole existence of the race, say five hundred thousand or a million years, and the primitive human mind is ever with us; finally, we are all born into an elaborate civilization, the constant pressure of which we can by no means escape.—JAMES HARVEY ROBINSON, *The Mind in the Making*.

50B. Repetition and Parallelism

The use of repetition and of parallel phrasing and structure in expressing thoughts parallel in meaning will strengthen coherence within the paragraph. Note the deliberate use of repetition and parallelism in the following passages.

24. This second course is fairly simple. It requires that man eliminate the source of the trouble. Let him dissociate himself, carefully and completely, from civilization and all its works. Let him systematically abolish science and the tools of science. Let him destroy all machines and the knowledge which can build or operate those machines. Let him raze his cities, smash his laboratories, dismantle his factories, tear down his universities and schools, burn his libraries, rip apart his art. Let him murder his

scientists, his lawmakers, his statesmen, his doctors, his teachers, his mechanics, his merchants, and anyone who has anything to do with the machinery of knowledge or progress. Let him punish literacy by death. Let him eradicate nations and set up the tribe as sovereign. Let him, in short, revert to his condition in society in 10,000 B.C. Thus emancipated from science, from progress, from government, from knowledge, from thought, he can be reasonably certain of prolonging his existence on this planet.—NORMAN COUSINS, *Modern Man Is Obsolete*.

25. Believe me when I say that totalitarianism has shown what democracy's high schools must teach. We shall teach whatever dictatorship abhors; we shall teach whatever the dictator most fears; we shall teach that by which he is destroyed. We shall teach the humane studies which exalt the humanity of man. We shall teach the liberating knowledges which free and exalt his mind. We shall teach whatever confirms faith in the dignity of the common man and the preciousness of every soul. We shall teach such moral and spiritual values as will humanize and liberalize the minds of men. When we have done these things as well as we can, we shall then take time to teach the neutral and useful skills associated with bread-winning. We have a way of life to win first, and if we do not win it, black and bitter will be the bread we shall eat then. There is a proverb which has been ascribed both to an anonymous Greek poet and to the prophet Mohammed, which runs: "If thou hast, of all the world's goods, but two loaves of bread remaining, sell one and buy hyacinths to feed thy soul." I am for letting some of the bread go and buying the hyacinth of liberty.—WILLIAM H. CORNOG, "Bread and Hyacinths," *School and Society*.

26. Then the moon blazed down upon the vast desolation of the American coasts, and on all the glut and hiss of tides, on all the surge and foaming slide of waters on lone beaches. The moon blazed down on 18,000 miles of coast, on the million sucks and scoops and hollows of the shore, and on the great wink of the sea, that ate the earth minutely and eternally. The moon blazed down upon the wilderness, it fell on sleeping woods, it dripped through moving leaves, it swarmed in weaving patterns on the earth, and it filled the cat's still eye with blazing yellow. The moon slept over mountains and lay like silence in the desert, and it carved the shadows of great rocks like time. The moon was mixed with flowing rivers, and it was buried in the heart of lakes, and it trembled on the water like bright fish. The moon steeped all the earth in its living and unearthly substance, it had a thousand visages, it painted continental space with ghostly light; and its light was proper to the nature of all the things it touched: it came in with the sea, it flowed with the rivers, and it was still and living on clear spaces in the forest where no men watched.—THOMAS WOLFE, *Of Time and the River*.

50C. Transitional Devices

In every well-written paragraph, coherence is increased by the use of transitional devices. These include not only conjunctions and such clearly transitional words and phrases as *next, thus, secondly, moreover, consequently, nevertheless, finally, indeed, in addition, on the other hand, to be sure,* and *in the meantime,* but also personal pronouns such as *he, it,* and *they* and the demonstrative pronouns and pronominal adjectives *this, that, these,* and *those,* which link the sentences in which they appear to earlier sentences in which their antecedents have been used. Careful examination of such words and phrases in almost any good paragraph will show that they perform a much more important function than the casual reader realizes.

50D. Analysis of Sample Paragraph

A detailed analysis will make clear the varied means by which coherence is secured in Paragraph 27.

27. (*a*) We have said that glaciers are in continual, slow motion down the valley; yet in temperate climates they do not reach the sea—they do not reach beyond a certain point, called the lower limit of glaciers. (*b*) Under constant conditions the snout of the glacier remains unmoved at this place, even though the glacier is in constant current-motion. (*c*) This apparent anomaly may be explained thus: (*d*) The glacier may be regarded as under the influence of two opposite forces. (*e*) Gravity urges it by slow motion downward, and, if this acted alone, the glacier would run into the sea. (*f*) But the ice is constantly melted, more and more, as the glacier presses downward into warmer regions; if this acted alone, the point of the glacier would retreat to the summit-snow. (*g*) Now, where these two forces—one tending to lengthen, the other to shorten the glacier—balance each other, is found the lower limit of the glacier where the snout rests unmoved. (*h*) Sometimes, after a succession of cool, moist years, or a succession of heavy snowfall years, the melting is less rapid or the motion more rapid, and the snout of the glacier will slowly advance, perhaps invading cultivated fields and overturning houses. (*i*) Sometimes, on the contrary, from more rapid melting or less rapid motion, the snout will recede, strewing debris in its former bed. (*j*) But, whether the snout stands still, or moves forward, or moves backward, the matter of the glacier is moving constantly down-

ward. (*k*) In this respect, glaciers are like rivers in certain dry regions. (*l*) These rivers rise in the mountains, run a certain distance, but never reach the sea—never pass a certain point where the supply is balanced by waste from evaporation.—JOSEPH LE CONTE, *A Compend of Geology.*

The first clause of Sentence *a* repeats from an earlier paragraph a thought that is to be kept in mind throughout the new paragraph, and the words *we have said* serve as a link between the two. Then the clause beginning with *yet* tells the reader that in temperate climates glaciers, in spite of being in continual motion downward, never reach the sea. Since this apparent contradiction is the theme of the entire paragraph, the first sentence is clearly a topic sentence. Note that the use of *they* twice in the second clause, referring to glaciers, tightens the coherence between clauses, and that when *they do not reach the sea* is to be made more specific, parallel structure is used: *they do not reach beyond a certain point.*

Sentence *b* is introduced by a phrase, *under constant conditions,* which prepares the way for the later introduction of special conditions in Sentences *h* and *i.* The *this* in *this place* takes the reader back to the *certain point* defined in (*a*) as the *lower limit of glaciers.* The clause at the end reminds the reader that even though the snout of the glacier remains unmoved, the glacier is in continual slow motion as stated in Sentence *a.* The repetition of the word *glacier* in this and subsequent sentences is itself of importance in holding the paragraph together.

In what is called Sentence *c* even though it ends with a colon rather than a period, the pronominal adjective *this* reminds the reader of the apparent contradiction described in Sentence *b,* and the final word *thus* points forward to the explanation to be made in the next four sentences. Sentence *d* introduces the two opposing forces which produce the apparent anomaly and which the writer properly elects to present by the method of dual development in the next three sentences. The first of the two forces alluded to, that of gravity, is promptly explained in Sentence *e,* where *it,* referring to *glacier,* and *this,* referring to *gravity,* provide additional coherence. The second force, that of the slow melting of the glacier, is explained in Sentence *f,* and since it has an effect opposite to that of gravity, the sentence is properly introduced by *but.* The pronoun *this,* referring to the process of melting, strengthens the coherence.

Sentence *g* explains the *apparent anomaly* of Sentence *c* as a balance between two opposing forces. Note the transitional effect of *now*; the use of *these, one, the other,* and *each other*; the use of parallel structure in the phrases that fall between the two dashes. Note also the almost identical repetition of *lower limit of the glacier* from Sentence *a* and *the snout rests unmoved* from Sentence *b.*

Sentences *h* and *i* describe special conditions under which the snout of the glacier may advance beyond or recede from the lower limit described in Sentence *b* as remaining fixed "under constant conditions." Note the transitional use of *sometimes* and the effectiveness of using the word to introduce both sentences, which are parallel in thought even though they describe opposite rather than similar effects. In Sentence *i* the phrase *on the contrary* notifies the reader at once that forces and results opposite to those in Sentence *h* are to be described. There is close parallelism between *the melting is less rapid or the motion more rapid* of Sentence *h* and *from more rapid melting or less rapid motion* of Sentence *i*; between *the snout of the glacier will slowly advance* and *the snout will recede;* and between the phrases with which the two sentences end.

The opening word *but* in Sentence *j* prepares the reader for the reminder that no matter what the circumstances, the statement made in the opening clause of the paragraph holds true: *the matter of the glacier is moving constantly downward.* In the description of the three possible contingencies the writer properly adopts parallel structure: *whether the snout stands still, or moves forward, or moves backward.* The opening phrase of Sentence *k, in this respect,* links it firmly with the statement made in Sentence *j.* In the final sentence, the phrase *these rivers* forms a link with Sentence *k,* and the parallelism in *never reach the sea* and *never pass a certain point* reminds the reader of the parallelism in the almost identical statement made about glaciers in Sentence *a* and emphasizes the similarity between glaciers and certain rivers stated in Sentence *k*. Further, this final sentence, by making exactly the same statement about these glacier-like rivers that was made about glaciers in Sentence *a,* drives home the central thought of the entire paragraph—that glaciers, though they "are in continual, slow motion . . . do not reach beyond a certain point."

Experienced writers in part follow unconsciously rather than consciously the procedures described in this detailed analysis, but such a study as has just been made should be helpful to the student who wishes to learn how to construct effective paragraphs.

EXERCISE

Prepare a careful analysis, like that made of Paragraph 27, above, of any one of the paragraphs numbered 8, 20, 28, 30, 33, 35, 36, 44, 50, 52, 55.

51. METHODS OF PARAGRAPH DEVELOPMENT

There are almost innumerable methods of developing the thought and arranging the materials of a paragraph so as to achieve effective structure, and the experienced writer does not follow set rules. Nevertheless, it is advisable to identify and illustrate a number of methods that are frequently employed and that you should keep in mind as you embark upon paragraphs of your own. You will perceive that the same idea might be developed effectively by any one of several methods, and also that there is some overlapping among the methods described; but the important thing to remember is that every successful paragraph is built on some sort of pattern and is the product of careful planning. If you note the pains taken by experienced writers in building paragraphs, you will be willing to expend greater effort upon your own work and will be less easily discouraged by difficulties.

51A. Linear Development

Often the material of a paragraph calls for a simple step-by-step development in a straight line. This may be called the linear method of development. It is similar to the method of obtaining coherence through logical order described in Section 50A, and the illustrative paragraphs there (Paragraphs 17–23) are also appropriate here. Adopt the linear method when you wish to present a series of steps or thoughts or particulars in logical sequence, as in the following examples.

28. The common law began its development in medieval England. When a case came before the royal justices in the Middle Ages they tried to ascertain the prevailing custom bearing on the subject and decide the question in accordance with it. Theoretically they did not make the law, but merely formulated the practices of the community into legal rules and gave them an official sanction. As a matter of fact they did make law, for they interpreted the customs and had the power to select some and discard others, especially if there was a conflict. When another case involving the same point was brought before the judges, they generally followed the rule laid down in the decision of the first case. If, however, it was thought that the original finding was incorrect or that conditions had changed, they would override the previous decision and work out a new doctrine. Thus flexibility was always possible—one of the best features of the common law. In this way a body of precedents was built up and a set of legal doctrines developed. When an entirely novel case came up, some "general principle" of the common law was evoked in its determination.—CHARLES A. BEARD, *American Government and Politics.*

29. Chill the blood, as Sir Joseph Barcroft did by lying naked in an icy room while an assistant watched. For a time the body tries to combat the cold. Barcroft's mind told him to get up, walk, keep his blood in circulation. But he refused for the sake of science. Then the mind gave up the battle. He stretched out his legs. He felt warm. "It was as if I were basking in the cold," he says. He was content to lie still, blissfully indifferent to a death from which his vigilant assistant saved him. His mind had ceased to watch over him.—WALDEMAR KAEMPFFERT, *Science Today and Tomorrow.*

51B. Dual Development

Frequently the material of a paragraph suggests some form of dual development: comparison to show the similarities between two persons or objects or ideas; contrast to show differences between two sides of a person's character, or between surface appearance and the truth; a combination of comparison and contrast.

Observe the readily identifiable means of dual development adopted by the writers of the following paragraphs.

30. The effect of historical reading is analogous, in many respects, to that produced by foreign travel. The student, like the tourist, is transported into a new state of society. He sees new fashions. He hears new modes of expression. His mind is enlarged by contemplating the wide diversities of laws, of morals, and of manners. But men may travel far, and return with minds as contracted as if they had never stirred from their own market-town. In the same manner, men may know the dates of many battles and the genealogies of many royal houses, and yet be no wiser. Most people look at past times as princes look at foreign countries. More than one illustrious stranger has landed on our island amidst the shouts of a mob, has dined with the King, has hunted with the master of the stag-hounds, has seen the guards reviewed and a knight of the garter installed; has cantered along Regent Street, has visited St. Paul's and noted down its dimensions; and has then departed, thinking that he has seen England. But of the vast and complex system of society, of the fine shades of national character, of the practical operation of government and laws, he knows nothing. He who would understand these things rightly must not confine his observations to palaces and solemn days. He must see ordinary men as they appear in their ordinary business and in their ordinary pleasures. He must mingle in the crowds of the exchange and the coffee-house. He must obtain admittance to the convivial table and the domestic hearth. He must bear with vulgar expressions. He must not shrink from exploring even the retreats of misery. He who wishes to understand the condition of mankind in former ages must proceed on the same principle. If he attends only to public transactions, to wars, congresses, and debates, his studies will be as unprofitable as the travels of those imperial, royal, and serene sovereigns who form their judgment of our island from having gone in state to a few fine sights, and from having held formal conferences with a few great officers.—THOMAS BABINGTON MACAULAY, "History," *Edinburgh Review.*

31. In 1763, Great Britain attained a height of power and dominion which led many Englishmen to conclude that a new Roman Empire had been brought into being through the genius of William Pitt and the valor of British arms. France and Spain, united by the Family Compact, had been decisively defeated, and a large part of North America and India had been brought under British control. A period of "prosperity and glory unknown to any former age" seemed to be opening for Great Britain and her colonies. Yet those Englishmen who in 1763 regarded themselves as the heirs of Rome soon perceived a new and highly disquieting resemblance between Britain

and Rome: the British Empire seemed about to go the way of the Roman Empire. It appeared probable that the same generation of Englishmen which saw the empire reach its highest point of grandeur would be the witness of its decline and fall. So swiftly did fortune turn that William Pitt, who had brought Great Britain to the zenith, died in the House of Lords fifteen years later in one of England's darkest hours.—JOHN C. MILLER, *Origins of the American Revolution.*

32. In 1940, those of us who were in Washington as civilians were concerned mostly with the technological conservatism of the men in uniform. I will relate no stories to prove the point. The conflict between the professors and the "brass" is too well known. Most of the versions do less than justice to the military man and give too much credit to the professor. Be that as it may, what I am concerned with is not the technological conservatism of the men in uniform in 1940 but the almost fanatic enthusiasm for research and development of their successors in 1952. It is a phenomenon not unlike that of an old-fashioned religious conversion. The Defense Department, in regard to research, is not unlike the man who sprang onto his horse and rode madly off in all directions.—JAMES B. CONANT, *Modern Science and Modern Man.*

33. Let us remind ourselves first of the recent expansion of our horizon. In space, our Western field of vision has expanded to take in the whole of mankind over all the habitable and traversable surface of this planet, and the whole stellar universe in which this planet is an infinitesimally small speck of dust. In time, our Western field of vision has expanded to take in all the civilizations that have risen and fallen during these last 6,000 years; the previous history of the human race back to its genesis between 600,000 and 1,000,000 years ago; the history of life on this planet back to perhaps 800,000,000 years ago. What a marvelous widening of our historical horizon! Yet, at the same time, our field of historical vision has been contracting; it has been tending to shrink within the narrow limits in time and space of the particular republic or kingdom of which each of us happens to be a citizen. The oldest surviving Western states—say France or England—have so far had no more than a thousand years of continuous political existence; the largest surviving Western state—say Brazil or the United States—embraces only a very small fraction of the total inhabited surface of the earth.—ARNOLD J. TOYNBEE, *Civilization on Trial.*

34. Ours is a paradoxical world. The achievements which are its glory threaten to destroy it. The nations with the highest standard of living, the greatest capacity to take care of their people economically, the broadest education, and the most enlightened morality and religion exhibit the least capacity to avoid mutual destruction in war. It would seem that the more

civilized we become the more incapable of maintaining civilization we are. —F. S. C. NORTHROP, *The Meeting of East and West.*

35. If I were to try to sum up in a phrase the main difference between the Chinese and ourselves, I should say that they, in the main, aim at enjoyment, while we, in the main, aim at power. We like power over our fellowmen, and we like power over Nature. For the sake of the former we have built up strong states, and for the sake of the latter we have built up Science. The Chinese are too lazy and too good-natured for such pursuits. To say that they are lazy is, however, only true in a certain sense. They are not lazy in the way that Russians are; that is to say, they will work hard for their living. Employers of labor find them extraordinarily industrious. But they will not work, as Americans and Western Europeans do, simply because they would be bored if they did not work, nor do they love hustle for its own sake. When they have enough to live on, they live on it, instead of trying to augment it by hard work. They have an infinite capacity for leisurely amusements—going to the theater, talking while they drink tea, admiring the Chinese art of earlier times, or walking in beautiful scenery. To our way of thinking, there is something unduly mild about such a way of spending one's life; we respect more a man who goes to his office every day, even if all that he does in his office is harmful.—BERTRAND RUSSELL, *Sceptical Essays.*

36. The U.S. is the world's greatest democracy, but its fundamental law was written mainly by aristocrats and conservatives who feared the people. The U.S. is the world's most tireless advocate of the principles of freedom, equality, tolerance, and due process of law. Yet it is peculiarly susceptible to wholly undemocratic outbursts of mob violence resulting in lynchings, repression, and vigilantism; and every so often it produces a Ku Klux Klan or a Black Legion, and it supports a fair share of indigenous fascist movements. The U.S. is a law-abiding nation, which recorded 1,400,000 major crimes in 1937 and has a hard time finding jail space to house the criminals. It has a divine faith in the power of legislation. It spends more money on making laws and governing itself than any other country, outside of the U.S.S.R., and it takes a peculiar satisfaction in circumventing or ignoring its own laws. The U.S. is the arch-enemy of injustice throughout the world, and sounds off at frequent intervals on the iniquities of foreign governments, foreign philosophies, and foreign methods based on persecution, imperialism, and force; yet it tolerates the most brutal exploitation of certain classes of its own people and shrugs nonchalantly at the organized persecution of unpopular characters. So close to the frontier that many a living man has filed notches in his gun, the U.S. has canonized its most colorful banditti—Jesse James and Billy the Kid are typical heroes—and exhibits a thinly disguised admiration for its Dillingers and Baby Face Nelsons.—*Fortune.*

37. Fundamentally Grant was superior to Lee because in a modern total war he had a modern mind, and Lee did not. Lee looked to the past in war as the Confederacy did in spirit. The staffs of the two men illustrate their outlook. It would not be accurate to say that Lee's general staff were glorified clerks, but the statement would not be too wide of the mark. Certainly his staff was not, in the modern sense, a planning staff, which was why Lee was often a tired general. He performed labors that no general can do in a big modern army—work that should have fallen to his staff, but that Lee did because it was traditional for the commanding general to do it in older armies. Most of Lee's staff officers were lieutenant colonels. Some of the men on Grant's general staff, as well as the staffs of other Northern generals, were major and brigadier generals, officers who were capable of leading corps. Grant's staff was an organization of experts in the various phases of strategic planning. The modernity of Grant's mind was most apparent in his grasp of the concept that war was becoming total and that the destruction of the enemy's resources was as effective and legitimate a form of warfare as the destruction of his armies. What was realism to Grant was barbarism to Lee. Lee thought of war in the old way as a conflict between armies and refused to view it for what it had become—a struggle between societies. To him, economic warfare was needless cruelty to civilians. Lee was the last of the great old-fashioned generals, Grant the first of the great moderns.—T. HARRY WILLIAMS, *Lincoln and His Generals.*

51C. Details

Presenting a series of details bearing upon the central theme of a paragraph is often the most effective method of amplifying the thought. If skillfully chosen and arranged, as in the paragraphs that follow, such details cohere to form a unified whole. Moreover, the details make for concreteness and vividness, and their cumulative effect is impressive.

38. You may regard his [Aaron Burr's] career, even more than most, as a series of big and little losses. He was born in 1756. With Jonathan Edwards as his grandfather and the president of Princeton College as his father, he might seem to have inherited an almost suffocating odor of sanctity; but he soon lost it. He lost his parents in early childhood, and he was brought up under what his Edwards uncle regretfully called "a maple-sugar government." As a mere boy, he went with Arnold to Quebec, and followed this with other military distinction; but he lost his health and the favor of Washington and with these the chance of becoming a great soldier. He practised law successfully, but was drawn into politics and showed a wonder-

ful gift for the seamy side of them. He lost the presidency in 1801 by a tie-vote with Jefferson and was thus shifted into that graveyard of greater hopes, the vice-presidency. He lost the governorship of New York, chiefly through the activity of his constant opponent Hamilton. Whereupon he fought and killed Hamilton and by so doing lost the respect of most respectable people. He then schemed to create an empire in the Southwest by robbing and possibly ruining his own country. He lost this vast dream hope, and though he was acquitted of treason in a famous trial, he lost what public confidence had been left to him. Money he was always losing, by extravagance, by generosity, by indifference, by windy speculation. He spent four years, from 1808 to 1812, in the most disreputable Bohemian exile in Europe, and at length crept home. Long before, he had lost a charming and beloved wife. He now lost his grandson, whom he worshiped, and the exquisite daughter who worshiped him. It might seem as if he had nothing left to lose. But he kept on for twenty-five years longer, losing what little trifles life could still take from him. At the very end he married a rich widow and lost first her money and then her affection. And before his death, in 1836, he lost even the use of his limbs. Yet in this crowding, mountainous accumulation of losses, he rarely lost his patience, and never that heaven-bestowed gift of amusing himself.—GAMALIEL BRADFORD, *Damaged Souls*.

39. The people of Soapland are subject to a set of special ills. Temporary blindness, preceded by dizzy spells and headaches, is a common affliction of Soapland people. The condition usually clears up in six or eight weeks, but once in a while it develops into brain tumor and the patient dies. One script writer, apparently forgetting that General Mills was the sponsor of his serial, had one of his women characters go temporarily blind because of an allergy to chocolate cake. There was hell to pay, and the writer had to make the doctor in charge of the patient hastily change his diagnosis. Amnesia strikes almost as often in Soapland as the common cold in our world. There have been as many as eight or nine amnesia cases on the air at one time. The hero of "Rosemary" stumbled around in a daze for months last year. When he regained his memory, he found that in his wanderings he had been lucky enough to marry a true-blue sweetie. The third major disease is paralysis of the legs. This scourge usually attacks the good males. Like mysterious blindness, loss of the use of the legs may be either temporary or permanent. The hero of "Life Can Be Beautiful" was confined to a wheel chair until his death last March, but young Dr. Malone, who was stricken with paralysis a year ago, is up and around again. I came upon only one crippled villain in 1947: Spencer Hart rolled through a three-month sequence of "Just Plain Bill" in a wheel chair. When their men are stricken, the good women become nobler than ever. A disabled hero is likely to lament his fate and indulge in self-pity now and then, but his wife or sweetheart never com-

plains. She is capable of twice as much work, sacrifice, fortitude, endurance, ingenuity, and love as before. Joyce Jordan, M. D., had no interest in a certain male until he lost the use of both legs and took to a wheel chair. Then love began to bloom in her heart. The man in the wheel chair has come to be the standard Soapland symbol of the American male's subordination to the female and his dependence on her greater strength of heart and soul. —JAMES THURBER, "Soapland."[1]

40. Thus, glancing round the bookshop, we make other such capricious friendships with the unknown and the vanished whose only record is, for example, this little book of poems, so fairly printed, so finely engraved, too, with a portrait of the author. For he was a poet and drowned untimely, and his verse, mild as it is and formal and sententious, sends forth still a frail fluty sound like that of a piano organ played in some back street resignedly by an old Italian organ-grinder in a corduroy jacket. There are travellers, too, row upon row of them, still testifying, indomitable spinsters that they were, to the discomforts that they endured and the sunsets they admired in Greece when Queen Victoria was a girl. A tour of Cornwall with a visit to the tin mines was thought worthy of voluminous record. People went slowly up the Rhine and did portraits of each other in Indian ink, sitting reading on deck beside a coil of rope; they measured the pyramids; were lost to civilization for years; converted Negroes in pestilential swamps. This packing up and going off, exploring deserts and catching fevers, settling in India for a lifetime, penetrating even to China and then returning to lead a parochial life at Edmonton, tumbles and tosses upon the dusty floor like an uneasy sea, so restless the English are, with the waves at their very door. The waters of travel and adventure seem to break upon little islands of serious effort and lifelong industry stood in jagged column upon the floor. In these piles of puce-bound volumes with gilt monograms on the back, thoughtful clergymen expound the gospels; scholars are to be heard with their hammers and their chisels chipping clear the ancient texts of Euripides and Aeschylus. Thinking, annotating, expounding goes on at a prodigious rate all around us, and over everything, like a punctual, everlasting tide, washes the ancient sea of fiction. Innumerable volumes tell how Arthur loved Laura and they were separated and they were unhappy and then they met and they were happy ever after, as was the way when Victoria ruled these islands.—VIRGINIA WOOLF, *The Death of the Moth and Other Essays.*

51D. Illustration

Often the most natural method of paragraph development is through illustration. In Paragraphs 41, 42, and 43 the pattern is

[1] From an article originally in *The New Yorker.* Copr. 1948 James Thurber.

a general statement followed by a single illustration. The writer may elect to use two illustrations, as in Paragraphs 44 and 45, or a series of illustrations, in which event the method is much the same as that of development by means of details (see pp. 304–6).

41. Travel, as everybody knows, is for the time being a mighty leveler of social distinctions, particularly when its concomitants throw the voyagers together while at the same time isolating them from the rest of the world. Think of the smoking room of a small steamship with only three or four dozen passengers. These men might live side by side in one row of brick houses for a hundred years and scarcely know each other's faces. Break the shaft, keep them at sea for an extra week, and, if they aren't careful and if the cigars hold out, they will empty their hearts to one another with an indiscretion that may shock them to death when they remember it ashore. —GEORGE LYMAN KITTREDGE, *Chaucer and His Poetry.*

42. Analogies are handy and useful things, necessary to many of the sciences and fruitful in everyday life, but they do not constitute proof. The old grasshopper-ant fable is an example. You undoubtedly remember the grasshopper who played all day and let the future take care of itself and the ant who chided him for his lack of foresight. The analogy lies, of course, in the application of the fable to people, of whom some are like the gay grasshopper and others like the frugal ant. But the fable, whatever its value, is not proof that the person who enjoys life is always worse off than the saving soul with his eye on the next depression.—WILLIAM HUMMEL AND KEITH HUNTRESS, *The Analysis of Propaganda.*

43. A simple experiment will distinguish two types of human nature. Gather a throng of people and pour them into a ferryboat. By the time the boat has swung into the river you will find that a certain proportion have taken the trouble to climb upstairs, in order to be out on deck and see what is to be seen as they cross over. The rest have settled indoors, to think what they will do upon reaching the other side, or perhaps lose themselves in apathy and tobacco smoke. But leaving out those apathetic, or addicted to a single enjoyment, we may divide all the alert passengers on the boat into two classes—those who are interested in crossing the river, and those who are merely interested in getting across. And we may divide all the people on the earth, or all the moods of people, in the same way. Some of them are chiefly occupied with attaining ends, and some with receiving experiences. The distinction of the two will be more marked when we name the first kind practical, and the second poetic, for common knowledge recognizes that a person poetic or in a poetic mood is impractical, and a practical person is intolerant of poetry.—MAX EASTMAN, *The Enjoyment of Poetry.*

44. Many of the natural wonders of the earth owe their existence to the fact that once the sea crept over the land, laid down its deposits of sediments, and then withdrew. There is Mammoth Cave in Kentucky, for example, where one may wander through miles of underground passages and enter rooms with ceilings 250 feet overhead. Caves and passageways have been dissolved by ground water out of an immense thickness of limestone, deposited by a Paleozoic sea. In the same way, the story of Niagara Falls goes back to Silurian time, when a vast embayment of the Arctic Sea crept southward over the continent. Its waters were clear, for the borderlands were low and little sediment or silt was carried into the inland sea. It deposited large beds of the hard rock called dolomite, and in time they formed a long escarpment near the present border between Canada and the United States. Millions of years later, floods of water released from melting glaciers poured over this cliff, cutting away the soft shales that underlay the dolomite, and causing mass after mass of the undercut rock to break away. In this fashion Niagara Falls and its gorge were created.—RACHEL L. CARSON, *The Sea Around Us*.

45. Quite obviously, the book's informal character prevents it from always giving a complete picture. For example, most narratives of transcontinental staging have a long chapter on the buffaloes; Mark Twain dismisses the whole subject with the tale of Bemis's affair with the buffalo bull —a tale which develops into one of the funniest pieces of prose in the English language because of the author's superb use of the western dead-pan manner of telling a tall story. Instead of methodically describing Salt Lake City and the Mormons, Mark Twain delights the reader with his impossible yarns about Brigham Young's too numerous children, and then sidles off into a derisive dissection of the Book of Mormon, which he characterizes: "It is chloroform in print. If Joseph Smith composed this book, the act was a miracle—keeping awake while he did it was, at any rate." Here, in the buffaloes and the Mormons, are two topics that in less inspired hands might well have developed into solemnly informative chapters, but it would require a pedestrian mind indeed to prefer orthodox narrative to what Mark Twain offers: sheer fantasy, so skillfully handled that it appeals to all men in all times.—RODMAN W PAUL, "Introduction" to *Roughing It*.

51E. Analogy

A special form of the development of paragraphs through illustration is the method of analogy, in which light is thrown upon one thing or idea through a pointing out of the resemblance between certain of its attributes and those of another thing or idea, usually a more familiar one. Paragraphs 46 and 47 are examples.

46. If you are at the beach, and you take an old, dull, brown penny and rub it hard for a minute or two with handfuls of wet sand (dry sand is no good), the penny will come out a bright gold color, looking as clean and new as the day it was minted. Now poetry has the same effect on words as wet sand on pennies. In what seems almost a miraculous way, it brightens up words that looked dull and ordinary. Thus, poetry is perpetually "re-creating language." It does this in several ways. It may coin new words: it may help to bring into common use words which, before, had only been used by experts—technical, scientific words, for instance: it may put common words into new contexts, introduce them to other ordinary words they had not met before, as a good hostess introduces strangers to each other at a party and makes them interest one another: it may enrich the value of words by giving them new associations—for instance, when Tennyson, writing a poem about an eagle looking down from a cliff, said, "The wrinkled sea beneath him crawls," he was able to give a most vivid picture of what the sea looks like from a great height by bringing into a new association two quite ordinary words, "crawled" and "wrinkled."—CECIL DAY LEWIS, *Poetry for You.*

47. Time passes and, their honeymoon over, the cats begin to tell us things about humanity which even the lid of civilization cannot conceal in the world of men. They tell us—what, alas, we already know—that husbands soon tire of their wives, particularly when they are expecting or nursing families; that the essence of maleness is the love of adventure and infidelity; that guilty consciences and good resolutions are the psychological symptoms of that disease which spasmodically affects every male between the ages of eighteen and sixty—the disease called "the morning after"; and that with the disappearance of the disease the psychological symptoms also disappear, so that when temptation comes again, conscience is dumb and good resolutions count for nothing. All these unhappily too familiar truths are illustrated by the cats with a most comical absence of disguise. No man has ever dared to manifest his boredom so insolently as does a Siamese tom-cat, when he yawns in the face of his amorously importunate wife. No man has ever dared to proclaim his illicit amours so frankly as this same tom caterwauling on the tiles. And how slinkingly—no man was ever so abject—he returns next day to the conjugal basket by the fire! You can measure the guiltiness of his conscience by the angle of his back-pressed ears, the droop of his tail. And when, having sniffed him and so discovered his infidelity, his wife, as she always does on these occasions, begins to scratch his face (already scarred, like a German student's, with the traces of a hundred duels), he makes no attempt to resist; for, self-convicted of sin, he knows that he deserves all he is getting.—ALDOUS HUXLEY, *Music at Night.*

51F. Definition

Moving toward full clarity by more precise definition constitutes in itself an important method of paragraph development. Usually a paragraph in which the thought is thus amplified consists of much more than just a dictionary definition. In Paragraph 48 the definition proper is followed by a series of concrete examples, and the method thus becomes similar to that of multiple illustration. In Paragraph 49 the definition of a detective story is not presented in a single statement but is built up by implication through a series of ingredients of such a story. This and Paragraph 50 show that authors sometimes amplify and strengthen a definition by explaining what something *is not* as well as what it *is* (see also Section 51K, Elimination). The writer of Paragraph 51 cites two familiar instances.

48. By *genteelism* is here to be understood the substituting, for the ordinary natural word that first suggests itself to the mind, of a synonym that is thought to be less soiled by the lips of the common herd, less familiar, less plebeian, less vulgar, less improper, less apt to come unhandsomely betwixt the wind and our nobility. The truly genteel do not offer *beer,* but *ale;* invite one to *step,* not *come,* this way; take in not *lodgers,* but *paying guests;* send their boys not to *school,* but to *college;* never *help,* but *assist,* each other to potatoes; keep *stomachs* and *domestics* instead of *bellies* and *servants;* and have quite forgotten that they could ever have been guilty of *tooth-powder* and *napkins* and *underclothing,* of *before* and *except* and *about,* where nothing now will do for them but *dentifrice, serviette, lingerie, ere, save, anent.*—H. W. FOWLER, *A Dictionary of Modern English Usage.*

49. I will confess to the reader that I also have wished to write a detective story. I once thought of a very good murder, but it was so skillfully planned that I have never been able to see how it could be found out and the crime brought home to the culprit. For years I have racked my brains, but I have never found an answer to the riddle. And now I have given it up as a bad job. Meanwhile I studied this form of fiction with care and I came to certain conclusions which I now venture to set before the reader. The story is the chief thing. The characters should be natural, but it is unnecessary to go into them in any detail. Their idiosyncrasies are only of consequence if they are essential to the story. You do not want to know their opinions on art, life, or the immortality of the soul. Love-making is merely tiresome, and the amorous attachment of one person to another is only op-

portune if it is a possible motive for an action. It is an insufficient, because too obvious, cause to lead to the unravelling of the mystery. The writing should be good, but the detective story is no place for elegances of style. Nothing should hold you up. The scene must be set, but you do not want to be bothered with descriptions of scenery. For my own part I think a detective story should deal with a murder. I am unwilling to excite myself over the robbery of a great red ruby or the theft of a secret treaty. But I do not think murder should be exaggerated. A second murder following on the first cools my ardour and a third leaves me sceptical. No, give me one corpse, a beautiful woman in evening dress stabbed to the heart or an eminent politician with his head bashed in, and let me look forward to three hundred pages of suspense and I am happy. But the writer must play fair with me. He must give me clues which I pounce upon, but which lead to nothing, and clues which if I were quick enough (but I am not) would lead me to the discovery of the villain. He must give me a sporting chance. The culprit must be one of the principal persons brought on the scene; he must not be someone who has been so kept in the background that I cannot be expected to have thought of him, nor someone, like the plumber who had come in to repair the bathroom tap, who has nothing to do with the story. The motive for the murder must be sufficient to make it reasonable that the murderer should risk his neck for it. The interest should be held till the end and when truth is out the author should finish with the least possible delay.—W. SOMERSET MAUGHAM, *Fifty Modern English Writers.*

50. Geology is the science which treats of the past conditions of the earth and of its inhabitants. It is, therefore, a history of the earth. It is closely allied to physical geography, but differs in this: Physical geography treats only of the present forms of the earth's features; geology also, and mainly, of their gradual formation, or evolution from former conditions. It is also closely allied to natural history, but differs in this: Natural history is concerned only with the present forms and distribution of animals and plants, while geology is chiefly concerned about previous forms and distribution, and their changes to the present forms and distribution. In a word, geography and natural history are concerned about how things are; geology, about how they became so.—JOSEPH LE CONTE, *A Compend of Geology.*

51. A dilemma is a situation, in logic or in life, from which there is literally no way out. If one turns one way, he is lost; if he turns another, the second horn of the dilemma catches him. The trial lawyer who demands that the witness "answer yes or no" when either answer will damage the witness's case is making use of the dilemma. Perhaps the best example of all is the ancient vaudeville wheeze: "Have you stopped beating your wife yet?" Either answer is an admission of guilt, and the form of the question

allows no further possibilities.—WILLIAM HUMMEL AND KEITH HUNTRESS, *The Analysis of Propaganda.*

51G. Repetition

A writer may amplify a statement by repeating it in different words or showing that it holds true under different circumstances. We have already seen the effectiveness of repetition as a means of securing coherence (see Section 50B), but in Paragraph 52 every sentence embodies expression of the writer's central point: the scientist's refusal to give blind obedience to authority. You can easily perceive, however, that each sentence does more than simply repeat: it carries the thought forward as well as reiterating it.

52. The improver of natural knowledge absolutely refuses to acknowledge authority, as such. For him, scepticism is the highest of duties; blind faith the one unpardonable sin. And it cannot be otherwise, for every great advance in natural knowledge has involved the absolute rejection of authority, the cherishing of the keenest scepticism, the annihilation of the spirit of blind faith; and the most ardent votary of science holds his firmest convictions, not because the men he most venerates hold them; not because their verity is testified by portents and wonders; but because his experience teaches him that whenever he chooses to bring these convictions into contact with their primary source, nature—whenever he thinks fit to test them by appealing to experiment and to observation—nature will confirm them. The man of science has learned to believe in justification, not by faith, but by verification.—THOMAS HENRY HUXLEY, "On the Advisableness of Improving Natural Knowledge."

51H. Cause and Effect

It is sometimes appropriate to build a paragraph by detailing the causes of an event or situation, or its effects. Thus in Paragraph 53 the oblivion in which the Pilgrims and their story long rested is explained; in Paragraph 54, some of the results of the Methodist revival are set forth; in Paragraph 55, the principal motives that lead to research; in Paragraph 56, the causes of emigration from Europe to America; and in Paragraph 57, the effect of Judea's geographical position upon her history.

53. The Pilgrims themselves were to blame in large part for the fog that so long obscured them, for they and their immediate descendants were

singularly careless of their fame. Simple and humble folk of plebeian origin, they read no earth-shaking import into what they were doing. They erected no monuments to themselves and their prowess, leaving behind regrettably few memorials of any kind, whether inscribed on paper or in stone. Used to toil and hardship, many of them illiterate, few with any formal schooling, they performed as best they could the homely day-to-day tasks that had to be done, content to let history come after them. They did not even bother to keep town records until 1632, twelve years after the landing.—GEORGE F. WILLISON, *Saints and Strangers.*

54. The great body which he [John Wesley] thus founded numbered a hundred thousand members at his death, and now counts its members in England and America by millions. But the Methodists themselves were the least result of the Methodist revival. Its action upon the Church broke the lethargy of the clergy; and the "Evangelical" movement, which found representatives like Newton and Cecil within the pale of the Establishment, made the fox-hunting parson and the absentee rector at last impossible. In Walpole's day the English clergy were the idlest and the most lifeless in the world. In our own day no body of religious ministers surpasses them in piety, in philanthropic energy, or in popular regard. In the nation at large appeared a new moral enthusiasm, which, rigid and pedantic as it often seemed, was still healthy in its social tone, and whose power was seen in the disappearance of the profligacy which had disgraced the upper classes, and the foulness which had infested literature, ever since the Restoration. A new philanthropy reformed our prisons, infused clemency and wisdom into our penal laws, abolished the slave trade, and gave the first impulse to popular education.—JOHN RICHARD GREEN, *History of the English People.*

55. There are many highly respectable motives which may lead men to prosecute research, but three which are much more important than the rest. The first (without which the rest must come to nothing) is intellectual curiosity, desire to know the truth. Then, professional pride, anxiety to be satisfied with one's performance, the shame that overcomes any self-respecting craftsman when his work is unworthy of his talent. Finally, ambition, desire for reputation and the position, even the power or the money, which it brings. It may be fine to feel, when you have done your work, that you have added to the happiness or alleviated the sufferings of others, but that will not be why you did it. So if a mathematician, or a chemist, or even a physiologist, were to tell me that the driving force in his work had been the desire to benefit humanity, then I should not believe him (nor should I think the better of him if I did). His dominant motives have been those which I have stated, and in which, surely, there is nothing of which any decent man need be ashamed.—G. H. HARDY, *A Mathematician's Apology.*

56. The impulse of migration may be described, negatively, as an impulse of escape. The American fled from a Europe where he could find no satisfying fulfillment of his energies and was confronted by conflicts and dilemmas that had no easy solution. The groups who came to all parts of the New World were, in general, those who were most acutely discontented with their status in European society and who had the least hope of being able to improve it. The Hispanic colonies were settled mainly by impoverished members of the lower nobility and by adventurers from the lower classes. Unable to achieve aristocratic status at home, they hoped to win riches, land, and glory for themselves in America. Most of the early immigrants to the United States came from the petty bourgeoisie in the English cities or from the yeoman farmers; a few were motivated primarily by the desire to put into practice novel religious or political ideas, but the majority expected to improve their economic condition. The later migration from the other European countries into both North and South America was similar in character, including some religious and political refugees, but consisting mainly of ambitious younger sons of the bourgeoisie and of oppressed and land-hungry peasants from Ireland, Germany, Scandinavia, Italy, and the Austrian and Russian empires. All sought in the New World an environment where they could act more freely, without being restricted by traditional forms of authority and discipline or by a scarcity of land and natural resources.—HENRY BAMFORD PARKES, *The American Experience.*

57. The position of the land of Judea and of Jerusalem, its capital, is a peculiar one. The country is a band-shaped strip between the Mediterranean to the west and the desert beyond the Jordan to the east; through it lies the natural high-road between the Hittites, Syria, Assyria, and Babylonia to the north and Egypt to the south. It was a country predestined, therefore, to a stormy history. Across it Egypt, and whatever power was ascendant in the north, fought for empire; against its people they fought for a trade route. It had itself neither the area, the agricultural possibilities, nor the mineral wealth to be important. The story of its people that these scriptures have preserved runs like a commentary to the greater history of the two systems of civilization to the north and south and of the sea peoples to the west.—H. G. WELLS, *The Outline of History.*

51J. Question and Answer

Beginning with a question and then proceeding to answer it is an effective method of development under certain circumstances. It is widely used in explanation and argument. Sometimes a paragraph may consist almost entirely of a series of related questions that are not meant to be answered or are answered in paragraphs that follow.

58. Was Japan already beaten before the atomic bomb? The answer is certainly "yes" in the sense that the fortunes of war had turned against her. The answer is "no" in the sense that she was still fighting desperately and there was every reason to believe that she would continue to do so; and this is the only answer that has any practical significance.—KARL T. COMPTON, "If the Atomic Bomb Had Not Been Used," *Atlantic Monthly.*

59. Who are those who are really disloyal? Those who inflame racial hatreds, who sow religious and class dissensions. Those who subvert the Constitution by violating the freedom of the ballot box. Those who make a mockery of majority rule by the use of the filibuster. Those who impair democracy by denying equal educational facilities. Those who frustrate justice by lynch law or by making a farce of jury trials. Those who deny freedom of speech and of the press and of assembly. Those who press for special favors against the interest of the commonwealth. Those who regard public office as a source of private gain. Those who would exalt the military over the civil. Those who for selfish and private purposes stir up national antagonisms and expose the world to the ruin of war.—HENRY STEELE COMMAGER, "Who Is Loyal to America?" *Harper's Magazine.*

60. How about our other apparently insoluble problems? Why does our nation want to manufacture and sell to the people within its borders at higher prices the things it could import more cheaply from elsewhere? Why, if it continues to send away more of its natural resources, more of the products of its soil's fertility, more of the products of its labor than it receives in exchange from other nations, does it consider that it has a "favorable" balance of trade? And why, when we are all agreed that lower trade barriers between nations are necessary to world peace, do we have the difficulties we do in lowering any of the barriers? Why do people speak bitterly about the illiteracy and ignorance of Negroes and then use their illiteracy and ignorance as grounds for opposing any measures for ameliorating their condition? Why, above all, when every nation is agreed that another world war would be unthinkably awful and must be avoided at all costs, are the major powers breathlessly making preparations for another war? The world is full of such paradoxes.—S. I. HAYAKAWA, *Language in Thought and Action.*

51K. Elimination

It is often helpful in analyzing a topic or a term to point out first what it *is not.* The effectiveness of such procedure as an aid in definition has already been illustrated (see Section 51F), and the additional examples that follow show how a whole paragraph may be devoted to a process of elimination. The writer of Paragraph 61 is interested in making clear by examples several things that war is not, intending to proceed with an explanation of what it is. Paragraph 62 has a similar plan with regard to the topic of loyalty. The writer of Paragraph 63 shows that no one of four elements is effective by itself and advocates a combination of them.

61. How does war look when pinned out in the biologist's collection? In the first place, he is able to say with assurance that war is not a general law of life, but an exceedingly rare biological phenomenon. War is not the same thing as conflict or bloodshed. It means something quite definite: an organized physical conflict between groups of one and the same species. Individual disputes between members of the same species are not war, even if they involve bloodshed and death. Two stags fighting for a harem of hinds, or a man murdering another man, or a dozen dogs fighting over a bone, are not engaged in war. Competition between two different species, even if it involves physical conflict, is not war. When the brown rat was accidentally brought to Europe and proceeded to oust the black rat from most of its haunts, that was not war between the two species of rat; nor is it war in any but a purely metaphorical sense when we speak of making war on the malaria mosquito or the boll-weevil. Still less is it war when one species preys upon another, even when the preying is done by an organized group. A pack of wolves attacking a flock of sheep or deer, or a peregrine killing a duck, is not war. Much of nature, as Tennyson correctly said, is "red in tooth and claw"; but this only means what it says, that there is a great deal of killing in the animal world, not that war is the rule of life.—JULIAN HUXLEY, *On Living in a Revolution.*

62. It is easier to say what loyalty is not than to say what it is. It is not conformity. It is not passive acquiescence in the status quo. It is not preference for everything American over everything foreign. It is not an ostrich-like ignorance of other countries and other institutions. It is not the indulgence in ceremony—a flag salute, an oath of allegiance, a fervid verbal declaration. It is not a particular creed, a particular version of history, a particular body of economic practices, a particular philosophy.—HENRY STEELE COMMAGER, "Who Is Loyal to America?" *Harper's Magazine.*

63. The cultivation of learning alone produces not a university but a research institute; sole concern with student life produces in these days either an academic country club or a football team maneuvering under a collegiate banner; professional education by itself results in nothing but a trade school;

an institution concerned with general education, even in the best liberal arts tradition, divorced from research and training for the professions is admittedly not a university but a college. Therefore, to my mind, the future of the American university depends primarily on keeping a balance between these four traditional elements of strength. These four elements were the basis of the properly balanced plan in a time when universities were flourishing; they must continue to be in balance if the American university is to fulfill its proper functions in the times that are to come.—JAMES BRYANT CONANT, *Education in a Divided World.*

51L. Transitional Paragraphs

Transitions from one subdivision of a long paper to the next are often made through special transitional paragraphs, usually short, which look back and point the way clearly forward. The following paragraphs serve this useful transitional function.

64. So far we have been proceeding negatively by eliminating the ordinary words. You discover some of the important words by the fact that they are *not ordinary for you.* That is why they bother you. But is there any other way of spotting the important words? Are there any positive signs which point to them?—MORTIMER J. ADLER, *How to Read a Book.*

65. Now why does the average American student need to learn how to read a book? Why does he approach *Hamlet* or *Crime and Punishment* with a mixture of awe and bravado, and usually look up from it with such puzzled delight and half-understood emotion? Manifestly because he has been ill taught at school. And, so far, that is nobody's fault: certainly not his; but there are two main reasons for the fact.—GILBERT HIGHET, "The American Student as I See Him," *The American Scholar.*

66. Now I should like to examine a little more closely the procedures employed by the scientists today in physics, in chemistry, in biology, and in the application of science for practical ends in the whole area of the natural sciences. If in so doing, I appear to be underlining the obvious, I hope I shall be forgiven; for although a discussion of the so-called scientific method is almost a standard topic in a university, what I have to say is so antithetical to much of the current doctrine that I venture to present it in some detail here.—JAMES B. CONANT, *Modern Science and Modern Man.*

52. ADEQUATE PARAGRAPH DEVELOPMENT

It should have become clear from discussion of the paragraph to this point that whatever the pattern adopted, the successful paragraph requires adequate development of a central theme. The paragraphs of an inexperienced writer are likely to be scrappy because he does not realize the need of amplifying his statement or does not know how to go about it. Thoughtful study of the means of development that have been presented should help you out of this difficulty. Look, for example, at the following paragraph from a student theme:

> Mr. Barnes, who taught history, was the best teacher I had in high school. He had a thorough knowledge of his subject, his classes were always interesting, and he never embarrassed his students or acted superior to them. He kept order without arousing resentment.

There is nothing wrong with the paragraph so far as it goes; the trouble is that it remains inadequately developed. Yet the student writer had at hand a number of possible ways of amplifying his subject effectively. He might have used the method of dual development by contrasting Mr. Barnes with another teacher, setting forth a series of ways in which the two differed. He might have retained the opening sentence as it is and cited instances to confirm the statements made in the second and third sentences. He might have begun with a definition of a successful teacher and then showed how Mr. Barnes merited the description. It is not important which of these or several other possible methods the writer chooses to employ; what is important is that the reader be told more about Mr. Barnes and that the material be arranged in an effective pattern.

EXERCISES

A. Each of the following topic sentences can be developed into a full paragraph. The instructor may require you to indicate appropriate methods of development for all the sentences and to develop one or more of them into unified, coherent paragraphs in accordance with the pattern or patterns chosen. In this exercise you should aim at a paragraph length of perhaps 175–200 words.

1. If in high school I had known as much about college as I know now, I could have spared myself some of my present difficulties.

2. The present commercialization of college athletics is generally admitted to be an evil, but getting rid of that evil is not an easy matter.
3. A person who devotes himself exclusively to his studies is missing some important potential benefits of a college education.
4. Why do so many students who found high-school work easy run into serious difficulty in college?
5. Whether one believes that fraternities (or sororities) should be encouraged on a college campus or forbidden depends in part upon the experience which he or people of his acquaintance have had with them.
6. Trifles often have significant effect upon decisions of great importance.
7. Childhood troubles are usually unimportant in comparison with those of later life, but they do not seem so to the child.
8. The prospective purchaser of a secondhand automobile should look for defects that do not appear on the surface.
9. No matter where a college is situated, the writers of the college catalogue can find advantages to call attention to.
10. To a certain extent every college student bears the reputation of his college in his own hands.
11. Politics in high school and college are accompanied by some of the same evils that afflict politics in national life.
12. Freshman regulations help to develop college spirit.
13. A college in which freshman regulations are enforced has not reached maturity.
14. Though college girls universally complain of the rigidity of dormitory rules, they will feel differently some years from now when their own daughters are in college.
15. A too rigid system of dormitory regulation defeats its own purpose.
16. It is no wonder that fewer and fewer adults are going to the movies.
17. A country auction is a scene of great variety and interest.
18. The teacher, like the umpire, is usually right; but not always.
19. Pitching is eighty per cent of baseball.
20. My choice of a career has undergone a series of changes.
21. The parole system is sensible but potentially dangerous.
22. A demagogue is one who tries to employ the fears and prejudices of the people for his own selfish ends.
23. Stubbornness is what the other fellow is guilty of when we are showing the courage of our convictions.

B. From the illustrative paragraphs quoted in this chapter, select two which contain examples of topic sentences and two which contain examples of clinching sentences. Defend your choice in some detail. Do not cite paragraphs which have already been indicated as examples of the use of topic or clinching sentences!

C. Leaving Paragraph 27 out of consideration, cite from the illustrative paragraphs two instances of the use of each of the following devices to improve coherence: (1) pronoun or pronominal adjective; (2) repetition of key nouns; (3) parallelism; (4) single transitional words such as *next, then, however;* (5) transitional phrases such as *on the other hand, in the meantime, in other words*; (6) repetition of sentence patterns.

Chapter 7

DICTION

53. THE ENGLISH LANGUAGE: A BRIEF SKETCH OF ITS HISTORY[1]

The student of English, whether a native speaker of the language or a new learner, is particularly fortunate in his subject: English is by far the richest of all languages in variety and flexibility, and it is the easiest of all languages to learn. No other language can match its vast word hoard or its fundamental simplicity of structure.

These advantages are the result of special conditions that have favored the growth of English as a world language. At present nearly two hundred million people are native speakers of English. Many more millions speak it as a second language, and knowledge of it is commonly required or recommended in the schools of nearly all civilized nations, so that it is possible for speakers of English to make their wants known almost the world over without recourse to any other tongue. The present influence and prestige of this speech are immense. Though its future is unpredictable, it would appear to be the one language best fitted to become a common speech for all nations, not necessarily a speech to replace all others, but one to serve as a second language, a universally understood means of communication.

How the English language has arrived at this estate is a fascinating story, but too long and complicated for more than the

[1] The authors wish to acknowledge a special debt to Professor A. C. Baugh's *A History of the English Language* (New York: Appleton-Century-Crofts, Inc., 1935) for many details of information. See also p. 329 for other references.

briefest summary here. English is part of the extensive Indo-European family of languages made up originally of the related languages Indian (Sanskrit and its kindred languages), Iranian, Slavic, Baltic, Albanian, Armenian, Hittite, Tocharian, Greek, Italic, Celtic, and Teutonic. Teutonic, the group to which English belongs in origin, was made up of three divisions in its early development, namely, North, East, and West Teutonic. West Teutonic in turn became divided into Low and High Teutonic dialects, so named because of their geographical situations: Low Teutonic was spoken in the lowlands in what is now northern Germany and Holland, and High Teutonic (High German or Deutsch) in the mountainous south (Bavaria, Austria).

53A. Old English (449–1150)

Some time toward the middle of the fifth century (Bede sets the date at A.D. 449 in his *Ecclesiastical History of the English People*), three Low Teutonic tribes, the Angles, Saxons, and Jutes, invaded Britain, as the island was then called, and after subjugating many of the British people (the Celts) and driving the rest back into Wales, Cornwall, or Scotland, established their rule over that part of the island now known as England. This series of events marks the beginning of English history and the English language. The Anglians, who were the most numerous of these people and who gave their name to "England" and "English," settled in those parts of England extending from the Humber River (or the Scottish border) to the banks of the Thames. The Jutes inhabited what is now known as Kent. The Saxons settled in the rest of England south of the Thames, excluding Wales and Cornwall.

The dialects spoken by these people, together with their literature, are known by the general name of Old English or Anglo-Saxon. Old English, like all the other Teutonic and Indo-European languages, is spoken of as a synthetic language. A synthetic language depends on suffixes indicating case, gender, and number (for nouns and adjectives) and tense, person, number, and mood (for verbs) to establish the relationship of words in sentences. Thus the words in the Latin sentence *Caesar Vercingetorigem superavit* (Caesar conquered Vercingetorix) might be arranged in any possible order and still convey the same meaning, thanks to the accusative (or objective) case ending *-em* and the verbal suffix *-vit* indicating the past tense. In Middle and Modern English, however, as we shall see, word order is rather narrowly limited. To say in English, "Caesar Vercingetorix conquered," is ambiguous; to say, "Vercingetorix conquered Caesar," is false. But in Old English, though the inflectional system was breaking down, writers, if not speakers, still relied on inflectional suffixes to establish exact shades of meaning.

Somewhat like Latin and Greek, which are highly inflected languages, and very like modern French and German, Old English had a formal declension of nouns, pronouns, and adjectives with inflectional suffixes for the nominative, genitive, dative, and accusative cases, and a rather elaborate inflection of verbs, the inflectional suffixes indicating person, number, tense, and mood.

In this period the vocabulary was predominantly Teutonic. Professor Baugh tells us that not more than twenty words in Old English appear to be of Celtic origin, and though the Latin contribution to the vocabulary is made up of very important words, not more than four hundred and fifty appear to have been added from that source. The Danish invasions in the eighth, ninth, and tenth centuries gradually added about nine hundred words to the native stock (exclusive of numerous dialect words), but these of course are Teutonic. In 1066 when the Norman William the Conqueror defeated Harold at Hastings and became King of England, England was a Teutonic land, its people speaking a language essentially as Teutonic as German, Netherlandish, or Danish.

Old English possesses the richest body of literature of its time, including the noble heroic epic *Beowulf,* the heroic poems *Widsith, Waldere, Brunanburh,* and *Maldon,* the elegiac poems, including *The Wanderer, The Sea Farer,* and *Deor's Lament,* the Christian narrative poems by Cynewulf and other authors, and the prose translations of Alfred (including Boethius' *Consolation of Philosophy,* Gregory's *Pastoral Care,* and Bede's *Ecclesiastical*

History). These works have been preserved only in the West Saxon dialect, since (it is assumed) the Anglian versions were destroyed in the Danish invasions.

53B. Middle English (1150–1500)

For three hundred years after the Norman Conquest the official language of England was French. English was still the main language of the people, but those who wished to prosper at court or otherwise to win the favor of their governors (either French or Saxons favored by the French) found it desirable to learn French, and for a long time people of the upper classes were largely bilingual. In time, however, as the French invaders came to identify their interests with England and became assimilated by the English, the English language once more resumed its former position as the official language of the realm (1362). But this English was notably different from Old English. Its inflections were now greatly reduced. Where Old English nouns were declined through four cases, both singular and plural, the new Middle English, as represented by the East Midland dialect of Chaucer, had usually only two forms in the singular and two in the plural. In short, the inflection of the noun, as will be seen in the following illustration, had become very like that of modern English:

	OLD ENGLISH	MIDDLE ENGLISH	MODERN ENGLISH
	Singular	*Singular*	*Singular*
NOM.	stan	stoon	stone
GEN.	stanes	stoones	stone's
DAT.	stane		
ACC.	stan		
	Plural	*Plural*	*Plural*
NOM.	stanas	stoones	stones
GEN.	stana	stoones	stones'
DAT.	stanum		
ACC.	stanas		

The nominative forms in Middle and Modern English serve without change for dative and accusative uses; early evidence of transition to this simpler state may be seen in the fact that in Old English the nominative and the accusative were frequently the same in form (as in the illustration above).

The personal pronoun (*I, you, he, she, it, we, they*) maintained a fairly full inflection, through the nominative, possessive, and objective (dative—accusative) cases in the masculine, feminine, and neuter genders, singular and plural; and this pronoun was to maintain this relatively full inflection down to the present.

Nowhere is the breaking down of the old inflectional system more striking than in the adjective. In Old English the adjective was inflected through four (sometimes five) cases, both singular and plural, and three genders, masculine, feminine, and neuter. There were two systems of this full inflection, commonly known as the strong and weak declensions. The definite article *the* had as many as nineteen inflectional forms. In Middle English the strong and weak inflections of the adjective retained only two forms each, one for the singular and one for the plural, as follows:

	Singular	*Plural*
STRONG:	good	goode
WEAK:	goode	goode

The definite article was reduced in Middle English to one form as at present.

Comparable changes were being made in the conjugation of verbs. The Old English strong verbs (such as *ride, bid, sing, bear, eat*) were reduced in number from an estimated 333 to approximately 68 verbs distinctly strong in form and 13 of mixed strong and weak forms. Many of the lost verbs disappeared completely, but others (about 81) were transformed to the classification known as weak verbs, which form their past tenses by the addition of the suffix *-ed* or *-t* to the present form. The number of weak verbs was greatly multiplied. The habit of transforming nouns into verbs with past tenses in *-ed* now became very common, a practice that was to accelerate rapidly in modern English. The inflection of verbs, which had begun to break down in Old English, was reduced yet further in Middle English.

We speak of the Middle English period as a period of leveled inflections; by this term we mean that the inflectional endings marking the synthetic state of the language had gradually been eliminated, and users of the language had come to rely on word order to make clear the relationship of words in a sentence. In other words, Middle English was rapidly becoming an analytic language. An analytic language is one which expresses its meaning through the arrangement of the words in the sentence, with the aid of prepositions and auxiliary verbs. The case endings of nouns in the synthetic stage of the language are lost and their meaning is supplied by the use of prepositions; and aspects of mood and tense, formerly indicated by verbal suffixes, have their meanings supplied by the auxiliary verbs, *will, shall, may, can, must, would, should, might,* and *could.*

Hardly less important is the enormous increase in the vocabulary at this time through the introduction of thousands of new words borrowed from French and Latin, representing every phase of human activity. At the beginning of the Middle English period, the language was Teutonic both in grammar and in vocabulary. By the end of the period in 1500, the grammar was still basically Teutonic (though greatly simplified), but the vocabulary was made up of Teutonic and Romance (French and Latin) words. The fundamental word stock was and would remain Teutonic (Old English); but the greater part of our words having to do with the church, the army, government, education, the arts and sciences, and all the refinements of living, including the arts of cooking and clothing, are derived from either French or Latin, as will be found by reference to a dictionary, and most of the more commonly used borrowings of these sorts came into our language in this period.

Some time toward the close of the Middle English period, a very strange phenomenon developed, now known as the Great Vowel Shift, which was to have a remarkable effect on the pronunciation of the language. The long vowels of Old and Middle English were pronounced essentially like the same vowels on the continent, like the long vowels of French, German, and Latin.

When the shift was completed, in the modern period, these same vowels were pronounced as they are today. The results may be illustrated by the following examples of the change:

OLD ENGLISH	MIDDLE ENGLISH	MODERN ENGLISH
nāme (*a* as in German *Mann*)	name (*a* as in *ah*)	name
stān (*a* as in *father*)	stoon (*oo* like *aw* in *law*)	stone
fēt (*e* like *a* in *fate*)	feet (*ee* like *a* in *fate*)	feet
rīdan (*i* like *ee* in *reed*)	ride (*i* like *ee* in *reed*)	ride
sōna (*o* as in *bone*)	sone (*o* as in *bone*)	soon
hūs (*u* like *oo* in *loose*)	hous (*ou* like *oo* in *loose*)	house

The Great Vowel Shift may be regarded as placing the chief stumbling block in the way of new learners of the language. Any European of today could have pronounced the vowel sounds of Chaucer's time correctly and without effort; but the new student of Modern English must learn a new set of sound values for the otherwise familiar vowel symbols.

Though some dialects of Middle English present complexities, the greater part of Middle English literature may be fairly easily read and appreciated by the modern student. This is particularly true of the great works of Chaucer and Malory. Other famous pieces of literature, such as *Sir Gawain and the Green Knight, The Pearl,* and *Piers Plowman,* are more difficult, but good translations are available. The Middle English period is the age of the romances of chivalry and courtly love, of dream-vision poems, of miracle and morality plays.

53C. Modern English (1500 to the Present)

Before the occurrence of the Great Vowel Shift we think of our language as Middle English. The development of the shift marks the beginning of the Modern English period, the period of Lost Inflections. Modern English is largely an analytic language. Only a few inflectional endings survive. Thus the s-plural of our nouns and our possessives in *'s* represent old inflectional endings; and of course the nouns that do not conform to this pattern, such as *man, men; ox, oxen; child, children,* point likewise to other old inflectional endings. The pronouns, because inflectional endings were constantly being used with these words, retain, as observed before, a relatively full inflection. Today, save in dialect, *thou, thy,* and *thee* are no longer in use. Otherwise our pronouns are not greatly different from those of Old and Middle English. Adjectives now have only one form, save for the plurals of *this* and *that,* namely *these* and *those.* The verb, which had a fairly full inflection earlier, now possesses only a few inflectional endings. The suffixes *-est, -eth* inherited from Middle English and still used in early Modern English and, to some extent, in later poetic practice, are now rarely used, and we have only the singular third person ending in *-s,* the present participle ending in *-ing,* and the inflectional variations of the strong and weak verbs in the past tense and past participle to remind us of the once much more elaborate inflection of the verb.

On the other hand, the gain in simplicity in the inflection of our verbs is counterbalanced by the complexity of the very elaborate system of auxiliary verbs, forms of *may, can, must, shall, will, be, do,* and *have,* used with the infinitive or participial forms of other verbs, by means of which we express mood and tense meanings which in Old English might have been conveyed by inflectional endings.

But the gain in the transformation of English from a synthetic to an analytic language (it is the only great Western world language that is analytic) far outweighs any of its disadvantages. English speakers need never worry whether they are using the right adjectival ending to agree with a feminine or masculine or neuter noun. Thanks to our system of natural gender as opposed to that of word gender, they need not even worry about the gender of nouns.

Another advantage of Modern English is its vast vocabulary, which lends itself with marvelous flexibility to every possible need for vocal expression and communication. Since it makes free use of Latin and Greek, which have international currency in Western world scholarship, it is therefore an advantageous language for science and learning. In business, trade, and commerce it imports terms from other languages almost as freely as it imports articles, and in turn exports its English terms all over the world. It is capable of expressing the richest and deepest emotion, the most delicate fancy, the most abstract and refined thought. At its worst it is a language of clichés and jargon; at its best it is the language of genius, of Shakespeare, Milton, Wordsworth, Coleridge, Keats, Hopkins, Yeats, and other celebrated poets in an unending procession of greatness.

The outstanding fact about Modern English has been its steady growth, which was the outcome of England's colonial expansion and the rise of the United States as a world power. It is now the national language of Great Britain, of the British Commonwealth of Nations, including Canada, Australia, New Zealand, and South Africa, and of the United States and its possessions. Though it is no longer the official language of India, most educated people in India know it as a second language. Indeed, the educated in nearly every nation take pride in their ability to speak English.

Despite dialectal differences in various regions of the English-speaking nations, the standard English of one nation is readily comprehensible in every other. American and British peoples freely enjoy the same works of literature. People in Melbourne, Auckland, Vancouver, New York, San Francisco, London, and Johannesburg read in their daily news a language that is almost equally intelligible everywhere English is spoken. Minor differences in idiom and vocabulary exist from land to land, but in the main the language of educated users of English is predominantly the same everywhere.

REFERENCES

"A Brief History of the English Language," *Webster's New International Dictionary* (2d ed.), lxxxii-xc.

Baugh, Albert C. *A History of the English Language.* New York: Appleton-Century-Crofts, Inc., 1935.

Kennedy, Arthur G. *Current English.* New York: Ginn and Company, 1935.

Marckwardt, Albert H. *Introduction to the English Language.* New York: Oxford University Press, 1942.

Robertson, Stewart. *The Development of Modern English* (2d ed.), revised by Frederick G. Cassidy. New York: Prentice-Hall, Inc., 1954.

54. TYPES OF DICTIONARIES

54A. Unabridged Dictionaries

Our language is well provided with dictionaries to suit every need, from large unabridged works that record most of the words in the language down to pocket-sized ones of very limited scope, from dictionaries carefully defining best usage to special dictionaries of dialects, of technical words and phrases, and of slang. The following unabridged dictionaries are planned to answer most of our questions about the meaning and use of words:

Webster's New International Dictionary of the English Language (2d ed.). Springfield, Mass.: G. & C. Merriam Co., 1934; latest reprint, 1953.

New Standard Dictionary of the English Language (1st ed.). New York: Funk & Wagnalls Co., 1913; latest reprint, 1953.

The New Century Dictionary of the English Language. 2 vols. New York: Appleton-Century-Crofts, Inc., 1953.

These dictionaries offer definitions of most of the words in the language and also serve as very useful works of reference for facts about people, places, and things. Thus *Webster's New International Dictionary* now lists 600,000 words, of which 552,000 are main vocabulary entries. The introductory pages include a valuable preface on the history, scope, and aims of the dictionary, a history of the English language, an extensive study of pronunciation, and a section devoted to rules for spelling. The main text of the dictionary itself in addition to its definitions includes much encyclopedic information about literary and mythological characters, geographic, historic, scientific facts and allusions, foreign language quotations, pictorial illustrations, and other helpful knowledge. The concluding pages offer sections explaining abbreviations used in printed literature, the arbitrary signs used in the various arts and sciences, and finally special geographical and biographical dictionaries, both giving the accepted pronunciations of their terms.

Other dictionaries of special value are those that trace the history of words. The greatest of these is the *New English Dictionary on Historical Principles* (often referred to as *N. E. D.*), also known as the *Oxford English Dictionary* (*O. E. D.*), which was published in installments from 1884 to 1933 (ten volumes and a supplement). This work attempts to record all the words found in English texts from the time of Chaucer to the present, with a history of each word, its different spellings, uses, and meanings, illustrated by quotations beginning with the earliest written occurrences down to the present. This dictionary is particularly important to those who wish to understand more fully the literature of any period. Thus, *nice, fond, naughty, prevent,* and *humor* conveyed meanings to Shakespeare quite different from those that will at once occur to most college freshmen of today. This dictionary records the history and usage of 240,165 main terms, exclusive of those in the supplement. A valuable abridgment of this work, the *Shorter Oxford English Dictionary* (two volumes), was published in 1936 (corrected reprint, 1947).

A Dictionary of American English on Historical Principles (University of Chicago Press, 1938–1944) records in like fashion words and expressions peculiarly American in origin and usage.

54B. Collegiate Dictionaries

The most conveniently useful of all dictionaries are the collegiate dictionaries. Though the relatively small size of these works limits their service, they will answer most demands made upon them, and every student should own one and refer to it constantly. These dictionaries list and define the most commonly used words and expressions and also contain much encyclopedic information. Be sure to secure the latest edition. Well-known dictionaries of this type are the following:

The American College Dictionary. New York: Random House, 1947; Harper & Bros., 1948.

Funk & Wagnalls New College Standard Dictionary. New York: Funk & Wagnalls Co., 1947.

Macmillan's Modern Dictionary (rev. ed.). New York: The Macmillan Co., 1947.

Thorndike-Barnhart Comprehensive Desk Dictionary. New York: Doubleday & Co., Inc., 1951.

Webster's New Collegiate Dictionary (2d ed.). Springfield, Mass.: G. & C. Merriam Co., 1949.

Webster's New World Dictionary of the American Language (College ed.). Cleveland: World Publishing Co., 1953.
The Winston Dictionary (Advanced, College, or Encyclopedic ed.). Philadelphia: John C. Winston Co., 1945.

54C. Special Dictionaries

Other dictionaries that will prove helpful in special problems of meaning and usage are these:

Fowler, H. W. *Dictionary of Modern English Usage.* Oxford: Clarendon Press, 1926, 1930, 1937.
Hall, John R. Clark. *A Concise Anglo-Saxon Dictionary* (3d ed.). Cambridge University Press, 1931.
Horwill, H. W. *Dictionary of Modern American Usage.* Oxford: Clarendon Press, 1935.
Kurath, Hans, and Kuhn, S. M. (assoc. ed.). *Middle English Dictionary.* In preparation. Parts E and F issued 1953–54. University of Michigan Press.
Partridge, Eric. *Dictionary of Slang.* New York: The Macmillan Co., 1950.
The Roget Dictionary of Synonyms and Antonyms. New York: G. P. Putnam's Sons, 1931.
Skeat, W. W. *Etymological Dictionary of the English Language* (4th ed.). Oxford: Clarendon Press, 1910.
Stratmann, F. H. *Middle English Dictionary.* Re-edited by Henry Bradley. Oxford: Clarendon Press, 1891.
Vizetelly, F. H., and DeBekker, L. J. *Desk-Book of Idioms and Idiomatic Phrases.* New York: Funk & Wagnalls Co., 1923.
Webster's Dictionary of Synonyms. Springfield, Mass.: G. & C. Merriam Co., 1942.
Weekley, Ernest. *A Concise Etymological Dictionary of Modern English.* London: Secker & Warburg, 1952.
Wright, Joseph. *English Dialect Dictionary.* 6 vols. London, 1898–1905.

55. USE OF THE DICTIONARY

Dictionaries serve best those who know how to make full use of their resources. For this reason it is important to get the habit of reading definitions completely. For every main entry a good dictionary records its spelling or spellings, its pronunciation and syllabication, its grammatical function or functions, its etymology or derivation, its general meaning or meanings, its special meanings and restricted uses, and often a list of its synonyms. In studying these features you will find helpful the accompanying explanatory sample page from *Webster's New Collegiate Dictionary.*

55A. Abbreviations

First of all, you should be familiar with the abbreviations used by your dictionary in presenting its information. Explanatory lists of these abbreviations may be found by consulting the contents page. In the *American College Dictionary* (abbreviated as *ACD*), a list of etymological and language abbreviations is found on the inside page facing the back cover, and a brief etymological list is given also at the bottom of every other page in the text; see the text itself for other abbreviations. In *Webster's New Collegiate Dictionary* (abbreviated as *NCD*), a complete list of the abbreviations used in the text is given on pages xxi–xxii immediately preceding the text.

55B. Spelling

The dictionary establishes the accepted spelling and accepted variant spellings (if any) of each word. It tells us how to spell the grammatical variations of many such words as the plurals of nouns and the principal parts of verbs. The authority of the dictionary may be regarded as absolute for the spelling of words except for some allowable variations in the spelling of dialect and technical terms. In general, when two spellings of any word are given, the first is regarded as preferred by most writers. Likewise American spelling is always used rather than British. See *ACD,* pp. xxviii–xxix, xl, Section 7; *NCD,* p. xviii, p. 1197.

55C. Pronunciation

The dictionary records for each term by means of diacritical marks or phonetic spelling the pronunciations approved by present, national, and reputable usage, and for a great part of our vocabulary the authority of the dictionary once more may be accepted as final, since all dictionaries and most speakers of the language everywhere pronounce these words in very much the same way. But, as reference to the "Guide to Pronunciation" in *Webster's New International Dictionary* (pp. lix–lxxviii) will show, even the dictionaries themselves disagree about the pronun-

Pronunciation

pawner

pawn'er (pôn'ẽr), **pawn'or** (pôn'ẽr; pôn·ôr'), *n.* *Law.* One who pawns or pledges anything as security.

Centered Period for Syllabic Division

pawn'shop' (pôn'shŏp'), *n.* A pawnbroker's shop.

paw·paw' (*see* PAPAW), *n.* Var. of PAPAW.

Subject Label

pax (păks), *n.* [L.] **1.** Peace; — deified by the Romans. **2.** *R.C.Ch.* A tablet bearing a figure or symbol of Christ, the Virgin Mary, or a saint, which in medieval times was kissed by the priest and the people, before the Communion.

‖**pax vo·bis'cum** (vō·bĭs'kŭm). [L.] Peace (be) with you.

pax'wax' (păks'wăks'), *n.* [For *faxwax*, fr. AS. *feax* hair + a word akin to *weaxan* to grow.] In many mammals, the median ligament of the back of the neck, composed of yellow elastic tissue and used in supporting the head.

Principal Parts

pay (pā), *v. t.;* PAYED (pād); PAY'ING. [OF. *peier, poier,* fr. L. *picare* to pitch, fr. *pix* pitch.] To smear or coat, as a vessel's bottom, a seam, etc., with a waterproof composition, as of tallow, resin, etc.

pay (pā), *v. t.;* PAID (pād) or, *Obs.* exc. in sense 6, PAYED; PAY'ING. [OF. *paier,* fr. L. *pacare* to pacify, appease, fr. *pax, pacis,* peace.] **1.** To satisfy (one) for service rendered, property delivered, etc.; remunerate. **2.** To give (something due) in return, satisfaction, or requital; also, to discharge indebtedness for; settle, as a bill. **3.** To make compensation or retaliation for. **4.** To give, offer, or make, freely or as fitting; as, to *pay* court or a visit. **5.** To be profitable to; also, bring in as a return. **6.** To pass out, as a rope; — now with *out* or *away.* — *v. i.* **1.** To give a recompense; make payment. **2.** To be profitable; to be worth the expense, effort, or the like.

Idiomatic Usage

Discriminated Synonyms

Syn. **Pay, compensate, remunerate, satisfy, reimburse, indemnify, repay, recompense, requite** mean to give money or its equivalent in return for something. **Pay** implies the discharge of an obligation incurred; **compensate,** as here considered, a making up for services rendered or help given; **remunerate,** more clearly, a paying for services rendered; **satisfy,** paying a person that which is asked or required by law; **reimburse,** a return of money that has been expended; **indemnify,** a reimbursing for loss suffered through fire, accident, damage by war, or the like; **repay,** a paying back in kind or amount; **recompense,** often, a compensating for services rendered but, sometimes, for losses or injuries sustained; **requite,** a reciprocating or retaliation, often but not necessarily in kind.

Verb Phrase

pay off. **1.** To pay; specif., to pay in full and discharge. **2.** To requite. **3.** To allow to run off, as a thread or cord. **4.** *Colloq.* To yield full return, either to one's advantage or disadvantage; also, to attain full effectiveness. **5.** *Naut.* To turn (a vessel) to leeward.

pay'nim (pā'nĭm), *n.* [OF. *paienisme* heathendom, fr. LL. *paganismus* paganism.] *Archaic.* Pagans or pagan countries; also, a pagan; an infidel, esp. a Mohammedan.

Usage Label

pay'off' (pā'ôf'), *n.* *Chiefly Colloq.* **1.** Act or time of paying employees' wages. **2.** Repayment or accrual for settlement at the outcome of an enterprise; reward or retribution. **3.** Climax of an incident or enterprise; specif., the denouement of a narrative. **4.** Decisive fact or factor resolving a situation, bringing about a definitive conclusion; as, the opinion of the Tax Court on taxability is the *payoff.* — *adj.* *Colloq.* Yielding results in the final test; rewarding or decisive.

Foreign Word

pay'roll' (pā'rōl'), *n.* A paymaster's list of persons entitled to pay, with the amounts due to each; also, the amount necessary, or the money, for distribution to those on such a list.

Capitalization

‖**pay'sage'** (pā'ē·zàzh'), *n.* [F.] A landscape or a landscape picture.

PC (pē'sē'). [patrol craft.] *U. S. Navy.* A fast patrol craft equipped with submarine-detection devices, 3-inch gun, machine guns, antiaircraft guns, and depth charges.

Word Story

pea (pē), *n.; pl.* PEAS (pēz) or PEASE (pēz) (see *Note* below). [AS. *pise,* pl. *pisan,* fr. LL. *pisa,* fr. L. *pisum,* pl. *pisa,* fr. Gr. *pison, pisos.* The vowel may have been influenced by OF. *peis,* fr. L. *pisum.* The final *s* was misunderstood in English as a plural ending.] **1.** Any plant of a family (Fabaceae, the pea family) of herbs, shrubs, and trees, the fruit of which is a true pod or legume. **2.** The round, smooth or wrinkled, edible seed borne severally in dehiscent pods by a vine (*Pisum sativum*) of this family; also, the similar angular seed of a related plant (*P. arvense*). **3.** Any of various leguminous plants or their seeds, resembling the common pea; as, the sweet *pea,* cow*pea,* etc. **4.** Something like a pea, as in size.

Plural Form

☞ The plural *peas* was formerly used to indicate a definite number, as contrasted with the collective plural *pease;* the tendency now is to use *peas* as plural in all senses.

Antonym

peace'ful (-fŏŏl; -f'l), *adj.* **1.** *Now Rare.* Pacific; peaceable. **2.** Possessing, enjoying, or marked by, peace; tranquil; also, of or pert. to peace. — **Syn.** See CALM. — **Ant.** Turbulent. — **peace'ful·ly,** *adv.* — **peace'ful·ness,** *n.*

Biblical Term

peace offering. A propitiatory gift; esp., *Bib.*, a ceremonial propitiatory sacrifice.

peace officer. A civil officer whose duty it is to preserve the public peace, as a sheriff, constable, or policeman.

peace pipe. The calumet.

peach (pēch), *v. t.* [ME. *apechen*, fr. AF.] *Obs.* To impeach; indict. — *v. i. Obs. exc. Slang.* To turn informer; to blab.

peach, *n.* [OF. *peche, pesche*, fr. LL. *persica*, fr. L. *Persicum* (sc. *malum*) Persian apple, peach.] **1.** Any of a family (Amygdalaceae, the peach family) of trees and shrubs distinguished by the single pistil

Hyphened Word

peacock blue. A color, bluish green-blue in hue, of medium saturation and low brilliance. See COLOR. — **pea′cock′-blue′,** *adj.*

pea′fowl′ (pē′foul′), *n.* The peacock or peahen.

peag (pēg), *n.* Also **peage** (pēg). Wampum.

Noun Phrase in Alphabetic Place

pea green. A color, yellowish yellow-green in hue, of low saturation and medium brilliance. See COLOR. — **pea′-green′,** *adj.*

pea′hen′ (pē′hĕn′), *n.* The female of the peacock.

pea jacket. [Prob. fr. D. *pij, pije*, coat of a coarse woolen stuff.] A sailor's thick loose woolen double-breasted coat.

peak (pēk), *v. i.* To grow thin and sickly.

peak, *n.* [Var. of 1st PIKE.] **1.** The sharp or pointed end of anything. **2.** [For earlier *pike*, fr. Sp. & Pg. *pico.*] Specif.: **a** *Now Local.* A headland or promontory. **b** The top of a hill or mountain ending in a point; one of the crests of a range; often, the whole mountain, esp. when isolated. **c** The projecting front part of a cap or the like. **3.** The topmost point; summit; also, the highest point, as in a graph; maximum. **4.** *Naut.* **a** The upper aftermost corner of a fore-and-aft sail. **b** The narrow part of a vessel's bow or stern, or the part of the hold in it. **5.** A point formed by the hair on the forehead; — chiefly in ***widow's peak***, orig. such a point on a woman's forehead, now often a similar point on a man's forehead. — **Syn.** See SUMMIT. — *v. t.* To cause to come to a peak; specif., *Naut.*, to raise to a position perpendicular, or more nearly so, as a gaff.

Special Meaning

Subject Label

peaked (pēkt; pēk′ĕd; -ĭd), *adj.* **1.** Pointed; having a peak. **2.** (*pron. usually* pēk′ĕd; -ĭd) [From PEAK to grow thin.] *Chiefly Colloq.* Thin; emaciated.

peal (pēl), *n.* [Shortened fr. APPEAL.] **1.** *Bell Ringing.* **a** Loosely, a set of bells tuned to the tones of the major scale for change ringing. **b** A complete set of changes on a given number of bells; esp., the series on seven bells. **c** Any shorter performance than a full set of changes; as, a wedding *peal*. **2.** A loud sound, or a succession of loud sounds, as of bells or thunder. — *v. i.* To give out peals; resound. — *v. t.* **1.** *Obs.* To assail or din, as with noise or loud sounds. **2.** To sound forth in or as in a peal or peals; noise abroad.

pe′an (pē′ăn). Var. of PAEAN.

pea′nut′ (pē′nŭt′; -nŭt), *n.* A Brazilian herb (*Arachis hypogaea*) of the pea family, of erect habit, whose peduncles bend after fertilization and push the pods into the ground, where they ripen; also, the nutlike seed of this plant. **peanut oil** is expressed from these seeds; **peanut butter** is made from these seeds roasted, ground, and moistened.

pear (pâr), *n.* [AS. *pere, peru*, fr. LL. *pera, pira*, fr. L. *pirum*, pl. *pira.*] **a** The fleshy pome fruit of a tree (genus *Pyrus*, esp. *P. communis*) of the apple family. **b** The tree bearing this fruit.

Variant Spelling

pearl (pûrl), *n.* [OF. *perle*, fr. ML. *perla, perula.*] **1.** A dense concretion, lustrous and varying in color, formed as an abnormal growth within the shell of some mollusks, and used as a gem. **2.** Something resembling a pearl in shape, size, color, beauty, or value. **3. a** Mother-of-pearl; nacre. **b** In full **pearl blue.** The color of mother-of-pearl, a nearly neutral gray (slightly bluish) of high brilliance. See COLOR. **4.** *Print.* A size of type (5 point). See TYPE. — *v. t.* **1.** To adorn with pearls. **2.** To form into small round grains, as barley. **3.** To give to or suffuse with a pearly luster. — *v. i.* To fish or search for pearls. — *adj.* **1.** Of, like, or set with pearls. **2.** Formed into small round grains; as, **pearl barley; pearl tapioca.** — **pearl′er,** *n.*

pearl. Var. of PURL.

pearl′ash′ (pûrl′ăsh′), *n.* Purified potash. See POTASH, 1.

pearl gray. The color of a fine pearl, an early neutral gray of high brilliance. See COLOR. — **pearl′-gray′** (-grā′; 2), *adj.*

pearl′ite (pûrl′īt), *n.* [*pearl* + *-ite.*] **1.** *Metal.* The readily fusible alloy of carbon and iron, containing 0.85 per cent carbon. **2.** *Petrog.* = PERLITE. — **pearl·it′ic** (pûrl·ĭt′ĭk), *adj.*

pearl′y (pûr′lĭ), *adj.*; PEARL′I·ER (-lĭ·ẽr); -I·EST. Of or like pearl or mother-of-pearl; adorned with or abounding in pearls.

Cross Reference

pearly nautilus. See NAUTILUS, 1.

pear′main (pâr′mān), *n.* [OF. *permain, parmain.*] An apple of one of several different varieties.

peart (pẽrt; pyẽrt), **peart′ly.** Dial. vars. of PERT, etc.

peas′ant (pĕz′ănt; -′nt), *n.* [OF. *païsant, païsent*, fr. *païs, pays*, land, country, fr. LL. *pagensis*, fr. L. *pagus* country district. See

Etymology

ciation of at least eleven hundred words, many of them common words familiar to educated people. Furthermore, educated speakers of different countries, regions, and even communities differ on the sound values of many words, as all lexicographers admit. The editors of *Webster's New Collegiate Dictionary* (p. ix), for example, say:

> The standard of English pronunciation, so far as a standard may be said to exist, is the usage that now prevails among the educated and cultured peoples to whom the language is vernacular; but since somewhat different pronunciations are used by the cultivated in different regions too large to be ignored, we must frankly admit the fact that, at present, uniformity of pronunciation is not to be found throughout the English-speaking world, though there is a very large percentage of practical uniformity.[2]

When, then, is a pronunciation correct? The same editors give the only possible answer (p. ix):

> When the essential facts are considered, "correctness of pronunciation" must be a flexible term. It is perhaps as accurate a definition as can be made to say that a pronunciation is correct when it is in actual use by a sufficient number of cultivated speakers.[2]

When more than one recognized pronunciation exists for a word, the lexicographers indicate the pronunciation that they find used most commonly by listing it first; but the other recorded pronunciations are acceptable, as the same editors remark (p. xviii):

> When two or more pronunciations are recorded, the general rule has been to place first the one that has been selected as preferable. Each form entered, however, has the support of good usage, and in some cases this usage is nearly or quite equally divided.[2]

For more detailed discussion of pronunciation see *ACD,* pp. xxii, xxxix; *NCD,* pp. vii–xviii, xvii, Section 2.

55D. Syllabication

Syllabication is also indicated for all primary entries. This division of a word into syllables is made on the basis of their

[2] By permission. From *Webster's New Collegiate Dictionary*, copyright 1949, 1951, 1953, by G. & C. Merriam Co.

uttered sound values, and is a valuable aid in learning both the spelling and the pronunciation of words. Always follow the divisions of the syllabication given in the dictionary when it is necessary to divide a word in manuscript. See *ACD*, p. xl, Section 1; *NCD*, p. xviii, Sections 1, 2. See also Section 43B in this textbook.

55E. Grammatical Function of Words

The dictionary indicates the function or functions of every word defined. Many words may serve a variety of functions in a sentence, and the definitions are arranged according to these functions. Thus the word "command" has seven definitions as a verb and seven meanings as a noun, all in good use, though two of the noun uses are special, as indicated by their labels (*Military, British*). On the other hand, some words are limited (at least in formal and informal use) to one part of speech: for example, "suspicion" and "contact" are primarily nouns; "buy" and "invite" are primarily verbs. The student who wishes to use "suspicion" and "contact" as verbs or "buy" and "invite" as nouns in a passage of formal writing should not do so without studying his dictionary and considering the possible effect of his usage on his readers.

In addition to indicating the part of speech, the dictionary also gives variant inflected forms of the nouns and verbs and indicates whether verbs are transitive or intransitive. When no plural is given for a noun, it is understood that the noun forms its plural by adding *-s* or *-es*. The principal parts of strong verbs are given (*sing, sang, sung*); for weak verbs (those forming the past tense in *-ed*), only the present form is ordinarily given. See *ACD*, p. xl, Sections 3, 4; *NCD*, pp. xviii–xix, Sections 3, 4.

55F. Etymology

The dictionary also gives the etymology or history of the origin of the word, its early forms in the Teutonic background of our language or in other languages. Knowledge of the etymology of words may help you in several ways. It is a means of widening your intellectual horizons. To know that "weird" traces back to Anglo-Saxon *wyrd*, referring to a goddess of fate or destiny, throws new light on the "weird sisters" in *Macbeth.* Is it surprising to find that a "good fellow" is etymologically one who is willing to share his property, or, in current terms, to "pick up the checks"? What mental gymnastics are suggested by the fact that *mission, missive, mess* (as in a dirty *mess, mess* hall, *mess* of beans), *message, messenger,* and *Mass* (Christ*mas*) all relate to the Latin *missus, missum* ("sent")! And one could multiply examples.

But most important of all the etymological relationships are those of our prefixes and suffixes (see Section 55K below). Armed with a knowledge of these, one is able to recognize the special meaning or application of many words. Thus knowing the meanings of *trans-* (a Latin prefix meaning "across") and the suffixes *-able, -ible* (derived from Latin *habilis*) helps us in recognizing the sense of such words as *transferable, translatable, transmutable, transmittible, transformable, transportable.* It is good to familiarize yourself with the meanings of these important elements in word formation.

For discussion of the treatment of etymologies, see *ACD,* pp. xxiii–xxiv, xl, Section 8; *NCD,* p. xix, Section 5.

55G. Definitions

The dictionary gives us definitions of the various meanings of each word. The arrangement of these definitions varies with the dictionary used. The Merriam-Webster dictionaries give first the early meanings of words, those closest to the primary root-meaning, and then the more recent meanings. Other dictionaries usually give the present or more recent meanings first. Get the habit of reading all the definitions of the words you look up in the dictionary: to understand the various uses that a word has and the limitations put upon its use will extend your knowledge of language. Notice also that your dictionary lists idiomatic uses of each verb after the main definition. Thus after "break" has been defined in its several meanings, *Webster's New Collegiate Dictionary* gives further definitions of the idioms *break down, break in, break on the wheel,* and *break up.* See *ACD,* p. xl, Section 6; *NCD,* p. xix, Section 6.

55H. Labels of Usage

Many definitions are preceded by italicized labels (usually abbreviated) that indicate restrictions put on the use of the word. Some of these labels (*Colloq., Slang*) indicate that the word defined may ordinarily be used only in conversation and in informal contexts; others (such as *Mus., Math., Med., Law*), that the word has special application in various fields; others (*Obs., Archaic*), that the word is no longer commonly used or is borrowed from older usage; and still others (such as *Brit., U.S. colloq., Western U.S.*), that the word has geographical limitations of usage. See *ACD,* p. xl, Section 5; *NCD,* pp. xix–xx.

55J. Synonyms

The dictionary also lists synonyms for many words. A synonym is etymologically a "with-name," a word that may be associated with another word in likeness of meaning. It must be understood that no two words have precisely the same meaning, but many words may have meanings so similar that one may be substituted for the other, sometimes to great advantage. The choice of the right word among several synonyms is an important test of a writer's taste and judgment: one must try to select the best word for the given situation. Often, of course, no satisfactory substitute for a word exists (see Elegant Variation, page 395). If one is talking about the philosophic meaning of pleasure, for example, no other single term describes the general concept behind the word as well as *pleasure* itself, and the writer will use that term unhesitatingly as often as he wishes to name the general concept.

On the other hand, many varying situations will call for the use of the synonyms that *Webster's New International Dictionary* offers for *pleasure: satisfaction, happiness, cheerfulness; gaiety, mirth, merriment, jollity, hilarity, delectation, delight, gladness, joy,* and *enjoyment.* The dictionary not only lists synonyms but also distinguishes shades of meaning (see those given for the last five synonyms above). When you look for synonyms, study these distinctions carefully. See *ACD,* pp. xxv–xxvi, xl, Section 10; *NCD,* p. xx, Section 7.

Though collegiate dictionaries give synonyms for many words, the unabridged dictionaries offer more. Still better for the purpose is a good dictionary of synonyms (see *Webster's Dictionary of Synonyms* or *The Roget Dictionary of Synonyms and Antonyms,* listed in Section 54C).

55K. Prefixes and Suffixes: Word Formation

Another special feature of the dictionary is the information it gives about prefixes and suffixes. Separate words themselves in origin, prefixes and suffixes are word elements that may be added to other words or word roots to give them new meanings. A prefix is, as the name suggests, added before the word or word-root (for example, *unpleasant* is composed of the prefix *un* + *pleasant*). A suffix is added to the end of the word (thus *pleasantly* is formed by the word *pleasant* + the suffix *-ly*).

A great part of our vocabulary is formed by means of these prefixes and suffixes; indeed the possibilities of word formation by adding these elements to other words are almost endless. A. G. Kennedy [3] finds, for example, that at least eighty words have been formed on the one Latin word root *ced* through the use of fifteen prefixes and twenty-five suffixes.

Your dictionary lists in their alphabetical places each of these word-forming elements. Familiarity with them will speed the growth of your vocabulary. Those listed below are the ones most commonly used. Study them and their meanings and the examples given of their use in word formation.

55K1. Prefixes. (Observe that some of these prefixes, such as *ad-, com-,* and *dis-,* are modified in form by certain letters following them: *ad-* becomes *ac-* when the root following it begins with *c;* thus instead of *adcommodate*, we have *accommodate*; instead of *comlect,* we have *collect,* etc.)

[3] *Current English* (Boston: Ginn & Co., 1935), p. 346.

LATIN PREFIX	MEANING	EXAMPLES
a-, ab-,	from, away	avocation, absent
ad- (ac-, af-, ag-, an-, ap-, ar-, as-, at-)	to, toward	advice, accept, affix
ante-	before	antebellum, antecedent, antedate
circum-	around	circumference, circumlocution
com- (co-, col-, con-, cor-)	with, together	coexist, collate, commit
de-	from, away from (of negative force)	demerit, denatured, despite
dis- (di-, dif-, div-)	apart, away (of negative force)	disappear, differ, diverge
ex- (e-, ef-)	out of, out (sometimes of negative force)	extort, effect, event
in- (il-, im-, ir-)	in, into, on	illustrate, immediate, include
in- (il-, im-, ir-)	not	illegible, immortal, indistinct
mal- (male-)	ill, bad	malefactory, malpractice, malevolent
non-	not	noncommittal, nondescript, nonsense
ob- (oc-, of-, op-)	toward, against, completely	obdurate, occasion, offend
per-	through, thoroughly	perfect, perennial, pervade
pre-	before	prefix, preface, prelude
pro-	before, in behalf of, for	propose, proceed, pronoun
re-	back, again	recede, return, review
sub- (suc-, suf-, sug-, sup-, sus-)	under	subject, succeed, suggest
super-	over, above	supercargo, superfluous, supersede
trans-	across, over	transform, transmute, transport

GREEK PREFIX	MEANING	EXAMPLES
a-, an-	not	atom, atrophy, anemic
ana-	up, backward	analysis, anagram, anachronism

GREEK PREFIX	MEANING	EXAMPLES
anti-	against	antibody, anticline, antiphonal
cata-, cath-	down, away, against	catastrophe, cathedral, catholic
epi-, ep-, eph-	upon	epilogue, epoch, ephemeral
eu-, ev-	well, good	eugenics, euphony, evangelist
ex-, ec-	out of	eclipse, exodontist, exotic
homo-	common, the same	homonym, homogeneous, homogenous
hyper-	over, above	hyperbole, hyper-critical, hypertrophy
mono-	one	monogamy, monologue, monotone
neo-	new, recent	neoclassical, neologism, neophyte
para-	beside, beyond	paradox, paragraph, parody
peri-	around	perimeter, periodic, periphrastic
poly-	many	polyandry, polyp, polyphonic
proto-	first	protocol, protoplasm, prototype
syn- (sy-, syl-, sym-)	with, at the same time	synonym, system, syllogism

55K2. Suffixes (Latin, French, Greek).

NOUN SUFFIX	MEANING	EXAMPLES
-acy	quality, state, office	accuracy, efficacy, primacy
-age	relationship, condition, place	acreage, language, yardage
-al	belonging to, pertaining to	adjectival, rebuttal, refusal
-ant, -ent	a person or thing acting as agent	agent, combatant, servant
-ary	pertaining to, of the nature of	library, notary, secretary
-ation, -ition	action, state, quality	ambition, annihilation, exploration
-ate	office or function	concentrate, consulate, delegate

NOUN SUFFIX	MEANING	EXAMPLES
-ic, -ics	of or pertaining to	critic, logic, physics
-ion, -sion, -tion	act or process, condition	rebellion, tension, mention
-ism	action, state, characteristic of	Americanism, fascism, hypnotism
-ist	action or conduct	bigamist, organist, socialist
-ment	result, action, process	achievement, argument, increment
-or	state, quality, agent	aviator, donor, successor

ADJECTIVE SUFFIX	MEANING	EXAMPLES
-able, -ible	capacity, fitness, given to	capable, edible, honorable
-ant, -ent	adjective of present participial origin	fluent, errant, pleasant
-ate, -ite	adjective of past participial sense	definite, desolate, fortunate
ic, -ical	of or pertaining to	classical, mystic, poetic
-itious	of the nature of, characterized by	fictitious, nutritious, repetitious
-ive	nature or quality	active, creative, massive
-ous (-ious)	possessing the quality of	famous, gracious, poisonous

VERB SUFFIX	MEANING	EXAMPLES
-ate	used to form verbs from nouns	concentrate, regulate, donate
-fy	to make	amplify, beautify, terrify
-ize	to subject to, to render, practice	botanize, colonize, satirize

EXERCISES

1. Give the preferred spellings of the following words:

   advertise, advisor, centre, colour, honour, judgement, mould, practise (verb), programme, skilful, sulphur, theatre, traveler

2. Give the spelling of

   a) the third person singular of the following verbs:

   carry, hurry, marry, tarry, worry

b) the plurals of the following nouns:

alumnus, ax, banana, beech, catastrophe, category, cherry, chimney, deer, fish, ox, phenomenon, tomato, thesis

3. Using the phonetic spelling and the diacritical marks of your dictionary, give the pronunciation of the following frequently mispronounced words:

accidentally	data	news
acumen	decadent	often
adult	despicable	offensive
advertisement	exquisite	perspiration
amateur	February	precedence
arctic	forehead	program
asked	grievous	student
athletics	impious	vagary
conscience	irreparable	valet
coupon	mischievous	

4. Break the following words into syllables:

accommodate	irreparable	psychology
aspiration	irrelevant	separate
awry	preface	tedious
charade	process	terrible
etiquette	promulgate	weathered
interesting	provost	

5. Insert hyphens where needed in the following words or write them as one word or separate them as the dictionary instructs you:

baseball	fancy ball	lovebird
basketball	football	lovingcup
basal metabolism	hightension	lovingkindness
basrelief	hightide	loudspeaker
fancy free	hillbilly	lowspirited

6. Look up the etymology of each of the following words and explain how the present meaning of each is related to the original meaning:

acumen	cattle	intoxication
arrive	chivalry	lynch
calculate	convince	pansy
candidate	curfew	prevent
carouse	daisy	recalcitrant
carrousel	deliberation	zest

7. Look up the grammatical functions of the following words. For the nouns, give the plural forms; for the verbs, note whether the verb is transitive (*v. t.*) or intransitive (*v. i.*), and the principal parts:

alas	datum	oh
alternately	domino	run
be	doughty	they
because	drink	whom
before	eat	where
dainty	egoist	

8. *a*) How many definitions does your collegiate dictionary list for each of the following words: get, go, make, take?
   b) How many idioms are added after the main definitions of each of these words?
   c) Write sentences using the following words correctly:

   improvise, idiosyncrasy, unique, paucity, harass, esoteric, Lilliputian, longevity, nuzzle, obscurant

9. Though most (not all) of the following words are acceptable in standard English, all have limits placed on their use in certain meanings as indicated by the special labels (*Archaic, Obs.*, etc.) following them. Indicate after each word the label or labels limiting its use, and the sense involved.

braces	enthuse	flattop
brae	episcopal	let
brave	facial	lift
chemist	fair and square	porridge
damsel	first	prevent
demerit	first rate	scalawag
demesne	firm	toff

10. Give three or more synonyms for each of the following words and distinguish between the meanings of these synonyms:

amuse	get	regard
approbation	give	responsible
explicit	liberal	sorrow
fashion	pose	tire (verb)
freedom	possible	

11. This exercise should be done with your dictionary and with the lists of prefixes and suffixes given in Section 55K.

a) Using your dictionary, find five examples in addition to those given above for each of the following prefixes:

com-, dis-, in-, non-, pre-, pro-, re-, sub-, trans-, mono-, para-.

b) Add three examples to each of the lists of example words given for the noun suffixes.

c) Add three examples to each of the lists of example words given for the adjective and verb suffixes.

d) Using the following word roots, *ced-, cred-, duc-, fer-, fect-, fin-, mit-, tract-,* and referring to the list of prefixes and suffixes in Section 55K, form as many words as you can employing both prefixes and suffixes. Verify your words in your dictionary. Underscore each prefix and suffix as follows: educate, effective.

e) The following prefixes, *for-, mis-, out-, over-, un-, under-,* and suffixes, *-dom, -ed, -en, -er, -ful, -hood, -ing, -ish, -less, -like, -ly, -ness, -ship, -ster, -some,* are derived from Old English (Anglo-Saxon). Using the lists of Latin and Greek prefixes and suffixes in Section 55K as a model, make a list of these Old English combining forms, indicate their meaning, and give three or more examples of word formations for each.

12. This exercise is designed to acquaint you with some of the encyclopedic resources of your dictionary. In *ACD* most of this information is incorporated into the text; see also the contents page and the index for additional information. In *NCD* biographical and geographical materials are to be found in special sections along with other subject matter (see the contents page); see the main text for other information.

a) Where are the following places, how are their names pronounced, and why are they well known?

Agincourt, Donnybrook, Downing Street, Drachenfels, Elsinore, Eniwetok, Haleakala, Hyde Park, Mecca, Tanagra

b) Who were the following, when did they live, and why were they famous?

Pavlova, Savonarola, Sarah Siddons, George Sand, Erasmus, Copernicus, Cyrano de Bergerac, Charles Dodgson, Parnell, Jan Christian Smuts *c*) Are the following mythical or historical? Briefly identify each.

Adonis, Medusa, Loki, Thor, Cuchullin, Freya, Lao Tse, Frederick Barbarossa, Genghis Khan, Ashurbanipal, Orpheus, Pegasus, Charon, phoenix, centaur, chimera, Janus, Montezuma, Rabindranath Tagore, Apollyon

d) What does your dictionary tell you about the following characters, works, groups, and beliefs?

Don Quixote, Domesday Book, Junior League, Abelard, Talmud, Goneril, Ophelia, Faust, New Thought, Nibelungenlied, Oxford movement, positivism

e) (1) Where does your dictionary list signs and symbols for the various sciences (astronomy, biology, chemistry, etc.)?
(2) Where does your dictionary list proofreaders' marks?
(3) Find explanations or tables for the metric system and Roman numerals in your text.
(4) Where does your dictionary list information about colleges?

56. GOOD USAGE

Our first and lasting concern about our language in writing and speech must always be whether it is in present and appropriate use.

56A. Present Usage

Since language changes from age to age, indeed even from day to day, it is necessary that we keep abreast of current usage. We should avoid expressions that recall bygone eras, obsolete and archaic words and phrases, and even outmoded phrases of last year. On the other hand, we should not step too far into the future by hastily adopting all the latest new words and phrases. Pope's sage advice may be applied here:

> In words, as fashions, the same rule will hold;
> Alike fantastic, if too new, or old:
> Be not the first by whom the new are tried,
> Nor yet the last to lay the old aside.

Our writing should not be an imitation of the works of writers of the past: their styles were for their ages, not for ours. However much we may admire them, we cannot be like them, nor should we try to be. Moreover, we should not follow eccentric fashions of the present. It should be our aim to use diction that is generally acceptable to and used by educated persons of the present. As in our activities, we should try to retain what is good from the past and to think forward.

56B. Appropriate Usage

The second test of good usage includes the first and extends it. Good English must be appropriate to the thought and to the audience. Pope emphasizes both of these points when he says,

> Expression is the dress of thought, and still
> Appears more decent, as more suitable.
> A vile conceit in pompous words expressed
> Is like a clown in regal purple dressed;
> For diff'rent styles with diff'rent subjects sort,
> As several garbs with country, town, and court.

In brief, our words must be appropriate to our subject matter, and they must also be chosen with regard for our audience. To speak correct English is to speak as the situation demands. This does not mean that an educated man must speak illiterate English to an uneducated audience. It means that he should use simple (but good) English that will be entirely intelligible to them. And when he is addressing an educated audience, his English may be more allusive and complex to match their habits of thought.

Implicit in all this discussion is the theme of change: language, like all other things, is subject to continuous change. How can rules be set down for what can never be fixed? Absolute rules cannot be given; but when specific problems of good usage are involved, we can observe the practices of good writers and speakers of our own time and make recommendations that will serve to guide us adequately so long as we do not make the mistake of thinking that our conclusions are unalterable laws.

What is good English, then? Professor Robert C. Pooley defines it as follows:

Good English is that form of speech which is appropriate to the purpose of the speaker, true to the language as it is, and comfortable to speaker and listener. It is the product of custom, neither cramped by rule nor freed from all restraint; it is never fixed, but changes with the organic life of the language.[4]

57. LEVELS AND VARIETIES OF ENGLISH USAGE[5]

English, like all other languages, has its special levels and varieties of expression. Comprehensively, from a cultural point of view, two large levels may be recognized, namely standard English and nonstandard English. Both of these levels include several varieties of expression, each of which fulfills a special function. Thus the level of standard English includes such functional varieties as colloquial (conversational) English, speechmaking, expository essays and articles, legal and scientific studies, poetry, and fiction. Depending on situation and subject matter, these functional varieties may be classed as either formal or informal, as, for example, formal or informal conversation, formal or informal essays.

Each classification has its own merits. Formal English is not better—or worse—than informal English. Each has its own place. Just as one would not wear dungarees to a formal dance, so one should not write informal English in meeting the requirements of a formal research paper or course thesis; in turn, formal evening dress is not suited to a hike: one should not use formal English when the situation clearly demands informal English. On the other hand, the two classes are not usually exclusive of each other. Informal expressions slip into formal writing, and a great part of our written and spoken discourse is a mingling of the two styles. But most writing may be distinguished as either mainly formal or mainly informal.

[4] *Teaching English Usage* (New York: Appleton-Century-Crofts, Inc., 1946), p. 14.

[5] The authors are deeply indebted to John S. Kenyon's article, "Cultural Levels and Functional Varieties of English," *College English*, X (1948–49), 31–36. The classifications presented in this section follow the pattern outlined by him except for the substitution of the term *nonstandard* for *substandard*. For other helpful studies see p. 356.

58. STANDARD ENGLISH

Standard English is the language of the educated. The functional varieties of standard English, as observed earlier, fall into two general classes, formal and informal English. These large classifications together with two special varieties, namely standard colloquial English and literary English, require our attention. First let us consider the nature of the general classes, informal and formal English.

58A. Standard Informal English

Standard informal English is good English in its everyday clothes. It is marked by its conversational tone and manner, and is commonly used in personal sketches, autobiographies, feature articles, familiar essays, friendly letters, political and other popular speech-making—in all communication in which a conversational tone may be employed, including conversation itself. Good informal expository English may freely use the contractions and idioms of good conversational English. The writer or speaker often addresses the reader or hearer directly in terms of the first or second person. The paragraphs are usually short rather than long. Sentence patterns are relatively short and simple as compared with those of formal English, though long ones may be used. Compound sentences are more common than complex ones. Elliptical sentences occur. Good informal English may use slang and dialect terms with more freedom than formal English, but uses them selectively for certain effects. The following passage by Lee Strout White illustrates several of these characteristics:

> Springtime in the heyday of the Model T was a delirious season. Owning a car was still a major excitement, roads were still wonderful and bad. The Fords were obviously conceived in madness: any car which was capable of going from forward into reverse without any perceptible mechanical hiatus was bound to be a mighty challenging thing to the human imagination. Boys used to veer them off the highway into a level pasture and run wild with them, as though they were cutting up with a girl. Most everybody used the reverse pedal quite as much as the regular foot brake—it distributed the wear over the bands and wore them all down evenly. That was

the big trick, to wear all the bands down evenly, so that the final chattering would be total and the whole unit scream for renewal.

The days were golden, the nights were dim and strange. I still recall with trembling those loud, nocturnal crises when you drew up to a signpost and raced the engine so the lights would be bright enough to read destinations by. I have never been really planetary since. I suppose it's time to say good-bye. Farewell, my lovely!—From *The New Yorker*, May 16, 1936.

A few parts of this passage are essentially formal in phrasing, but its tone as a whole is familiar and tends to be conversational. Thus *bound to be a mighty challenging thing, run wild with them, cutting up with a girl, most everybody, that was the big trick, I suppose it's time to say good-bye,* and *you drew up to a signpost* are all colloquial expressions. (How would you say them formally?) It must be emphasized again that such colloquial expressions as these are good English when properly employed, as in this informal passage. Formal English must avoid them if it is to remain formal; where they enter they bring their casual manners with them.

58B. Standard Formal English

Though our modern formal English tends toward informality as a result of an increasing adoption of terms formerly regarded as strictly colloquial, the difference in tone between the formal English of most textbooks and scientific and learned studies and informal English is always recognizable. A great part of our most serious writing is expressed in formal English. Articles in learned journals, theses, books on scholarly subjects, and many business and official letters and documents use essentially formal English. The language of your history, sociology, and science texts, the language of almost any text in which the emphasis is placed on ideas and facts, is largely formal; the language of this text, like that of most composition texts, is both formal and informal—formal in its development of idea, but informal in its personal approach.

Formal English may sometimes be entirely dignified and learned, but it may also incorporate some elements from other varieties of standard English at the will of the user. Ordinarily formal English avoids the contractions, the elliptical constructions, the personal approach of informal English, and the use of slang and dialect terms. Its paragraphs are often long and are carefully organized. Its sentence patterns are varied; they tend to be long, complex, and are often linked to each other by connectives. Parallel constructions are frequently employed. The following passages are examples of contemporary formal English.

(1) If civilization is to advance, education from the earliest years must develop ideals of love rather than hate, human brotherhood rather than class, racial, or national conflicts, peace rather than war, service rather than selfishness. It must instill reverence not only for truth, but also for beauty and righteousness. Doubters and cynics will say that these ideals are pleasant dreams, impossible of realization, but the well-known fact that they have been made real in many persons, families, and communities shows that they are possible of fulfillment and that it is only necessary to extend this process of education to wider and larger groups to bring a new and better spirit into the world.—EDWIN GRANT CONKLIN, *Man, Real and Ideal.*

Note the tendency to long, complex sentences and parallel structures, such as *ideals of love rather than hate, human brotherhood rather than class, racial, or national conflicts, peace rather than war, service rather than selfishness.* No contractions, elliptical constructions, colloquial words and phrases, or slang terms are used. The approach is impersonal.

(2) Glass can be made out of hundreds of substances ranging from the sand of a sea beach to sugar from a grocery store. Any material which can be melted and then cooled to rigidity without crystallizing will form a glass. Those jaw-jeopardizing bits of hard candy which children like are true pieces of glass, but windows of such glass would dissolve in the first rainstorm. A much more permanent variety is made by mixing quartz sand crystals with chemicals such as lime and soda, and melting them together to form a liquid stone which, when cold, is transparent, permanent, hard, and resistant to heat and electricity, properties which have been found so useful that without them our civilization could scarcely have reached its present form. —GEORGE RUSSELL HARRISON, *Atoms in Action.*

Notice again the tendency to long, complex sentence structure; but parallel constructions are fewer and less obvious. The diction of both passages is relatively simple, but that of this passage is more concrete as a result of the physical subject matter. Notice how this author also completely avoids the colloquial. Where he writes *jaw-jeopardizing bits of transparent hard candy,* Lee Strout White would probably have written the colloquial *jawbreakers.* Again, as in the first passage, there are no contractions, no elliptical sentences, and the approach is largely impersonal.

58C. Standard Colloquial English

Every educated person speaks his mother tongue in at least two ways, and the difference between the dignified [formal] and the colloquial style is considerable.—G. L. KITTREDGE.

In its broadest sense, standard colloquial English is the language of the conversation of the educated and varies, according to need, from the completely formal to extreme informality. But taken more narrowly, as in the usual dictionary definition and as used in this text, colloquial English may be considered distinctly informal. Thus *Webster's New Collegiate Dictionary* defines the term:

col·lo′qui·al (kŏ·lō′kwĭ·ăl), *adj.* Pertaining to, or used in, conversation, esp. familiar conversation; acceptable and correct in ordinary conversation, friendly letters, or informal speeches, but unsuited to formal speech or writing; hence, informal. — **col·lo′qui·al·ly,** *adv.* — **col·lo′qui·al·ness,** *n.*

Colloquial English is a term covering all the devices peculiar to conversation, such as virtual or elliptical sentences, contractions, various idiomatic expressions (see Idiom, Section 60), and many former slang words that have gradually crept into informal usage. After a slang expression *has been around long enough* (colloquial), it sometimes, but not always, becomes part of standard colloquial English. Thus such terms as *O.K., dumb* (for *stupid*), *cute, cunning* (for *pleasing*), *crib* (to cheat), *cut* (to snub), *fix* (noun: *plight*), *fit to be tied, flabbergast, fellow* (person), *fussbudget, hunk,* were originally slang expressions that have won colloquial ranking. Many educated people freely use these words and hundreds like them in daily conversation, but would not think of letting them intrude into their formal writing. With the passage of time, however, such words may even win formal ranking (see Slang, Section 66).

58D. Literary English

Literary English may be defined as standard English written by persons of high skill or genius. The qualities of standard English, both formal and informal, appear in their best form in literary English, from which examples may be chosen for illustration of desired objectives in standard English. A study of such examples will help you to realize your own aims. You will observe that all our good literature, whether past or present in composition, is either informal or formal in tone. Informal literary English is the language of the *Canterbury Tales,* the plays of Shakespeare, Anderson, O'Neill, Eliot, and Fry, the writings of Swift, Addison and Steele, Fielding, Sterne, Dickens, and Mark Twain, and of modern fiction. Formal literary English is the language of the prose works of Bacon, Milton, Newman, Mill, Arnold, and great documents of state and great addresses, such as the Declaration of Independence and the Gettysburg Address.

59. NONSTANDARD ENGLISH

Nonstandard English is a broad term designating the speech habits of the illiterate, the careless, and those whose schooling and other opportunities for education have been limited.

59A. Illiterate English

Illiterate English is language marked by obvious grammatical errors, double negatives, and other redundancies, such as *have went, he done gone, I is, ain't, youse, knowed, I seen, set down* (for *sit* or *sat down*), *he laid* (for *he lay*), *he raised up* (*rose up*), *I says, can't never, can't hardly, this here, that there.* The use of such language brands the speaker or writer as uneducated unless of course he is presenting a character who speaks in these terms.

59B. Dialect English

A second variety of nonstandard English is dialect English. This is the language of dialect terms, phrases, and sentence construction, ways of expression whose habitual use will often identify one as coming from some particular section of the country (New England, the South, the Southwest, etc.) or as having some particular language background (Pennsylvania Dutch, Swedish, Irish, Yiddish, etc.). Everyone is familiar with such terms as the following from their use in his own region or their occurrence in narrative employing dialect: *admire* (for *like*), *aim to* (for *intend*), *angleworm, fish worm* (for *earthworm*), *biscuit bread, corn pone* (corn bread), *feist* or *fyce* (a small dog), *ground hog, clough-jogger* (woodchuck), *galluses* (suspenders), *guess* (think), *ham meat, hant* (ghost), *hear tell, poke* (bag), *rare-ripes* (early onions), *reckon* (think), *rowen* (a second-growth crop of grass), *run* (stream), *shoat* (young hog), *shuck* (husk), *stoop* (porch), *tote* (carry). And all will remember reading or hearing sentences illustrating the ways in which peoples of different national origins reshape English to suit their speech habits, sentences such as these:

IRISH:	Sure and it was a fine sight the men in green and the crowd wild.
YIDDISH:	Gimme fa twenty fi cents some slices cornbiff.
PENNSYLVANIA DUTCH:	Go down here once 'n turn the corner around and you'll be there.

Words and sentences such as these lend color to stories interpreting the culture of a region. Some of them may be used occasionally in standard informal English, but they should be avoided as a general rule in formal English.

59C. Slang

Still another variety of nonstandard English is speech marked by the excessive use of slang. Though slang may be used, with discretion, in informal English, and upon rare occasion in formal

English, the frequent use of slang marks one as either careless or uneducated. (See Slang, Section 66.)

REFERENCES FOR STUDY

Fries, C. C. "Usage Levels and Dialect Distribution," *American College Dictionary,* pp. xxvii–xxviii.

Kenyon, John S. "Cultural Levels and Functional Varieties of English," *College English,* X (1948–49), 31–36.

Pooley, Robert C. "Levels in English Usage," *Teaching English Usage* (New York: Appleton-Century-Crofts, Inc., 1946), pp. 16–24.

EXERCISES

A. Indicate the levels and functional varieties of usage represented by each of the following passages.

1. Point out the characteristics that help to classify them.
2. Are there any sentences and phrases in the informal selections which could be included without change in a formal context?
3. Are there any informal expressions in the formal passages?
4. Are there any slang phrases in any of these passages?
5. Are there any passages representing illiterate usage?

a) The United States is operating peacefully and constructively and with some success through Point Four in India and other lands, and through the Voice of America in many tongues. The first is a plan to assist, the second is a device to penetrate curtains. But everyone knows that Point Four and the Voice of America are infinitesimal weighed in the general scale of activities. They hardly tip the scale at all, and they are not highly regarded in circles that believe the Big Stick is sufficient in itself. It seems to us that there will be no rift in the clouds as long as we're content merely to keep one bomb ahead of the enemy and to communicate with the Russian people by maintaining diplomatic relations with the big wheels of the Soviet Union. Talking with Soviet diplomats (and we've listened to a lot of it in the U. N.) is like talking with an educated bird: plenty of noise, never any real conversation. We must somehow keep the bird engaged, and at the same time get through to the millions in the cage.—From "The Talk of the Town," *The New Yorker.*

b) Brief and powerless is Man's life; on him and all his race the low, sure doom falls pitiless and dark. Blind to good and evil, reckless of destruction, omnipotent matter rolls on its relentless way; for Man, condemned today to lose his dearest, tomorrow himself to pass through the gate of darkness, it remains only to cherish, ere yet the blow falls, the lofty thoughts that ennoble his little day; disdaining the coward terrors of the slave of Fate, to worship at the shrine that his own hands have built; undismayed by the empire of chance, to preserve a mind free from the wanton tyranny that rules his outward life; proudly defiant of the irresistible forces that tolerate, for a moment, his knowledge and his condemnation, to sustain alone, a weary but unyielding Atlas, the world that his own ideals have fashioned despite the trampling march of unconscious Power.—BERTRAND RUSSELL, "A Free Man's Worship," *Mysticism and Logic*.

c) Ours is the century of the uneducated Common Man, of the perpetually adolescent Common Man, of the Common Man unskilled in the art of living. Untaught in the wisdom of the race, he is incompetent either to rule or to be ruled: He is blatantly vulgar, ill-mannered, boorish, unsure of himself, hungry for happiness, not a man so much as a boy who has outgrown his britches. For this he is not to blame. The blame rests on his schoolmasters.

Ortega y Gasset once called the Common Man as we today have him "the Vertical Intruder," the barbarian who has invaded civilization from the basement and proceeds to play havoc with the salon. If only when he broke through we had said, "Welcome! Now you are here, we shall teach you not merely to own the place but also how to get the most out of living in it." Instead of that, we turned the place over to him without introducing him to the amenities of the drawing room and encouraged the poor devil to muck around in it without having learned how to enjoy it.—BERNARD IDDINGS BELL, *Crisis in Education: A Challenge to Complacency*.

d) That man, I think, has had a liberal education who has been so trained in youth that his body is the ready servant of his will, and does with ease and pleasure all the work that, as a mechanism, it is capable of; whose intellect is a clear, cold, logic machine, with all its parts of equal strength, and in smooth working order; ready, like a steam engine, to be turned to any kind of work, and spin the gossamers as well as forge the anchors of the mind; whose mind is stored with a knowledge of the great and fundamental truths of Nature and of the laws of her operations; one who, no stunted ascetic, is full of life and fire; but whose passions are trained to come to heel by a vigorous will, the servant of a tender conscience; who has learned to love all beauty, whether of Nature or of art, to hate all vileness, and to respect others as himself.—T. H. HUXLEY, "A Liberal Education and Where to Find It," *Lay Sermons*.

e) "A mile farther on," he said, "you passed Ye Olde Waffle Shoppe." "I did," I said. "And about three miles farther on," he continued, "you're going to come to a big frame house that sets back about fifty yards from the road under some oak trees. It's been made into another oldy shoppy, and they try to give the impression that the place used to be a roadside tavern. It never was. Woman from Indiana comes down here and runs the place every summer. She brings an old man with her, a kind of feeble old fellow. He don't do anything but sit around all summer and do his best to look like a retired sea captain."—DON MARQUIS, "All Arted Uppe," *American Magazine.*

f) But then me and Luke's about as muddy as the team, and the women thought it was awful to go into town to the preacher's that way. So before we reached town—right down there by the crick, in what's Hubberts' pasture now—they made us fellers git out; and the girls they took sticks and whatever they could find handy, and tore a big chunk out of their underskirts—women wore plenty of clothes them days—and they made us fellers stand up and hev the mud scraped off our pants—and then when we's cleaned up a little, we went along to the preacher's and got married. —RUTH SUCKOW, "Golden Wedding," *Iowa Interiors.*

B. Each of the following sentences contains one or more words not appropriate to their context. Identify each inappropriate expression, explain why it is inappropriate, and substitute a word or words suitable to the thought.

1. Fresh and smiling, she trudged in, shedding a smell from her fur neckpiece, which she removed as she entered.
2. You have already informed us that you work in the State Department. What sort of work do you do for this outfit?
3. In 1867 the United States Government acquired Alaska from Russia. This was perhaps the most advantageous buy in the history of diplomacy.
4. She was tall, stately, like some fabulous Grecian goddess, much the prettiest girl he had ever laid eyes on.
5. Hotspur was the big wheel of the opposing crowd, but Vernon was really smarter.
6. He felt humiliated, rejected, sore at the way Jancis had kept him on the hook.

60. IDIOM

Idiom is a word of several associated meanings as the following definition shows:

id'i·om (ĭd'ĭ·ŭm), *n.* [F. and L.; F. *idiome,* fr. L. *idioma,* fr. Gr. *idiōma,* fr. *idioun* to make a person's own, fr. *idios* one's own, proper.] **1.** The language peculiar to a people (a tongue), or to a district, community, or class (a dialect). **2.** The structural form peculiar to any language. **3.** An expression in the usage of a language, that is peculiar to itself either in grammatical construction or in having a meaning which cannot be derived as a whole from the conjoined meanings of its elements (as, *the more the merrier, a picture of the king's, to make friends with him*). **4.** A form of expression characteristic of an author.

The third of these meanings relates to good usage and is the meaning of special interest to us here. As this meaning indicates, idioms do not always conform to the formal rules of grammar. Thus in the third example given, "to make friends with him," *make,* ordinarily a transitive verb, has instead the value of a linking verb (like *become*), and *friends* takes on a plural form because of a reciprocal meaning implicit in the construction. The point may be clarified by comparing a formal statement of the idea with the informal idiom:

FORMAL: I wished to make him my friend *or* become his friend (not friends).
INFORMAL: I wished to make friends with him.

A large number of expressions may be regarded as having grammar peculiar to themselves, each having a private grammar of its own. In short, though they do not conform to the ideal logic of grammar, they have become nonetheless an accepted part of our language. On the other hand, one must not conclude that grammatical English is not idiomatic. Actually much of grammatical English has an idiomatic set form which one is obliged to follow, and most idiomatic English is conventional in its grammar.

Our definition tells us also that the meaning of an idiom cannot always be derived from the meanings of its separate elements. Thus the definitions of the words *turn* and *down* in the idiom "turn down" will not in themselves suggest the special idiomatic meaning of *reject* or *refuse.* One could multiply examples indefinitely; consider the separate part-meanings and the whole meanings of the following expressions: "quite a few," "many a person," "counting out (or up) the votes," "to lose his head," "come under," "give in," "carry on," "keep moving," "keep making fun," "look down on," "make up." A new learner of the language is certain to find confusing the difference between the meaning of the separate parts of these expressions (and hundreds like them) and their complete idiomatic meanings. Since the native user of the language hears them frequently from infancy, he somehow absorbs them into his nature; their use and meaning become instinctive with him. Observe that most of these expressions, though used constantly, do not grow old and do not come under the reproach of being clichés or slang. We could not express our thoughts easily without them. Their use tends to make our communication informal, but they occur from time to time in most formal contexts.

H. W. Fowler ("Cast-Iron Idioms," *Dictionary of Modern English Usage*) points out that analogy is constantly at war with idiom; that is, many idioms are constantly being changed in common speech by analogy with other expressions. In time some idioms that are now regarded as faulty may become accepted in good formal usage. Thus the substitution of *and* for the sign of the infinitive *to* in the verbal phrase "try and think" is so widespread now as to be acceptable in conversation; and *different than* rather than *different from* seems to be gradually establishing itself as an acceptable informal expression. But these two expressions and many others commonly heard are not yet approved for formal English. The most common of these unaccepted idioms and their approved equivalents are listed below. In general, avoid using the expressions in the first list in formal and informal writing except when you wish to use them as representing a character's speech.

FAULTY IDIOM: either nonstandard or limited to conversational use	ACCEPTED IDIOM correct for both formal and informal use
all-around	all-round
all of a sudden	suddenly
a lot of	many
all the faster	the faster, fast as
angry at (someone)	angry with (someone)
any place, any wheres	anywhere

as a fact	as a matter of fact, in fact
as regards to	as regards, regarding
blame it on (someone)	blame (someone) for it
cannot help but admire	cannot help admiring
can't seem to remember	cannot remember
die with	die of
different than	different from
doubt if	doubt whether
entertain to	entertain at
feel of	feel
frightened of	afraid of; frightened by, at
graduated (high school)	graduated from (high school)
has, have got to	must
in back of	behind
in search for	in search of
inside of a year	within a year
in the year of 1953	in the year 1953 *or* in 1953
kind of a	kind of
no doubt but that	no doubt that
not let on	not reveal, not admit
off of	off, from
out loud	aloud
over with	over
plan on	plan to
still and all, still in all	all in all
superior than	superior to
treat on	treat of
try and (win, think, do, etc.)	try to (win, etc.)
the true fact of the matter is	the fact is
very interested	very much interested
want in, out, off	want to get in, get out, get off

The form of idioms, as indicated above, is so rigidly prescribed by convention that Fowler speaks of them as "cast-iron" idioms. Thus usage prescribes that we agree with a person, but agree to a proposal. We are angry with someone, but angry at an offense. Study the following list of idioms and make your usage correspond to it. If you are doubtful about other idioms that you use, form the habit of consulting the Glossary (see Section 72) or your dictionary (under the key word of the expression) or Fowler's *Dictionary of Modern English Usage* about them. Observe that in using most of these idioms correctly, you must make sure that the right preposition follows the noun, adjective, or verb.

accuse of
acquit of
adverse to
adequate for
agree to (a plan)
agree with (a person)
agree in (a belief)
agreeable to
angry at (an offense)
angry with (a person)
averse to
bring up
blame for
capable of
contrast with
correspond to (a thing)
correspond with (a person)
desire for
desirous of
differ from (a thing)
differ with (a person)
different from
disagree with
distaste for
envious of
expert in
identical with
independent of
jealous of
listen to
oblivious of
plan to
prefer to
stay at (home)
sensible of
sensitive to
separate from
superior to
treat of
try to
unequal to
vary from
variant of
variance with

EXERCISE

Correct the faulty idioms in the following sentences.

1. He must not let on that he and not Christian was the true lover.
2. The true fact is that he has the lowest bacterial count for his milk than any that comes to the University dairy.
3. Still and all, she was different than anything Joe had seen in the East or anywheres else, for that matter.
4. I cannot help but admire Professor Cornwall. He is an all-around athlete, quite different than the usual professor of English.
5. I can't seem to remember when he graduated high school, but I doubt if it was in the year of 1948.
6. The fact of the matter is that she came to college in search for a husband; and there is no doubt but that she will get him.
7. A man so very interested in philosophy as Dr. Benham has got to be much superior intellectually than the usual professor.

8. She has entertained us to dinner so often that I have got to plan on inviting her and her husband soon.
9. As a fact, in back of his smooth, smiling façade was a deep-seated ill will, a kind of resentment that almost amounted to hatred.
10. If you find him irritable when he is awakened, blame it on his fatigue; try and be gentle with him.

61. QUALITIES OF WORDS

61A. Denotation and Connotation

Our diction should be clear and precise when we wish to explain anything; it should be richly suggestive when we wish to create a mood or appeal to the emotions. Hence we must inquire into the nature of words themselves, their qualities of denotation and connotation, of abstract and general, concrete and specific statement, of imagery. The *denotation* of a word is its primary meaning, its literal meaning as it identifies the object or idea (the referent) for which it stands. Many words may be said to have only denotative meaning. Thus each of the words in the great vocabulary of technical and scientific terms (such as *oxygen, perihelion, hypotenuse, carburetor*) has one simple primary meaning. But nearly all other words have more than one shade of meaning—that is, they have a literal or denotative meaning, but other meanings are associated with the simple meaning. This suggestivity of a word, its quality of associated meaning or meanings, is its *connotation.* For example, *steed* and *nag* have the same basic referent (*horse*); likewise, the pairs *girl* and *lass, brook* and *run, mother* and *mamma, man* and *guy,* have their basic referents. But no one will make the mistake of writing of Sir Gawain's *nag* unless he is writing burlesque; and no one will use *lass, run, mamma,* or *guy* in a formal context. In short, as remarked above, words must be appropriate to the occasion: they must be chosen to fit the subject matter, the situation, and the audience.

Some words have agreeable or even romantic connotations: *love, home, serenity, peace, harmony, knighthood, dragon, princess.* Many of them symbolize codes of ideal behavior, beliefs: *justice, honor, truth, goodliness, God.* Others have unpleasant associations: *leer, scab, scuttle, dirt, drab, treachery, weasel.* From earliest childhood all of us are more or less aware of the power of words, of their double-edged power of sustaining or injuring the one who uses them. It is very important, then, to understand fully what words mean, both their literal and their often manifold associative meanings.

61B. Abstract and General Words; Concrete and Specific Words

All words may be further categorized as abstract and general or concrete and specific. The classification is not fixed: all abstract words may be regarded in some sense as general, but many general words are not abstract; all concrete words are specific in some sense, but many are general in relation to other concrete words.

Words expressing ideas and naming the qualities of physical things are abstract. Thus *virtue, honor, sweetness, brightness, color* are abstract. Words naming the classes to which objects belong are general: *vegetation, animal, people, cattle.* Concrete words are image-making words, sensory words: *tree, horse, man, cow.* But concrete words such as these are general in relationship to the following words which are both concrete and specific: *elm, Morgan colt, Mr. Walsh, Jersey cow.* All these could be made more specific still through the use of attributes: *the Washington Elm, the two-year-old Morgan colt, Provost Walsh, the Jersey cow named Annabelle Storrs.*

Abstract words and general words have their proper and indispensable use in our language, a use different from that of specific and concrete words, but not less important. Nearly all the terms describing our complex structure of society are abstract and general, and most of our thinking must be done in part in these terms.

Indeed, so useful and necessary are these terms that unless we are perpetually on guard our writing may become too abstract and lose touch with reality; at the worst it may be afflicted with the disease called *jargon* (see Section 69). But writing (and speech) awakes and lives through the use of concrete and specific terms. If you must express your thought abstractly, follow it if you can with a concrete illustration. If it is possible to express the thought effectively in concrete terms, always prefer the concrete to the abstract.

EXERCISES

A. Explain the denotation and connotation of the following pairs of synonyms:

politician, statesman	cereal, porridge
ghost, apparition	painter, artist
beau, lover	poet, bard
door, portal	sword, rapier
chariot, cart	gay, debonair
mirror, looking glass	effeminate, womanish
butcher, meat-cutter	anger, wrath

B. The following sentences are abstract statements of famous concrete proverbs, verse quotations, and other well-known statements. For example, the following abstract statement, "Doing a thing when it should be done will often prove economically beneficial," has as its concrete original the proverb "A stitch in time saves nine." (1) Try to identify the concrete originals for each passage, and consider their superiority to the abstract statements. (2) For those that you cannot identify, give concrete restatements of your own.

a) Persons of like nature tend to seek each other's company.
b) All that has a high degree of brilliance and luster is not precious metal.
c) A pleasing appearance is only a matter of superficiality.
d) A timorous person constantly experiences the apprehension of his demise; a courageous person has only one experience of this sort.
e) One should always act at exactly the right moment for action.
f) To what a distance that small instrument of light sends its reflection! In just this fashion shows a worthy action in a maleficent universe.
g) Eighty-seven years ago our ancestors originated on this continent a formerly unheard of type of state, based on the idea of freedom, and maintaining as a sacred obligation the idea of a fundamental human equality.
h) If he requests sustenance, will you present him with a hard mineral substance?

i) Constructions of masonry do not constitute a place of confinement for criminals, nor do ferrous strips of metal make a restraining enclosure.

j) Conduct, benignant illuminating Influence! conduct me onward in the surrounding dismal atmosphere.

k) A good reputation for a person of either sex, my esteemed nobleman, is the thing of greatest spiritual value to him. The person who obtains surreptitiously the monetary sum I carry with me, obtains matter of no worth.

62. IMAGERY AND FIGURES OF SPEECH

A special quality of many words is their power to evoke images; that is, they summon up in the mind pictures of the objects that they represent. All concrete words are image-making, and it is this quality that makes them the principal medium of poetry. Most abstract words were originally concrete and hence image-making. Thus the verb *educate* meant originally *to lead out of,* and an educated person is one led out of ignorance into knowledge. Consider the original meanings of such abstract words as *extort, contort, appetite, petition, chivalry, cordial, defalcate, sarcasm* for the pictures they create.

The appeal of concrete words lies in the images they fashion in the mind, images of sight, sound, taste, smell, and touch—visual, auditory, gustatory, olfactory, and tactile images, as in those summoned up by the following words: *stallion, thunder, syrup, orange, velvet.* Some writers have demonstrated the beauty of words alone by simply listing words without any connectives in a metrical rhyming pattern. It was this beauty of words in themselves that prompted many of Gertrude Stein's experiments with language, among them the famous definition, "A rose is a rose is a rose." Concrete words, then, are rich in their own right, but they are richer still when they are used to modify one another (as in adjective and noun combinations), when they are repeated or echoed in sound to secure a pictorial or tonal effect, and when they are contrasted. These qualities may be studied in the following poem by Louis MacNeice:

MORNING SUN

Shuttles of trains going north, going south, drawing
threads of blue,
The shining of the lines of trams like swords,
Thousands of posters asserting a monopoly of the good,
the beautiful, the true.
Crowds of people all in the vocative, you and you,
The haze of the morning shot with words.

Yellow sun comes white off the wet streets but bright
Chromium yellows in the gay sun's light,
Filleted sun streaks the purple mist,
Everything is kissed and reticulated with sun
Scooped-up and cupped in the open fronts of shops
And bouncing on the traffic that never stops.

And the street fountain blown across the square
Rainbow-trellises the air and sunlight blazons
The red butcher's and scrolls of fish on marble slabs,
Whistled bars of music crossing silver sprays
And horns of cars, touché, touché, rapiers' retort, a
moving cage,
A turning page of shine and sound, the day's maze.

But when the sun goes out, the streets go cold, the
hanging meat
And tiers of fish are colorless and merely dead,
And the hoots of cars neurotically repeat and the tiptoed feet
Of women hurry and falter whose faces are dead;
And I see in the air but not belonging there
The blown grey powder of the fountain grey as the ash
That forming on a cigarette covers the red.

For the moment, let us omit the first stanza and look at the rest of the poem. In the last three stanzas, the pictorial adjective-noun and noun-phrase combinations, such as *yellow sun, wet streets, whistled bars of music, scrolls of fish on marble slabs,* and the equally rich verb and verbal structures, *comes white off the wet streets, scooped-up and cupped in the open fronts of shops, rainbow-trellises the air,* together with the repetitions of *sun, touché,* and *dead,* and the contrast of sight and sound between the second and third stanzas and the last, all help to create the impression of the day as a "turning page of shine and sound." All these words are concretely effective; each arouses an image. But observe that something new has been added. The sun does not merely *shine*: it is *filleted*—its rays are like bands or streamers of ribbon through the purple mist. The shop windows *scoop up* or *cup* the sunlight instead of merely reflecting it. It *bounces* (like a ball) on the chromium and windows of the cars. The sounds of the horns of cars thrust into the air like fencers' rapiers. Words have taken on a new meaning: the day has become a *turning page*; a heap of fish becomes *scrolls of fish*. The blown spray of the fountain has become *blown grey powder*. Literally we know that water spray is not *powder*, that a day is not a *page*. But in these expressions our meaning is no longer literal: words have taken on a new and important meaning not found in the dictionary, a figurative meaning. This extension of meaning, the transfer of an image to a new value, is what is known as a figure of speech.

Now let us return to the first stanza. What extensions of meaning can you find in it? In addition to those already indicated, can you find any other images with extension of meaning in the rest of the poem?

62A. Simile

The most common and most important figures of speech are *metaphor* and *simile*. Simile expresses a likeness between objects of different classes and is commonly introduced by *like, as, as if,* or *as when*. It may be short or long. The terms of a simile must be different from each other in classification: to say that a man looks like Einstein is certainly not simile; it may be a mere statement of fact. Or if we compare a pain to the feeling caused by a knife cut ("It hurts like a knife"), such a comparison is once more a mere statement of fact, not a true figure of speech. But the difference between the classes of the things compared must not be so extreme as to be absurd or the result will have the effect of slang: "We got on together like a house afire." Observe the scope and variety of the following similes and note how they are introduced:

Without pity the world of men would distintegrate like an exploding star.—ARTHUR KOESTLER.

Perhaps as many as thirty bonfires could be counted within the bounds of the district. And as the hour may be told on a clock face, so did the men recognize the locality of each fire by its angle and direction, though nothing of the scenery could be viewed.—THOMAS HARDY.

From close to, the drill towers no longer looked like trees, but like a swarm of giant mosquitoes, standing on their high, spidery legs and sucking through their long proboscises the black blood of the earth. —ARTHUR KOESTLER.

Then he turned to Jabez Stone and a smile broke over his face like the sunrise over Monadnock.—STEPHEN VINCENT BENÉT.

62B. Metaphor

Metaphor boldly states that the objects compared are identical. For this reason, metaphor is more vivid and direct than simile, and it is consequently used much more than any other figure of speech. We are ordinarily aware of our use of simile because of its deliberate manner of introduction into our sentences, but all of us commonly use metaphor without even knowing that we are using it. The writer who recognizes the metaphoric powers of language will of course gradually come to use metaphor consciously to achieve his purposes. Metaphor may occur in several parts of speech; it is particularly effective in verbs. Study these examples:

ADJECTIVE-NOUN PHRASES: The distant city was a glittering jewel, and shadowy trees about her became huge vases of spreading ferns.—ROBERT WHITEHAND.

VERB: Inside, the crimson room bloomed with light.—F. SCOTT FITZGERALD.

VERB, NOUN, AND ADJECTIVE METAPHORS, AND SIMILE: Something was making him nibble at the edge of stale ideas as if his sturdy physical egotism no longer nourished his peremptory heart.—F. SCOTT FITZGERALD.

VERBAL ADJECTIVE AND NOUN: The sidewalks became tossing seas of umbrellas. —STEPHEN CRANE.

VERB, ADVERBIAL PHRASE, AND ADVERB: For now we see through a glass darkly.—ST. PAUL.

NOUN WITH MODIFIERS: Science today is an iceberg, with only a fraction —perhaps one sixth—of its bulk now visible above the ocean of military security.—JOHN MC PARTLAND.

Since simile and metaphor are essentially alike except for the formal way in which simile is introduced, the term *metaphor* is often used to embrace both terms in general discussion of the figures, as in the sections following.

62B 1. Structure and Nature of Metaphor. A metaphor or a simile has two parts, the idea and the image with which it is compared. Thus in "My love is like a red, red rose," Burns does not mean that his love is literally like a red rose; rather he is conveying an idea or impression of the loved one. This idea or impression is considered as like the concrete image of a rose (that is, like some aspect or aspects of a rose). And in the metaphor *barked* in "The lieutenant barked his orders," the same principle operates: The impression of the lieutenant's voice is like the barking of a dog—that is, certain characteristics of that barking, its staccato quality.

Observe, as indicated above, that the objects compared are fundamentally unlike. The likeness is not between the objects considered as a whole, but in some shared characteristic or characteristics, as in the following metaphoric statements of the same idea:

She came into the room like a galleon under full sail. (Simile)
Impressive and stately, she sailed into the room. (Metaphor)
She sailed into the room like a stately galleon. (Metaphor and simile combined)

Here the likeness lies in the manner of the woman's entrance into the room, which suggests the stateliness and assured movement of a romantic sailing ship. Perhaps something of a resemblance exists also between the free-flowing garments of the woman and the billowing sails of the ship. But here the likeness ends. In actuality the woman of course does not look like a ship, and she walks, she does not sail. All good metaphors have this comparison and contrast: the objects compared are of different classes but have some like quality or qualities.

As we have seen, metaphors are not restricted to poetry. Our prose and our daily conversation are full of them. The language of slang, as already indicated, is highly figurative; even our good colloquial expression and almost all our writing of every sort, formal and informal, excluding only technical scientific statement, use metaphor freely. It is an unusual paragraph that does not contain at least a few figures of speech either openly evident or partially hidden in its texture. Consider the following expressions taken from casual conversation:

> He sank his teeth into the steak.
> Well, I guess that wraps it up.
> He threw cold water on my suggestion.
> Don't bite the hand that's feeding you.
> Cornell swamped us last night.
> His eyes devoured her.
> What's eating you?
> Her tongue ran like a millrace.
> Don't fence me in.
> His cold glance swept the room.
> There is a landmine in every deal he makes.
> His remarks set off a chain reaction in the audience.
> Her eyes blazed with hate (*or* darted fire).

Some of these metaphors are slang, most are clichés, but all represent transfers of meaning, and all illustrate our natural tendency to think in terms of metaphor.

Why do we use metaphor? We use it because we find it helpful, even necessary, in the expression of our thought. When we use imagery, we are defining the unknown by reference to the known. An abstract paraphrase of the idea we have in mind when we use a figure of speech is almost never as true a communication of meaning as the figure is. Try your hand (metaphor) at restating in purely abstract terms Burns's very simple simile "My love is like a red, red rose" or "The lieutenant barked his orders" or Viscount Montgomery's metaphor representing Canada as a hinge of pure gold between the Old and New Worlds, and observe the superiority of the images in vividness and meaning. So superior are the figures in conveying our meaning that most of us would unblushingly use even trite figures rather than abstract terms in writing and speaking. This is one of the dangers we must guard against: though it is perhaps better to use an outworn figure, especially in conversation, than to be unnecessarily abstract, it is better still to try for freshness in imagery. (See Clichés, Section 67.)

62B 2. Fading and Dead Metaphor. Some figures are vivid and easily recognizable as figures. Others have become so much used that we no longer think of them as having a figurative meaning; they represent what are called fading and dead metaphors (notice the metaphors *fading* and *dead* which describe them). Our language is filled with such metaphors, words that once had a rich concrete denotation but now no longer summon up any concrete images. Consider the following: *cold* glance, *dead* reckoning, good *taste* (in clothes or books), *dark* sorrow, *bitter* anguish, *sweet* girl, *bright* smile. A fading or dead metaphor is not to be condemned as poor English (notice the dead metaphor *poor*) unless it is trite or hackneyed. (See Clichés, Section 67.)

EXERCISES

A. List all the metaphors and similes that you can find in MacNeice's "Morning Sun" on page 367.

B. Identify all metaphors and all similes in the following sentences, and briefly indicate whether you think them effective and why.

1. Dry leaves periwheel down the cliff at their backs, float up on the updraft of the fire, slip off, fall again.—STUART DODGE.
2. For a moment Joel felt as if all the joy inside him had been blown out.
3. Having secured a light, he crippled the match and threw it on the floor.
4. Heavy clouds sulked in the black sky, occasionally allowing wisps of sifted moonlight to penetrate into earth-view, adding to the eeriness below.
5. From the silken sky appeared dark curlicues that, coming close, resembled birds. Great white birds they were, which circled, dipping their pointed, streamlined wings.

6. She felt warm, and the lump in her throat grew heavy like bread eaten hot from the oven.
7. She is like a trained seal, balancing a lot of objects on her nose.
8. I worked so hard sandpapering the old chair that I wore the tread off my fingers.
9. The free world cannot trade on a one-way street.
10. The Post Office is to be reorganized in a businesslike way as far as is humanly possible, but it is a back-breaking task.
11. In the game of life you may hold the best cards, but in the end you lose to two fellows holding spades.—WALTER WINCHELL.
12. Hotspur is a smart alec who has learned to wash behind his ears, but forgotten to wipe the soap away.
13. This salary scale would seem to guarantee fruition in our battle for top academic recognition.
14. But underneath, free from clothes and the ceremonies of court, we see in Richard II a hollow shell—an éclair covered with chocolate but with no cream or substance inside.
15. Fred Friendly is the only man I know who can take off without warming up his motors.—E. R. MURROW.
16. It is now up to all North Campus dormitories to unite in a concerted effort to straighten out the débris.
17. As he opened the door, the two years fell away like a cobweb from a cleaning woman's broom.—STEVE MC NEIL.
18. He watched the swallows dip to the ground like eager little sea gulls skimming over water.
19. Yesterday afternoon I had my ears pinned back by a young woman who called up, madder than a rain-soaked tomcat.—STEVE MC NEIL.
20. The communist peace-balloon had barely risen when it sprung a bad leak last week.—*Newsweek*.
21. The alarm clock shot a needle of sound through the open window into the silence that shawled the little Chelsea garden.—PENELOPE CONNER, *Seventeen*.

62C. Mixed Imagery

A mixed image is like the coelacanth, the fish-animal that stopped short in its evolution untold ages ago. Similarly the mixed image, judged by purely rational standards, stops short in its development into an organized harmonious form. A notorious example of a mixed image is that of the congressman who is reported as having said: "I smell a rat. In fact, I see it floating about in the very air. But I shall nip it in the bud."

Not all mixed images are bad. Shakespeare occasionally uses a mixed image whose disordered effect reflects the turmoil and disorder in the mind of the character speaking it, as when Hamlet says, "Or to take arms against a sea of troubles"; and the deliberately mixed imagery of some modern prose may be justified by some comparable explanation. But in writing exposition, always try to avoid an incongruous juxtaposition of images. Ordinarily one can easily eliminate such faults from his writing because they call obvious attention to themselves; sometimes, however, one may be trapped by them, particularly when he associates unwittingly a supposed dead metaphor with another living metaphor of a different sort. In such circumstances the dead metaphor comes alive and sticks out like a sore thumb. The sentence immediately preceding is an example of this mixing of images.

Do not mistake a mere succession of images as constituting mixed imagery. When Shakespeare in a series of images calls England an "earth of majesty," a "seat of Mars," an "other Eden," a "fortress built by Nature," a "precious stone set in the silver sea," he is not mixing imagery, but using a succession of images to amplify an idea. So long as the images in any such construction are harmonious in creating the effect desired, they may be used together if they are actually needed for the effect. If any of the images can be omitted without a sense of loss, it should, of course, be omitted. (See Fine Writing, Section 70.)

Select the image that is closest to your concept. Discard any image or images that conflict with your chosen image.

EXERCISE

The following sentences are examples of mixed imagery. Identify the separate images, note whether they are metaphors or similes, and write new versions of the essential thought, retaining any satisfactory image but eliminating the others.

1. The yellow cabs, like quickened snails, weave through the wet night with rhythmic wipers working behind the streaks of white that stretch before their lights.

2. Because of its growing prestige the University has been able to capture some topdrawer professors.
3. The Italian regime is clearly on tenterhooks. Their goose is cooked to a turn.
4. At last I have built my Rubicon and burnt it behind me.—Cited by *The New Yorker* from *Home Garden.*
5. These factors act as an effective pair of scissors that soon eliminates most of the barriers that men put up to keep themselves apart.
6. The department has become badly infiltrated with dead wood, and needs a thorough overhauling.
7. Holy Cross rolled to an early lead and then bit off a late Wake Forest rally to whip the Southern Conference Champions.
8. The sun beating down on Raven City like the breath of hell filtered through the thin rising dust like silver slivers.
9. It is not Hoyle for traders to talk the market up or down themselves, but they are long since expert in adjusting market sails for the winds of rumor that come sweeping periodically from the horse's mouth.—Cited by *The New Yorker* from *The New York Times.*
10. Like a mad engineer, pouring coal in the furnace of a locomotive headed for a precipice, the ruling heads are permitting the lower brackets to sink in a quagmire of high prices.—Cited by *The New Yorker* from a letter to *PM.*
11. The tempos were all correct and the balances proper, but the work tended to tread water for lack of a plain emotional trajectory.—Cited by *The New Yorker* from *The New York Herald Tribune.*
12. Let us nip this political business in the bud before it sticks to us like a leech!—Cited by *The New Yorker* from *The San Francisco Chronicle.*

63. SOUND

Another quality of words is their sound, their tonal effect on our hearing and our response to that effect. Alexander Pope in his *Essay on Criticism* discusses this feature of language as it appears in verse:

> 'Tis not enough no harshness gives offense,
> The sound must seem an echo to the sense:
> Soft is the strain when Zephyr gently blows,
> And the smooth stream in smoother numbers flows;
> But when loud surges lash the sounding shore,
> The hoarse rough verse should like the torrent roar.

In the last four lines Pope tries to make the sound of the diction, that is, the sound of the separate words and their rhythm in combination, suggest first the nature of a gentle breeze and then the roar of the surge pounding the shore; he is, as he says, making the sound "seem an echo to the sense." In like manner R. C. Scriven is making the sound fit the sense when he writes of the bees as singing:

> In honey-soaked June our velvet shuttles flew,
> Our velvet shuttles flew through sun-threads loomed on light,
> Through sun-threads loomed on light! O not in Xanadu,
> O not in Xanadu fabrics so flower-bright!
>
> —"Bee Song," *Punch*, September 24, 1952.

This attempt to suggest or even to imitate in words the sound we hear is technically known as *onomatopoeia,* and language of this sort is called *onomatopoeic* or *onomatopoetic.* Though onomatopoeia is a poetic device, it is very common also in prose. Whenever a writer describes his impressions of a thunderstorm, the waves on a seashore, some giant machine in action, or any phenomena of sound, he is certain to use some onomatopoetic words and phrases. Thus Arthur Koestler uses such diction in describing the sounds made by a hearse damaged by rioters as it hurries through the streets:

> . . . all the time more fragments of glass were falling out of the hearse and breaking on the pavement with a high-pitched tinkling which punctuated the echo of the muffled rumbling of the wheels.—*The Age of Longing.*

Whenever you use such words as *bang, break, boom, buzz, crash, howl, hush, hiss, meow, murmur, mutter, pound, rattle, roar, screech, sputter, squeal, thunder,* you are using onomatopoetic diction.

63A. Euphony

Euphony means *pleasing sound.* As a term it includes effective onomatopoeia. All onomatopoetic effects, whether harsh or mellow, please the mind if they are well done and suited to their context. But euphony also refers to the sound of language in general: Are your sentences natural in rhythm? Are their diction and phrasing agreeable to the ear when read aloud (the best test for euphony)? If so your writing is euphonious.

63B. Cacophony

The opposite of euphony is *cacophony*—or *ugly sound*. Cacophony is lumpy language, like badly cooked oatmeal. When words in prose draw attention because of their alliteration or careless repetition of sounds, when sentence rhythm is bumpy (see "cobblestone rhetoric," p. 394), your writing is cacophonous. In calling your attention to this fault, your instructor may choose to refer you only to *euphony,* since he wishes you to make your cacophonous sentence or phrase over into a euphonious one.

FAULTY: Various vessels plying to and from enemy ports are subject to search and seizure in a peaceful blockade.

IMPROVED: Vessels sailing to and from enemy ports may be searched and seized in a peaceful blockade.

FAULTY: From my study of the Renaissance, I have carefully gleaned considerable helpful knowledge which I have found applicable in practically every course I have taken.

IMPROVED: From my study of the Renaissance I have gained much information that has proved helpful in most of my courses.

OR: My study of the Renaissance has helped me in most of my courses.

FAULTY: It was one of those very still and crystal-clear sort of silent evenings when your own solitary footsteps seem to be the only certain sound in the world. (Observe the hissing of the *s*-sounds in this sentence.)

IMPROVED: The evening was clear and still, so quiet that only my own footsteps broke the absolute silence.

EXERCISE

Rewrite the following sentences, eliminating or reducing the number of alliterative words, or other words of the same sound pattern (including adverbs in -ly, repetitions of the -ing ending, words of unintentional rhyme) and structures that sound clumsy or jolting when read aloud.

1. Deeply absorbed in himself, he ordinarily would have been unaware of how slowly and heavily he was trudging along.
2. The responsibilities attendant upon being a superintendent had carved a notable change in his apparel and appearance.
3. Until the end of my sophomore year of my high-school career, my mind was still living in a wondrous bewildering world of make-believe.
4. The women of that time dressed the silliest of all; they wore hats that were really only half-hats and did not cover the ears at all.
5. There was no close noise, but in what at first seemed silence, gradually, dimly I discerned the swishing of the water on the beach, the singing of the distant birds, the ringing of far-off hammer blows falling steadily, the harsh mewing of the gulls, and the splashing of the fish.
6. Everything but the clearness of her face before me seemed so unreal that I began to have doubt about the actuality of my own reality.
7. Now the spring sun had returned to refuel the futile battle, giving sustenance to the few plants that grew through the thick mulch, and strengthening the alder in its thickening leafy infiltration.

64. VIVIDNESS

One of the writer's fundamental aims, as we have seen, is to capture and hold attention. One of the best ways of achieving this aim is to make sure that your diction has life and vigor. Use words that arouse sense impressions—concrete nouns, fresh adjectives, mobile verbs, and newly minted metaphors. Of course you are coming to realize that clichés and overworked adjectives have as little value as smooth-worn pennies, and far from holding attention, will not even gain it.

64A. Image-Making Words

Don't say *horse* if a special horse is your subject; name him exactly. Say: *Morgan colt, stallion, palamino, nag, pacer, saddle-horse.* Don't say *fish*: say *trout, black bass, codfish, catfish, sailfish, salmon, tuna, pike, carp, guppy.* Don't say *red* or *pink*: say *scarlet, crimson, carnelian, burgundy, rose, Venetian-red, Indian-*

red, auburn, carrot, flame-colored, brick-red, blood-red, ruby, garnet, carmine, maroon, cerise, cherry, vermilion. Don't say *play*: say *comedy, tragedy, tragicomedy, melodrama, farce, fantasy*—or if the situation suggests it, name the play itself: *Much Ado About Nothing, The Importance of Being Earnest.* In short, prefer the concrete and the specific to the general and the abstract. (See Section 61B.)

64B. Fresh Adjectives

Use fresh adjectives, but use them carefully. Do not overload your nouns with them (see Wordiness, Section 71). Above all, avoid using counter adjectives (words that take the place of the exact adjectives) like *pleasant, nice, fine, beautiful, pretty, dull,* or slang adjectives like *swell, lousy.* Persons of impoverished vocabularies make *nice* do the work of *agreeable, altruistic, amenable, amiable, beautiful, beneficent, benign, bounteous, bountiful, charitable, comfortable, cordial, courteous, courtly*—and you will observe that this list covers only adjectives beginning with the first three letters of the alphabet.

64C. Mobile Verbs

Don't say *go* or *move*: say *amble, run, hurry, rush, crawl, creep, saunter, writhe, wiggle, leap, bound, trot, gallop, hurtle*—or any other of the many words that will describe the observed action exactly. On the other hand, avoid the trap of Elegant Variation (p. 395); thus in dialogue it is usually better to pepper your writing with *said* than to strive for variety with *exclaim, murmur, pout, reply, retort,* though now and then such a writer as Henry James may use these words effectively to give color to statements.

64D. Sparing Use of Adverbs

Though it is better to say, "He talked slowly," than merely to say, "He talked," it is better still to say, "He drawled," than to say, "He talked slowly," if the meaning fits. Don't say *spoke loudly*, say *roared, ranted, raved, thundered, snarled.* A snake does not merely move *stealthily* or *sinuously*; it *slithers, writhes, flows.*

In short, let the verb work for you. Always ask yourself: Is it possible to replace the verb and adverb I am using with a more specific verb? Justify to yourself every adverb that you use.

Do not make the mistake of thinking, however, that the single concrete verb is always better than a verb phrase: Compare the two following versions of a biblical passage and observe the superiority of the second:

> He cometh forth like a flower and withers.
> He cometh forth like a flower and is cut down.

64E. Figures of Speech

Use figures of speech derived from your own experience. Study the section on Figures of Speech in this chapter (Section 62), together with the exercises, and then try to enliven your own writing with effective imagery based on your own observation of life. Once more, do not overload your sentences with figures of speech and do not mix them, but use them whenever your meaning will be made richer and clearer through their use. Often good figures of speech will suggest themselves; but cultivate the habit of inventing them to give color to your writing. Some of your inventions of this sort may not be successful, but only through such attempts can you learn how to use imagery effectively. Study the following examples of relatively abstract statement and see how much more vivid the sentences become when their thought is expressed in figures of speech:

ABSTRACT: The sensation of touching the bird's feet was disagreeable to her.

SIMILES: "Or the feel of his feet, I won't be able to stand it. They'll be cold, naked, unbearable, like a sick thing's or a dying baby's fingers."—KAY BOYLE.

ABSTRACT: The columns of infantry moved slowly over the terrain without engaging the enemy.

METAPHOR: But the long serpents crawled slowly from hill to hill without bluster or smoke.—STEPHEN CRANE.

ABSTRACT: The artist, whether productive or not, must use much time in contemplation.

METAPHOR: Whether or not he produces anything, this contemplation is the hall-mark of the artist. He who values it is one, the rest can never be. It is his gelatine, his queen-bee jelly, the compost round his roots; the violent are drawn to such a man by the violence of his serenity.—CYRIL CONNOLLY, *The Unquiet Grave.*

Observe that the last is made more vivid also through the use of effective repetition (*violent . . . violence*) and paradox (*violence of his serenity*). (See Repetition, Section 65, and Imagery, Section 62.)

EXERCISE

Impart life to the following sentences by following the recommendations given above.

1. The dog ran swiftly round the track after the mechanical device and quickly overtook it.
2. The evening had been very pleasant: he had enjoyed the play, and the conversation had moved along nicely.
3. This instructor is a man of many hobbies, as may be seen by looking about his study.
4. My high-school teacher was a man of handsome appearance, fine scholarship, and splendid character.
5. Mr. West was a somewhat dark, short man with an attractive smile and a cheerful demeanor; he gave a very good lecture.
6. The diagnosis of his condition was favorable. It was reported that he might be able to return home shortly.
7. All the girls sang as they worked, and though Carol did not know the words, she tried to hum the tunes.
8. This rather attractive little spot has taken on a fascinating atmosphere.
9. The room was cool and inviting to the weary mind; a rest was welcome after the strenuous hours of drudgery.
10. The task was monotonous and unending; Ross began to think how wonderful a swim would be, when noon came.

65. REPETITION

See also Sections 4B1, 26B, 27C, 51G.

65A. Effective Repetition

In the hands of a skilled writer repetition may be used to emphasize thought, to make it more vivid, or even to create a mood. The writer may repeat single words, phrases, or clauses; sometimes he may simply repeat structural form (see Parallelism, Section 24). Consider, for example, how James Joyce employs repetition in the following passage in creating a rhythmic mental image (and metaphor) of snow falling over a vast landscape:

> . . . snow was general all over Ireland. It was falling on every part of the dark central plain, on the treeless hills, falling softly upon the Bog of Allen and, farther westward, softly falling into the dark mutinous Shannon waves. It was falling, too, upon every part of the lonely churchyard where Michael Furey lay buried. It lay thickly drifted on the crooked crosses and headstones, on the spears of the little gate, on the barren thorns. His soul swooned slowly as he heard the snow falling faintly through the universe and faintly falling, like the descent of their last end, upon all the living and the dead.—JAMES JOYCE, "The Dead," *Dubliners*.

Notice the repetition of the clause *it is falling,* of the phrases (with skillful transposition) *falling softly, softly falling, falling faintly, faintly falling,* and the repetition of structural patterns throughout the passage.

Repetition is also frequently needed for clarity. Though the careful writer tries to eliminate ineffective repetition, it is often necessary to repeat the subject of discourse and other key words and phrases. Thus the writer of an essay on dogs must unhesitatingly repeat the word *dog* rather than resort to such clichés as "man's best friend," "faithful companion," "canine comrade," or other evasions of the exact word (see Elegant Variation, p. 395). And a discussion of *repetition* must *repeat repetition* much as it is *repeated* in this section.

65B. Faulty Repetition

See Economy, Section 27C.

Unless repetition is justified as desirable for emphasis or necessary for clarity, it is ineffective and should be avoided. Eliminate such repetition from your writing by using pronouns and synonyms, and by rephrasing the sentences. Study the following examples of faulty repetition and their revisions. Notice that faulty repetition is one of the several types of wordiness.

FAULTY: The very heart of student activities is the Student Union. It is at the Student Union that you meet your friends. Almost every member of the student body comes to the Student Union at some time during the week to attend lectures or other entertainments. (45 words)

REVISED: The Student Union is the center of activities. Here one meets friends, plays games, attends lectures, listens to music. (19 words)

FAULTY: Professor Garrigus is on the approved list of official judges that will judge milking Shorthorn cattle at fairs and shows during this year. (23 words)

REVISED: Professor Garrigus is one of the official judges for the Shorthorn milking contests this year. (15 words)

EXERCISE

Most of the sentences below exhibit faulty repetition. A few illustrate effective repetition. (*a*) Rewrite the faulty sentences, either eliminating the bad repetition or making it effective. (*b*) Identify the sentences containing effective repetition and explain briefly why you think them satisfactory.

1. Whenever the valves are involved, and this probably happens always in a case of carditis, the mitral valve is involved frequently and heavily, and the other valve is involved less frequently and heavily.
2. When I was a child Sunday afternoons were not anticipated very eagerly. Sunday afternoons were quite the longest, dullest afternoons of the week.
3. The beginning of the Atomic Age has brought less hope than fear. It is a primitive fear, the fear of the unknown, the fear of forces man can neither channel nor comprehend. This fear is not new; in its classical form it is the fear of irrational death.
4. There are still several systems in use at the present time, and this is the cause of considerable confusion, but it seems probable that these systems may be resolved into one system in the near future. It is more than likely that the system left will be the Braille system.

5. One day one section has the early classes and on the following day the other section has the early classes.
6. But most of all he liked candy; he liked candy that was red or white or green or yellow; he liked candy in sticks or balls or squares. He liked sweet candy, sour candy, and spicy candy.
7. Each afternoon Charles walked Mrs. Mentor's little poodle for an hour. He walked down Center Street; he walked on Main Street past the shops showing sporting goods and dry goods, then he turned and walked toward the Park, where he and the poodle walked for a short time. Then they walked home.
8. A man flying combat planes must be kept free from worry in order to be fit because when flying a combat plane a man has to feel relaxed and unworried.
9. Keepers of books, keepers of print and paper on the shelves, librarians are keepers also of the records of the human spirit—the records of men's watch upon the world and on themselves.

66. SLANG

See also Section 59C.

Slang has been defined as a "peculiar kind of vagabond language hanging on the outskirts of legitimate speech, but continually shaping or forcing its way into the most respectable company."[6] It takes its origin from "the effort of ingenious individuals to make the language more pungent and picturesque —to increase the store of terse and striking words, to widen the bounds of metaphor, and to provide a vocabulary for new shades of meaning."[7] Though born of the desire to startle, slang tends to defeat itself by its own extravagance. One can cry wolf once too often: startling phrases frequently repeated become clichés.

Ask your best friend what slang is. He might well answer, "Talking like the other fellows." Slang, as he sees it, is a language that one assiduously learns from early childhood on to adulthood so that one can belong to the gang. Though often witty and clever when it was invented, as group language it becomes little more than a ticket to casual fellowship, the cliché that masks the per-

[6] J. B. Greenough and G. L. Kittredge, *Words and Their Ways in English Speech* (New York: The Macmillan Co., 1901).

[7] H. L. Mencken, *The American Language* (New York: Alfred A. Knopf, Inc., 1936).

sonal ("you can't be too different"), rather than the incisive expression of the individual mind.

The world of slang is a comfortable world to belong to—but when you come to college, you are preparing for serious citizenship in a larger world. This is not to say that you will now find it necessary to give up the use of slang. Actually you may find it desirable to use current slang, with judgment, at certain times. But your large task now is to master the style of writing that will win you fellowship in the world of educated men and women, a style that may be formal or informal as occasion demands, but one that avoids slang entirely (highly formal English) or uses it sparingly (informal English).

Slang, as has been indicated, is not just slang words; it is a whole language by itself. It has its own special vocabulary which includes many words of good lineage that are either extended beyond their accepted meanings or given new meanings (*square, kosher, swell, goldbrick, dead pan, apple-polishing, daisy, jerk, sharp, crumb, beef, horse's mouth, old hat, keen, tomato, hotdog, hot, hot air*) and words that are coined anew, sometimes representing new forms but more often based on the shortening, telescoping, or other reshaping of familiar words (*jazz, blurb, quiz, rap, Veep, cuke, glads, champ, G. I., brunch, socialite, cinemactress, hassle, blessed-event, Renovated*).

Slang shows itself also in phrases and sentence structure. Such expressions as "Aw gwan!" "Beat it!" "Scram!" "off his rocker," "belongs in the looney bin," "Shoot the works," "Tell it to the marines," "I'm from Missouri," "He blew his stack," will suggest numerous other phrases and sentences in which the literal meaning is distorted and given a new meaning.

Slang shows the natural human love for figures of speech, such as simile, metaphor, synecdoche, metonymy, and exaggeration. Thus a drunkard is as "tight as a drum" (simile); Joe Louis gave boxing "a shot in the arm" (metaphor); a girl is a *skirt* (synecdoche) or a *dame* or *doll* (metonymy); a girl sends *bushels of love* (exaggeration). Slang owes its picturesqueness, vigor, and raciness to this feature of language.

But slang is a dangerous language, a language you must learn to use with caution and, on certain occasions, avoid entirely. It is well called the lazy man's language, for it offers a special stereotyped vocabulary of terms and phrases to fit all ordinary situations. Once one has learned this special list of phrases, one is tempted to use them on all occasions rather than to take the trouble of thinking out more exact words and expressions. To say that Jack is a "good sport" implies much that cannot be said otherwise in short compass. But this is one of the objections to many slang terms: they are often large, but general and somewhat vague in meaning. A letter of recommendation must specify as exactly as possible the qualities of Jack's character. Is he trustworthy? reliable? honest? sincere? likable? All these characteristics and more or only a few may afford the reason why Jack is a "good sport"; or perhaps "good sport" simply means that Jack can be "touched" for a "buck" or two when needed. Just as we do not measure fine airplane parts with ordinary rulers, so our more serious writing and thinking require the exact word, the word specially selected to fit the thought.

Slang is also a transitory language. None of us, except on whimsical impulse, would use such exclamations as "Gadzooks!" "Odd's bodykins!" "Zounds!" We know that these expressions are dead except as they re-create a past age. Even the slang of our modern era demonstrates its ephemerality. "Oh, you kid," "the bee's knees," "the cat's pajamas," "apple sauce," and other slang phrases of the 1920's are outmoded and often meaningless today. The slang of O. Henry now needs an interpreter; Damon Runyon's is rapidly fading from popular comprehension. One may safely predict that tomorrow nearly all our current slang will be forgotten. This is one of the perils of slang: not only does its vocabulary fade and wilt like flowers in a child's May-basket, but its use also tends to date the user and classify him socially.

Though most slang perishes in the period of its creation, some gradually makes its way into literary and even formal usage. Such words as *mob* (from *mobile vulgus,* the fickle crowd), *hoax* (*hocus*), *sport* (for *disport*), *cad, sham, canter, gin* (from *ge-*

neva), *bus, cab* were once considered as slang. But the number of slang words from any period that become recognized as standard English is exceedingly small. Do any of the other slang phrases cited in this section seem likely to become established as reputable? Can you think of any other examples in our present usage that promise to live? Consider the chances of the following: *all washed up, make like an usher* (football player, etc.), *jalopy, And how, blurb, kayo, I can take it, I get you, click* (to succeed), *blah, S.A., punch-drunk, whoopee, lounge-lizard, doll* (girl), *B.M.O.C.*

Of course, if you are writing a story presenting a character who makes much use of slang, you will write as befits his nature. Use slang where the situation calls for slang. But:

In all formal writing avoid slang.

In informal writing use it sparingly and with discretion.

In personal interviews, especially when you are applying for work, avoid slang so far as you can do so without becoming stilted in your conversation.

These recommendations mean that though you may still retain a knowledge of slang, you must not let it rob you of the ability to express yourself well in good formal and informal English. If it seems necessary for you to try to eliminate slang altogether from your speaking and writing vocabulary to achieve this aim, there will be no harm in doing so. A beginner does well to set himself exact standards from which he may ultimately vary with good judgment—after he has established good habits of speaking and writing.

67. CLICHÉS (Trite Expressions)

A cliché is a worn-out or hackneyed or trite expression, one worn threadbare with use. Each expression of this sort was once new and had an appeal that made it popular; but much repetition has dimmed its luster. Nearly all slang becomes trite, and much jargon also comes under this classification. Whenever words gather into familiar clusters, we have clichés. Clichés usually impoverish style: each cliché takes the place of some other expression that might have vigor and freshness.

One cannot always avoid clichés. In conversation in particular the familiar worn-out phrase will release the speaker from the hard necessity of thinking that is required for fresh and vigorous expression. But the good conversationalist will try to eliminate clichés from his speech (or enliven them: see below); and the careful writer will try to remove them from his writing unless he is using them in narrative to exhibit the speech of a character addicted to the cliché habit.

Like jargon, which has many trite phrases (see Jargon, Section 69), clichés usually represent an attempt to dignify or decorate everyday ideas much better represented by unadorned words, as for example, *institution of higher learning* (for *college*), *playful as a kitten* (*playful*), *devouring element* (*fire*). The right names of things are almost always better than the substitutes for them; and if you use a figure of speech (see Simile, Metaphor, Sections 62A, B), be sure that it is fresh and appropriate.

The following list of clichés will remind you of many others that you have heard or read. Notice that these clichés are frequently figures of speech, metaphors, or similes that have lost all vitality from overuse.

acid test
after all is said and done
at one fell swoop
at a loss for words
beat a hasty retreat
bitter end
blazing inferno
bolt from the blue
bored to death
bow to the inevitable
breathless silence
bring order out of chaos
budding genius
burn the midnight oil
conspicuous by his absence
classic performance
goes without saying
good square meal
in the last analysis
in conclusion
last but not least
long arm of the law
memorable occasion
mine of information
partake of refreshments
point with pride
psychological moment
put in an appearance
quick as a flash
reigns supreme
rendered a selection
sadder but wiser

depths of despair
dire necessity
doomed to disappointment
downy couch
drastic action
festive occasion
financially embarrassed
finger of suspicion
stellar role
table groaned
tired but happy
view with alarm
wended my way
without further ado
words fail to describe
worked like a Trojan

Can clichés ever be effective? Yes, says Professor George Arms ("Clichés, Extended or Otherwise," *The Saturday Review of Literature,* November 30, 1946, 9 ff), and he points to numerous clever uses of clichés by gifted writers who by slightly altering the familiar phrasing have produced amusing effects. Here are a few examples:

> At the drop of a brass hat.—FRED B. MILLETT.
>
> To gild the lily with radiator paint—EARNEST HOOTON.
>
> . . . poor Henry James always chews more than he can bite off.—MRS. HENRY ADAMS.
>
> . . . politicians talking themselves red, white, and blue in the face. —CLARE BOOTH.
>
> For the milk of human kindness the most obvious substitute is soft soap.—STUART CHASE.

Such wit will enliven conversation and informal writing; but don't lie awake nights refashioning clichés for your college courses. Try to manage without them.

Two final cautions:

1. If you decide to use a cliché, don't apologize for it. It will not smell any the fresher for quotation marks or apologetic words.

2. Avoid such much-used quotations as "To be or not to be," "full of sound and fury," "Et tu, Brute!"—and all stale allusions.

EXERCISES

A. Revise the following sentences, replacing the trite phrases with fresh expressions of your own invention. Observe that not all the parts of some of these sentences are trite. Again, some may be effectively shortened.

1. Al, the big Greek bartender, leaned against the bar staring at nothing through the gray haze that rose from the cigarette that dangled precariously from the corner of his mouth.
2. Joe was his childhood idol—a tall, square-shouldered Russian immigrant, with handsome, clean-cut features and a winning smile.
3. Almost quick as a wink both of us had done what people call "justice" to the meal spread before us, perhaps even better than that, to the extent of "injustice" to our overburdened stomachs.
4. Now, to tell the truth, I didn't have much interest in seeing those redwoods, though I usually like places of scenic grandeur and awe-inspiring beauty.
5. After having "cleaned up" so much good food, we didn't mind "cleaning up" the few dishes which had served as a humble means to that noble end.
6. After working in the tobacco field all day, like the village blacksmith, you have earned your night's repose.
7. Rose was pretty as a picture as she sat there, curled up with a good old-fashioned mystery story.
8. Some people claim that reading books is the greatest cultural influence, and still others maintain that you can get the most in the quickest split second time by listening to lectures, but what I always say is, "There's nothing more broadening than travel."—SINCLAIR LEWIS.
9. There is nothing like the Grand Old Party for doing the right thing in the way of good clean government: a new broom sweeps clean.
10. I now give to you that stalwart leader, that great champion of the principles of our democratic forebears, that red-blooded, one hundred per-cent American, the next President of the United States!

B. Make a list of twenty trite phrases that you have heard or have used yourself. Arrange opposite each expression its equivalent in good English.

68. EUPHEMISMS

A *euphemism* is an attempt to modify an unpleasant thought by substituting mild or polite words or phrases for the exact word or words. Euphemisms unfortunately tend in time to become as coarse as the words they are substitutes for; thus *mistress* (for *concubine*), *expectorate* (*spit*), *perspiration* (*sweat*) are no longer any more refined than the rude words.

It is proper, however, to use euphemisms at certain times (and wiser: *misrepresent,* or *tell a fib,* is better on occasion than *lie*). Do not offend your reader or listener unnecessarily. But in your writing so far as decency permits, use the exact word. These are examples of euphemisms:

went to his reward, passed away, passed on (died)
grim reaper (death)
laid to rest (buried)
abdomen (belly)
limbs (legs)
intoxicated (drunk)
halitosis (bad breath)
funeral director (undertaker)
paying guest (lodger)
fellow worker (employee)
depression (hard times)
underprivileged (poor)
casualties (the killed and injured)

69. JARGON

The worst fault that writers (and speakers) of formal English commit is the abuse of language known as jargon. This is the way a writer of jargon might define the term: "Jargon is the obfuscation of intellection through the utilization of polysyllabic diction and periphrastic constructions." Reduced to English, this sentence means: "Jargon darkens meaning through the use of long words and circumlocution." Arthur Quiller-Couch in a famous essay ("On Jargon") defines it more picturesquely as a perpetual "shuffling around in the fog and cotton-wool of abstract terms."

Though nearly every educated person is guilty of writing jargon at times, professional men in particular are subject to the failing and have frequently been ridiculed for it, as in the following rephrasing of part of Lincoln's Gettysburg Address by a college professor, written, he says, "so that professors can understand it":

> Eight and seven-tenths decades ago the pioneer workers in this continental area implemented a new group based on an ideology of free boundaries and initial conditions of equality.
>
> We are now actively engaged in an over-all evaluation of conflicting factors in order to determine whether or not the life expectancy of this group or of any group operating under the stated conditions is significant. We are met in an area of maximum activity among the conflicting factors. The purpose of the meeting is to assign permanent positions to the

units which have been annihilated in the process of attaining a steady state. This procedure represents standard practice at the administrative level.

From a more comprehensive viewpoint we cannot assign—we cannot integrate—we cannot implement this area. . . .[8]

And here are Lincoln's direct and moving words for ease of comparison:

Fourscore and seven years ago our fathers brought forth on this continent a new nation, conceived in liberty, and dedicated to the proposition that all men are created equal.

Now we are engaged in a great civil war, testing whether that nation, or any nation so conceived and so dedicated, can long endure. We are met on a great battlefield of that war. We have come to dedicate a portion of that field as a final resting-place for those who here gave their lives that that nation might live. It is altogether fitting and proper that we should do this.

But in a larger sense, we cannot dedicate—we cannot consecrate—we cannot hallow this ground. . . .

The parody is absurd, but as its author implies, much professional writing is equally bad. (Observe incidentally that Lincoln does not avoid long words where they will enrich his thought.)

In an attempt to get rid of jargon the Federal Security Agency[9] urges its employees to avoid unnecessarily long, technical, or highbrow words that suggest that the writer is pompous and trying to show how much he knows. The agency recommends that its workers write

NOT LIKE THIS	BUT LIKE THIS
a substantial segment of the population	many people (a large group)
fully cognizant of	know well
interpose an objection	object
comprising numerous agricultural units	made up of many farms
hold in abeyance	wait (postpone action)
promulgate the regulation	issue the regulation
effectuate (implement) the policy	carry out the policy
pursuant to your request	as you requested

[8] *Tech Training,* November, 1951.

[9] Milton Hall, "Better Writing," No. 2, Federal Security Agency, Social Security Board.

NOT LIKE THIS	BUT LIKE THIS
prior to . . . subsequent to	before . . . after
secure (ascertain) the data	get the facts
interrogate the claimant	ask (question) him
purports to construe	explains (tries to explain)
encounter difficulty in	find it hard to
precludes the institution of appeal processes	does away with the need for . . .
marked discrepancy	clear difference
initiate (institute) a project	begin . . .
consummate the arrangement	make or complete . . .
in the initial instance	in the first place
of the order of magnitude	about

One should avoid all phrases like those in the first column above when it is possible to substitute simpler phrases for them. This bad habit of "officialese" or "gobbledygook," as former Congressman Maury Maverick names it, shows itself in many terms. Quiller-Couch warns us to beware of such "woolly abstract nouns" as *case, instance, element, factor, character, nature, condition, persuasion, degree,* of such phrases as *as regards, with regard to, in respect of, in connection with, according as to whether, as such.* A longer list could be made of other currently popular words and phrases of jargon; one thinks of such expressions as *contact* (*talk with, get in touch with*), *implement, over-all, accelerate, behooves, utilize, due to* (or *owing to*) *the fact that, along the lines of, end-result, asset, relative to, as a matter of fact.*

The cure for many of these is simply to be more direct and concrete. Consider the following examples of jargon and their revisions:

JARGON: In case you find that the problem is of a difficult nature, try to solve it along the lines of the example presented on this page.

REVISED: If you find the problem difficult, try to solve it by following the example given on this page.

JARGON: I shall contact him tomorrow relative to the change in prices and ascertain what can be done in connection with their reduction.

REVISED: I shall talk with (telephone, cable, get in touch with) him tomorrow about the change in prices and find out whether they can be reduced.

Jargon is not merely the use of big or pretentious words. It expresses itself also in syntax or the relationship of words in the sentence. Thus the writer of jargon likes to use passive constructions because he mistakenly believes that they give his thought dignity, whereas in actuality they only make it stilted or pompous. He says, "It is argued that the Taft-Hartley bill needs modification," when he means, "Some argue that the Taft-Hartley bill needs modification." Or he uses a noun construction of the same passive nature where an active construction would be better, as in the introductory clause of the following sentence:

> It is the sense of the faculty that no academic credit should be given for courses in typewriting.

> REVISED: The faculty rules (recommends, thinks, urges, believes) that no academic credit should be given for courses in typewriting.

Observe that the subordinate clause in this sentence illustrates the proper use of the passive voice (see Passive Voice, Section 15C 3). It is quite correct to use the passive when you wish to stress the thing or idea being discussed rather than an agent. But otherwise always prefer the active voice whenever you can use it without awkwardness. In general, try to avoid lifeless introductory constructions like those given above.

Yet another example of jargon in sentence structure is found in the massing of nouns (usually abstract) in a series of successive prepositional phrases. (The sentence just given illustrates the fault.) Marjorie True Gregg in *The Saturday Review of Literature* names this fault in style "cobblestone rhetoric" on the ground that the sentence rhythm bumps from one phrase to another. She cites as an example:

> If there were a uniform condition with reference to the distribution of population it would be necessary to move forward to a recognition of the desirability of such a readjustment.

Note that there are five bumpy prepositional phrases in this sentence, considering *with reference to* as a compound (and bad) preposition. The sentence is so foggily worded that its meaning is difficult to discover; but it may mean something like the following:

> If population could be distributed uniformly, doubtless it should be done.

It is not necessary to get rid of all such phrases, as this revision does, but avoid a series of these if possible.

Quiller-Couch also calls attention to another fault of jargon which he names Elegant Variation. Elegant Variation (the epithet *elegant* is ironic) is the practice of using various synonyms in order to avoid repeating a necessary word. This practice is frequently seen in inferior sports writing and bad oratory. Thus in sports articles, the University of Connecticut basketball team may be named successively "the Huskies," "the Nutmeggers," "the boys from Storrs," to avoid the use of the term "Connecticut team." The reporter may speak of himself as "this writer," "your reporter," to avoid the use of the natural pronoun *I*. Orators used to speak of the late Senator Taft as "Mr. Republican," "the Senator from Ohio," "the great Buckeye statesman," to avoid saying "Mr. Taft." In general, in good formal and informal writing call people, ideas, and objects by their right names, and do not hesitate to repeat those names as often as is needed for clarity.

EXERCISE

Rewrite the following sentences in good formal or informal English, your choice of level being determined by the sense of each passage.

1. Since I plan to major in languages, a suggestion from a language professor is an invaluable bit of advice which in my case must be respected, and, incidentally, heeded.
2. The factors which are involved in causing rheumatic fever are not too well known.
3. Even the direction in which I drove was quite different, and my mind, being decidedly refreshed, bore that appreciative characteristic which enables one fully to enjoy the blends of man-made and natural phenomena.
4. The four of us displayed eagerness to participate in the laudable change of subject.

5. A student persisted in saying that in his opinion the instructor should be more interested in course achievement than campus application, and that this would be a highly effective means of improving the student-teacher relationship.
6. It is obvious from the difference in elevation with relation to the short depth of the property that the contour is such as to preclude any reasonable development potential for active recreation.—Cited by W. E. FARBSTEIN, "Overfine Words," *The New York Times Magazine.*
7. England anticipates that, as regards the current emergency, personnel will face up to the issues, and exercise appropriately the functions allocated to their respective occupation groups.—A. P. Herbert's satiric rewriting of a famous order by Lord Nelson.
8. Verbal contact with Mr. Blank regarding the attached notification has elicited the attached representation intimating that he prefers to decline the assignment.—Cited by W. E. FARBSTEIN.
9. The above case was an extreme example that undoubtedly applies only to a few maladjusted individuals.
10. At any rate his motivation is decidedly positive in the direction of his staying awake.

70. "FINE WRITING"

The temptation to decorate one's writing with flowery terms and glittering phrases is natural, born of the desire to gain attention and to impress the reader. But one of the fundamental things that a writer must learn is that decoration in itself is not art. The imagery of good writing must be an essential part of the meaning. More adjectives than are needed to convey the thought effectively, more figures of speech than the thought requires, or figures that are not suited to the thought mark the decorative, redundant style known as "fine writing." The name is ironic: it means writing that the author admires (why else would he write it?) but that the critic smiles at.

The opposite of "fine writing" is dull writing. You should not let fear of "fine writing" drive you to the opposite extreme. Use imagery, use adjectives where your thought is improved by them, but guard against excess. Present your thought as vividly as you can with due regard to subject and situation, but don't hang it with ornaments. Here is an example of a style glittering with false jewels:

> Joan fought her big loose handbag halfway through the recital of that letter, wrested a wisp of lace and linen from it and turned imploringly toward the judge, trying to dam the spatter of sudden tears.
>
> She was in a purple sweater and a black skirt today, and wore a purple coat that diffused its royal color into her cascade of auburn hair, and petted her cheeks with lilac shadows.—From the *Chicago Sun*, as quoted by *The New Yorker*.

What is the cure for such a passage? One is tempted to say, throw it away. Most writing of this sort should be discarded. Now and then some "fine writing" can be saved by careful pruning, elimination of excess adjectives and figures of speech; but many phrases, sentences, and passages of this sort have such slight value as to be almost worthless.

The following rewriting of the passage represents an attempt to retain the main sense with as much color as the situation allows:

> Halfway through the reading of the letter, Joan looked imploringly at the judge, took a handkerchief from her handbag, and dabbed at her eyes.
>
> Today she wore a purple sweater, a black skirt, and a purple coat that accented her flowing auburn hair.

But first thoughts are often best. Throw it away!

EXERCISE

Rewrite the following examples of "fine writing," discarding all adjectives, adverbs, and figures of speech that seem merely decorative to you. Change or discard pretentious words. Retain any words, phrases, or images that enhance the meaning.

1. And now to cap the structure of my thought fittingly and substantially with a golden dome of conclusion.
2. The water which at one time roared with unruly gaiety dons a cloak of humbleness edged with a placid dignity.
3. Night descended with its great black wings, sending all the timid little people scurrying to their nooks and crannies in the city's concrete canyons.

4. For days the landscape had been in the clutches of old Father Winter; everywhere the bearded trees creaked with ancient groanings, and little bespectacled ponds reflected the moon.
5. Most of the factories and stores in town had suspended their activities before noon, and the workers had hurried with their families to the soothing beaches and lakes seeking mitigation of the torrid weather.

71. WORDINESS

See also Economy, Section 27.

Wordiness is a many-headed evil. It is using two or more words where one would do. It is using clauses that can be reduced to phrases, phrases that can be reduced to words. It is repeating the same thought unnecessarily in different words (tautology). It is one of the chief enemies of good writing, and though you may easily eliminate many other faults, this one will continue to vex you, requiring constant attention.

Fortunately, some types of wordiness are easily detected. Thus tautology is usually self-revealing, as in the phrases "audible to the ear," "return back," "true fact," "ascend up," "many in number"; and with a little effort it can be recognized when it occurs in sentences such as this one: "This explosion was novel and unusual; it had never happened before."

Expletive (*there is, there are*) constructions, dependent clauses, and phrases can be reduced or at times struck out entirely without loss in meaning and with gain in effect. Study the following examples:

WORDY: There are many men who are dominated by lust for power. (11 words)

REDUCED: Many men are dominated by lust for power. (8 words)
Many men lust for power. (5 words)

WORDY: It is certain that the Dodgers, who are the pride of Brooklyn, will win the pennant. (16 words)

REDUCED: The Dodgers, the pride of Brooklyn, will win the pennant. (10 words)

WORDY: If it were possible for the house mothers in the fraternities to serve meals, it would eliminate a large number of students who at present have joined the ranks of the common people and stand in line. (37 words)

UNINTENTIONAL HUMOR AND SNOBBERY REMOVED: If meals could be served at fraternity houses, the long lines at the dining halls could be greatly reduced. (19 words)

WORDY: Something must be done about the transportation facilities that are being offered at the University. I am sure that the whole student body joins me in a plea for more efficient and cheaper bus transportation. (35 words)

REDUCED: The University must improve its bus service. All the students agree that we should have better schedules at cheaper rates. (20 words)

WORDY: The calculator, which is made of durable plastic, is of a size which will fit into anyone's shirt pocket. (19 words)

REDUCED: The calculator, made of durable plastic, fits into a shirt pocket. (11 words)

Form the habit of going through each theme and getting rid of *it is* and *there are* constructions. Examine every clause beginning with *who* or *which* and ask if it can be reduced to a phrase or a word. If you have repeated any word or phrase, or repeated the meaning of any expression in other words, get rid of the repetition unless it effectively emphasizes or clarifies the thought (see Faulty Repetition, Section 65B). Examine your work for excess adjectives and adverbs. Make sure that your adjectives are needed, and substitute active verbs for verb-adverb combinations. (See Vividness, Section 64.)

Nearly all jargon is wordy. Here is a well-known example, from a list of instructions prepared by the Office of Civilian Defense in 1942:

> Such preparations shall be made as will completely obscure all Federal buildings and non-Federal buildings occupied by the Federal Government during an air-raid for any period of time from visibility by reason of internal or external illumination. Such obscuration may be obtained either by blackout construction or by termination of the illumination. (52 words)

President Roosevelt is credited with the following clarification and simplification of the statement:

> Tell them in buildings where they have to keep the work going, to put something across the windows. In buildings where they can afford to let the work stop for a while, turn out the lights. (36 words)

Finally, one special caution on wordiness: Say what you have to say without preamble or apology. Don't say that you are going to say it.

STATEMENT WITH PREAMBLE: First of all, I would like to state the theme of this play. It is the idea of love, false and true. (22 words)

REVISED: First, the theme of this play is one of true and false love. (13 words)

EXERCISE

Retaining the essential meaning and any words or phrases that help in expressing that meaning effectively, eliminate as many words from the following sentences as you can. Indicate after each sentence the number of words in the original sentence or sentence groups and the number in your revised sentence or sentences, as in the examples above.

1. As a matter of fact, progress involves a state of mind and heart and attitude rather than something characterized by the efficiency of machines; it is a philosophy that considers manual labor to be distinctly advantageous rather than one that disapproves of such labor as deleterious and harmful.
2. "A friend in need is a friend indeed" is a saying that suits my friend. He is good-natured and will help anyone who is in need of help. He will never hesitate to come to the aid of a friend. Of the many friends whom I have he is the one who is far more outstanding than the others.
3. The atmosphere of serenity that surrounds and envelops this family has its ultimate origin at least in part in the mental condition of stability of the father and the mother, who lead a life shaped by themselves and founded on intimate knowledge of their own capacities.
4. The reason why I broke the Portland Vase was because I had a headache that day and I didn't feel well, and anyway I didn't like it; it was too ornate and it irritated me.

5. The candidate dressed in morning clothes placed a wreath on the tomb of the unknown soldier after alighting from his car while newsmen took pictures of the ceremony and passers-by craned their necks to see who the dignitary was, dressed in striped pants.
6. It is obvious that the Monroe Doctrine was an effective instrument of policy, since for an indefinitely long period of time no power of any sort dared to encroach on the American continents.
7. The destitute, poverty-stricken old man had cats all over the place. Poorer than any church mouse, he had cats from the time of the Flood in unbroken family lines; white, black, piebald, and tortoise-shell, they roamed over chairs and under the rickety, ramshackle bed and climbed the broken stairway at our approach, looking at us with yellow, flat, noncommittal eyes.
8. The herb garden would have tickled a witch of Salem—rest her soul!—For there the gardener and owner had gathered and assembled all the herbs familiar to the sorcerer, such herbs as dogbane, rue, monkshard, nightshade, and poisonous and magical herbs of every variety used in witchcraft; needless to say, the effect made the thoughtful visitor wonder a little about the perpetuator of all this strange agriculture.
9. Except for his eyes, sharp and black as pitch, and the strange threatening atmosphere of immenseness he diffused, Sloan could be lightly described as a clean-cut, soft-spoken man of thirty-odd years who moved with a grace and balance rare among horsemen.
10. Judy was a very sweet-looking girl. She was thin. Her eyes were big and full. Her hair was cut short and she wore bangs. She was dressed very plainly, and she looked like every other girl in the orphanage.

72. GLOSSARY OF USAGE

The words and phrases listed here are often the cause of errors. The glossary of course is not complete, but it includes most of the problems of usage likely to trouble you. It should be supplemented on occasion by reference to a dictionary. Since usage is constantly shifting, some of the judgments expressed here are necessarily tentative and would not be universally accepted.

For explanations of such words as "colloquial" and "illiterate" see Sections 57–59 on the levels and varieties of usage. See also the index for page references to explanations of grammatical terms.

A, an. *A* is used before a consonant sound, *an* before a vowel sound: *a* crow, *a* lake, *a* road; *an* accident, *an* event, *an* octopus. Note that *a* is used before words beginning with the sound "yiu" even though the initial letter is a vowel: *a* European country, *a* unicorn. Note that *an* is used before words beginning with *h* if the *h* is silent: *an* hour, *an* honor, but *a* heart, *a* history, *a* hobby.

Accept, except. Verbs sometimes confused. *Accept* means "receive," "assent to." *Except* means "exclude." "He accepted my apology and excepted me from the general punishment." *Except* may also be a preposition meaning "with the exception of."

Accidentally. This is the correct spelling—not "accidently."

A.D. Abbreviation of *Anno Domini*, "in the year of our Lord." Used before a year when there is need to specify that the year is in the Christian era rather than prior to it: "Nero was slain A.D. 68."

Ad. To be avoided in writing. See *Want ad*.

Admission, admittance. *Admission* differs from *admittance* in implying the granting or sale of certain privileges: *admission* to a club or theater. *Admittance* implies nothing beyond actual entrance.

Affect, effect. Sometimes confused. *Affect* is almost always a verb, meaning "act on, impress, produce an effect on" or "make a show of, pretend." *Effect* is either a verb, meaning "accomplish, execute," or a noun, meaning "result."

> The prolonged drought will *affect* the price of food.
> He *affected* remorse that he did not feel.
> A military clique tried to *effect* a revolution.
> The love affair had an unfortunate *effect* upon his grades.

Aggravate. Means "intensify, make worse." "The tight bandage aggravated the injury." The colloquial use in the sense of "provoke, irritate," though widespread, should be avoided.

Ain't. To be avoided in speech as well as writing.

Alibi. Strictly, a plea of having been elsewhere when an act was committed, but the colloquial use in the sense of "excuse" is well established.

All right. This is the correct spelling—not "alright."

All the farther, all the longer, etc. Colloquial in the sense of "as far as, as long as," etc. This colloquial use, though widespread, is still objectionable in formal speech as well as in writing.

> CORRECT: This is as far as we shall go.
> One hour is as long as you may have for shopping.

Allude, refer. *Allude* means "suggest indirectly." *Refer* means "mention specifically."

> The teacher named no names, but the class knew that he was alluding to me.

The teacher referred to Waterloo as one of the turning-points of history.

Allusion, illusion. Sometimes confused, though in no way similar in meaning. An *allusion* is an indirect reference or suggestion: "He made an allusion to her habit of biting her nails." An *illusion* is a deceptive appearance or a false impression: "A mirage is an optical illusion." "Youth is full of illusions."

Almost, most. The abbreviated form *most* is colloquial.

COLLOQUIAL: Most everyone we know will be there.
That child seems to cry most all the time.
FORMAL: Almost everyone we know will be there.
That child seems to cry almost all the time.

Already, all ready. Sometimes confused. The adverb *already* means "before a specified time, previously": "The mail has already been delivered." In the phrase *all ready,* the adjective *ready* means "prepared": "The mail is all ready to go."

Alright. See *All right.*

Altogether, all together. Sometimes confused. The adverb *altogether* means "completely, without exception": "I am altogether opposed to your platform." The phrase *all together* means "in a group" or "in all": "At last we were all together again." "The football candidates numbered only twenty all together." "All together, there were only four of us willing to go."

Alumnus, alumni; alumna, alumnae. *Alumnus* (singular) and *alumni* (plural) refer to male graduates; *alumna* (singular) and *alumnae* (plural) refer to female graduates. The proper term for male and female graduates together is *alumni.* Modern usage condones the extension of these terms to include all former students of an institution, not just graduates.

A.M., P.M.; a.m., p.m. To be used only with a specific hour: "4:20 P.M." Not to be substituted for "in the morning, in the afternoon." Both capitals and small letters are correct, provided the writer is consistent.

Among, between. Strictly, *among* implies more than two objects or persons, whereas *between* implies only two: "Divide the money among the three boys." "Divide the money between Tom and Fred." But in informal writing this distinction is often ignored.

Amount, number. *Amount* refers to quantity (flour, money, sugar, water), *number* to a collection of individual items (barrels, pennies, soldiers).

And etc. *And* is obviously redundant before *etc.* (Latin *et cetera*), which means "and others, and so forth."

Anybody, anyone. Pronouns to be distinguished from *any body, any one:* "I shall talk with anybody who answers [*not* any body who answers]."

These days any body of water large enough to float a canoe is called a lake.

Anyone can learn to swim.

I have no preference for any one golf course.

The same distinction applies to *everybody, every body; everyone, every one; somebody, some body; someone, some one.*

Anyway. Overused as a transitional or introductory device.

Anyways, anywheres. Not to be used for *anyway, anywhere.*

Apt, likely, liable. *Apt* implies an inherent, habitual tendency: "He is apt to take offense easily." *Likely* implies simple probability: "He is likely to arrive at any minute." *Liable* implies something undesirable: "If you stand up you are liable to upset the canoe." *Liable* may also mean "responsible": "Williams asserted that he was not liable for the debts of his estranged wife."

As. As a conjunction, less precise than *because, for, since.*

Because [not *as*] he had proved untrustworthy, I refused to bargain with him.

You are too late, for [not *as*] they have already started.

Since [not *as*] you do not believe me, look for yourself.

As should not be used instead of *that* or *whether:*

I do not know that [not *as*] he is exactly a coward.

I do not know whether [not *as*] I shall come.

As, like. See *Like, as.*

As . . . as. In formal writing, *so . . . as* is preferable to *as . . . as* in negative statements: "She is as pretty as her sister," but "She is not so pretty as her sister." This distinction, however, is ignored by many writers.

Asset. Strictly, "property subject to the payment of legal obligations." The colloquial use in the sense of "advantage," though widespread, is objectionable in formal writing.

At. Redundant and illiterate in such sentences as "Where are you at?" and "He did not know where he was at."

Awful. Colloquial (and overworked) in the sense of "very bad."

Awfully. Colloquial (and overworked) in the sense of "extremely."

Back of, in back of. Colloquial for *behind.*

Bad, good. These are adjectives, not adverbs: "He did badly [not *bad*]." "He did well [not *good*]." But *bad* and *good* are correctly used as predicate adjectives following verbs such as *feel, look, smell, sound, taste:* "Jenny does not look good today." "This candy tastes bad."

Balance. Except in the sense of *bank balance,* regarded as colloquial for *remainder,* but widely used.

B.C. Abbreviation of "before Christ," used following any year of the pre-Christian era: "The year of Alexander's death was 323 B.C."

Because. Not to be used to introduce a noun clause (see Section 12E).

FAULTY: Because you lost the match is no reason for getting angry at me.
CORRECT: That you lost the match is no reason for getting angry at me.
FAULTY: The reason he is angry is because he lost the match.
CORRECT: The reason he is angry is that he lost the match.
He is angry because he lost the match.

Beside, besides. Sometimes confused. *Beside* is almost always a preposition meaning "by the side of": "Please sit beside me." *Besides* may be either an adverb or a preposition. As a simple adverb it means "in addition" ("He told me all this and more besides"); it may also be a conjunctive adverb meaning "moreover" ("Henry was embarrassed; besides, he was bored"). As a preposition it means "in addition to" ("I shall know no one there besides the members of the immediate family").

Between. See *Among, between.*

Bunch. Colloquial in the sense of *group* when applied to people.

Bust, busted, bursted. Colloquial or slang forms of the verb *burst,* the principal parts of which are *burst, burst, burst.* But in the following special instances the use of *bust* is widespread: bronco-*buster,* trust-*busting,* to *bust* an officer (reduce his rank, usually to that of private).

But, hardly, only, scarcely. Any of these words used with a negative forms a double negative.

NONSTANDARD: I don't have but one Saturday class.
STANDARD: I have but one Saturday class.
I have only one Saturday class.
NONSTANDARD: She can't hardly see.
STANDARD: She can hardly see.
NONSTANDARD: He hasn't been absent only once.
STANDARD: He has been absent only once.
NONSTANDARD: He didn't eat scarcely any dinner.
STANDARD: He ate scarcely any dinner.

But that, but what. The use of *but what* for *but that* is colloquial.

FORMAL: I am not sure but that you are right.

Sometimes the *but* in the phrase *but that* is superfluous and clumsy.

FAULTY: I do not doubt but that you are right.
IMPROVED: I do not doubt that you are right.

Calculate. U.S. dialectal in the sense of *guess, intend, think.*

Can, may. Strictly, *can* means "to be able to, know how to," *may* means "to have permission to." "Can he run the half-mile in two minutes?" "May I enter the half-mile run?"

Cannot (can't) help but. Colloquial, though widespread.

COLLOQUIAL: I cannot (can't) help but pity him.
FORMAL: I cannot help pitying him.
I cannot but pity him.
I can but pity him.

Cannot (can't) seem to. Colloquial for *seem unable to.*

COLLOQUIAL: He cannot (can't) seem to understand you.
FORMAL: He seems unable to understand you.

Case. Overworked and often unnecessary.

FAULTY: The procedure is different in the case of beginners.
IMPROVED: The procedure is different for beginners.

Censor, censure. To *censor* means specifically to "examine with a view to eliminating undesirable material"; to *censure* means more broadly to "condemn, find fault with."

Claim. Colloquial (but widely used) in the sense of *assert, maintain.*

INFORMAL: He claimed that he was not at fault.
FORMAL: He maintained that he was not at fault.

Coincident. Adjective, meaning "contemporaneous, concurrent." Never use it for the noun *coincidence.*

Common, mutual. *Mutual* implies an interchange of feeling or interest: "mutual admiration," "in mutual agreement." *Common* implies only an equal sharing or belonging: "a common friend," "common property." Thus "a mutual friend" is technically incorrect, though widely used.

Complected. U.S. dialectal for *complexioned.*

Considerable. Colloquial as a noun.

COLLOQUIAL: He earned considerable during the summer.
FORMAL: He earned a considerable amount during the summer.

Contact. Colloquial as a verb.

COLLOQUIAL: I shall contact him at once.
IMPROVED: I shall see (interview, get in touch with) him at once.

Contemptible, contemptuous. *Contemptible* means "deserving of contempt." *Contemptuous* means "expressing contempt."

His conduct was contemptible.
She was contemptuous of her poorer classmates.

Continual, continuous. *Continual* means "repeated, regular, very frequent" but implies interruption. *Continuous* means "without cessation, without interruption."

Throughout the speech there were continual bursts of applause.
The continuous ripple of the stream made me drowsy.

Could of. Illiterate for "could have." Other illiteracies are *should of, would of, may of, might of, must of.*

Council, counsel. *Council* means "assembly" or "administrative body." *Counsel* means "advice" or, especially in law, "one who gives advice."

Credible, creditable, credulous. *Credible* means "capable or worthy of belief." *Creditable* means "praiseworthy, respectable." *Credulous* means "apt to believe readily, easily imposed upon."

His story did not sound credible.
The players gave a creditable performance.
Children are by nature credulous.

Cute. Derived from *acute,* it is colloquial even in the original sense of "keen, clever, shrewd." By careless speakers and writers it is used wrongly (and with deplorable frequency) to mean *pretty* or *attractive,* or to express vague though enthusiastic approval.

Data, phenomena, strata. Plurals of *datum, phenomenon, stratum.*

Deal. Colloquial and overworked in the sense of *business transaction, agreement, arrangement.*

Differ from, differ with. *Differ from* means "be unlike." *Differ with* means "disagree with."

English customs often differ from American customs.
I must respectfully differ with you about hazing.

Disinterested, uninterested. *Disinterested* means "unbiased, not influenced by regard for personal advantage." *Uninterested* means "lacking in interest, not caring." Thus a judge should be disinterested but certainly not uninterested.

Don't. Acceptable as a contraction of *do not* except in formal writing. Incorrect, of course, as a contraction of *does not.*

Due to. Colloquial in a prepositional phrase modifying a verb: "Due to illness I left early." Here "because of" or "on account of" is preferable. But "due to" is correct when "due" is a predicate adjective: "His failure was due to indolence." In other words, when "due" modifies a noun or pronoun, "due to" is correct.

COLLOQUIAL: Due to the lateness of the hour we parted abruptly.
FORMAL: Because of the lateness of the hour we parted abruptly.
Our prompt parting was due to the lateness of the hour.

Dumb. Mute, speechless. Colloquial in the sense of *stupid.*

Effect, affect. See *Affect, effect.*

Elegant. Colloquial (and objectionable) in the sense of *excellent, delicious.*

Emigrate, immigrate. *Emigrate* means "move away from a country." *Immigrate* means "move into a country."

Eminent, imminent, immanent. *Eminent* means "distinguished." *Imminent* means "impending, about to happen." *Immanent* means "indwelling, inherent."

Enthuse. Colloquial (and objectionable) in the sense of *to be enthusiastic.*

Etc. Redundant when used after *such as.*

FAULTY: He likes outdoor sports such as baseball, swimming, hunting, etc.

CORRECT: He likes outdoor sports such as baseball, swimming, and hunting.

Everybody, everyone. See *Anybody, anyone.*

Except, accept. See *Accept, except.*

Expect. Colloquial in the sense of *suppose.*

COLLOQUIAL: I expect you think me tactless.

IMPROVED: I suppose you think me tactless.

Extra. Colloquial (and objectionable) in the sense of *very, unusually.*

COLLOQUIAL: Today is extra warm for April.

IMPROVED: Today is unusually warm for April.

Fact. (1) The phrase *the fact that* can (and should) often be condensed to *that* or eliminated entirely.

FAULTY: I have been warned of the fact that some risk is involved.

IMPROVED: I have been warned that some risk is involved.

FAULTY: He left because of the fact that he was bored.

IMPROVED: He left because he was bored.

(2) The phrase *the fact of the matter* is trite and wordy.

FAULTY: The fact of the matter is that Brisson lacks humility.

IMPROVED: The truth is that Brisson lacks humility.
Brisson lacks humility.

(3) The phrase *true facts* is redundant. If something is a fact, it is true.

Factor. An omnibus word that is overworked. Usually a more precise word can be found: *element, circumstance, influence.*

Farther, further. *Farther* usually applies to distance, *further* to degree.

He can jump two feet farther than I.
Let us not discuss it further.

Only *further* is idiomatic in the sense of *more:* "We need further information." (See also *All the farther.*)

Faze. Colloquial for *trouble, disconcert, upset.*

Fellow. Colloquial for *person, boy, man.*

Fewer, less. *Fewer* applies to number, *less* to amount: fewer marbles, fewer people, fewer problems; less money, less sugar, less unhappiness.

Field. The phrase *the field of* is usually wordy.

WORDY: I plan a career in the field of engineering.
IMPROVED: I plan a career in engineering.

Figure. Colloquial for *believe, expect, think.*

Fine. Overworked as a term of approval: fine day, fine girl, fine surprise. Usually a more precise adjective can be found. *Fine* is colloquial in the sense of *well:*

COLLOQUIAL: My watch runs fine now.
IMPROVED: My watch runs well now.

Fix. As a noun, colloquial in the sense of *predicament, dilemma.* As a verb, colloquial in the sense of *arrange* (to *fix* one's hair), *repair* (to *fix* the television set), *punish* ("I'll *fix* him").

Folks. Colloquial for *relatives* or *family.*

Formally, formerly. *Formally* means "in a formal manner." *Formerly* means "heretofore, previously."

Former, latter. *Former* refers to the first member of a pair, *latter* to the second member. Neither word is used properly in reference to a member of a series of three or more.

Funny. Means "laughable, humorous." Colloquial in the sense of "strange, queer": "It's funny that we have heard nothing from her."

Further, farther. See *Farther, further.*

Gentleman, lady. Not to be used indiscriminately for *man, woman.* But it is of course conventional to address an audience as "Ladies and Gentlemen."

Get. Colloquial or slang in many expressions such as "That music gets me," "Now you'll get it for being late," "Let's get going." Redundant (and colloquial) in "We have got to finish promptly" (Improved: "We have to finish promptly"). The past participle of *get* is either *got* or *gotten.*

Good. (1) Overworked as a term of approval. Use a more specific word. (2) An adjective, not an adverb: "He plays well" (not "He plays good").

Good and. Colloquial as an intensive: "I am very tired," not "I am good and tired."

Grand. Overworked as a term of approval. See also *Fine.*

Guess. Colloquial in the sense of *believe, suppose, think.*

Had of. Illiterate. "I wish I had [not *had of*] known that earlier."

Had ought, hadn't ought. Illiterate. "She ought [not *had ought*] to have come with us." "They ought not [not *hadn't ought*] to have broken training rules."

Hanged, hung. When the death penalty is referred to, the proper form of the past tense and past participle of *hang* is *hanged;* otherwise the form is *hung.* "The man was sentenced to be hanged," but "I have hung your coat in the closet."

Hardly. See *But, hardly, only, scarcely.*

Healthful, healthy. *Healthful* means "conducive to health"; *healthy* means "having health." Thus, *healthful* climate, but *healthy* children.

Heighth. Illiterate for *height.*

Herself, himself, myself, yourself. Intensives not to be substituted without reason for the personal pronouns *she, her, he, him, I, me, you.*

Honorable, Reverend. As titles of respect, to be accompanied by *The* and the full name or initials or the title of the person concerned: *The Honorable Mr. Gregory, The Honorable Daniel H. Gregory* [not *Honorable Gregory* or *The Honorable Gregory*]; *The Reverend Dr. Kerr, The Reverend Ellis P. Kerr* [not *Reverend Kerr* or *The Reverend Kerr*].

Human. Colloquial as a noun. Use *human being* instead.

Illusion, allusion. See *Allusion, illusion.*

Immigrate, emigrate. See *Emigrate, immigrate.*

Imply, infer. *Imply* means "suggest"; *infer* means "draw a conclusion." "You implied that I was not telling the truth." "He inferred from the conversation that the partners were no longer friendly."

In, into. *In* implies "presence within, inside." *Into* implies "transition from without to within." Thus, "He is in the room," but "They walked into the room."

In back of. See *Back of.*

Incident, incidence. The noun meaning "event," "occurrence," or "episode" is *incident,* never *incidence.*

Incidentally. This is the correct spelling—not "incidently."

Incredible, incredulous. *Incredible* means "unbelievable." *Incredulous* means "unbelieving."

Individual. Not to be substituted carelessly for *person.* To be used only when there is need to emphasize the individual member of a group. Thus, "Tyranny makes no allowance for the rights of the individual," but "He is an odd person [not *individual*]."

Infer, imply. See *Imply, infer.*

Ingenious, ingenuous. *Ingenious* means "possessed of ingenuity, clever." *Ingenuous* means "frank, candid."

Into, in. See *In, into.*

Irregardless. Illiterate (or humorous) for *regardless.*

Is when, is where. Not to be used in definitions (see Section 13D2).

FAULTY: A Texas Leaguer is when a ball drops between the infielders and the outfielders.

CORRECT: A Texas Leaguer is a hit dropped between the infielders and the outfielders.

A hit that drops between the infielders and the outfielders is called a Texas Leaguer.

FAULTY: A dilemma is where you have to choose between equally unsatisfactory alternatives.

CORRECT: A dilemma is a situation requiring choice between equally unsatisfactory alternatives.

Its, it's. *Its* is the possessive form of *it* ("The dog wagged its tail"). *It's* is a contraction of *it is* or *it has* ("It's a warm day," "It's been a warm day"). See also Section 14J 2b.

Just. Colloquial, overworked, and usually redundant in the sense of *very, extremely.* "His performance was splendid [not *just splendid*]."

Kind, sort. Singular nouns, modified by singular adjectives and requiring singular verbs: "This kind of day is ideal for swimming." "That sort of thinking is absurd." Plural forms of course exist but are seldom needed: "You must make a choice among these kinds of ice cream."

Kind of, sort of. Colloquial for *rather, somewhat:* "Jack seemed rather [not *kind of*] bitter," "My enthusiasm has somewhat [not *sort of*] dwindled."

Lady, gentleman. See *Gentleman, lady.*

Later, latter. The frequent confusion in student writing between later ("more late") and latter ("the second member of a pair") is usually the result of careless spelling rather than misunderstanding.

Latter, former. See *Former, latter.*

Lay, lie. *Lay* (past tense, *laid;* past participle, *laid*) is a transitive verb, requiring an object: "Lay the book down." "He laid the book on the table." *Lie* (past tense, *lay;* past participle, *lain*) is an intransitive verb, used without an object: "I shall lie here for a few minutes." "The book lay where he had left it." "The dog has lain still for half an hour." (See also Section 15B 3a(3).)

Lead, led. The form of the past tense and past participle of *lead* is *led.*

Learn. Not permissible in the sense of *teach.*

Leave, let. *Leave* means "depart, depart from, cause to remain": "He left at noon." "He left me without a word." "He left the book on the table." *Let* means "allow, permit": "Let me go." "The mother let the child do as he pleased." Note that "Leave me" (that is, "Go away from me") is correct whereas "Leave me go" is incorrect; and that "Let me be" is correct whereas "Leave me be" is incorrect.

Less, fewer. See *Fewer, less.*

Liable. See *Apt, likely, liable.*

Lie, lay. See *Lay, lie.*

Like, as, as if, as though. In comparisons, the preposition *like* is used if only a noun or pronoun follows; the conjunction *as* is used if an indicative clause follows; the conjunction *as if* or *as though* is used if a conditional clause follows.

> The rumor spread like fire. He looks like me.
> Do as I tell you.
> He looked as if (as though) he had been stunned.

Likely. See *Apt, likely, liable.*

Line. The phrase *in the line of* (*along the line of*) is both colloquial and wordy.

> FAULTY: Please show me what you have in (along) the line of sport shoes.
> IMPROVED: Please show me what you have in sport shoes.
> I am interested in a pair of sport shoes.

Locate. Colloquial in the sense of *settle.*

Loose, lose. Sometimes confused, though often the error is simply one in spelling. *Loose* as a verb means "release, set free"; *lose* means "suffer the loss of, mislay." *Loose* may also be an adjective meaning "not fastened, free."

Lot, lot of, lots of. Colloquial in the sense of *much, many, great amount (number) of, great deal of.*

> I have thought much [not *a lot*] about it.
> He has lost a great deal [not *a lot*] of money.
> Many [not *lots of*] visitors come to view the grave.

Lovely. Overworked as a term of approval: lovely dinner, lovely speech, lovely time. Often a more precise adjective can be found.

Luxuriant, luxurious. *Luxuriant* means "profuse in growth": luxuriant foliage. *Luxurious* means "given to luxury, pertaining to luxury": luxurious habits of living, luxurious furniture.

Mad. Colloquial in the sense of *angry.* In formal English *mad* means "insane."

May, can. See *Can, may.*

May have, might have. *Might* is the past tense of *may.* In a conditional statement requiring the use of *may have* or *might have, may have* is correct if there is uncertainty as to the outcome, whereas *might have* is correct if the outcome is settled. Thus, "what *may* have been" refers to something that perhaps has happened but perhaps has not happened, whereas "what *might* have been" refers to something that is known *not* to have happened. "The door *may* have been locked" implies that perhaps the door has been locked but perhaps it has not, whereas "The door *might* have been locked" implies that the door has already been found *not* to have been locked. (On the use of *might* as a future tense see Section 15B 3c.)

May of, might of. See *Could of.*

Mighty. Colloquial in the sense of *very.*

Moral, morale. *Morale* is a noun meaning "mental state, attitude, spirit." Do not confuse it with the noun or adjective *moral.*

The moral of this story is obvious.
He is a man of loose morals.
He is not a moral man.
The morale of the students is high.

Most, almost. See *Almost, most.*

Must of. See *Could of.*

Mutual. See *Common, mutual.*

Myself. See *Herself, himself, myself, yourself.*

Nice. Overworked as a term of approval: nice day, nice girl, nice time. Usually a more precise adjective can be found.

No account, no good. Colloquial in the sense of *worthless.*

No doubt but that. The *but* is superfluous.

REDUNDANT: There is no doubt but that he will succeed.
IMPROVED: There is no doubt that he will succeed.

Nowhere near. Colloquial in the sense of *not nearly.*

COLLOQUIAL: It is nowhere near so cold as it was.
IMPROVED: It is not nearly so cold as it was.

Nowheres. Illiterate for *nowhere.*

Number, amount. See *Amount, number.*

Off of. The *of* is superfluous: "The egg rolled off [not *off of*] the table."

O. K. Colloquial.

Only. See *But, hardly, only, scarcely.*

Opinion. The phrase "in my opinion" is overworked and often superfluous. A reader assumes that any discussion of ideas or controversial subject matter embodies the writer's own views, and frequent repetition of qualifying phrases like "in my opinion" not only is irritating but suggests timidity and self-distrust.

Party. Except in legal language, *party* should never be used to refer to an individual. Thus, "This is the person [not *party*] I told you about," but "In a lawsuit the two parties are called the plaintiff and the defendant."

Per. Objectionable except in commercial and technical writing: "My class in mathematics meets four times a week [not *per week*]."

Phenomena. Plural of *phenomenon.*

Phone. Colloquial for *telephone.*

Photo. Colloquial for *photograph.*

Piece. Colloquial in the sense of *short distance.*

Plenty. Colloquial when used as an adverb, as in "plenty tired," "plenty large enough."

P.M. See A.M.

Point of view, viewpoint. That is, "the point from which one views a situation." Not to be loosely substituted for "opinion, view."

> Her opinion was influenced by prejudice.
> I expressed my views freely.
> My point of view (viewpoint) is naturally different from that of a participant in the quarrel.

Poorly. Colloquial in the sense of *in poor health.*

Practicable, practical. *Practicable* means "capable of being accomplished": "Barton's scheme is not practicable." *Practical* is the opposite of theoretical: a practical man, a practical farmer, practical problems.

Prejudiced toward. Some students use this idiom to mean "biased in favor of," whereas it means to most readers "biased against." The correct idioms are "prejudiced in favor of" and "prejudiced against."

Pretty. Overworked as an adverb meaning "rather, fairly" (pretty cold, pretty weary) and as an adjective expressing approval (pretty landscape, pretty sunset). Usually a more precise term can be found.

Principal, principle. *Principal* is either (*a*) an adjective meaning "chief, leading" or (*b*) a noun meaning "head, chief officer, chief participant" or "capital sum placed at interest." *Principle* is always a noun meaning "fundamental truth, rule of conduct, method of construction or operation."

> The principal speaker was the principal of Westwood School.
> My banker advised me not to withdraw any of my principal.
> She believes in the principles of Christianity.
> He is a man of principle.
> The principle of this machine is simple.

Proposition. A noun, colloquial in the sense of *project, scheme, suggestion, undertaking.* Never correctly used as a verb.

Quiet, quite. The frequent confusion in student writing between *quiet* and *quite* is usually the result of careless spelling rather than misunderstanding.

Quite. An adverb meaning "completely, entirely," as in "quite done," "quite mistaken." Colloquial (and overworked) in the sense of "to a considerable extent or degree": "quite pretty," "quite angry."

Quite a few, quite a lot. Colloquial for "several, "much," "many."

Raise, rise. Sometimes confused. *Raise* is a transitive verb: "He raises corn. He raised corn. He has raised corn." *Rise* is an intransitive verb: "The sun rises. The sun rose at five o'clock. The sun has risen." (See also Section 15B 3a(3).)

Real. Colloquial in the sense of *very,* as in "real late," "real thoughtful."

Reason is because. A statement beginning "The reason . . . is . . . " should logically be completed by a clause beginning with "that" (noun clause) rather than one beginning with "because" (adverbial clause).

FAULTY: The reason he is ill is because he overate.
IMPROVED: The reason he is ill is that he overate.

But the adverbial clause is correct in the following sentence: "He is ill because he overate." (See also Section 12F.)

Reckon. Dialectal in the sense of *think, suppose, guess.*

Red up. Dialectal for *clean up, put in order, tidy up.*

Refer, allude. See *Allude, refer.*

Remember of. The *of* is superfluous: "I remember [not *remember of*] seeing it there."

Respectfully, respectively. *Respectfully* means "in a respectful manner"; *respectively* means "in the order listed."

He nodded respectfully.
Yours respectfully.
The blue coat and the green sweater belong to Jane and Sue, respectively.

Reverend. See *Honorable, Reverend.*

Right. Colloquial or dialectal in the sense of *very:* "I shall see you very [not *right*] soon."

Rise, raise. See *Raise, rise.*

Said. Objectionable as an adjective except in legal language.

FAULTY: I mounted said pony and rode away.
CORRECT: I mounted the pony I have described, and rode away.

Same. Objectionable as a pronoun except in legal language.

FAULTY: Please pay the bill and get a receipt for same.
CORRECT: Please pay the bill and get a receipt for it.
Please pay the bill and get a receipt.

Scarcely. See *But, hardly, only, scarcely.*

Seldom ever. The *ever* is superfluous: "I seldom [not *seldom ever*] see her." But *seldom if ever* and *hardly ever* are correct.

Set, sit. Sometimes confused. *Set* (past tense, *set;* past participle, *set*) is a transitive verb, requiring an object: "She set the plant down." "I have set the table." *Sit* (past tense, *sat;* past participle, *sat*) is an intransitive verb, used without an object: "I sit where I please." "They sat together." "We have sat here for an hour." But in two common uses *set* takes the place of *sit:* "The sun sets in ten minutes." "That hen is setting." (See also Section 15B 3a(3).)

Set-up. Colloquial in the sense of *arrangement, situation, plan.* Slang when used to mean "easy victory, easily defeated opponent."

Shall, will. See Section 15D 3.

Should, would. See Section 15D 3.

Should of. See *Could of.*

Show up. Colloquial in the sense of either *make an appearance* or *expose:* "He appeared [not *showed up*] at last." "We threatened to expose him [not *show him up*]."

Sit, set. See *Set, sit.*

Size up. Colloquial for *appraise, form a judgment about* (as in "He sized up the situation." "We tried to size up the newcomer.").

Sleep in. Colloquial in the sense of *sleep late.*

So. (1) The use of *so* as a co-ordinating conjunction or conjunctive adverb makes for loose sentence structure. Rearrangement of the sentence to eliminate *so* will usually result in improved structure and more specific phrasing.

FAULTY: The game was delayed by rain, so we had to leave before the end.

IMPROVED: Because the game was delayed by rain, we had to leave before the end.

FAULTY: You seem to be in a bad humor, so I shall drop the subject.

IMPROVED: Since you seem to be in a bad humor, I shall drop the subject.

(2) As a subordinating conjunction, *so* is colloquial in the sense of *so that.*

FAULTY: Be sure to let me know the cost so I may pay my share.

IMPROVED: Be sure to let me know the cost so that I may pay my share.

(3) *So* should be used as an intensive only when followed by a clause of result (a *that* clause).

FAULTY: I am so confused. [*So* in this sense is sometimes called a "feminine intensive."]

IMPROVED: I am confused.
I am very much confused.
I am so confused that I cannot think straight.

Some. (1) Colloquial when used adverbially in the sense of either *somewhat* or *moderately, a little.*

COLLOQUIAL: The report made me feel some better.
IMPROVED: The report made me feel somewhat better.
COLLOQUIAL: Though nearly twelve, she still plays with dolls some.
IMPROVED: Though nearly twelve, she still plays with dolls a little.

(2) Slang when used as an adjectival intensive ("That was some speech you gave us").

Someone. See *Anybody, anyone.*

Someway. Colloquial for *somehow.*

Somewheres. Illiterate for *somewhere.*

Sort, kind. See *Kind, sort.*

Sort of, kind of. See *Kind of, sort of.*

Strata. Plural of *stratum.*

Such. Should be used as an intensive only when followed by a clause of result (a *that* clause).

FAULTY: He is such a handsome boy. [*Such* in this sense is sometimes called a "feminine intensive."]
IMPROVED: He is a very handsome boy.
He is such a handsome boy that everyone notices him.

Sure. Colloquial for *surely, certainly:* "She certainly [not *sure*] is beautiful." "They surely [not *sure*] were angry."

Sure and. Colloquial for *sure to:* "Be sure to [not *and*] write to me."

Suspicion. Incorrect as a verb: "We suspected [not *suspicioned*] that he was somehow involved in the theft."

Swell. Slang when used as an adjective indicating enthusiastic approval: a swell time, a swell teacher.

Take and. Illiterate.

NONSTANDARD: Now I take and draw a wavy line here.
They took and tore down the sign.
STANDARD: Now I draw a wavy line here.
They tore down the sign.

Take in, off, on. Colloquial: "We decided to see [not *take in*] a movie." "He imitated [not *took off*] Mr. Bronson perfectly." "There is no need to complain [not *take on*] so violently."

Take (took) sick. Colloquial for *become (became) sick.*

That, this. Colloquial when used as adverbs: "I did not know she was so tall [not *that tall*]." "I am so [not *that*] tired I can hardly stand." "I did not expect to be so late [not *this late*]."

That there, these here, this here, them there, those there. Illiterate. In all such expressions the *here* or *there* is redundant.

Their, there, they're. The frequent confusion among these words in student writing is usually the result of careless spelling rather than misunderstanding.

These kind (sort), those kind (sort). See *Kind, sort.*

Toward, towards. Both are correct. *Toward* is more common in the United States, *towards* in Great Britain.

True facts. Here *true* is redundant.

Try and. Colloquial for *try to:* "Won't you try to [not *and*] be prompt hereafter?"

Unique. Means "unlike any other, the only one of its kind," and therefore cannot logically be compared: "I never saw a more unusual [not *unique*] specimen." "He is the most extraordinary [not *unique*] person I have ever known." But see Section 16F3.

Used to. The spelling *use to* is illiterate.

Very. (1) The use of *very* to modify a past participle is regarded as unidiomatic, though there are exceptions. For example, "I am very tired" is not only acceptable but standard, whereas in the following sentences an additional adverb such as *much* is needed: "I was very *much* irritated by his question." "The bandstand was very *gaily* decorated." See also Section 17C 4.

(2) Often the intensive *very* tends to weaken rather than strengthen the word modified. Thus "a gloomy day" is more effective than "a very gloomy day," and "a grimly determined team" is more effective than "a very grimly determined team." This weakening effect becomes pronounced if *very* is overused. You would do well to examine critically every use of it in your work.

Viewpoint. See *Point of view.*

Wait on. Dialectal in the sense of *wait for:* "We decided not to wait for [not *on*] Richardson any longer."

Want ad. Colloquial. Avoid in formal English.

Want in, off, out, etc. Dialectal: "They want to come in" [not *want in*]. "I want to get off" [not *want off*]. "The baby wants to get out" [not *wants out*].

Want that. The use of a *that* clause as the object of *want* is illiterate.

NONSTANDARD: They want that I should start tomorrow.
STANDARD: They want me to start tomorrow.

Ways. Colloquial for *way* or *distance:* "They went with us a little *way*" [not *ways*].

What. See *But that, but what.*

When, where. See *Is when, is where.*

Where. Colloquial in the sense of *that:* "I see that [not *where*] the mayor is trying to prevent an investigation of the police force."

Where at. Illiterate. "Where am I?" [not *Where am I at?*].

Whether or not. Often the "or not" is superfluous: "Let me know whether you can come" [not *whether or not you can come*].

Which, who, that. *Which* refers only to things, *who* only to persons, and *that* to either things or persons.

While. Careful writers avoid the use of *while* in the sense of *although, though, whereas:* "Though [not *while*] I agree with you, I deplore your rashness." "Our neighbors are tireless gardeners, whereas [not *while*] we believe in letting nature take its course."

Who's, whose. Sometimes confused. *Who's* is a contraction of *who is* or *who has; whose* is a possessive pronoun: "Who's going to tell me whose fingerprints these are?"

Will, shall. See Section 15D 3.

Would, should. See Section 15D 3.

Would of. See *Could of.*

Your, you're. *Your* is a possessive pronoun; *you're* is a contraction of *you are:* "You're going to regret your decision."

Yourself. See *Herself, himself, myself, yourself.*

Chapter 8

SPELLING

Errors in spelling are probably more frequent than any other kind. Yet, though almost everyone misspells a word occasionally, there is no excuse for the habitually poor speller. People who spell badly are inclined to take refuge in one or both of two contentions—that there is nothing they can do about it, and that spelling does not matter much anyway. Both contentions are false. Anyone can improve his spelling if he is willing to work. And, perhaps unfortunately, spelling does matter. Though the cynical may be right in saying that only English teachers notice and care about many kinds of errors, spelling errors somehow stand out in a way to catch the eye of even the careless or ignorant reader and prejudice him against the writer. People who are themselves weak in spelling will be found to show little mercy toward the spelling errors they detect in the writing of others. Therefore it is incumbent upon the poor speller to strive to conquer his weakness. And though teachers and textbooks can help, success or failure will depend almost entirely upon his own efforts.

Carelessness is the cause of a large majority of the spelling errors found in student writing. If you are a poor speller and are determined to become a good one, you must resolve first of all to renounce carelessness. Second, though English spelling is regrettably inconsistent, you must learn and apply the few rules that will help you with certain categories of words. And finally, you must identify and conquer your particular weaknesses. It is likely that your troubles come not from the misspelling of a large number of words that you use occasionally but from the repeated misspelling of a comparatively small number that you use frequently. If you will grimly and painfully learn to avoid these particular errors, you will have taken an important step toward mastering your spelling difficulties.

73. CARELESSNESS

The student who is too indifferent and too foolish to check his work for spelling errors deserves to fail. Week after week, some students turn in papers marred by errors that they would readily detect in the writing of others. It is absurd to spend several hours on a theme and then not bother to give it the careful proofreading that an additional ten or fifteen minutes would permit.

Again, carelessness accounts for the repeated misspelling of certain words that would cause no difficulty if the writer gave a moment's thought to their structure. For instance, no one is likely to misspell the word *unnatural* if he reflects that it is formed by the addition of the prefix *un-* to the root word; nor is anyone likely to misspell the word *keenness* if he reflects that it is formed by the addition of the suffix *-ness* to the root word. Even casual attention to the process by which such words are formed will help with such similar examples as *dis*appoint, *dis*satisfied, *mis*apply, *mis*spell, *un*even, *un*noticed, care*ful,* free*ly,* formal*ly,* and clean*ness.*

Another form of carelessness that causes errors in spelling is failure to pronounce accurately. A student who all his life has been saying "supprise" instead of "surprise" is not likely to spell the word correctly. An extreme example of this kind of carelessness is the writing of "should of" or "might of" for "should have" or "might have" because the writer has always pronounced the phrases in a slovenly way. Other misspellings that occur frequently because of faulty pronunciation are *sophmore* (for *sophomore*), *goverment* (for *government*), *temperment* (for *temperament*), *canidate* (for *candidate*), *quanity* (for *quantity*), *fraility* (for *frailty*). Improbable as it may seem, every experienced teacher of English is likely to have found in the work of at least one college student the absurd phrase *take for granite* instead of *take for granted.*

Finally, carelessness often results in the confusion (and hence misspelling) of words identical or similar in sound but different in meaning. Possibly the most familiar examples are *affect* and *effect, principal* and *principle*; others are *coarse* and *course, complement* and *compliment, formally* and *formerly, loose* and *lose, stationary* and *stationery, weather* and *whether.*

74. RULES OF SPELLING

Because modern English spelling is so inconsistent, there are few rules that are of help to the student, and even these may have exceptions. Nevertheless, knowledge of the principal rules that do exist is of value.

74A. Words in *ei* and *ie*

In words in which the sound is *ee, i* generally comes before *e* except after *c: achieve, believe, chief, reprieve, wield;* but *ceiling, deceive, perceive.* Exceptions: *either, neither, leisure, seize, weird.* In words in which the sound is other than *ee, e* generally comes before *i: eight, freight, neighbor, veil, height, sleight, foreign.* Exceptions: *friend, sieve.* Memorizing and applying this rule and its exceptions will enable you to spell correctly a large group of words that cause widespread trouble.

74B. Final -e Followed by Suffix

Generally, final *-e* is retained before a suffix beginning with a consonant: *care, careless; hate, hateful; like, likely, likeness; excite, excitement; nine, ninety.* Some exceptions: *abridge, abridgment; acknowledge, acknowledgment; awe, awful; due, duly; judge, judgment; nine, ninth; true, truly; whole, wholly; wise, wisdom.* The final *-e* in such words as *care, careless* and *hate, hateful* is an indication that the main vowel is long (compare *car* and *hat*).

Generally, final *-e* is dropped before a suffix beginning with a vowel: *insure, insurable, insurance; continue, continuation; hide, hiding; fame, famous.* Some exceptions: (1) words in which *c* followed by *a* or *o* is pronounced like *s: notice, noticeable* (but compare *noticing,* with a suffix beginning with *i*); *service, serv-*

iceable (but compare *practice, practicable,* where *c* is not pronounced like *s*); (2) words in which *g* followed by *a* or *o* is pronounced like *j*: *change, changeable* (but compare *changing*); *courage, courageous* (the present participle of *singe* must be spelled *singeing* to avoid confusion with the present participle of *sing*); (3) *dye, dyeing* (compare *die, dying*); (4) *hoeing, shoeing, toeing* (dropping of *-e* would result in mispronunciation); (5) *acreage, mileage.*

74C. Doubling of Final Consonant

A single final consonant followed by a suffix beginning with a vowel is doubled only if the consonant is preceded by a single vowel and is in an accented syllable: *stop, stopped, stopping* (but compare *stooping*); *refer, referred, referring* (but compare *reference,* in which the accent has shifted to the first syllable). Exception: *excellence, excellent.* The doubled consonant in an accented syllable is an indication that the vowel is short (compare *mop, mopping* with *mope, moping; whip, whipped* with *wipe, wiped*).

74D. Final -y

Generally, final *-y* following a consonant is changed to *i* before any suffix except one beginning with *i*: *pity, pitiable; apply, appliance; defy, defied; twenty, twentieth; many, manifold; beauty, beautiful; hardy, hardihood;* but *apply, applying; defy, defying; baby, babyish.* This rule, however, does not apply consistently. For instance, in *beauty, beauteous* and *pity, piteous* the final *-y* becomes not *i* but *e,* and in *lady, ladylike, ladyship* the final *-y* is retained.

Generally, final *-y* following a vowel is retained before a suffix: *play, played, player, playful, playing; employ, employed, employer, employing, employment.* But there are important exceptions: *day, daily; gay, gaily, gaiety; lay, laid* (but note *laying*); *pay, paid; say, said.*

74E. Plurals

Though most plurals are formed regularly by the addition of *-s* to the singular, there are so many exceptions that full treatment here is impossible. Nevertheless, you will find helpful the following summary of the principal rules and exceptions. Reference to the dictionary will solve problems in the spelling of plurals not covered here.

(1) Most plurals are formed by the addition of *-s* to the singular (*apes, books, combs, dogs*), but *-es* is added if the pronunciation of the plural requires an extra syllable (*ashes, brushes, crosses, duplexes*). Though all nouns ending in *-o* preceded by a vowel add only *-s* (*cameos, radios*), some nouns ending in *-o* preceded by a consonant add *-s*, some *-es: altos, pianos, zeros,* but *cargoes, echoes, heroes.* Obviously, when in doubt you should consult the dictionary.

(2) Nouns ending in *-y* preceded by a consonant change *-y* to *i* and add *-es: babies, buggies, fairies, follies, harpies, zanies.* This is true also of nouns ending in *-quy,* in which *u* is equivalent to the consonant *w: colloquies.* Nouns ending in *-y* preceded by a vowel (other than the *u* in words ending in *-quy*) retain the *-y* and add *-s: trays, boys, keys, valleys.*

(3) Nouns ending in *-ff* add only *-s: sheriffs, tariffs.* Some nouns ending in *-f* add only *-s* (*beliefs, chiefs, proofs, roofs, waifs*), but in many others the *-f* is changed to *-ve* before the *-s* (*calf, calves; half, halves; leaf, leaves; loaf, loaves; self, selves; shelf, shelves; thief, thieves; wolf, wolves*). In most nouns ending in *-fe* the *-fe* is changed to *-ve* before the *-s* (*knife, knives; life, lives; wife, wives*), but some such nouns simply add *-s* to the plural (*fifes, safes*). You should learn as many of these plurals as possible individually, and consult the dictionary whenever you are in doubt.

(4) A few common English words retain plurals dating from times when the language was much more heavily inflected than it is today: *brethren, children, feet, geese, lice, men, mice, oxen, teeth, women.*

(5) A few foreign words not fully naturalized retain the foreign plural (for example, *alumni, alumnae,* sing. *basis* plu. *bases, crises, criteria, data, hypotheses, phenomena, strata, synopses, theses*). A few words have both English and foreign plurals (for example, *appendixes, appendices; curriculums, curricula; formulas, formulae; indexes, indices; memorandums, memoranda*).

75. MASTERING INDIVIDUAL DIFFICULTIES

The only way in which a poor speller can become a good one is by concentrating upon the mastery of those words which he has misspelled once and will undoubtedly misspell again and again if he does not conquer them.

Consultation of the dictionary—even repeated consultation—is not in itself enough. If you discover that you are uncertain about the spelling of a word or have actually misspelled it in a theme, you should begin by looking up the correct spelling and entering the word in a special list. You should study the word to determine whether there are any clues that will help you with it in the future. Do any of the rules just cited apply to it? Is there anything in the derivation of the word to help fix the correct spelling? Can you obtain a clue from observing the relationship of the word to the one from which it is derived (*preparation,* from *prepare*)? Can you obtain a clue from breaking the word into parts (*extraordinary*)? Has careless pronunciation caused the error? Have you confused one word with another (*its, it's; quite, quiet*)?

There remains one step—the most important of all. Since the list formed by the recommended procedure will contain words that will certainly continue to give trouble unless you master them, you must study them until you know each one as well as you know your own name. If you do so (and you may be surprised at the small number of words that you have to learn in this way), you will no longer be a poor speller. True, you will still have difficulty with unfamiliar words you meet unless you look them up, but mastery of the fifty or a hundred or two hundred words on your special list will insure you against any serious trouble with spelling.

76. LIST OF COMMON WORDS FREQUENTLY MISSPELLED

The following list of course does not include all words likely to cause trouble, but if a student plagued by poor spelling can strengthen himself to the point of never erring on these words, he can rest assured that he has become at least an adequate speller and probably an unusually good one. The teacher may wish to give a test based on this list early in the year and then repeat the test at the end of the year.

abbreviate
abridgment
abscess
absence
academic
accept
access
accessible
accessory
accidentally
accommodate
accumulate
acknowledgment
acquaintance
acquiesce
acquire
acquit
acquittal
acreage
across
acute
address
adjacent
adjective
adjourn
admission
admittance
adolescence
advice
advise
adviser
aerial
aeroplane
aesthetic
affect
afraid

aggravate
aggregate
agreeable
aisle
all right
allot, allotted
allotment
allusion
ally
almighty
almost
already
altar
alter
although
altogether
always
amateur
analogy
analysis
analyze
angel
angle
annual
anoint
antarctic
anxious
apostle
apparatus
apparel
apparent
appearance
appoint
appropriate
arctic
arguing

argument
around
ascend
ascertain
assassin
asylum
athlete
athletic
attack, attacked
attendance
audience
auxiliary
awful

bachelor
balloon
banana
barbarous
barrel
beggar
beginning
believable
benefit, benefited
berth
birth
boisterous
boundaries
bouquet
breath
breathe
bridal
bridle
brilliant
buoy, buoyant
bulletin
bureau

business

calendar
cancel, canceled
candidate
canvas
canvass
capital
capitol
caucus
cavalry
ceiling
cemetery
censor
censure
cereal
certain
change, changing
changeable
chaos
chassis
chauffeur
chief
choose, chose
cigarette
clothes
coarse
coincidence
colonel
column
coming
commission
commit, committed
committee
comparatively
compel, compelled
competent
competition
complement
complete
compliment
concede
conceivable
conceive
concur, concurred
concurrence
confer, conferred
conference
confidence
connoisseur
conscience
conscientious
conscious
contemptible
contemptuous
continuous
control, controlled
convalescent
convenience
corps
corpse
correspondence
council
counsel
course
credible
creditable
crescent
cruelty
customary
cylinder
cynical

dairy
deceased
deceive
decency
decision
defendant
defer, deferred
deference
definite
deity
delegate
deliverance
descendant
descent
description
desert
desirable
despair
desperate
dessert
develop
development
device
devise
diabetes
diary
dictionary
die, dying
difference
dine, dining
diphtheria
disappear
disappoint
disastrous
discipline
disease
dissatisfied
dissipate
dissolve
divide
divine
dose
doze
drought
dual
duel
dye, dyeing

ecstasy
effect
effervescent
efficient
eighth

elicit
eligible
embarrass
emigrate
eminent
emphasize
endeavor
endurance
enemy
enmity
enthusiasm
environment
equip, equipped
equivalent
escape
especially
ethyl
exaggerate
exceed
excel, excelled
excellent
except
excitement
exercise
exhaust
exhibit
exhilarate
existence
expel, expelled
expense
experience
extinct
extraordinary

fain
faint
fallacy
familiar
fascinate
February
feign
feint
fiend
fiery
finally
financier
forehead
foreign
foremost
foresee
forfeit
formally
formerly
forth
forty
fourth
frailty
friend
furthest

gaiety
gallant
gamble
gambol
garage
generally
gorilla
government
governor
grammar
grandeur
grievous
guarantee
guard
guidance
guilt
gymnasium

handkerchief
harass
height
hero, heroes
heroine
hesitancy
holy
hop, hopping
hope, hoping
hospitable
hospital
hostel
hostile
human
humane
hurried
hygiene
hypocrisy
hypocrite

icicle
idle
idol
idyl
illicit
imaginary
imitation
immanent
immediately
immigration
imminent
impetuous
implement
impromptu
inaugurate
incidentally
inconspicuous
incredible
incredulous
increment
independence
indict
indispensable
infer, inferred
inference
influential
ingenious
ingenuous

innate
innocence
innocuous
inoculate
instance
instructor
intellectual
intelligence
intentionally
intercede
interest
intrigue
irrelevant
irreparable
irresistible
island
isthmus
its
it's
itself

jealous
jeopardize
judgment

khaki
kindergarten
knowledge

laboratory
larynx
later
latter
lay, laid, laying
lead, led
leisure
library
license
lie, lay, lain, lying
lieutenant
lightening
lightning

likelihood
likely
literature
livelihood
lively
lonely
loneliness
lovely
loose
lose
loyalty

machinery
magazine
magnificence
maintain
maintenance
maneuver
manual
marriage
mathematics
mean, meant
medicine
mileage
miniature
minimum
minute
mischievous
misspelled
momentous
moral
morale
mortgage
murmur
muscle
musician

naïve
necessary
neighbor
neither
nicety

nickel
niece
ninety
ninth
notable
noticeable
nuisance

obedience
obscene
obsession
obstacle
occasionally
occur, occurred
occurrence
official
officious
ominous
omission
omit, omitted
omniscient
once
oneself, one's self
opinion
opportunity
optimism
ordinance
ordnance
original
outrageous

pageant
pamphlet
paraffin
parallel
paralysis
parliament
particularly
partner
pastime
patience
peaceable

peculiar
pedal
peddle
pedestal
perceive
peremptory
perform
permanence
permissible
perseverance
persistence
personal
personnel
perspiration
persuade
phenomenon
physics
physique
picnic, picnicking
piece
piteous
plain
plan, planned
plane, planed
playwright
pleasant
pneumatic
pneumonia
poison
politician
possession
practicable
practical
prairie
precede
precedence
precious
prefer, preferred
preference
prejudice
preparation
presence

prevalent
primitive
principal
principle
privilege
probably
procedure
proceed
professor
pronounce
pronunciation
prophecy
prophesy
prove
psalm
pseudonym
psychic
psychology
pursue
pursuit

quantity
quiet
quite

recede
receipt
receive
recognize
recommend
recur, recurred
recurrence
refer, referred
reference
regard
reign
rein
relieve
religious
remember
reminiscences
rendezvous

renunciation
repel, repelled
repetition
representative
requital
reservoir
resistance
respectable
respectfully
respectively
restaurant
resurrection
resuscitate
rheumatism
rhyme
rhythm
ridiculous
rogue
route

sacrilegious
safety
sandwich
scenic
scent
schedule
science
secretary
seize
semester
senior
sense
separate
sergeant
serial
severely
shepherd
sheriff
shine, shining
siege
sieve
sign

significant
similar
simile
sincerely
singular
sit, sat
sizable
sleeve
society
soldier
soliloquy
soothe
sophisticated
sophomore
speak
species
speech
specimen
sphinx
stationary
stationery
statistics
statue
stature
statute
stop, stopped
stratagem
strategy
strength
strenuous
stretch
strictly
studying
succeed
superintendent
supersede
supplement
suppress
surprise
susceptible
suspicion
syllable
symmetrical
synonym

temperament
temperature
tendency
testament
than
their
then
there
therefore
they're
thorough
through
to
tonsillitis
too
track
tract
tragedy
transcend
treachery
tremendous
truly
twelfth
tyranny

umbrella
unanimous
until
unusual
urban
urbane
usage
usually

vacancy
vaccinate
vacillate
vandal
vanilla
vegetable
vengeance
vertical
veteran
veterinary
victual
vigilance
village
villain

waist
waive
warrant
waste
wave
weather
Wednesday
weigh
weird
where
whether
who's
wholly
whose
withhold
women
write, writing, written

yacht
yield
yoke
yolk
your
you're

Chapter 9

USE OF THE LIBRARY

77. THE LIBRARY AND THE STUDENT

The heart of a college or university is the library. The most important tool in research, it is one of the main criteria on which the standing of an educational institution is judged. A student who learns how to use the resources of a good library and who forms early the habit of library use possesses the essentials with which to acquire a liberal education.

The college or university library is maintained for the service of undergraduates, graduate students, and faculty. Though you as a freshman stand at the foot of the ladder, you will benefit all the more by an immediate start toward competence in the use of the library. The earlier you acquire such competence, the more years you will have in which to profit by it. Some students do not learn to use the library until their junior or senior year: that is a serious waste of time and opportunity. Some never learn: that is a calamity.

You should familiarize yourself promptly, therefore, with your college library. Learn the rules, and obey them scrupulously. Learn the location of the principal reference works and all the main categories of books. Ask questions of members of the staff, whom you will find ready to help and who are trained to save you time. If you form as a freshman the habit of frequenting the library, you will find yourself using it increasingly throughout your college career. Nor should you confine yourself to visits for borrowing or returning books, for looking up reference material, for study. Form the delightful habit of browsing—among current periodicals, among books newly received, in the sections devoted to fiction, to biography, to art, to history. Among the cherished memories of most college graduates are quiet hours spent in the library without specific purpose—hours apparently idle but rich in benefits not easily measurable.[1]

78. CLASSIFICATION

In most libraries in the United States, books and other published materials are classified and arranged according to one of two systems—the Library of Congress system and the Dewey decimal system. Discover promptly which is followed by the library of your college. Under either system each book is assigned a call number, and no two books are ever given an identical call number. The call number has two parts: the first is the class number; the second is the author and book number.

78A. Library of Congress System

In the Library of Congress system books are classified by subject into twenty-one main divisions, each represented by a capital letter.

A General Works
B Philosophy—Religion
C History—Auxiliary Sciences
D History and Topography (except America)
E America (general) and United States (general)
F United States (local) and America except the United States
G Geography—Anthropology
H Social Sciences
J Political Science
K Law
L Education
M Music
N Fine Arts
P Language and Literature
Q Science
R Medicine

[1] A set of films and recordings on "Library Orientation" prepared by Chicago Teachers College is available through the Society for Visual Education, Inc., in Chicago.

S Agriculture
T Technology
U Military Science
V Naval Science
Z Bibliography and Library Science

Subdivisions are indicated by additional letters and figures. For example, class numbers between E101 and E135 are assigned to books about the discovery of America. Again, class numbers between E151 and E810 are assigned to books about the United States, and the class number E806 is assigned to the biography of Franklin D. Roosevelt.

78B. Dewey Decimal System

In the Dewey decimal system books are classified by subject into ten main divisions:

000–099 General Works
100–199 Philosophy
200–299 Religion
300–399 Social Sciences
400–499 Linguistics
500–599 Pure Science
600–699 Applied Science
700–799 Arts and Recreation
800–899 Literature
900–999 History

Each main division is further divided into ten parts. For example, 900–999 History:

900–909 General Works
910–919 Geography
920–929 Biography
930–939 Ancient World History
940–949 European History
950–959 History of Asia
960–969 African History
970–979 North American History
980–989 South American History
990–999 History of Oceania

Each of these divisions may be further divided into ten parts. For example, 970–979 North American History:

970–970.9	General Works
971–971.9	Canada
972–972.9	Mexico–Central America
973–973.9	United States (general)
974–974.9	Northeastern States
975–975.9	Southeastern States
976–976.9	South Central States
977–977.9	North Central or Lake States
978–978.9	Western or Mountain States
979–979.9	Pacific States

Further subdivision is made possible by decimal expansion. For example, 973.9 is assigned to books on the United States in the twentieth century; 973.91, to books on the early twentieth century; and 973.917, to books dealing with the administration of Franklin D. Roosevelt and World War II. Such subdivision may be carried still further to any extent required.

Many libraries that use the Dewey system deviate from it in some ways. You may find that the capital letter B is used for biography and that biographical works on individual persons are classified alphabetically according to names of persons treated. Often works of fiction are all shelved together and simply arranged alphabetically according to names of authors.

79. THE CARD CATALOGUE

The card catalogue is the key to the book collection of a library. Each book is represented by at least two and usually three or more cards—one for author, one for title, and at least one for subject. Often books with common titles such as *The History of . . .* or *The Life of . . .* are not listed under title; and most works of fiction are listed only under author and title, not under subject. On the other hand, if a book covers a number of subjects there may be as many as four or five or even more subject cards. Thus if you know only the author of a book or only its title or only one of its principal subjects, you should have no trouble locating the work through the card catalogue. The books catalogued in your library under any subject constitute a partial bibliography of that subject.

Many libraries now use for most books author cards printed by the Library of Congress. Here is an author card for a book classified according to the Dewey system.

```
973.917  <= 1.
R24r
  2. => Rauch, Basil, 1908-  <= 3.
  4. =>      Roosevelt: from Munich to Pearl Harbor; a study in the
          creation of a foreign policy.  [1st ed.]  New York,
          Creative Age Press, 1950. <= 5.
  6. =>      xiv, 527 p.  22 cm.
  7. =>      "Reference notes": p. [497]-514.

  8. =>      1. Roosevelt, Franklin Delano, Pres. U. S., 1882-1945.  2. U. S.—
          For. rel.—1933-1945.    I. Title.

  9. =>      E807.R3  1950 <= 10.    973.917 <= 11.    50-6815 <= 12.

 13. =>      Library of Congress    ( )    [60] <= 14.
```

1. Call number.
2. Author's name, given in full.
3. Date of author's birth. If an author is dead, the date of his death is also given. The absence of such a date shows that the author was living at the time the card was printed.
4. Title. This line and the rest of the paragraph give the information that appears on the title page of the book.
5. Imprint. That is, place, publisher, and date of publication.
6. Collation. That is, a description of the technical features of the book. This book contains 14 pages of prefatory material numbered in small Roman numerals and 527 pages numbered in Arabic numerals. It is 22 centimeters high.
7. In this space the cataloguer may list any features of the book that make it especially valuable to the reader.
8. Headings under which this book is listed in the card catalogue in addition to the author card. The Arabic numerals indicate subject headings; the Roman numeral indicates a title heading.
9. Library of Congress classification.

10. Date of copyright.
11. Dewey classification.
12. Number used by libraries in ordering this card. This is called the "Library of Congress Card Catalog Number," and current practice is to print such a number on the copyright page (the back of the title page) of each book published.
13. Indicates that a copy is in the Library of Congress.
14. Printer's key for this card.

If a book has two or more authors, each specifically named on the title page, you will find a card for each author. Sometimes you will find an institution or society or government department rather than a person listed as author.

A title card is an author card with the title of the book typed above the name of the author, thus:

```
          Roosevelt: from Munich to Pearl Harbor
973.917
R24r   Rauch, Basil, 1908-
          Roosevelt: from Munich to Pearl Harbor; a study in the
        creation of a foreign policy. [1st ed.] New York, Creative
        Age Press, 1950.
```

In the card catalogue an article (*a, an, the*) is never regarded as the first word of a title: thus a book entitled *The Hero in America* is catalogued under *Hero*.

A subject card is an author card with a subject typed, usually in red, above the name of the author, thus:

```
          U.S. - Foreign relations - 1933-1945 -
973.917
R24r   Rauch, Basil, 1908-
          Roosevelt: from Munich to Pearl Harbor; a study in the
        creation of a foreign policy. [1st ed.] New York, Creative
        Age Press, 1950.
```

A book that contains information on several major subjects is represented in the catalogue by a card under each subject. Subject headings are as specific as possible. Look under *Children's literature* rather than under *Literature* for books for children; under

Taxation rather than under *Economics* for books on taxation; under the name of the place rather than under *History* for the history of a country or locality; under specific metals rather than under *Metals*. Remember, however, that a book on African history will have material on the history of Egypt, and that a book on light will have material on lenses; such general books may add to the material found under the specific headings *Egypt* and *Lenses*. Hence, if you cannot find what you want under the specific term, go to the next larger term.

Following some subject headings you will find guide cards directing you to other terms under which you may locate additional material. Such references are usually from a large topic to smaller ones, thus:

Church history—see also
- Abbeys
- Church and state
- Episcopacy
- Missions
- Papacy
- Protestant churches

Sometimes you will find a guide card directing you from one term to a slightly different term describing the same subject. For example: Appreciation of art—see Art criticism.

Periodicals may be located under subject or title, and many libraries keep a special file listing periodicals separately for easy reference. Current issues are usually shelved in a special periodical section or room.

80. REFERENCE BOOKS

Reference books form one of the most important parts of a library. They are specially planned to help you find answers to specific questions in the shortest possible time and to direct you to sources of further information. You will find most of the basic reference works in your library shelved together for convenient access in a central location.

The number of reference books is very large. The standard *Guide to Reference Books*[2] lists about 5,500 titles, but even so it is not complete. On the following pages is a selective list, arranged under subject headings, of some of the reference works that you are likely to find most useful. If you form an early acquaintance with them you will hold throughout your college years and afterward a key to most of the incredibly rich information available through the printed word.

80A. Dictionaries

Dictionaries, particularly the huge unabridged volumes, are among the most important reference works. They are far more than mere lists of words indicating spelling, pronunciation, meaning, and derivation. You may be astonished to discover how much information on a host of subjects is available in them. Even the smaller dictionaries of the collegiate variety supply basic information about such topics as notable persons living or dead, mythology, historical events, place names, population, and colleges and universities. For a detailed discussion of dictionaries and their use, see Section 54, Types of Dictionaries, and Section 55, Use of the Dictionary.

80B. General Encyclopedias

Encyclopedias are systematic summaries of basic information in all fields of knowledge, presented for nonspecialists. They are the most convenient starting point for the student looking for survey material or bibliographic references to sources of additional material.

Encyclopaedia Britannica. Probably the best-known encyclopedia. Scholarly, authoritative, especially strong in the humanities. Be sure to use the admirably detailed index in the final volume to locate discussion of minor topics. Supplemented annually by the *Britannica Book of the Year.*

Encyclopedia Americana. More informal in style. Especially strong in treatment of American subjects and of science and technology. Index

[2] Seventh ed., edited by Constance M. Winchell (Chicago: American Library Association, 1951). Another useful, more selective guide is Louis Shores, *Basic Reference Sources* (Chicago: American Library Association, 1954).

volume similar to that of the *Britannica.* Supplemented annually by the *Americana Annual.*

Collier's Encyclopedia. Especially strong in modern subjects. Richly illustrated, popular in style. Supplemented annually by *Collier's Year Book.*

Columbia Encyclopedia. Much briefer (single volume) than the others listed, but convenient when only basic information is needed. Well adapted for quick reference.

New Century Cyclopedia of Names. Gives essential facts about "more than 100,000 proper names of every description—persons, places, historical events, plays and operas, works of fiction, literary characters, mythological and legendary persons and places," etc.

For encyclopedias in special fields see subject areas below under Section 80L, Miscellaneous Reference Works.

80C. Atlases and Gazetteers

An atlas is a bound collection of maps, either contemporary or historical. The larger atlases are rich in statistical information. A gazetteer is an alphabetical list of place names, including basic information about location, population, etc.

Rand McNally Commercial Atlas and Marketing Guide. Annual. First (and more detailed) part devoted to the United States and its possessions, second part to the rest of the world. Especially valuable for information on agriculture, commerce, industry, marketing, transportation. Numerous statistical tables.

There are many other good modern atlases. Two of the best are the *Encyclopaedia Britannica World Atlas* and *Hammond's Complete World Atlas.*

Historical Atlas. 7th ed. By William R. Shepherd. New York: Henry Holt & Co., Inc., 1929. "The best of the smaller general historical atlases." Contains maps useful in the study of world history from 1450 B.C. to 1929.

Historical Atlas of the United States. Rev. ed. By Clifford L. and Elizabeth H. Lord. New York: Henry Holt & Co., Inc., 1953. Maps presenting political and economic history to 1950. Numerous statistical tables. Index.

Columbia Lippincott Gazetteer of the World. Ed. by Leon E. Seltzer. New York: Columbia University Press, 1952. An excellent, detailed modern gazetteer. Uses 1950 census figures.

Webster's Geographical Dictionary. Springfield, Mass.: G. & C. Merriam Co., 1949. A concise, useful list of more than 40,000 place names, with brief geographical and historical information.

80D. Yearbooks

Britannica Book of the Year. Annual supplement of the *Encyclopaedia Britannica.*

Americana Annual. Annual supplement of the *Encyclopedia Americana.*

Collier's Year Book. Annual supplement of *Collier's Encyclopedia.*

World Almanac and Book of Facts. Inexpensive storehouse of up-to-date information on a host of subjects, compactly presented. Not arranged alphabetically. Index in front.

Information Please Almanac. Similar to *World Almanac.* Index in back.

American Yearbook, 1910–19, 1925–50. No longer published. A record of political, economic, and social history and of progress in science and the humanities.

Political Handbook of the World. Up-to-date information about political events and changes in all countries.

Statesman's Yearbook. Concise information about all countries—political, historical, geographical, economic, etc. "The most useful of all the general yearbooks."

Statistical Abstract of the United States. Prepared by the Bureau of the Census. Contains hundreds of statistical tables on population, education, commerce, etc.

Yearbook of the United Nations. Summarizes the activities of the United Nations.

80E. General Lists of Books

United States Catalog: Books in Print January 1, 1928. Alphabetical arrangement under author, title, and subject, giving publisher, date of publication, price, etc.

Cumulative Book Index: A World List of Books in the English Language. Now published monthly except August, cumulated [3] at intervals. Supplements and keeps up to date the *United States Catalog.* Directory of publishers at back of each issue.

Publishers' Trade List Annual. A master collection of publishers' annual catalogues arranged alphabetically by publishers. A companion volume, *Books in Print,* is an author-title index to the contents of the complete *Publishers' Trade List Annual.*

[3] Current indexes of this sort are said to be "cumulated" when all entries in successive lists are assembled and re-indexed in a later master list.

80F. Biographical Dictionaries—General

Dictionary of American Biography. Contains basic biographical articles of considerable length on noteworthy Americans no longer living (through 1935). Excellent bibliographies. Valuable index volume includes listings by birthplace, educational institution, and occupation, as well as a detailed topical index to material within the biographies.

Dictionary of National Biography. The 63-volume main work, together with its supplements, is the most important source for British biography. Contains articles of considerable length on noteworthy British citizens no longer living from the earliest Britons to 1940. Bibliographies excellent but in older volumes somewhat out of date. The *Concise Dictionary of National Biography* (1930) is a convenient single-volume condensation of the larger work (through 1921).

Who's Who in America. Brief biographies of noteworthy living citizens of the United States. Biennial.

Who Was Who in America. Compiled at intervals from entries that had appeared in the current work while the persons listed, now dead, were still living.

Who's Who. Brief biographies of noteworthy living persons, chiefly British. Annual.

Who Was Who. Compiled at intervals from entries that had appeared in the current work while the persons listed, now dead, were still living.

Current Biography: Who's News and Why. Up-to-date articles of considerable length on prominent living persons of all countries. Informal in style, includes portraits. Published monthly except August, with an annual cumulation.

International Who's Who. Brief biographies of prominent living persons of all countries. Annual.

Webster's Biographical Dictionary. Springfield, Mass.: G. & C. Merriam Co., 1943. Concise biographies of more than 40,000 notable persons of all times. Useful for identification.

80G. Biographical Dictionaries—Special

The works in this group are concerned only with persons living at the time of publication. There are many similar publications listing persons prominent in various other fields (law, medicine, etc.). For works listing authors see below under "Literature," Section 80L.

American Men of Science. Latest ed., 1955.
Chemical Who's Who. Latest ed., 1951.

Directory of American Scholars. Latest ed., 1951.
Leaders in Education. Latest ed., 1948.
Who's Who in American Art. Latest ed., 1953.
Who's Who in Commerce and Industry. Latest ed., 1953.
Who's Who in Engineering. Latest ed., 1954.
Who's Who in Labor. Latest ed., 1946.
Who's Who in Music. Latest ed., 1953.
Who's Who in the Theatre. Latest ed., 1952.

80H. Indexes to Periodicals—General

Among the most valuable reference tools are indexes to the vast literature available in periodicals. Not only is information in current periodicals more up to date than that in books, but much specialized information is available *only* in the files of periodicals.

Reader's Guide to Periodical Literature, 1900 to date. The most widely used periodical index. Covers more than 100 publications, chiefly general and popular. Published twice monthly except July and August, when there are single issues. Cumulated at frequent intervals, with a permanent bound cumulation every two years. Alphabetical arrangement under author and subject, and sometimes under title. Notes presence of illustrations, tables, etc. Articles by a person are listed first, followed by articles about him (if any). List of full titles of periodicals indexed appears at the front of each issue.

International Index to Periodicals, 1907 to date. Devoted chiefly to the humanities, social sciences, and science. Covers more than 150 periodicals. Quarterly, with annual cumulations and a permanent bound cumulation every three years. Alphabetical arrangement under author and subject. List of full titles of periodicals indexed appears at the front of each issue. Notes presence of illustrations.

Poole's Index to Periodical Literature, 1802–1906. Published 1882–1908, including supplements. Reprinted in six vols., 1938. Alphabetical arrangement under subject only. Though long discontinued, still valuable for information concerning articles published in the years covered. This and the next item, however, are likely to be found only in large libraries with extensive periodical collections.

Nineteenth Century Reader's Guide to Periodical Literature, 1890–99, with Supplementary Indexing, 1900–22. Covers 51 periodicals, chiefly for 1890–99. Alphabetical arrangement under author and subject.

Annual Magazine Subject Index, 1907–49. Discontinued. Covers selected American and British periodicals for the years indicated. Alphabetical arrangement under subject. Has as a second part a *Dramatic Index*, covering articles on drama and theater.

80J. Indexes to Periodicals—Special

Agricultural Index, 1916 to date. Monthly, with an annual cumulation and a permanent cumulation every three years. A detailed subject index to agricultural periodicals and to related reports and bulletins.

Art Index, 1929 to date. Quarterly, with an annual cumulation and a permanent cumulation every three years. An index to material in periodicals and museum bulletins in the fields of archaeology, architecture, and arts and crafts.

Biography Index, 1947 to date. Quarterly, with an annual cumulation. An index to biographical material in books and magazines. Lists names alphabetically and also by profession and occupation. Notes presence of portraits.

Biological Abstracts, 1926 to date. Ten issues each year. Brief summaries of articles on theoretical and applied biology.

Book Review Digest, 1905 to date. Monthly except February and July, cumulated in August and again in an annual volume. A digest and index of book reviews selected from about seventy periodicals, chiefly general. Alphabetical arrangement under author, with a title and subject index. For each book gives title, number of pages, price, publisher, a brief description, excerpts from some reviews and references to others. Plus sign indicates a favorable review; minus sign, an unfavorable one.

Chemical Abstracts, 1907 to date. Semimonthly. Brief summaries of articles on subjects in and related to chemistry.

Dramatic Index, 1909–49. Discontinued. Covers articles on drama and theater for the years indicated.

Education Index, 1929 to date. Monthly except June and August, with cumulation annually and every three years. An author and subject index to a selected list of educational periodicals, books, and pamphlets.

Engineering Index, 1884 to date. Now published annually. A subject index to technical and engineering periodicals both American and foreign.

Facts on File, 1940 to date. Not an index, but a weekly classified digest of world news. Useful for current events. Frequent cumulative indexes, bound annual volumes.

Industrial Arts Index, 1913 to date. Monthly, with an annual cumulation. A subject index to a large list of engineering, industrial, and business periodicals, books, and pamphlets.

New York Times Index, 1913 to date. Now published twice a month, with an annual bound cumulation. A detailed subject index with plentiful cross references. Invaluable for locating contemporary accounts of daily events.

Official Index to "The Times," 1906 to date. A quarterly index to the London *Times.* Usually found only in large libraries.

Psychological Abstracts, 1927 to date. A monthly bibliography listing new books and articles in the field grouped by subjects, with a signed abstract of each item.

Public Affairs Information Service, 1915 to date. Weekly, with bimonthly and annual cumulations. A subject index to current books, pamphlets, and periodicals on political science, government, legislation, economics, sociology, etc. Good for pamphlet material especially.

Science Abstracts, 1898 to date. Monthly. Brief summaries of articles on scientific subjects. Issued in two sections: *A.* Physics; *B.* Electrical Engineering.

80K. Lists of Periodicals

Union List of Serials in Libraries of the United States and Canada. 2d ed. New York: The H. W. Wilson Co., 1943. Supplements, 1945, 1953. Comprehensive list of more than 115,000 current and defunct periodicals and of the files of each available in more than 600 libraries.

American Newspapers, 1821–1936: A Union List of Files Available in the United States and Canada. New York: The H. W. Wilson Co., 1937. Lists holdings in nearly 5,700 depositories.

N. W. Ayer & Son's Directory of Newspapers and Periodicals, 1880 to date. Annual comprehensive list, arranged geographically, covering the United States and its possessions, Canada, Bermuda, Cuba, Panama, and the Philippines. Gives names of editor and publisher, frequency of publication, political tendency, date of foundation, size, subscription price, and circulation.

Ulrich's Periodicals Directory. 7th ed. New York: R. R. Bowker Co., 1953. Classified list of about 14,000 periodicals, chiefly in North and South America and the British Empire. A valuable feature is that it tells where each periodical is indexed.

80L. Miscellaneous Reference Works

Agriculture

Agricultural Statistics, 1936 to date. Published annually by the United States Department of Agriculture. (From 1894 through 1935 included as part of the *Yearbook of Agriculture.*)

Standard Cyclopedia of Horticulture. By L. H. Bailey. 6 vols. New York: The Macmillan Co., 1914–17. Reissued 1947 in 3 vols.

ARTS AND ARCHITECTURE

Apollo: An Illustrated Manual of the History of Art Throughout the Ages. By SALOMON REINACH. Trans. by Florence Simmonds. Rev. ed. New York: Chas. Scribner's Sons, 1935.

Bryan's Dictionary of Painters and Engravers. New ed. 5 vols. New York: The Macmillan Co., 1903–5. Old.

Dictionary of American Painters, Sculptors, and Engravers. By MANTLE FIELDING. New York: Paul A. Struck, 1945.

Dictionary of Architecture and Building. By RUSSELL STURGIS. New York: The Macmillan Co., 1901. Old but standard.

Harper's Encyclopedia of Art: Architecture, Painting, Sculpture, Decorative Arts. New York: Harper & Bros., 1937.

CLASSICS AND MYTHOLOGY

FRAZER, SIR JAMES G. *The Golden Bough: A Study in Magic and Religion.* 3d ed. 12 vols. London: Macmillan & Co., Ltd., 1907–15. Supplement, 1936.

GAYLEY, CHARLES MILLS. *Classic Myths in English Literature and in Art.* Rev. ed. Boston: Ginn & Co., 1911.

Harper's Dictionary of Classical Literature and Antiquities. Ed. by HARRY THURSTON PECK. New York: Harper & Bros., 1897. Old but standard.

Oxford Classical Dictionary. Ed. by M. CARY and OTHERS. Oxford: Clarendon Press, 1949.

Oxford Companion to Classical Literature. By SIR PAUL HARVEY. Oxford: Clarendon Press, 1937.

ECONOMICS

See Social Sciences.

EDUCATION

Cyclopedia of Education. Ed. by PAUL MONROE. New York: The Macmillan Co., 1911–13.

Encyclopedia of Educational Research. Rev. ed. Ed. by W. S. MONROE. New York: The Macmillan Co., 1950.

Patterson's American Educational Directory, 1904 to date. Chicago: Educational Directories, Inc. Annual directory of public and private schools and colleges arranged by states, followed by a list of schools classified by types, etc.

ENGINEERING

See Science and Engineering.

Government of the United States

Official Congressional Directory, 1809 to date. Revised currently. Information about Congressional personnel, government machinery and agencies, diplomatic representatives, etc.

United States Government Organization Manual, 1935 to date. Now annual. Information on the organization, activities, and current officials of the various departments, bureaus, offices, commissions, etc., of the government.

Government Publications

The United States government is not only the world's largest publisher but also one of the most up-to-date and comprehensive. The number of government publications is tremendous, but the two selective works listed here will lead the student to the most significant ones. Many college and university libraries are regular depositories of government publications.

Subject Guide to United States Government Publications. By Herbert S. Hirschberg and Carl H. Melinat. Chicago: American Library Association, 1947.

United States Government Publications. By Anne M. Boyd. 3d ed. revised by Rae E. Reps. New York: The H. W. Wilson Co., 1949.

History

Cambridge Ancient History. Ed. by J. B. Bury and Others. New York: The Macmillan Co., 1923–29. This and the two other Cambridge histories are excellent reference histories, with each chapter written by a specialist and with bibliographies at the end of each volume.

Cambridge Medieval History. Ed. by H. M. Gwatkin and Others. 8 vols. New York: The Macmillan Co., 1911–36.

Cambridge Modern History. Ed. by A. W. Ward and Others. 13 vols. New York: The Macmillan Co., 1902–26. Now of course somewhat out of date.

Dictionary of American History. 2d ed. Ed. by James Truslow Adams. 5 vols. and index. New York: Chas. Scribner's Sons, 1942.

Documents of American History. 5th ed. Ed. by Henry Steele Commager. New York: Appleton-Century-Crofts, Inc., 1949. Contains important historical documents (treaties, declarations, addresses, etc.) of five centuries.

Encyclopedia of American History. Ed. by Richard B. Morris. New York: Harper & Bros., 1953.

Encyclopedia of World History. Rev. ed. By William L. Langer. 2 vols. Boston: Houghton Mifflin Co., 1948.

New Larned History for Ready Reference, Reading, and Research. Rev. ed. Ed. by Donald E. Smith and Others. 12 vols. Springfield, Mass.: Nichols, 1922–24.

Literature

See also Classics and Mythology.

American Authors, 1600–1900: A Biographical Dictionary of American Literature. Ed. by Stanley J. Kunitz and Howard Haycraft. New York: The H. W. Wilson Co., 1938.

American Novelists of Today. By Harry R. Warfel. New York: American Book Co., 1951.

Bookman's Manual: A Guide to Literature. 7th ed. By Hester R. Hoffman. New York: R. R. Bowker Co., 1954.

British Authors before 1800: A Biographical Dictionary. Ed. by Stanley J. Kunitz and Howard Haycraft. New York: The H. W. Wilson Co., 1952.

British Authors of the Nineteenth Century. Ed. by Stanley J. Kunitz and Howard Haycraft. New York: The H. W. Wilson Co., 1936.

Cambridge Bibliography of English Literature. Ed. by F. W. Bateson. 4 vols. New York: The Macmillan Co., 1941. Comprehensive. Supersedes the bibliographies in the *Cambridge History of English Literature.* A revision is in progress.

Cambridge History of English Literature. Ed. by A. W. Ward and A. R. Waller. 14 vols. and index. London: Cambridge University Press, 1907–16. Index issued 1927. Reissued 1933 without bibliographies. Now somewhat out of date.

Concise Cambridge History of English Literature. By George Sampson. New York: The Macmillan Co., 1941. Based on the longer *Cambridge History.*

Cassell's Encyclopedia of Literature. Ed. by S. H. Steinberg. 2 vols. London: Cassell & Co., Ltd., 1953. Greater part devoted to biographies of authors of all countries.

Columbia Dictionary of Modern European Literature. Ed. by Horatio Smith. New York: Columbia University Press, 1947.

Contemporary American Authors. By Fred B. Millett. New York: Harcourt, Brace & Co., Inc., 1940.

Contemporary British Literature. 3d ed. By Fred B. Millett. New York: Harcourt, Brace & Co., Inc., 1935.

Essay and General Literature Index, 1900 to date. A detailed author, subject, and title index to essays and articles in collections published since 1900. The author entry lists essays by an author, essays about the author, and criticisms of individual books. Strong in biography and criticism.

Granger's Index to Poetry. 4th ed. Ed. by Raymond J. Dixon. New York: Columbia University Press, 1953. Index to poetry in 577 collections by title and first line, by author, and by subject.

Index to Plays, 1800–1926. By Ina T. E. Firkins. New York: The H. W. Wilson Co., 1927. Supplement, 1935. Author index and title and subject index to plays in collections or separately published.

Index to Plays in Collections. 2d ed. By John H. Ottemiller. Washington, D.C.: Scarecrow Press, 1951. Author and title index to plays in collections that appeared between 1900 and 1950.

Literary History of England. Ed. by Albert C. Baugh. New York: Appleton-Century-Crofts, Inc., 1948. Also in 4-vol. ed.

Literary History of the United States. Ed. by Robert E. Spiller and Others. 2 vols. and bibliographical vol. New York: The Macmillan Co., 1948.

Literature of the American People. Ed. by Arthur Hobson Quinn. New York: Appleton-Century-Crofts, Inc., 1948.

Oxford Companion to American Literature. 2d ed. By James D. Hart. New York: Oxford University Press, 1948.

Oxford Companion to English Literature. 3d ed. By Sir Paul Harvey. Oxford: Clarendon Press, 1946.

Oxford Companion to the Theatre. Ed. by Phyllis Hartnoll. New York: Oxford University Press, 1951.

Oxford History of English Literature. Ed. by F. P. Wilson and Bonamy Dobrée. Several of the 12 projected vols. published so far. Oxford: Clarendon Press, 1945–47.

Play Index, 1949–1952. By Dorothy Herbert West and Dorothy Margaret Peake. New York: The H. W. Wilson Co., 1953.

Reader's Encyclopedia: An Encyclopedia of World Literature and the Arts. Ed. by William Rose Benét. New York: Thomas Y. Crowell Co., 1948.

Short Story Index: An Index to 60,000 Stories in 4,320 Collections. Compiled by Dorothy E. Cook and Isabel S. Monro. New York: The H. W. Wilson Co., 1943.

Twentieth Century Authors: A Biographical Dictionary of Modern Literature. By Stanley J. Kunitz and Howard Haycraft. New York: The H. W. Wilson Co., 1942.

Music

Grove's Dictionary of Music and Musicians. 5th ed. Ed. by Eric Blom. 9 vols. New York: St. Martin's Press, 1954.

Harvard Dictionary of Music. By Willi Apel. Cambridge, Mass.: Harvard University Press, 1944.

International Cyclopedia of Music and Musicians. Ed. by OSCAR THOMPSON. 5th ed. rev. by NICOLAS SLONIMSKY. New York: Dodd, Mead & Co., Inc., 1949.

Oxford Companion to Music. 7th ed. By PERCY A. SCHOLES. London: Oxford University Press, 1947.

MYTHOLOGY

See Classics and Mythology.

PHILOSOPHY AND PSYCHOLOGY

Dictionary of Philosophy and Psychology. Ed. by JAMES M. BALDWIN. 3 vols. in 4. New York: The Macmillan Co., 1910.

Dictionary of Psychology. Ed. by H. C. WARREN. Boston: Houghton Mifflin Co., 1934.

Encyclopedia of Psychology. Ed. by PHILIP L. HARRIMAN. New York: Philosophical Library, 1947.

QUOTATIONS

BARTLETT, JOHN. *Familiar Quotations.* 13th ed. Boston: Little, Brown & Co., 1955.

MENCKEN, H. L. *A New Dictionary of Quotations on Historical Principles from Ancient and Modern Sources.* New York: Alfred A. Knopf, Inc., 1942.

Oxford Dictionary of Quotations. 2d ed. New York: Oxford University Press, 1953.

STEVENSON, BURTON. *The Home Book of Quotations.* 5th ed. New York: Dodd, Mead & Co., Inc., 1947.

RELIGION

Catholic Encyclopedia. 17 vols. New York: Encyclopedia Press, 1907–22.

Encyclopedia of Islam. Ed. by M. TH. HOUTSMA and OTHERS. 4 vols. London: Luzac & Co., Ltd., 1911–38.

Encyclopaedia of Religion and Ethics. Ed. by JAMES HASTINGS. 12 vols. and index. New York: Chas. Scribner's Sons, 1908–27.

Jewish Encyclopedia. Ed. by ISIDORE SINGER. 12 vols. New York: Funk & Wagnalls Co., 1901–06.

New Schaff-Herzog Encyclopedia of Religious Knowledge. Ed. by SAMUEL M. JACKSON. 12 vols. and index. New York: Funk & Wagnalls Co., 1908–12.

Universal Jewish Encyclopedia. 10 vols. New York: Universal Jewish Encyclopedia, Inc., 1939–44.

SCIENCE AND ENGINEERING

Condensed Chemical Dictionary. 4th ed. Ed. by ARTHUR and ELIZABETH ROSE. New York: Reinhold Publishing Corporation, 1950.

Encyclopedia of Chemical Technology. Ed. by RAYMOND E. KIRK and OTHERS. New York: Interscience Encyclopedias, Inc., 1947–. In process: 12 vols. published to date. Articles written by specialists include excellent bibliographies. Up to date, broad in coverage, includes all kinds of technology. Begins to be a comprehensive encyclopedia of science and technology.

General Engineering Handbook. Ed. by C. E. O'ROURKE. New York: McGraw-Hill Book Co., Inc., 1940.

Glossary of Physics. Ed. by LEROY D. WELD. New York: McGraw-Hill Book Co., Inc., 1937.

Handbook of Chemistry and Physics. 35th ed. Ed. by CHARLES D. HODGMAN and OTHERS. Cleveland, Ohio: Chemical Rubber Publishing Co., 1953.

Handbook of Engineering Fundamentals. Ed. by O. W. ESHBACH. New York: John Wiley & Sons, Inc., 1936.

Handbook of Nature Study. 24th ed. Ed. by ANNA BOTSFORD COMSTOCK. Ithaca, New York: Comstock Publishing Co., 1939.

Materials Handbook. 6th ed. By GEORGE S. BRADY. New York: McGraw-Hill Book Co., Inc., 1947.

Radio Amateur's Handbook, 1926 to date. Revised annually. West Hartford, Conn.: American Radio Relay League.

Television Encyclopedia. By STANLEY KEMPNER. New York: Fairchild Publications, 1948.

Thorpe's Dictionary of Applied Chemistry. 4th ed. 11 vols. New York: Longmans, Green & Co., Inc., 1937–54.

Van Nostrand Chemist's Dictionary. Ed. by JURGEN M. HONIG and OTHERS. New York: D. Van Nostrand Co., Inc., 1953.

Van Nostrand's Scientific Encyclopedia. 2d ed. New York: D. Van Nostrand Co., Inc., 1947.

There are also standard, up-to-date handbooks in all the individual major fields of engineering—such as chemical, civil, electrical, mechanical, radio.

SOCIAL SCIENCES

Book of the States, 1935 to date. Chicago: Council of State Governments. Biennial. Information on "the structures, working methods, financing, and functional activities of the state governments, together with listings of state officials and members of the legislature."

Dictionary of Economics. 3d ed. By HAROLD S. SLOAN and ARNOLD J. ZURCHER. New York: Barnes and Noble, Inc., 1953. Inexpensive dictionary of definitions and explanations of terms relating to economic problems, theories, and practices.

Documents on American Foreign Relations, 1939 to date. Formerly published by World Peace Foundation; now published by Council on Foreign Relations (New York: Harper & Bros.). Annual collection of important documentary materials pertaining to United States foreign relations.

Economic Almanac, 1940 to date. Annual. New York: Industrial Conference Board. A statistical handbook covering such subjects as banking and finance, communication and transportation, prices, labor force, international economic statistics.

Encyclopedia of Banking and Finance. By GLEN G. MUNN. 5th ed. by F. L. GARCIA. Cambridge, Mass.: Bankers Publishing Company, 1949.

Encyclopaedia of the Social Sciences. Ed. by E. R. A. SELIGMAN and ALVIN JOHNSON. 15 vols. New York: The Macmillan Co., 1930–35.

White's Political Dictionary. By WILBER W. WHITE. New York: World Publishing Company, 1947.

Yearbook on Human Rights, 1947 to date. New York: United Nations. Annual survey of the constitutional and legal provisions of the countries of the world concerning the rights of the citizen.

SPEECH AND DEBATE

Reference Shelf, 1922 to date. New York: The H. W. Wilson Co. Issued irregularly, 5 or 6 numbers to a volume. Each number is devoted to a timely controversial question, with reprints of selected articles from books and periodicals giving background information and arguments on either side, followed by a comprehensive bibliography.

Speech Index: An Index to 64 Collections of World Famous Orations and Speeches for Various Occasions. By ROBERTA BRIGGS SUTTON. New York: The H. W. Wilson Co., 1935.

SPORT

Encyclopedia of Sports. Rev. ed. by FRANK G. MENKE. New York: A. S. Barnes & Co., 1953.

EXERCISE

This exercise is designed to help you learn to use reference books that will be useful to you in your college courses and throughout life. In considering each question assigned to you, decide upon the type of reference work likely to contain the answer, the specific book or books to be consulted, and then the proper approach to the work selected—for example, through the index or the table of contents. State not only the answer but also the source of your information. Many of the questions can be answered by means of various books and various methods of approach. In some books you will have to look up the explanation of the abbreviations used. Some of the questions are easy; a few are difficult; one or two may foil you. But do not give up easily.

The teacher may decide to assign a different set of questions to each student or each group of students and call for classroom discussion of answers and the methods used in finding them. Do not expect the teacher to know all the answers!

1. Where are the Palau Islands, and how are they governed?
2. Find the source of the following: "I have loved the stars too fondly to be fearful of the night."
3. Who commanded the force of United States Marines that captured John Brown at Harpers Ferry?
4. What was the response of contemporary critics to Sinclair Lewis's *Main Street?*
5. Did the word "hussy" always have its present meaning? Explain.
6. Locate a map showing the course of the Lewis and Clark expedition.
7. Name and give the home addresses of the United States Senators from your state, and name the administrative assistant or secretary of each.
8. Locate three recent articles on college students.
9. What was the numerical division between Republicans and Democrats in each house of Congress in 1927–1929 (70th Congress)?
10. Locate the text of the Dred Scott decision and cite at least one article discussing it.
11. The assassination of what royal personage at Sarajevo on June 28, 1914, precipitated World War I?
12. Locate one favorable review and one unfavorable review of Ernest Hemingway's *Across the River and Into the Trees.*
13. How many representatives does Illinois have in the lower house of the United States Congress?
14. Why would it be appropriate for an American author to write a patriotic poem entitled "The Ride of Samuel Prescott"?
15. List the authors and titles of three books in your college library on the Spanish Civil War 1936–1939.
16. Locate maps showing the proportion of slaves to the total population of the United States at intervals from 1790 to 1860.

17. When did the kingdom of Saudi Arabia receive its present name?
18. How did Laocoön meet his death?
19. Name the representative of your congressional district, and state where he was educated and when he was first elected to Congress.
20. Locate the text of the radio speech delivered by Edward VIII (the Duke of Windsor) on the occasion of his abdication.
21. Under what government department does the Forest Service belong?
22. Locate a recent biographical sketch with portrait of the famous clown Emmett Kelly.
23. The American actor DeWolf Hopper gained fame by his recitals of what well-known poem? Who wrote the poem?
24. Who referred to woman as "A rag and a bone and a hank of hair"?
25. Locate a discussion of the Reform Bill of 1832.
26. When and by whom was the Drury Lane Theatre built?
27. Locate a discussion of the present constitution and government of Austria.
28. Compile a bibliography of five recent essays or articles (not books) on the historical novel.
29. List the authors and titles of at least three works of music or literature making use of the Don Juan legend.
30. Who holds the National League record for the most home runs hit in a lifetime?
31. Locate a table showing the revenue and expenditure in a recent year of each city in the United States having a population of over 250,000.
32. Name at least eight states that contain a town or village named Bedford.
33. Which of the present Supreme Court justices were appointed by President Franklin D. Roosevelt?
34. Locate a brief bibliography of material about Jack Cade.
35. What was the electoral vote for President by parties (Democratic and Republican) in 1928? in 1936?
36. Locate a recent article on electrons.
37. What was the change in population of Miami, Florida, between 1910 and 1950?
38. Locate the text of the speech in which the speaker called December 7, 1941, "a date which will live in infamy."
39. What American writer made "Spoon River" famous?
40. What was the exact date of "Braddock's Defeat"?

Chapter 10

THE RESEARCH PAPER

In many of your college courses you will be asked to write fairly long expository papers on various problems. Your experience in writing such papers will not only increase your knowledge about some person, place, idea, or thing but also help prepare you for yet more important projects later. Though the methods used in investigative writing vary somewhat in different fields of work, essentially the same procedure is practiced in most, and you should follow that procedure now in writing your first research paper.[1]

81. CHOOSING A SUBJECT

What are you to write about? This may depend in part on the will and discretion of your instructor. He may wish you to investigate some topic chosen from your own favorite field of study or one chosen from a completely different field. If you avail yourself of permission to choose the former, you will have the advantage of some degree of familiarity with your subject to aid you in its development, and the results of your study will add to your knowledge of the field. If you choose the latter, you may profitably broaden the scope of your general education.

Whatever your choice, your first consideration must be, as always, the proper limitation of your subject (see Section 1A). Sometimes a subject is manifestly too broad: for example, "Political Parties in the United States" would require a large book for an adequate treatment. "The Republican (or Democratic) Party"

[1] For more detailed treatment of this subject see Ellen Johnson, *The Research Report: A Guide for the Beginner* (New York: The Ronald Press Company, 1951).

is also much too large a topic. "The Origins of the Democratic (or Republican) Party" or "The Attitude of the Republican (or Democratic) Party Toward International Trade" is a much more limited topic. Often only the course of the investigation of the subject itself will reveal the need of narrowing its scope.

The following list of subjects accordingly contains many topics that will be found, after study, to need limitation. Some may even incorporate several possible research papers. Most papers growing out of these general topics will represent in their final development certain limited aspects of the subjects, and should be given new titles indicating their modified nature.

The Comprehensive Examination in American Colleges
The St. Lawrence Waterway
The Diesel Engine
The Erie Canal
The Amino Acids
The New York Central Railroad
The Making of Leather
Rayon
Adrenalin
Henry Barnard and His Influence on Education
Robert Frost's Conception of Nature
Vitamins
Scholastic Aptitude Tests
Enzymes in the Digestive Processes
The Modern Olympic Games
Paint
The Beginnings of Monasticism
Witchcraft in Salem
The California Gold Rush
The "Bull Moose" Party
Bolívar
Socialized Medicine
Sinclair Lewis, the Satirist
The Gypsies
Thorndike's Animal Experiments
Alaska
The Restriction of Immigration in the United States
The Bank Holiday of March, 1933
The Rise of Group Tests for Measuring Intelligence
The Role of the Brain in Learning
The Winnetka and Dalton Plans of School Organization
The League of Nations
Yellow Fever
Penicillin
The "Activity Movement" in Education
The Use of Greenbacks in Financing the Civil War
The Population of the United States, Past, Present, and Future
Glass
The National Recovery Act
The Stream of Consciousness Technique
Aldous Huxley and the Novel of Ideas
The South of William Faulkner
The National Banking System before 1913
The Organization of the Federal Reserve Banking System

Artesian Wells
The United Nations
Nutritional Anemia
The Sulfa Drugs
Peat
The Honey Bee Colony as a Social Organization

82. MAKING A WORKING BIBLIOGRAPHY

When you have arrived at your subject, you are ready to begin getting information about it. One may know enough about a subject to be aware at once of the outstanding authorities who have written about it. More commonly, however, one must begin with very limited information. Let us assume that your project is of the latter sort. How shall you begin?

Most subjects are discussed at least partially in the general encyclopedias such as the *Encyclopaedia Britannica* and the *Encyclopedia Americana.* Almost every field of study, moreover, has its own reference books. Consult the lists in Chapter 9, "The Use of the Library," for basic works in your field. The articles on your topic in such works will not only give a quick digest of what is known about the topic but also—and this is their special value to you—refer you through their bibliographical data (usually at the end of each article or chapter) to important books and articles that will provide more detailed information. Remember that a search of subject cards in the card catalogue may provide a partial bibliography of the material available in your library. If you find no subject cards on your topic, try several broader topics under which it might be included. Remember too that you may find your topic indexed under a heading phrased somewhat differently.

You are now ready to begin building your working bibliography. On 3″ by 5″ cards copy each pertinent reference from the list at the end of the articles dealing with your subject in basic reference works and from library cards filed under your subject in the card catalogue. List each reference on a separate card, with the author's name on the first line in inverted order (the surname first, followed by a comma and the given name), and the title of the book or article on the second line. Be sure to give the full name of the author, not just his surname: it is unfair to your reader to oblige him to hunt through a long list of Andersons or Browns when a little care on your part would have enabled him to identify the author promptly. It is unwise to list only one given name if the author has two or more: there are many John Browns and William Smiths.

Your next step is to look up each reference entered on your author cards. Using the library card catalogue, copy in the upper right-hand corner of your cards the call number of each listed book or periodical that your library owns. Copying the call number will not only serve you at once in securing the volume if it is available but will save time when you wish to refer to it again. If the book or periodical is not available in your library, note the fact: later, if the missing book or article seems important, you would do well to record its unavailability in a footnote at a suitable place in your paper. Be sure to enter the volume number if the work listed is in several volumes or is a periodical.

Following the procedure established by your college library, obtain the volumes you wish to consult and take them to the reading room. If the work concerned is a book, copy from the title page any essential bibliographical information not already entered on your card: full name of author; full title of book, with all important words initially capitalized (library cards follow library conventions in omitting capitalization except for the first letter of the first word of a title and the first letters of proper names); place of publication, publisher, and date. It is conventional to omit the names of the publishers of out-of-print books or books dated before 1920. Make sure that you have entered the most recent date of publication, since important changes in paging and content often occur in new editions. The latest date on the back of the title page is the one you should record: it will serve to warn the reader who is using a different edition that he may expect to find differences. Your completed card will now look somewhat like this:

Call number here

Werne, Benjamin
The Law of Labor Relations
New York: Macmillan, 1951

If the work concerned is a periodical, the form will be somewhat different:

Call number here

Spoerl, Dorothy Tilden
"Some Aspects of Prejudice as Affected by
Religion and Education"
Journal of Social Psychology, XXXIII (1951), 69–76

There will be further slight variations of form for references to articles in encyclopedias or to stories or poems in collections.

Next leaf through the book or article to determine what, if any, material in it may be of use to you. Since this is a preliminary viewing, in which you are trying to orient yourself toward the subject as a whole, do not take full notes as yet. Simply indicate on your bibliography card whether the work offers promising material on some portion of your subject (name the portion, if possible) or whether it is only of doubtful value to you or of no value at all. If you can make no use of it, you will not need to consult it again, and you will of course exclude it from your final bibliography. Your bibliography card with its suggestive note or lead may now read somewhat like this:

Call number here

Bush, Douglas
The Renaissance and English Humanism
Toronto: University of Toronto Press, 1939
Good on theories of the nature of the Re-
naissance. Pp. 13–38.

At the end of the book or article (sometimes elsewhere) you will often find the bibliography that the author used. This bibliography, particularly if the work is a recent one of sound scholarship, may prove your best source of reference to other books and articles, affording many useful works to add to your list; and if the author has critically evaluated his bibliography, his comments may help to guide you in finding out which sources will be most valuable to you. Only after you have reviewed the bibliographies in the latest and best works dealing with your subject and added their suggestions to your list of references can you afford to feel content with your bibliography.

After proceeding as indicated above through your entire list, you should have begun to form some ideas regarding the possible extent and the main divisions of your subject. Probably the notes on your bibliography cards will constitute a set of headings that can be organized into a rough phrase outline. Scan them carefully to see whether you can associate those that clearly belong together. The order and the arrangement of these headings will depend on the nature of the subject, but a natural and logical order should soon occur to you. These headings will form the structural basis of your sentence outline and the completed paper itself.

83. HOW TO TAKE NOTES

With the headings of your topical outline in mind, you are now ready to take the notes that are to help you give substance and value to that outline.

83A. The Two Types of Notes

83A 1. Note of Digest or Summary. One type of note—much the more useful—represents a digest or summary *in your own words* of the author's material relating to your subject. This note should not be a patching together of phrases borrowed from the text. To avoid this serious offense, you should not look at the author's words while making your notes. Read the passage, think over what the author is saying, and then, turning away from his text, restate his meaning in your own words. It will of course be impossible to avoid using some of the author's key words, but you can keep from using clusters of his words and following his sentence structure.

After making your note, compare what you have written with the author's version to see if your version is free of phrases somehow remembered from the text. Change any such phrases that may remain, or if, as you may occasionally feel, an epithet or other brief phrase is too good to omit, be sure that all such borrowed phrases (which should be used sparingly) are put in quotation marks. Compare your note with the original yet once more to make sure that your summary accurately represents the sense of the author. For example, you must not take from a text material that fits your opinion without taking into account the author's possible objections to that opinion or repudiation of it that may follow in his next sentence or next paragraph or chapter. In short, keep the context of your notes in mind: be careful not to misrepresent the author. When you have completed the note, be sure to record accurately the page or pages from which it is drawn.

83A 2. Note of Exact Quotation. The second type of note is the exact quotation. This sort of note will lend color or emphasis to your thought, but it should be used with judgment. Except in argument, when it is often necessary to quote an author extensively, it is advisable as a rule to quote only when an author's phrasing is particularly succinct and admirable. Even when dealing with an author of unusual eloquence, do not let your writing become a patchwork of his expressions. This is your work that you are writing, not his. In quoting, be careful to restate exactly the author's expression of his thought, reproducing his spelling, punctuation, and other devices exactly as the text shows them. If the passage quoted has a misprint or misspelling in it, reproduce the apparent error with a correction following it inserted in brackets, or the symbol *sic* similarly inserted (see Section 86E). If the note involves poetry, be sure to arrange the lines exactly as you find them in your source.

As in the first type of note, you should be sure that your quotation does not misrepresent the views of your author: do not omit parts of a quotation that may run counter to the view you wish to present. Thus it is not valid to represent Washington as a champion of isolationism by quoting (or citing) the well-known passage in which he warns against entangling alliances unless you add that in the same address he makes provision for temporary alliances in times of great danger.

The proper introduction of quotations into your writing deserves careful study. So far as possible they should be neatly integrated with your own sentence structure. If a quotation is less than three lines in length, incorporate it with your text and set it in quotation marks. If it is three lines or more, separate it from your text by a space above and below (three spaces in width in typing), single-space the lines, and omit quotation marks. Usage varies somewhat as to the placing of the left margin of a quotation, but for prose quotations in typed or printed matter it is correct to keep the same margin as that of your own text. The white space above and below the quotation and the single-spacing of the lines are sufficient indication that the passage is quoted. In handwriting such passages should be set in at least a half-inch from the left margin and quoted.

83B. The Necessity of Exact Reference

In making either of these types of notes, carefully record the page or pages of the source of your information. Your reader will often wish to know exactly from where you have derived your facts and ideas, and a general reference to a chapter or section of a book will not be satisfactory.

83C. The Mechanics of Note-Taking

Practice varies as to the type of card used for note-taking. Some use the same size of card as the bibliography cards (3″ x 5″). Others prefer the larger 4″ x 6″ or 5″ x 8″ cards, and still others use full sheets of paper, 8″ x 11″. The 5″ x 8″ card offers sufficient space for most single notes and yet retains the advantages of a card when one is rearranging his notes and filing them.

Since you already have adequate bibliographical information on your bibliography cards, such information on your note card can be greatly simplified. Full names (unless duplicates exist) can be shortened to surnames, complete titles to a word; or if an author is to be represented by only one work in your paper, the title may be omitted altogether.

As you read and make your notes, use a fresh card for each new phase of the material you are summarizing and give it a heading to correspond with that of your topic outline. Thus if an article you are reading has as many as three or four separate divisions of thought that relate sharply to the separate divisions of your subject, you will make out as many different cards each having the author's name, brief title of the work (if needed), the topical heading, the page or pages of the reference, and the note (a summary or a quotation or both). By keeping the divisions of your subject matter thus distinct on separate cards you will be able quickly to rearrange all your notes finally in the pattern of your outline. If a note on a single topic is too long for a single card, add another card with the same heading. The one essential thing to remember in this connection is to limit your notes on any one card to one topic. When you encounter a new theme in your reading, use a new card with the proper heading from your tentative outline.

When you have finished taking all your notes, rearrange the cards, assembling them according to the headings of your outline. Reviewing the cards assembled under your first heading, you will find that they vary somewhat in value, and some of them you may decide to discard. Arrange the remaining cards in the order that seems most logical and effective for the general development of your thought. When you have arranged all the cards thus to conform to your basic plan, you are ready to build your formal outline, based on your topical outline and your assembled information.

84. SENTENCE OUTLINE

Only a well-developed sentence outline will afford a sure test of the validity of your arrangement of your subject matter. If your main headings can be shaped into controlling topic sentences, and the material under them be cast into roughly parallel structures (separate parallel sentences or parallel clauses or phrases subordinate to the main clause headings), you can be relatively sure that your paper will be well organized before you begin its final composition. The sentence outline will ordinarily be from a fourth to a third as long as the completed paper. It is, in effect, stripped of its numbering symbols, an abstract of the paper and needs only to be expanded with full details to become the final paper itself.

For more detailed discussion of the sentence outline see Section 6C 3. Also study the relation of the outline to the text in the illustrative research paper, Section 88B.

85. FIRST DRAFT

In the expansion of the outline into the completed paper, the main headings, now fully formed sentences in the outline, may of course serve as controlling topic sentences, though they may be rephrased at times to advantage. Perhaps your main divisions are substantial enough to call for subdivisions into several paragraphs. If so, such a main heading will serve as a main topic sentence controlling several paragraphs, the number depending largely on the number of subordinate parts. But the effect of choppiness is to be avoided. Subordinate parts that can be effectively united should not be paragraphed separately if they are very short .

In this first draft you will present your own ideas fully and make use of all the pertinent information from your body of notes. As you make use of this material, set down in parentheses the source (author, work, and page or pages) of each allusion or quotation. These temporary parenthetic references will serve to indicate where to place your symbol references to footnotes, and of course should be eliminated in the final draft. You will discover that you have accumulated too many illustrations of certain ideas and, now and then, some related material that does not fully fit the pattern of your thought but clearly has a pertinent value. Such material will often make interesting footnotes, either given in full detail, briefly digested, or referred to in passing. In any event, though you should give ample illustration of your ideas in the main draft, do not load your paper down with unnecessary details, and never let the main thread of the thought be broken by interpolations or digressions. The place for such material, if it is used at all, is in footnotes.

86. FOOTNOTES[2]

86A. The Types of Footnotes

When the first draft of the paper is written, your next concern must be the proper documentation of your material—or the footnotes, as they are conventionally called. Footnotes are of two main sorts, notes of reference and notes of added explanation or comment. The importance of the former has been sufficiently stressed: you must refer the reader to the exact page or pages of the source of your ideas each time that you use them. The value of the second type, the note of comment or explanation, is often not realized by students. This type of note gives you a chance to explain many technical terms whose definition in the text would impede the flow of your thought. It offers you a chance to discuss opposing views or theories that you cannot ignore but that also would interrupt the progress of your thought. It enables you to reinforce your ideas, as indicated above, with added illustrations, summarized or detailed, which would, if used in the text, slow down your thought and violate proportion. Notes of this sort that throw additional light on the subject can be both interesting and valuable. (For an illustration of the use of such notes, see pp. 487–89.)

86B. Arrangement of Footnotes

Footnotes may be related to the main text in one of three ways. They may be placed, as the name suggests, at the foot of the page to which they relate—a familiar practice in books and journals, but hard to accomplish in typing and handwriting. They may be inserted in the text at the point of reference and set off from the text itself by separating lines—a practice easy enough to follow and advantageous for quick communication, but unpleasing to the eye. They may be placed at the end of the paper. Unless your instructor recommends otherwise, use this third method. Obviously notes so placed are hardly "footnotes" in the original sense

[2] See *The MLA Style Sheet* (New York: The Modern Language Association of America, 1951) for a compact but detailed description of the majority practice of a large number of university presses and scholarly journals in the handling of footnotes.

of the name. Hence make a separate formal division of them with a capitalized title: NOTES. (See p. 487 for illustration of this method.)

86C. Numbering and Placing of the Footnote Symbols

There is only one approved system of numbering notes: the use of Arabic numbers, 1, 2, 3, etc., without a period. It is current practice both in printing and in typing to raise the number slightly above the printed line to which it refers, always after the punctuation, if any:

> The importance of one such function has almost certainly been overemphasized in the past: the employment of singing to cover entrances and exits.[8] The theory is that the nature of the platform stage made it desirable to relieve the awkwardness involved in a character's long walk to or from the door by assigning him a clever couplet or a snatch of song. It is illogical, however, to attribute to the Stuart dramatists a sense of embarrassment at the deficiencies of their stage when they knew no other stage and so hardly could have been conscious that their own was deficient.[9]
>
> —William R. Bowden, *The English Dramatic Lyric, 1603–1642* (New Haven, Conn.: Yale University Press, 1951), p. 70.
>
> [8] See, for example, Richmond Noble, *Shakespeare's Use of Song* (London: Humphrey Milford, 1923), p. 84, and Walker, "Popular Songs and Broadside Ballads" [unpublished dissertation]. pp. 61–81.
>
> [9] Most dramatists were, like Shakespeare, conscious of the limitations of their stage; but these limitations are inherent in any stage. Any inconvenience felt to arise from the location of the doors would have been remediable.

In handwriting, the footnote symbol is also placed slightly above the line, but because of the possibility of confusion with other parts of the handwriting it should be enclosed in parentheses or placed in a V-shaped mark.

86D. Structure and Punctuation of Footnotes

Footnotes, even if only phrase references without verbs, function as sentences and should be capitalized and punctuated accordingly. Explanatory footnotes should be written in complete sentences, governed by the same rules of technique that hold for all expository writing. One should not be expansive in footnotes; on the other hand, the footnote is no place for telegraphic style.

86E. Abbreviations

For economy of expression a number of abbreviations, several of them borrowed from Latin, are employed in footnotes. There follows a list of the most commonly used of these abbreviations, together with a few similarly used Latin words that are not abbreviated.

ca.	*circa,* about
cf.	*confer,* compare (Do not use cf. when you merely mean *see.*)
ed.	editor, edition, edited by
et al.	*et alii,* and others
et seq.	*et sequens,* and the following
f., ff.	and the following page(s)
ibid.	*ibidem,* in the same place (that is, the title cited in the note immediately preceding)
infra	below
l., ll.	line(s)
loc. cit.	*loco citato,* in the place cited (that is, in the same passage referred to in a recent note; never followed by a page number)
op. cit.	*opere citato,* in the work cited
p., pp.	page(s)
passim	here and there, throughout the work
q. v.	*quod vide,* which see
sic	thus (used in brackets to indicate a mistake in author's text)
supra	above
tr.	translator, translated by
vide	see
viz.	*videlicet,* namely
vol., vols.	volume(s)

Observe that *ca., et al., et seq., ibid., infra, loc. cit., op. cit., passim, sic, supra,* and *vide* are italicized, and that *infra, passim, sic, supra,* and *vide* are not abbreviated. Though you will encounter *et al., et seq., infra, passim, supra, vide* (sometimes *v.*) and *viz.* in your reading, most writers today commonly use their English equivalents. Many writers consider *op. cit.* an affectation and prefer to use instead the author's last name alone or his name and a short title.

86F. First References in Footnotes

The first reference to any work in a footnote should be fairly complete. If, as in your research paper, you plan to supply a formal bibliography with your work, you may ordinarily omit the name of the publisher, though it is always good practice to name the publisher of relatively recent works. The standard order of details may be illustrated by the following examples:

FOR BOOKS

[1] W. H. Clemen, *The Development of Shakespeare's Imagery* (Cambridge, Mass.: Harvard Univ. Press, 1951), p. 25.

[2] Harley Granville-Barker, *Prefaces to Shakespeare* (London: Sidgwick & Jackson, 1927), I, 206.

[3] G. L. Kittredge, ed., *The Complete Works of Shakespeare* (Boston: Ginn & Co., 1936), p. 36.

[4] Sir Sidney Lee, *A Life of William Shakespeare* (New York, 1917), p. 67.

FOR ARTICLES IN PERIODICALS

[5] W. Stacy Johnson, "The Genesis of Ariel," *Shakespeare Quarterly*, II (July, 1951), 221.

Observe carefully the punctuation of these notes. Book titles are italicized, the title of the magazine article is enclosed in quotation marks, place of publication and date are enclosed in parentheses, and each detail is separated from the following one by a comma. Note that no comma precedes the first parenthesis mark: the title of the work and its place and date of publication become one item through the use of parentheses. If volume number is given, the abbreviation *p.* is not necessary before the page number. Brackets are used for an unavoidable parenthesis within a parenthesis. Study the application of these instructions in the student paper in Section 88B.

86G. Subsequent References

Second and succeeding references are briefer than first references. (1) You may use the author's last name and the title of the work by itself; (2) you may abridge the title (if possible); (3) you may use the Latin terms *ibid., loc. cit., op. cit.* in place of the title;

(4) or better still, if your bibliography lists only one work by an author you may use simply the author's last name and the page number of the material to which you refer:

(1) Clemen, *The Development of Shakespeare's Imagery*, p. 37.
(2) Clemen, *Shakespeare's Imagery*, p. 37.
(2) Johnson, "The Genesis of Ariel," p. 221.
(3) Granville-Barker, *op. cit.,* I, 220.
(3) *Ibid.*, p. 223.
(3) *Loc. cit.*
(4) Clemen, p. 42.

Note that *ibid.* as used above refers to Granville-Barker, *op. cit.,* I. If one wished to refer to Granville-Barker again after an intervening note it would be necessary to repeat the name, since *ibid.* can be used only when no other references intervene. Note also that *loc. cit.* as used above refers to a specific page in a specific work and may not be used after an intervening note.

In general the tendency today is to cite the author's surname only, with the page number, in second and succeeding references (as in the student paper, Section 88B). If, however, one is using two or more works by the same author, it is necessary to cite the title of each work (abridged if possible in subsequent references). If the author's name or the name of his work is used in the main text, one may refer to the page alone: do not abbreviate *page* when referring to a single page in this type of note:

[1] Page 16.

Whatever method you use, be consistent. If you use *op. cit.* for subsequent references, use it throughout your notes. If you use the author's name and the page number, use that form only, except of course when two or more works by the same author are involved and you must add the title.

87. BIBLIOGRAPHY

When you have completed and verified the documentation, you should next prepare your formal bibliography, which will be the last division of your paper. You will of course ignore works that you did not make use of: all those that were useful will constitute the bibliography of the paper.

This bibliography may be divided into two sections, one devoted to books and pamphlets, and the other to encyclopedia, magazine, and newspaper articles. The works in each section should be arranged alphabetically according to authors, the last name being given first. The standard form is as follows (note carefully the punctuation, capitalization, italicizing for books, and quoting for articles):

For Books

Connolly, Cyril. *The Rock Pool.* Norfolk, Conn.: New Directions, 1936.

Walker, James Blaine. *The Epic of American Industry.* New York: Harper & Bros., 1949.

For Articles

Gideonse, Harry D. "An Unsentimental Look at India." *Harper's Magazine,* CCVIII (June, 1954), 78–84.

Pearce, Ray Harvey. "Wallace Stevens: The Life of the Imagination." *PMLA,* LXVI (September, 1951), 561–82.

88. FINAL DRAFT. A SAMPLE RESEARCH PAPER

88A. Revising and Writing the Final Draft

You are now ready to revise your first draft. Scan once more all the details of your work, its organization, its paragraphing, its sentence structure, and the mechanics of writing, with close attention to diction, grammar, punctuation, and spelling. Rereading the first draft may suggest that certain material you have used should be reduced to footnotes; occasionally some footnote may contain a point that should be incorporated in the text. Rereading may also reveal awkward sentences that need rephrasing, cumbrous passive structures that should be made active, dull passages that require the color of illustration. If you have any illustrative pictures, graphs, or drawings to make your text more appealing, this is the time to insert them. This is also the time to eliminate the parenthetic references to your sources, which you have now developed into carefully formed footnotes.

After having completed these revisions, you are ready to begin writing the final copy of your paper. You should of course write or type this copy with careful attention to the accepted rules for manuscript. Be sure to proofread your work thoroughly. Finally, arrange the several parts of your paper in a folder in the following order:

1. The Title Page
2. The Sentence Outline
3. The Paper
4. The Notes (unless put at bottom of page)
5. The Bibliography

The title page should bear, in addition to the title, your name, your class, and the date as indicated in the example immediately following.

88B. A Sample Research Paper

The student research paper following is not offered as a model that you are expected to imitate. Your research problem may result in a paper of fewer or more main divisions of thought, and you may have occasion to use fewer or more notes than this student has employed in documenting his ideas. But the organization of the paper and its general development may be suggestive to you. You may find it profitable to examine this paper in the light of the recommendations in this chapter to see how closely the student follows them.

THE AURORA BOREALIS

by

Paul A. Godwin
English 108 F2
March 29, 19—

CONTENTS

THE AURORA BOREALIS

I. Men have speculated about the nature of the aurora borealis for centuries.

   A. Aristotle realized that auroras were natural phenomena.

   B. Seneca offers a vivid description of them.

   C. In the late Renaissance they were confused with comets.

   D. Superstitious people have always considered them supernatural.

   E. Critical examination of auroras began in the eighteenth century.

II. The aurora borealis has three main classes of forms.

   A. One class is without ray structure.

      1. Of this type, homogeneous arcs are the commonest form and have the following characteristics:

         a) The arcs have various breadths.

         b) They may extend in parallels like rainbows across the sky.

         c) Isolated parts may appear.

         d) Their lower border is often sharply defined, but the upper limits are diffused.

         e) Upper arcs may curve back on themselves to form lower arcs.

         f) They may be relatively stable or they may pulsate rhythmically.

ii

2. A second form is made up of homogeneous bands.
   a) These resemble homogeneous arcs, but are irregular.
   b) They tend to move more rapidly than arcs.
3. A third form is made up of luminous surfaces.
   a) These are indistinct cloudlike areas.
   b) They may occur after brilliant rays and curtains.
   c) Like the homogeneous arcs they may pulsate rhythmically.

B. A second class of auroras shows ray structure.
1. Rays may appear singly.
   a) These rays vary in width and length.
   b) They are parallel to the lines of magnetic force.
2. These auroras often start as homogeneous forms.
   a) They break up into parallel rays of various lengths and widths.
   b) Arcs and bands of this type are similar to the homogeneous forms but composed of rays.
3. Bands of rays may form draperies.
4. Near the zenith they may form a corona.

C. The flaming aurora is the most impressive of the three classes.
1. It is composed of an undulating wave or waves of light rapidly moving toward the zenith.
2. It may have the effect of an invisible wave causing patches and rays to appear momentarily.

iii

III. The intensity and the color of the auroral light vary.

A. The total light is never strong.

1. Stars can be seen through it.

2. It is occasionally reflected on snow and water.

B. Auroras take on numerous colors.

1. The commonest is greenish-yellow.

2. Other colors are frequently seen, namely bluish white, violet gray, red, and reddish white.

3. The colors are often combined.

a) The draperies are of this type.

(1) The base is a reddish color.

(2) The body itself is of a greenish-yellow color.

b) The rays contain all colors.

4. Auroras also contain invisible colors, infrared and ultraviolet.

IV. The height of the aurora borealis is variable and difficult to ascertain.

A. The spatial position is calculated from photographs.

1. Photographs are taken simultaneously from two or more stations.

2. Position is calculated from the shift over the stars.

B. There is much variation in the height.

1. The height of the base varies.

a) The average height of the base is sixty to seventy miles.

iv

b) It occasionally reaches 125 to 250 miles.

c) It is rarely very low.

(1) It has been seen between an observer and a mountain.

(2) It seemed to come to the ground around a house.

(3) It occurs in small areas around the magnetic pole.

2. The upper limits are variable.

a) Rays sometimes extend up to 750 miles.

b) Auroras above 250 miles are in both sunlight and darkness.

V. The frequency of auroras varies with the latitude.

A. There is an area of maximum frequency.

1. This is a small oval around the magnetic pole.

2. It is approximately sixty degrees north latitude in the western hemisphere and seventy degrees north latitude in the eastern hemisphere.

B. Isochasms mark the diminishing frequency north and south.

1. The average number is one hundred a year in Norway.

2. It is one every ten years in the Mediterranean.

VI. The aurora borealis shows a tendency to recur at regular intervals.

A. There is an auroral cycle of 27.3 days.

1. There is close agreement with the period of solar rotation.

v

2. The period fluctuates.
   a) When the period is longer there are fewer auroras.
   b) When the period is shorter there are many auroras.
3. There is a relationship between the lunar cycle and auroral frequency.
   a) There is an increase in auroras when the moon is south.
   b) There is a decrease when the moon is north.

B. There is also an eleven-year cycle of auroral frequency.
   1. This cycle follows the sunspot cycle.
   2. It lags behind the sunspot maxima.

C. Auroras also have a double annual period.
   1. The greatest number occur in March and September.
   2. The maxima occur at the time of most sunspots.

VII. There are two main theories explaining auroral phenomena, namely the ultraviolet light theory and the corpuscular theory.

A. The ultraviolet light theory assumes the presence of neutral molecules of gas at the outer edge of the atmosphere.
   1. These molecules are thrust up by thermal impacts and fall back by gravity.
   2. The molecules strike ionized particles as they oscillate.

vi

a) They receive energy in this way.

b) This energy propels them 30,000 to 60,000 miles into space.

3. The molecules become ionized by ultraviolet light from the sun.
4. As charged particles, they are attracted to lines of force.

a) They move along these lines to polar regions.

b) They descend to low altitudes and become concentrated.

5. Auroral light is the result of two things.

a) One is the collision of activated nitrogen and oxygen atoms.

b) The other is the excited atoms becoming normal.

6. The variations in auroral displays are due to two causes.

a) One cause is found in winds of high altitude.

b) A second cause lies in the intensity and duration of ultraviolet flares emitted by the sun.

B. The corpuscular theory assumes that streams of particles come from the sun.

1. These streams have three characteristics.

a) They are electrically neutral.

b) They are relatively narrow.

c) The streams move at speeds from 600 to 1,200 miles a second.

vii

2. The particles become ionized while traveling to earth.
3. They strike particles of atmospheric gas.
   a) The molecules break up into ions and atoms.
   b) They become electrically charged.
4. These charged particles are affected by magnetic force.
   a) They move along lines of magnetic force to polar regions.
   b) They descend to low altitudes and become concentrated.
5. Auroral light is produced by molecular energy.
   a) Nitrogen and oxygen particles collide and break up into ions.
   b) The ions recombine into molecules.
   c) The process of recombination releases energy producing the aurora.
6. According to this theory, irregularities in auroras depend on the nature of the solar streams.
   a) Variations result from differences in the density, speed, length, and width of the streams.
   b) The stream variations themselves depend on the circumstances of the emission of particles from the sun.

THE AURORA BOREALIS

The aurora borealis, more commonly known as the northern lights, is principally a celestial phenomenon which is visible on the earth. Of all the lights of the night sky, none captures and excites the imagination as does the aurora borealis; and men have speculated about its nature for centuries. In ancient Greece the versatile Aristotle recognized the northern lights as a natural phenomenon in his discussion of "burning flames."[1] About three centuries later, Seneca, the Roman philosopher and naturalist, wrote a brief but remarkably accurate description of these celestial fires, as he termed them.[2] Both Aristotle and Seneca discuss them as associated with meteors and comets; hence it is not surprising that in the late Renaissance they should be confused with comets. At this period, and doubtless in all ages, superstitious people considered auroral displays as supernatural, portending wars, pestilence, and famine, or heralding the end of the world. Not until the eighteenth century, when Halley in 1716 noticed the association between magnetic disturbances and the northern lights, were auroral phenomena considered critically.[3]

Auroras are extremely variable; no two are exactly alike, and each individual display is constantly changing in appearance and brilliance.[4] In spite of the continual change, a number of general auroral forms are recognized. These are divided into three principal classes, those without any ray structure, those with ray structure, and the flaming aurora, composed of rapidly moving waves of light.[5] Any auroral display is made up of one or more of these forms.

There are several fairly distinct rayless forms. Of these, homogeneous arcs are the most common. The arcs of this type are of various breadths and may extend in parallels like a rainbow across the northern sky, though at times only isolated parts of arcs may appear. Their lower border is often sharply defined, but the upper limits tend to be diffused and hazy. The lower arcs may be formed at times by the upper arcs curving back on themselves.[6] These arcs may be relatively static or they may pulsate rhythmically. A second type of rayless auroras manifests itself in homogeneous bands. These bands somewhat resemble arcs, but are irregular and tend to move more rapidly. The bands may be narrow or wide; sometimes they appear folded and may suggest the effect of a curtain. Many times the rayless aurora has no definite shape but consists of indistinct, irregular, luminous cloudlike areas. These may follow the occurrence of brilliant rays or curtain-type auroras. Like the arcs and bands, these diffused surfaces may pulsate rhythmically, becoming alternately brilliant and dim or disappearing altogether.[7]

Auroras that show ray structure also have a variety of forms. They may be single rays of varying widths and lengths, parallel to the lines of magnetic force. Often they start as homogeneous forms which become brighter and break into parallel rays. Observations show that the rays do not deviate much more than ten degrees from being parallel to the lines of magnetic force; however, from the earth perspective makes the rays appear to converge.[8] Arcs and bands with ray structure are similar to homogeneous arcs and bands, but are constructed of parallel rays which may be close together or scattered. Long, brilliant bands of rays may take forms known as draperies. A yet more striking form is the corona formed by bands of rays or draperies converging towards the magnetic zenith.

The flaming aurora is the most impressive auroral form. It is composed of a rapidly moving, strong, undulating wave or waves of light moving towards the zenith. It may have the effect of an invisible wave which rhythmically causes patches and rays to appear momentarily[9] . . .

[At this point for the sake of space three pages of this paper have been omitted. For a digest of this subject matter, the reader may refer to the outline.]

It seems generally agreed that auroral phenomena have their origins in the sun. The direct relation which exists between auroral displays and solar rotation and the passage of sunspots across the solar equator can lead to no other conclusion;[29] but unfortunately the nature of the causal agent is still a mystery. A number of theories have been advanced to account for the relationship between the sun and the auroras; two of these have gained prominence, namely the ultraviolet light theory and the corpuscular theory. Both theories are similar in that they assume that charged particles explain auroral phenomena, but are quite opposed as to the source of the particles.[30]

The ultraviolet light theory assumes that on the outer edges of our atmosphere there are neutral molecules of gas (nitrogen, oxygen, helium) which are alternately driven upward by thermal impacts from below and then fall back as a result of the earth's gravity. As they oscillate up and down some of these molecules strike ionized particles, receiving energy from them.[31] This energy projects the neutral molecules and atoms from 30,000 to 60,000 miles into space.[32] The far-flung molecules are ionized by blasts of ultraviolet light emitted by the sun.[33]

The molecules, having been ionized, are now charged particles, and these particles are attracted to the earth's lines of magnetic force. The lines of force converge at the magnetic pole, and the ions moving along these lines descend to a low level and become concentrated.[34] As the ions become concentrated, collisions between the particles occur more frequently. It is the collision of activated nitrogen atoms with atoms of oxygen and excited oxygen atoms returning to their normal state which produces the light of the aurora borealis.[35] Variations in auroral displays are attributed to winds of the high altitude producing "fitful gusts and clouds of high flying atoms,"[36] and to differences in the intensity and duration of the flares of ultraviolet light.[37]

8

The corpuscular theory assumes that the sun emits a stream of electrically neutral particles. The stream of particles is relatively narrow and moves toward the earth at speeds varying from 600 to 1,200 miles a second.[38] As these particles travel through space, they in some way become ionized. These charged particles bombard the molecules of atmospheric gas, causing the molecules to ionize and break up into excited atoms. Since ions and activated atoms are charged particles, they are influenced by the earth's lines of magnetic force. The particles move along the lines of force to the polar regions where they become concentrated and, as in the ultraviolet theory, the ions and atoms collide and regroup into molecules with the attendant release of energy. This results in the luminosity of the aurora borealis.[39] According to this theory, the irregularities of auroras are a result of variations in the density, speed, length, and width of the solar stream. The stream variations depend on the circumstances of the emission of the particles from the sun.

9

NOTES

1. The Works of Aristotle, ed. W. D. Ross, Vol. III, Meteorologica, tr. E. W. Webster (Oxford: Clarendon Press, 1931). Books 1, 4, 5.
2. Physical Science in the Time of Nero: Being a Translation of the "Quaestiones Naturales" of Seneca by John Clark (London: Macmillan & Co., Ltd., 1910), pp. 37-41. Part of this description in a translation cited as taken from Angot (not in our library) is used by Sydney Chapman and Julius Bartels in the introduction to their study of auroras (Geomagnetism, [Oxford, 1940], I, 449).
3. "The Aurora of January 25-26, 1938," Nature, CXLI (1938), 234.
4. Some excellent descriptions of auroral displays are given in Chapman and Bartels, I, 450-53; see also the illustrations, pp. 454-59. Other rather good descriptions are found in S. S. Berry, "A Noteworthy Aurora," Science, XC (1939), 490-91; "The Aurora of January 25-26, 1938," Nature, CXLI (1938), 232-35; and C. Störmer, "Photographic Measurements of the Great Aurora of January 25-26," Nature, CXLI (1938), 955-57.
5. This classification, with its terminology, is based on that by Chapman and Bartels, I, 454-56.
6. Chapman and Bartels, I, 454.
7. Chapman and Bartels, I, 455.
8. C. W. Gartlein, "The Aurora Borealis," The Encyclopedia

10

Americana, II (1954), 557.

9. Chapman and Bartels, I, 456-57.

[For the sake of space the notes of the pages omitted in the body of the paper are not reproduced here.]

29. On the relationship of sun spots and auroras, see H. T. Stetson, "The Present State of Solar Activity and Associated Phenomena," *Science*, XC (1939), 483. So far as the proponents of the ultraviolet light hypothesis are concerned (see page 7 of the text) there is no marked seasonal variation. A fifty-five-year study between 1885 and 1938, however, shows March and September as months of maxima for sunspots and June and November as months of minima (Clayton, II, 402).

30. There have been other theories explaining auroral displays. Like rainbows and haloes, auroras were at one time thought to be the result of reflected or refracted light. The theory was invalidated when no true polarization could be found (Chapman and Bartels, I, 476). Another explanation regarded auroras as the result of the earth cutting through "cosmic lines of electric force" (Clayton, II, 397).

31. Maris and Hulburt, "A Theory of Auroras and Magnetic Storms," *Physical Review*, XXXIII (1929), 415.

32. Maris and Hulburt, p. 416.

33. Maris and Hulburt, p. 417.

34. Maris and Hulburt, p. 418.

35. "The Aurora of January 25-26 (1938)," *Nature*, CXLI (1938), 235.

36. Maris and Hulburt, p. 420.
37. Maris and Hulburt, pp. 422-25. Maris and Hulburt contend that the flares of ultraviolet light which cause auroras should also have some effect on comets.
    In studying the behavior of thirty-one comets from 1848-1927, they found this condition to be true (H. B. Maris and E. O. Hulburt, "Comets and Terrestrial Magnetic Storms," Physical Review, XXXIII [1929], 1046-60).
38. Chapman and Bartels, II, 852-54. The particles may be other than neutral. Some magnetic effects are accountable for only by positively charged particles and others by negatively charged particles.
39. The luminous effect of the passage of electricity through a vacuum tube containing a rare gas led to the hypothesis of similar phenomena in auroras. Early spectroscopic analysis seemed to bear this out.
    A green spectral line appeared in every spectograph of auroral light. In 1925 McLennan and Shrum identified the line as an oxygen line (Chapman and Bartels, I, 479). The analogy may still hold, however, since a small quantity of argon added to oxygen in the vacuum tube greatly increases the oxygen line. The line was also reproduced by rolling a mercury drop on the inside of a glass bulb containing neon with a trace of nitrogen and helium (G. Dejardin, "The Light of the Night Sky," Reviews of Modern Physics, VIII [1936], 20).

BIBLIOGRAPHY

BOOKS

Chapman, Sydney, and Bartels, Julius. Geomagnetism, Vols. I and II. Oxford: Clarendon Press, 1940.

Clarke, John. Physical Science in the Time of Nero. London: Macmillan and Co., Ltd., 1910.

Clayton, H. Helm. Solar Relations to Weather and Life, Vol. II. Canton, Mass.: Clayton Weather Service, 1943.

Humphries, William Jackson. Physics of the Air. New York: McGraw-Hill Book Co., Inc., 1929.

Petterssen, Sverre. Introduction to Meteorology. New York: McGraw-Hill Book Co., Inc., 1941.

Stetson, Harlan True. Sunspots and Their Effects. New York: McGraw-Hill Book Co., Inc., 1937.

ARTICLES

"The Aurora of January 25-26, 1938." Nature, CXLI (1938), 232-35.

Berry, S. S. "A Noteworthy Aurora," Science, XC (1939), 490-91.

Chapman, S. "The Audibility and Lowermost Altitude of the Aurora Polaris," Nature, CXXVII (1931), 341-42.

Corlin, A. "The Low Altitude Aurora of November 16, 1929, Nature, CXXVII (1931), 928.

15

Cummings, A. C. "A Low Aurora and its Effects on a Radio Receiver," Nature, CXXVII (1931), 108.

Dejardin, G. "The Light of the Night Sky," Reviews of Modern Physics, VIII (1936), 1-21.

Gartlein, C. W. "Aurora Borealis," The Encyclopedia Americana (1954), II, 557.

Maris, H. B., and Hulburt, E. O. "Comets and Terrestrial Magnetic Storms," Physical Review, XXXIII (1929), 1046-60. "A Theory of Auroras and Magnetic Storms," Physical Review, XXXIII (1929), 412-15.

Simpson, G. "Low Altitude Aurora," Nature, CXXVII (1931), 663.

Stetson, H. T. "The Present State of Solar Activity and Associated Phenomena," Science, XC (1939), 482-84.

Störmer, C. "Photographic Measurements of the Great Aurora of January 25-26," Nature, CXLI (1936), 955-57.

Chapter 11

LETTER WRITING

One important type of written communication is letter writing, which most of us practice daily in one form or another. Letters are mainly of two sorts, personal and business letters, and to write both kinds effectively should be the aim of every student.

89. PERSONAL (OR FRIENDLY) LETTER

Everyone writes personal letters of a sort, but very few of these letters are good or invite a second reading. Most are written with little regard for content, form, or style. A well-written personal letter not only informs and interests the reader but also develops the skill and the mentality of the writer: no one can write a good letter without growing intellectually.

The personal letter is informal in tone. There are no rigidly prescribed forms, but here as elsewhere order is desirable. Thus it is good to let the intended reader know when and where the letter was written, preferably at the beginning of the letter (the heading), to use the conventional salutation (*Dear John:* or *Dear Jane:*), and to close with the conventional complimentary close (*Sincerely yours, Yours cordially,* and variations). But the letter may be as informal as you wish. Use contractions freely and write very much as you talk. No one expects or wishes to receive from a friend a letter that reads like a formal exposition. But respect for order of thought is valuable here also. Develop the habit of thinking and writing in paragraphs. Punctuate with care, and look up the spelling of words of which you are unsure —unless you wish to give your reader the little thrill of superiority that will come to him as he smiles at your mistakes. One of the best ways to learn to write well is to write your personal letters with care. If you use slang at all, use it sparingly, and avoid trite words and phrases.

Most important of all is the sense of your letters, the ideas that you are conveying. The dull writer often contents himself with listing events and happenings. He writes that he has attended a lecture on poetry and enjoyed it, that he went to a dance and took a girl, and that the football team won its annual game with Sardis University. The good writer, so far as he has time for it, re-creates each experience. The reader of the letter enjoys with him some salient points of the lecture by E. E. Cummings, learns the nature of the Cinderella Ball and visualizes the scene, almost sees the girl, and hears the shouts of the crowd in the stadium as the team scores a touchdown on a trick play. When you write home get the habit of giving your readers little word pictures of your experiences.

90. BUSINESS LETTER

Business letters are for the most part more formal in tone than personal letters, and their forms are set by convention. The content of the letter is governed by the rules and principles of good exposition: a good business letter must be carefully planned, developed in logical paragraphs (these are ordinarily shorter than the usual paragraphs of expository themes and articles), carefully punctuated, and written in diction free from slang and hackneyed expressions. Its content must be deliberately aimed, without eccentricity, to arouse and hold the interest of the reader.

91. APPEARANCE AND FORM OF BUSINESS LETTERS

The first impression a reader has of a letter is that of its physical appearance. He will be aware, even if only subconsciously, of the quality of paper used and the way the message looks on the page. It is important, then, to use a good quality of paper and to write (preferably typewrite) your letter with utmost care for neatness and for effective arrangement on the page. Though allowance may be made for typing errors that can be corrected through erasure without marring the appearance of the letter, struck-over corrections are not acceptable. Any revisions or additions to a letter require its rewriting.

Business letters are generally written on good bond paper sheets 8½ inches by 11 inches in size. Half sheets (8½ by 5½ inches) are sometimes used for short letters, but more commonly such letters are written on 7½- by 10½-inch sheets, the size used mainly by executives. Business letters may conform to any one of the three generally approved styles of arrangement, semiblock style, block style, and indented style, examples of all of which follow. Consistency is necessary: do not mix styles in one letter. Whatever form you select, use it without variation.

The fourth example, the executive type of letter (so named because of its wide use by executives) may employ any of the three styles. Such letters usually place the inside address at the end of the letter (as in the example). They vary from the formal to the informal: the writer of Letter IV might have begun with a formal salutation (*Dear Mr. Gauthier*:) if he had wished to do so.

LETTER I: SEMIBLOCK STYLE

EADING
typed)

21 Parker Street
Boston 13, Massachusetts
January 31, 19--

NSIDE
DDRESS

Mr. Richard Parkhurst
Sales Director
American Handicrafts, Inc.
106 Park Street
New York 10, New York

ALUTATION

Dear Mr. Parkhurst:

ODY

On January nineteenth you asked me to prepare a report in which I would plan a campaign to advertise a retail store on South Street in Boston selling handicrafts and products of New England. I am now submitting my report, The Handicraft Society, for your consideration.

Since the store is a local one with no mail-order business, I have limited my investigation for schemes of promotion to Boston. To get up-to-date information I consulted several people in advertising agencies and representatives of three arts and crafts groups. As a result, I am recommending a basic program of newspaper advertising and window and counter display, combined with a public relations program of talks and lectures.

I hope that the suggestions I am making for the project meet with your approval.

OMPLIMENTARY
LOSE

Sincerely yours,

Abigail P. Hutchins

GNATURE

Abigail P. Hutchins

LETTER II: BLOCK STYLE

PRINTED HEADING

UNIVERSAL ENGINEERING COMPANY
389 MAIN STREET
BOSTON 8, MASSACHUSETTS

December 8, 19--

Underwood Supply Company
1109 Twenty-third Street
Chicago 21, Illinois

Attention of Sales Department

Gentlemen:

Will you please send us the following supplies listed in your catalogue No. 41:

5 packages of typing paper No. 2106 at $2.50 each package	$12.50
2 quart bottles of blue ink No. 208 at $2.75 each bottle	5.50
3 packages of carbon paper No. 616 at 50 cents each	1.50
	$19.50

Please send this order by parcel post as soon as possible to the address above. We are enclosing a postal money order for the total cost, $19.50.

Very truly yours,

UNIVERSAL ENGINEERING COMPANY

Felicia Hemans

Secretary to Mr. Roger Smart,
Purchasing Agent.

Enclosure

LETTER III: INDENTED STYLE

4300 Austin Street,
Portland 6, Oregon,
October 7, 19--.

Dr. Alexander Macheath,
Upper Brule Mission,
Foxville, South Dakota.

Dear Dr. Macheath:

On October fifth I mailed you five packages of clothing for your mission.

This clothing was contributed by members of the Young Adults' Club, the club for young working people of Emmanuel Church, Portland. The Reverend Mr. Richard Blackwell is our adviser, and Miss Hazel Sparks, chairman of the Women's Guild, has been active in collecting and packing the clothes.

We sincerely hope that this small contribution will be helpful to you.

Very truly yours,

Margaret P. Honeywell

Margaret P. Honeywell
Young Adults' Club

Copies to Miss Sparks
The Reverend Mr. Blackwell

LETTER IV: EXECUTIVE TYPE

Economics Department
UNIVERSITY OF TEXAS
AUSTIN, TEXAS

February 6, 19--

Dear Bob:

I should like you to meet Mr. William Landon, who was graduated last June with honors in economics. Mr. Landon did excellent work in all his courses with me and wrote one of the best theses I have had. We all think highly of him here.

Mr. Landon is moving to Memphis with his family and would like to find work with some firm that may be interested in securing a first-class accountant. I should appreciate your helping him if you are able to do so.

It would be very pleasant to see you again. Are you coming to the reunion in June? If so you must be sure to visit us.

Cordially yours,

John B. Borden

John B. Borden

Mr. Robert Gauthier, Secretary
The Chamber of Commerce
318 Lewis Avenue
Memphis, Tennessee

92. PARTS OF THE BUSINESS LETTER

As indicated above in the margin of Letter I (Semiblock Style), business letters have six parts: a heading, an inside address, a salutation, a body, a complimentary close, and a signature.

92A. The Heading

The heading of a business letter includes the address of the writer and the date of the writing. For a letter representing a person, the arrangement of the heading as given in any of the four letters is conventional, though if the letter is typed the heading may be centered at the top of the sheet if the writer wishes. Firms and organizations usually have a printed letterhead with the name and address centered at the top of the sheet, and one need only add the date, which may be centered about three spaces below the heading or placed to end at, and hence define, the right margin. If the heading is typewritten, it is arranged to end at the right margin as in Letter I.

It is important to observe the right punctuation of the heading. Observe that in Letters I and II only two commas are used, the first to separate city and state, the second to separate the day of the month and the year. This type of limited punctuation is known as open punctuation. In Letter III commas are used after every item of the address except the last, which ends with a period. This is called close punctuation. With both block forms the tendency is to use open punctuation; with the indented form, the custom is to use close punctuation. Whatever form (and consequent punctuation) is adopted for the heading should be observed uniformly also in the inside address and the address on the envelope.

Avoid abbreviations in the names of streets, states, and months (observe the practice in the letters above). Do not write *Ave., St., Rd.*: write *Avenue, Street, Road.* Do not write *Jan. 1st* (*2d, 3d,* etc.): write *January 1, 2, 3,* etc.). Do not write *1/20/19—*: write *January 20, 19—.* On the other hand, the British practice of writing *20 January 19—* has merit and may be used as an alternate form.

92B. The Inside Address

The inside address should begin at the left margin, four to eight spaces lower than the date as in the first three examples given. In long letters observe four spaces, six for those of medium length, and eight for short letters. In somewhat less formal letters, as in the executive type (Letter IV), the inside address may be placed at the end of the letter, four spaces lower than the signature, beginning at the left margin.

The inside address includes the title and name of the person, or the name of the organization to which the letter is written, and the place of residence or location (see the examples given). Use the form of a person's name that you believe he would use himself (always use his given names or initials). If a firm abbreviates any part of its name in its letterhead, follow its lead:

W. August, Inc.
Orlando, Florida

Be sure to use the appropriate title. Always use the title of doctors of medicine (surgery, dentistry, psychiatry, etc.), and place the title first: *Dr. A. L. Hepburn* (not: *A. L. Hepburn, M.D.*). In university circles instructors with the title of Doctor of Philosophy (Ph.D.) may be addressed as *Dr.* or *Mr.* (*Miss, Mrs.*), depending on the fashion of the university. The title *Professor* (not *Prof.*) may be used in addressing any teacher above the rank of instructor. Clergymen may be addressed according to the conventions of their churches:

The Rev. Mr. A. R. Nelson
The Right Reverend Dr. R. N. O'Brien

In addressing an official of any organization, always use his name unless you are instructed to do otherwise. Do not write:

The Chairman
The Committee of Admissions

Write:

Professor R. W. Sumner, Chairman
The Committee of Admissions

Brief titles following the name may be placed immediately after the name. If they are disproportionately long, however, they may be dropped to the second line of the address:

Mr. William E. Foxwell
Superintendent of Public Works
Winston-Salem, North Carolina

If you wish the letter called to the attention of some member of a firm or group, words to that effect may be placed below the address as in Letter II.

92C. The Salutation

The salutation begins at the left margin two or three spaces below the inside address. In addressing a person, use his title and his last name, prefaced by the proper term of salutation:

Dear Dr. Hinton:
Dear Professor Wentworth:
Dear Mr. [Miss, Mrs.] Snow:

If you wish to be very formal, you may write: *My dear Dr. Hinton:*. If you wish to be entirely impersonal or distant write: *Dear Sir:* or *My dear Sir:*. In addressing a company or an organization, write: *Gentlemen:* (not: *Dear Sirs:*). An organization composed of women should be addressed as *Ladies* or *Mesdames.* Regularly use the colon after the title: *Dear Mr. Weston:*. Commas may be used in more informal letters, but the colon can be used for all letters. No other marks of punctuation are permissible.

See also *Webster's New International Dictionary* (second edition), pp. 3012–14 for salutations to people of official rank and to clergymen.

92D. The Body

The size of the letter you plan to write determines the arrangement of the whole letter on the page. If what you have to say will occupy the greater part of a page or more, you should plan to begin the heading approximately one and a half inches from the top, and observe margins of one and a half inches on the left, a half inch on the right, and an inch at the bottom of the page. If your material clearly exceeds this amount of space, increase the margins at top and bottom so as to have at least two or three lines (preferably a paragraph) of the body on the second page. Avoid a single or "widow" line at the bottom of the page or at the top of the next page. A complimentary close and signature should not be crowded into the margin at the bottom of the page, nor should they be placed at the top of a second page by themselves.

The second page should have an identifying heading, including the name of the person addressed, the page number, and the date of the letter:

Professor William Elton 2 January 14, 19—

Use Arabic numbers only. The first page is not numbered.

For short letters the margins at top and bottom should be increased inversely to the size of the letter. Double-space very short letters.

The paragraph indention of the body of the letter depends on where one chooses to begin the first paragraph. Common practice for single-spaced letters is to begin two spaces below the salutation and ten spaces from the left margin (five spaces for double-spaced letters) and to use corresponding indentions for paragraphs. Another practice, that of unmodified block form, is to begin at the left margin and to indicate paragraphs only by means of additional spacing between paragraphs, as in Letter II.

Though allowance is made for a personal approach, most business letters are somewhat formal in tone, as observed above. Contractions are sparingly used. Slang, trite phrases, and jargon are carefully avoided. Though it is good to acknowledge receipt of a previous letter, do not use outworn formulas. Do not say: "Yours of the 21st received and contents duly noted." Say: "Thank you for your letter of January 21. We have been considering your suggestion that . . ." or begin yet more directly: "Your suggestion of January 21 that we meet in Phoenix is acceptable to some of us, but . . ." It should be re-emphasized that careful organization of thought is required. All the rules for good exposition apply in the writing of this, the substance of your letter. Vivid and correct expression, careful punctuation, and perfect spelling are necessary. There is no valid excuse for misspelling in any letter written by a college student. A poorly written letter is a lost opportunity.

Just as you avoid trite phrases in beginning your letter and in its text, avoid them also in the concluding lines. Do not say, "I beg to remain" or "Hoping that you will answer soon, I remain . . ." Such words are a waste of time. When you have come to the end of what you have to say, stop. Just like that.

92E. The Complimentary Close

The complimentary close also varies somewhat in arrangement. It may be aligned with the paragraph indention or the colon of the salutation. An extreme block form has it begin at the left margin, but most who use block form prefer to begin it more conventionally, as in the examples shown.

The complimentary close may be any of the following accepted phrases, those most commonly used being given first:

Very truly yours,
Yours very truly,
Sincerely yours,
Yours sincerely,
Yours truly,
Truly yours,
Cordially yours,
Faithfully yours,
Respectfully yours,

In informal letters *Sincerely yours* is most commonly used and is becoming increasingly used in nearly all types of business correspondence. You may use *Respectfully yours* when you have respect for the attainments of the one to whom you write, but *Sincerely yours* will suffice for letters even to persons of this sort.

Capitalize the first letter only of these phrases, and use commas after them.

92F. The Signature

The signature must be written (not typed) in ink (preferably black) about three spaces below the complimentary close, and it should be reasonably legible. To make sure that it can be read, place a typewritten signature four spaces below the written signature. The point of beginning depends on the length of the name. It is generally considered desirable to have the name end somewhere near the right margin, though practice varies. In extreme block form, of course, it would begin at the left margin, but this style is still an innovation.

It is customary for a married woman to sign her personal name, followed by her married name in parentheses:

Candace L. Martin
(Mrs. John R. Martin)

An unmarried woman may prefix *Miss* in parentheses: (Miss) Marion Sheridan. This practice is especially desirable if the name does not clearly indicate the sex of the writer.

92G. Folding the Letter

Procedure varies according to the type of stationery and envelope used.

Folding of the usual 8½- by 11-inch sheet for a No. 6¾ envelope (6½ by 3⅝ inches):

As the letter lies flat on the desk before you, bring the bottom of the sheet up to within a quarter-inch of the top; fold sharply with a pen or paper knife; then bringing the right end over to approximately two-thirds of the width of the sheet, fold it again; next, bring the left side over to about a quarter-inch of the second fold, and fold finally.

Folding for a No. 9 (8⅞ by 3⅞ inches) or No. 10 (9½ by 4⅛ inches) envelope:

Bring the bottom of the sheet up one-third of its length, and fold sharply; then bring the top down to about a quarter-inch from the first crease and fold again.

92H. The Envelope

The address on the envelope should correspond in style with that of the inside address. A block-style letter requires a block-style address; an indented style requires an indented address. The address should be centered vertically and horizontally. The return address may be block style for any type of letter. It may be written either in the upper left corner of the front of the envelope or centered on the back flap.

3. LETTER OF APPLICATION

The most important type of letter for most students is the letter applying for work. Though no set formula exists for such a letter, the letter following, with its personal data sheet, illustrates the type. Observe that the writer begins by telling the prospective employer how he learned of the position to be filled, and then states his candidacy (he might have reversed the order of these details, beginning with a request to be considered for the position and following it with a statement of his source of information about it). In a second paragraph he reviews his training, giving the principal facts about it, but reserving the details for the personal data sheet. In a third paragraph he summarizes his experience, once more reserving details for the data sheet. In a last paragraph he indicates his willingness to go to see the employer for an interview. If the employer lived at a great distance, the applicant might have chosen to close with a comment to the effect that more information could be had from the references supplied in his data sheet and that he could be reached by telephone at a certain address.

Study carefully also the organization of the data sheet.

A LETTER OF APPLICATION

17 Euclid Avenue
Syracuse, New York
April 18, 19--

Mr. Harry Parsons, Director
East Side Community House
7 Genesee Street
Buffalo, New York

Dear Mr. Parsons:

I have just learned from the University Employment Bureau that a position as assistant director of East Side Community House will be open July first. I should like to apply for that position.

I shall be graduated with a Bachelor of Arts degree from Syracuse University on June 12. My major work has been in sociology with as many courses in applied psychology as I could work into my schedule for my minor subject. I have made a special study of group activities and club organization and am keenly interested in the problems of the adolescent in today's world.

In addition to the theoretical knowledge gained in my study at Syracuse, I have had practical experience in club administration work as part of my course of study. For two years I have worked with the Syracuse Federated Boys' Clubs under Mr. Joseph Margolis, Sports Director. At least once a month I helped run the Saturday night social at the Pine Street Center. My summers since 19-- have been spent as camper or councillor at the camps listed in the enclosed personal data sheet.

For further information about my qualifications I refer you by permission to the University Employment Bureau and to the persons listed on my data sheet. I shall be glad to come to Buffalo for an interview with you. Since I have no classes on Friday afternoons and Saturdays, I could come to your office any time after three o'clock on Friday or at any hour convenient to you on Saturday.

Yours very truly,

Arthur M. Everett

Arthur M. Everett

Enclosure

PERSONAL DATA SHEET

Name: Arthur M. Everett
Permanent Address: 222 East Walnut Street, Syracuse, New York
Telephone Number : SA 6-6106

PERSONAL QUALIFICATIONS

Birthplace: Syracuse, New York — Date: June 5, 19--
Age: 22 years
Health: Excellent — Marital Status: Single

EDUCATION

1. Secondary: West Side High School, Syracuse, New York
   Affiliations: Outing Club, Camera Club, basketball and swimming teams

2. College: Syracuse University, Syracuse, New York, 19-- to 19--
   Affiliations: Sociology Club, Psychology Club, the Square Dancers; member University basketball and swimming squads, 19-- to 19--

EXPERIENCE

Assistant Scout Master, Syracuse Boy Scouts, 19-- to 19--; councillor, Onondaga Boys' Camp, 19-- to 19--; assistant coach in basketball and swimming, Syracuse Federated Boys' Clubs, 19-- to 19--; assistant, Saturday Night Social, Pine Street Center, 19-- to 19--

SPECIAL INTERESTS

Basketball, swimming, hiking, square dancing, photography

REFERENCES

Mr. John R. Foster, Placement Director, Syracuse University Employment Bureau

Mr. Joseph Margolis, Sports Director, The Syracuse Federated Boys' Clubs, 114 South Salina Street, Syracuse, New York

The Reverend Harold Hermans, St. Mark's Episcopal Church, 200 Euclid Avenue, Syracuse, New York

94. SOCIAL NOTES

94A. The Formal Note

Formal social notes follow a conventional pattern. They are always written in the third person. Dates and hours are written in full. Except for Mr., Mrs., and Dr., no abbreviations are used. The heading is placed at the lower left, and no inside address is used. The note should be handwritten (social notes are never typewritten) on formal correspondence cards or heavy white note paper of small size.

Mrs. Willard requests the pleasure of Mr. and Mrs. Sharpe's company at dinner on Friday evening, October the tenth, at seven o'clock.

125 Berkeley Street,
October the first.

Mr. and Mrs. Sharpe accept with pleasure the kind invitation of Mrs. Willard to dinner on Friday evening, October the tenth, at seven o'clock.

212 Ash Street,
October the third.

Mr. and Mrs. Sharpe regret that they are unable to accept the kind invitation of Mrs. Willard to dinner on Friday evening, October the tenth, at seven o'clock.

212 Ash Street,

October the third.

94B. The Informal Note

The formal note is often expressed more informally today, as in the following note (acceptances and regrets would be modified accordingly).

Dear Mrs. Harper:

We should be happy to have you and Mr. Harper dine with us on Friday, November the fifteenth, at seven o'clock. After dinner we should like your company at the lecture on Aztec art at the City Museum.

Sincerely yours,

Ellen Willard

24 Alton Road,

November sixth.

EXERCISES

1. Write a letter, semiblock style, asking for an interview with the president of your college regarding the establishment of a new student publication or some comparable problem.

2. Write a letter, executive type, to the editor of your college paper on some problem of current interest.

3. Acting as secretary of some college group, write an order in block style for supplies to some firm, properly identifying the goods ordered and indicating method of payment, shipment, etc.

4. Write a letter, semiblock style, with a personal data sheet, applying for work in some firm or organization.

APPENDIX

Appendix

DIAGRAMING SENTENCES

I. THE DIAGRAM: ITS DEFINITION AND PURPOSE

Though the structure of any sentence may be made clear by the direct analysis of the function of each of its words, phrases, and clauses, such an analysis may be made more vivid by the use of a diagram. A diagram is a visual device showing the grammatical relationships of words in a sentence. The sentences diagramed in this section are taken mainly from "The Structure of Sentences" (Chapter 2), and their diagrams may be studied concurrently with the definitions of the types they represent in that chapter. None of the forms is difficult, once you are able to identify the various parts of speech, phrases, and clauses; and practice in diagraming will help you to learn to identify these structural parts instantly. A diagram of any sentence will enable you to see just how the various parts of a sentence fit together.

II. THE SIMPLE SENTENCE AND ITS MODIFIERS

A. Subject and Predicate

Children play.

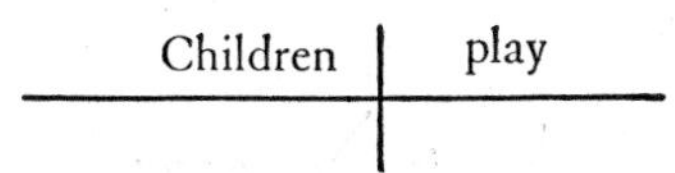

Children is the simple subject; *play* is the simple predicate.

B. Subject with Modifying Adjectives and Predicate with Modifying Adverb

Two little children played happily.

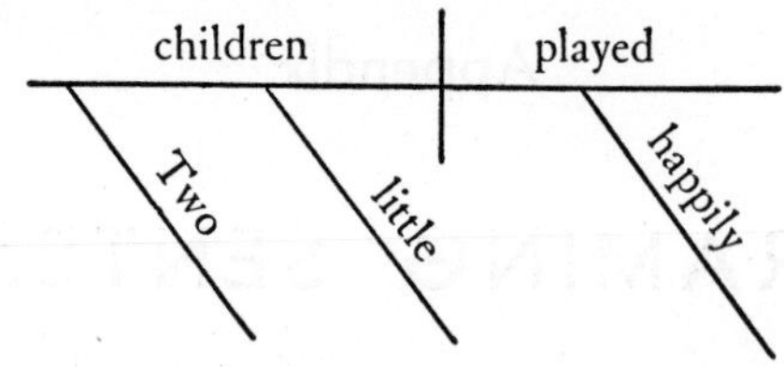

Two and *little* are adjectives limiting and describing the subject; *happily* is an adverb of manner modifying the verb.

C. Subject, Verb, and Subjective Complement (predicate noun, pronoun, or adjective after a verb or verbal of *being, seeming*)

Fred is a hero.

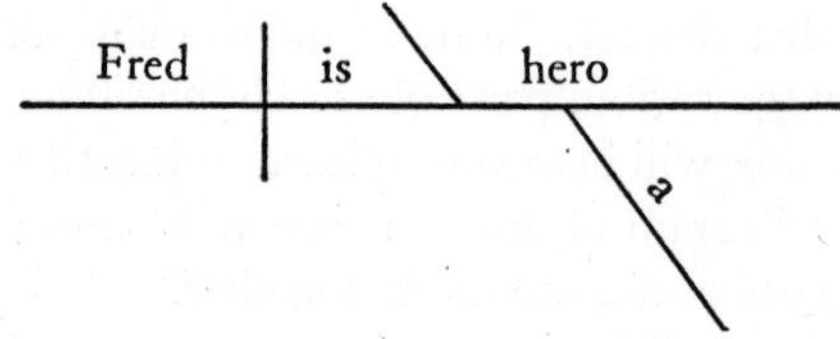

Hero is a subjective complement or, specifically, a noun completing the predicate *is; a* is a special form of the adjective, an indefinite article, modifying *hero*. Note the use of a line slanted to the left to indicate that a subjective complement follows.

Tom is angry.

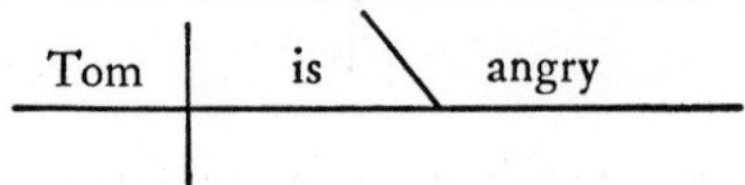

Angry is a subjective complement or, specifically, an adjective completing the predicate *is*.

D. Subject, Verb, and Direct Object

He hit me.

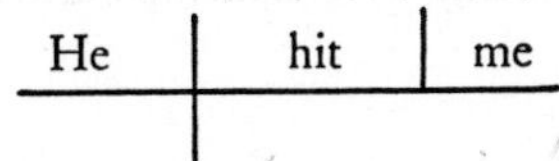

Me is the direct object of the transitive verb *hit.*

E. Subject, Verb, Direct Object, and Objective Complement

He called Fred a hero.

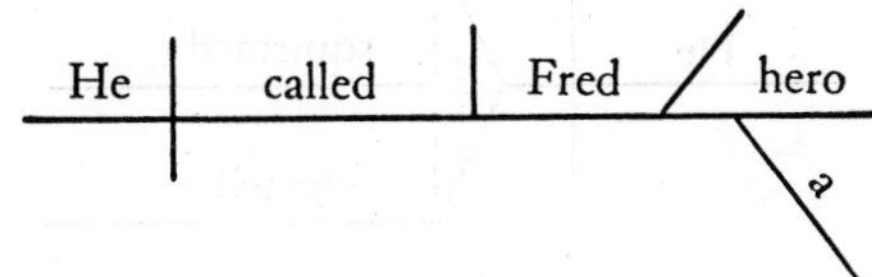

Fred is the direct object of *called; hero* is the objective complement of *Fred*. Observe the use of a line slanted to the right to indicate the objective complement.

F. Subject, Verb, Indirect Object, Direct Object

He gave Mary the necklace.

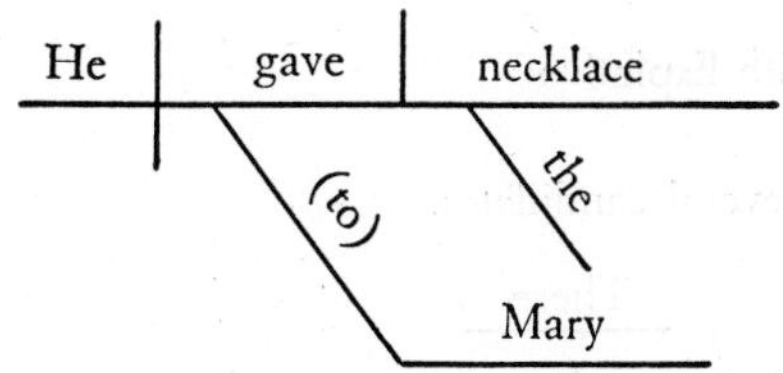

Mary is the indirect object of *gave,* as proved by the fact that *to* can be inserted before it; in the diagram *Mary* is seen as the object of the preposition *to* understood. *Necklace* is the direct object of *gave.*

G. (1) Compound Subject, Verb, and Subjective Complement
(2) Simple Subject and Compound Predicate

Dickens and Thackeray were contemporaries.

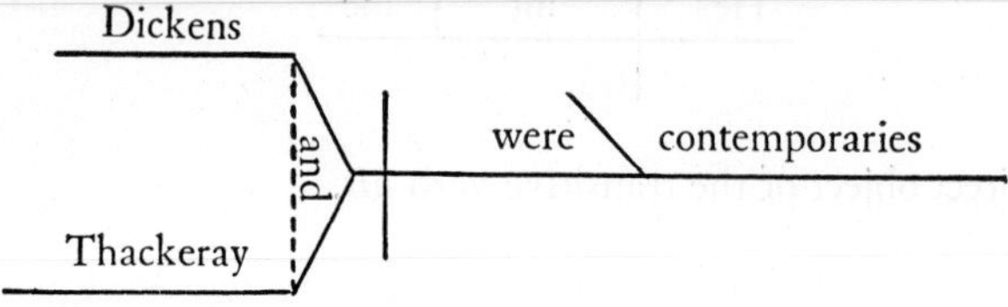

He sighed, squirmed, and fidgeted.

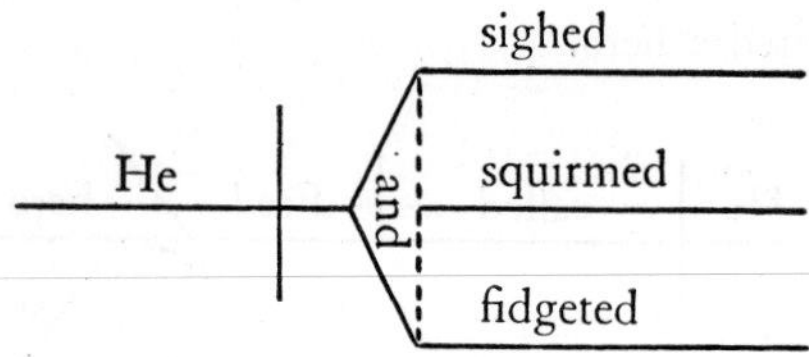

H. Compound Subject, Compound Predicate, and Direct Objects

John and William liked swimming but hated calisthenics.

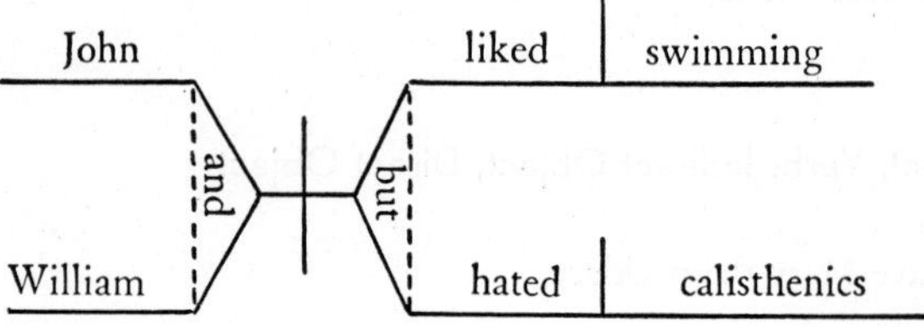

J. Sentence with Expletive

There are several candidates.

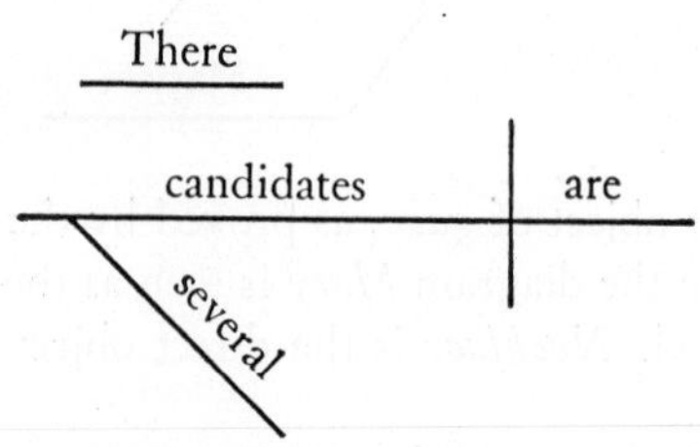

There is an expletive introducing the true subject, *candidates.* Since an expletive does not modify any part of the sentence, it is placed here above, but not connected with, the subject that it introduces.

K. Sentence with Absolute Construction

The spring being rainy, gardens were planted late.

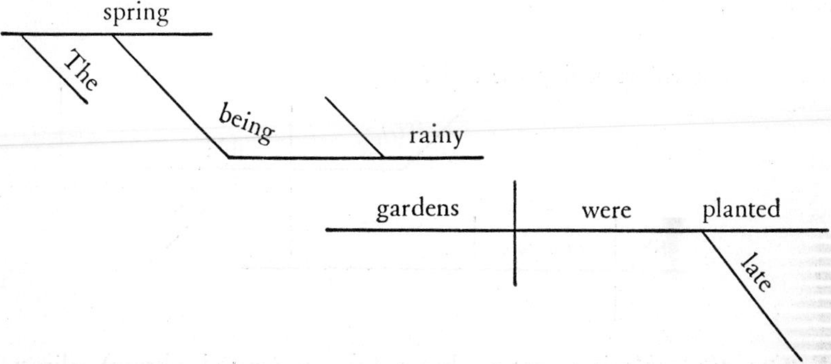

Since *The spring being rainy,* as an absolute construction, does not modify any single part of the sentence, it is placed above the sentence but separate from it to indicate its grammatical independence. (It is obvious that the construction does modify the general meaning of the sentence.) *Spring* is a noun, modified by the definite article *the* and the participial (adjectival) phrase *being rainy; rainy* is the subjective complement (predicate adjective) of *being.* Note how the participle is placed in this diagram. *Late* is an adverb of time.

III. PHRASES IN SENTENCES

A. Noun Phrases

1. Noun Phrase as Subject

Learning to swim is easy.

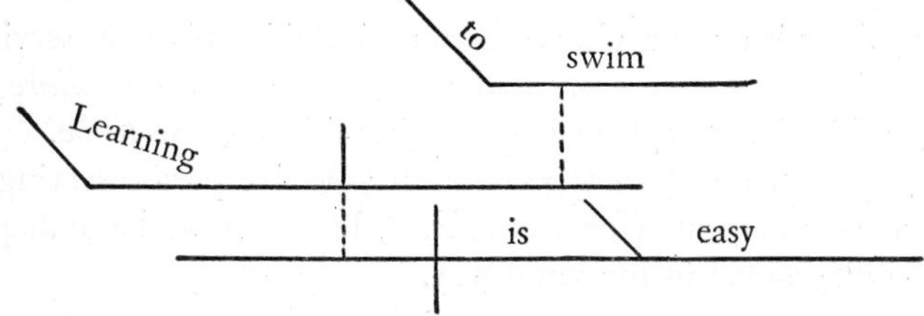

Learning to swim is a noun phrase, subject of the predicate *is easy*. *Learning* is a gerund (hence functions as a noun); *to swim* is an infinitive phrase, object of the verbal aspect of the gerund. Since the gerund is dominant in this phrase, the phrase is also known as a gerund phrase.

2. Noun Phrase as Direct Object of a Verb

She enjoys setting the table.

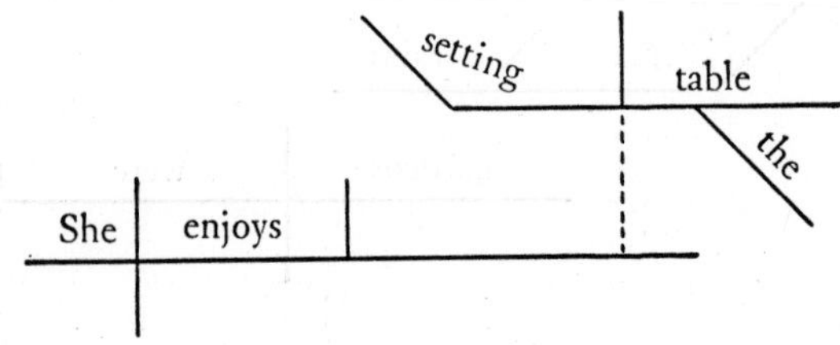

Setting the table is a noun phrase (also a gerund phrase), direct object of *enjoys*. *Table* is the direct object of the verbal aspect of the gerund.

3. Noun Phrase as Subjective Complement

He seems to be a failure.

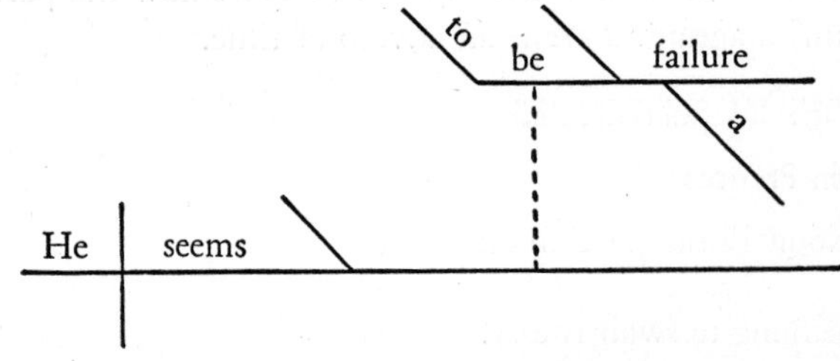

To be a failure is a noun phrase (also an infinitive phrase), serving as the subjective complement or predicate noun of *seems*. *Failure* is in turn the subjective complement of the infinitive phrase *to be*.

A sentence of the same type with an adjective phrase serving as a subjective complement (for example, "He seems to be unhappy") would be diagramed in the same way.

B. Adjective Phrases

1. The man at the door is a stranger.

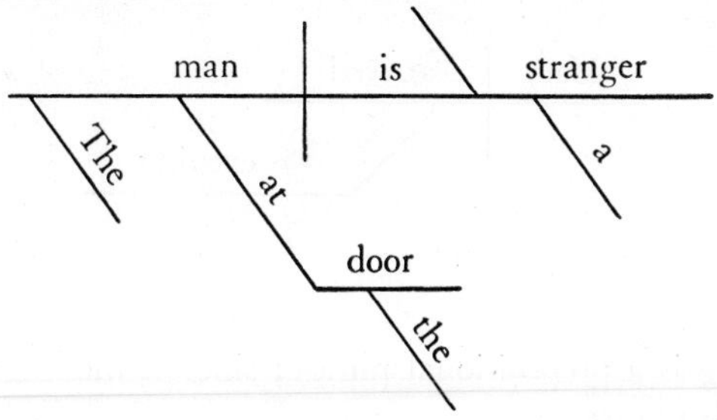

At the door is a prepositional phrase modifying *man* and hence an adjective phrase. *At* is a preposition; *door* is its object.

2. Exhausted by his efforts, he collapsed.

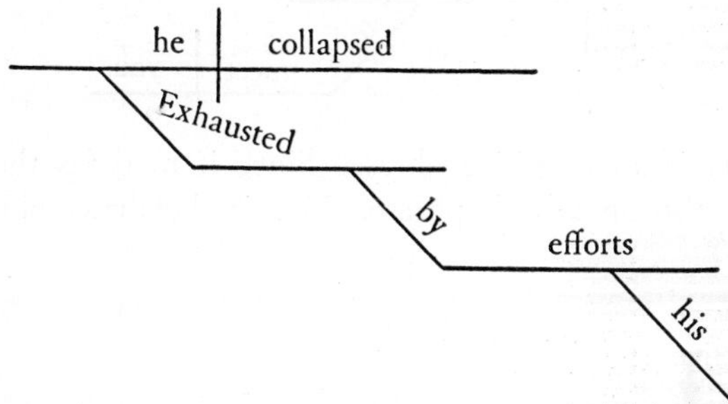

Exhausted by his efforts is a participial phrase, hence an adjective. *Exhausted,* the participle, modifies *he. By his efforts,* a prepositional phrase, is also an adverb phrase since it modifies the participle (an adjective).

3. She has a report to make.

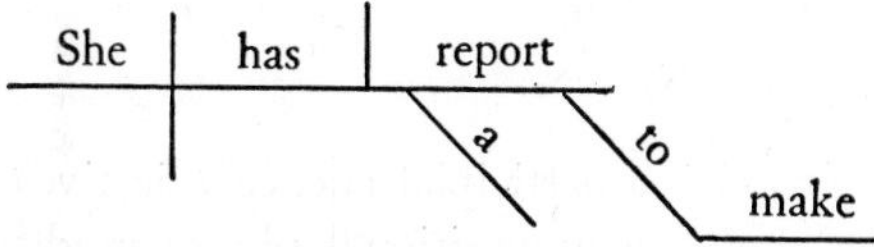

To make is an infinitive phrase, modifying *report* (a noun), and hence an adjective phrase.

C. Adverb Phrases

1. Mary arrived in the evening.

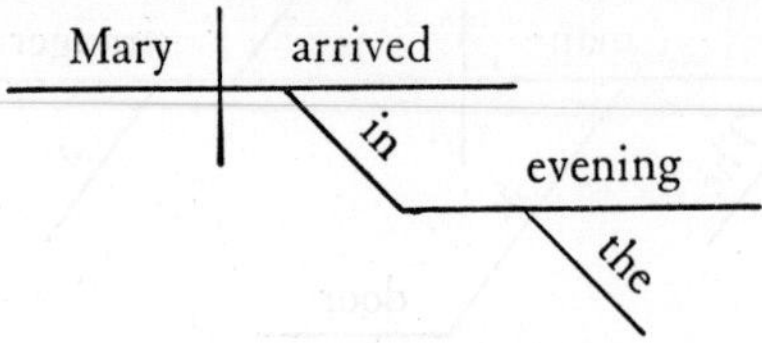

In the evening is a prepositional phrase; since it modifies *arrived* it is also an adverb phrase.

2. I am happy to meet you.

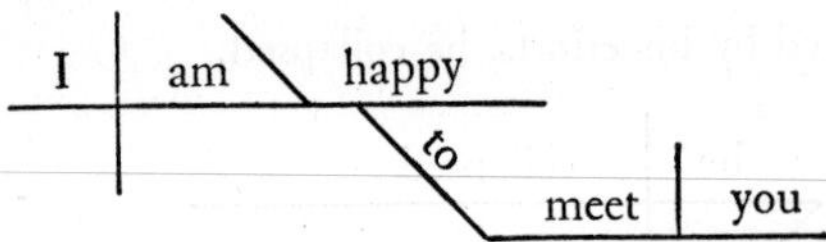

To meet you is an infinitive phrase. Since it modifies the adjective *happy,* it is also an adverb phrase. *You* is the direct object of the infinitive.

D. Adjective and Adverb Phrases

Drawing a deep breath, he dived into the pool to hunt the lost ring.

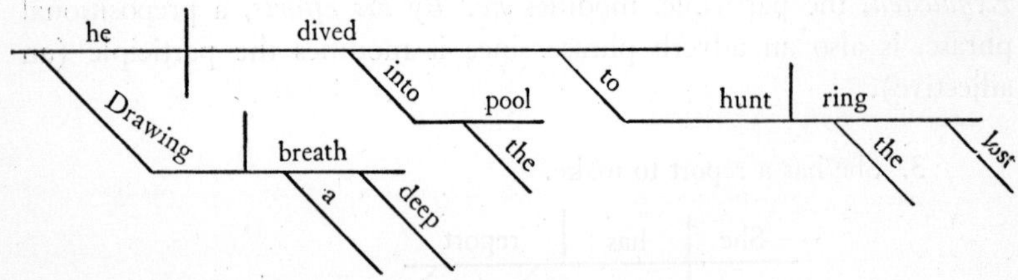

Drawing a deep breath is a participial (hence adjective) phrase modifying *he. Into the pool* is a prepositional phrase modifying *dived* and hence an adverb (of place). *To hunt the lost ring* is an infinitive phrase also modifying *dived* and hence an adverb (of purpose).

IV. CLAUSES IN SENTENCES

A. Noun Clauses

1. Noun Clause as Subject

That I broke my arm is true.

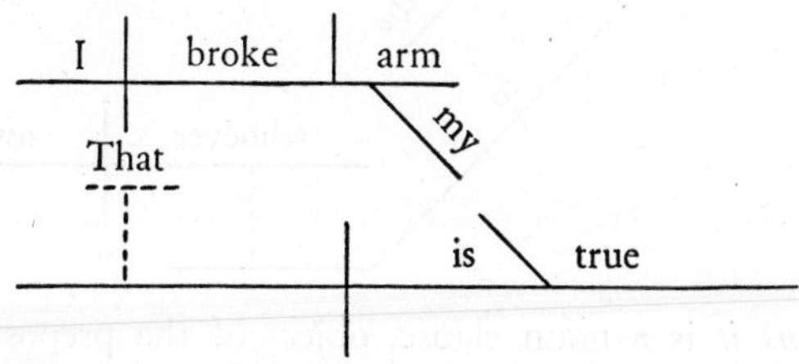

That I broke my arm is a noun clause, subject of *is. That* is a subordinating conjunction, introducing the noun clause.

2. Expletive with Noun Clause as Subject

It is a fact that he was defeated.

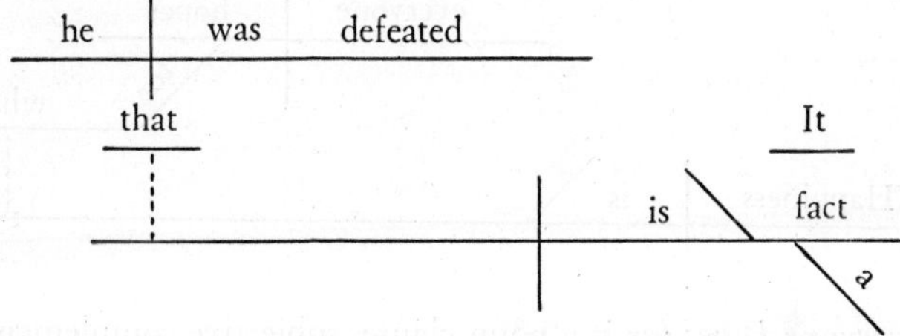

It is an expletive. *That he was defeated* is a noun clause, the true subject of *is*.

3. Noun Clause as Object of Verb

They charged that he had robbed the bank.

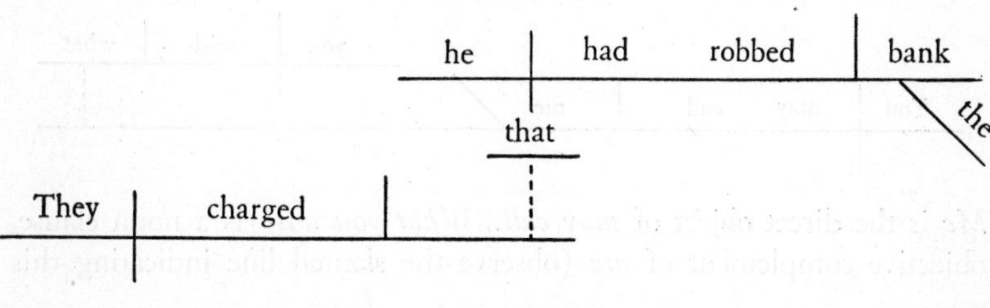

4. Noun Clause as Object of Preposition

I will give the book to whoever owns it.

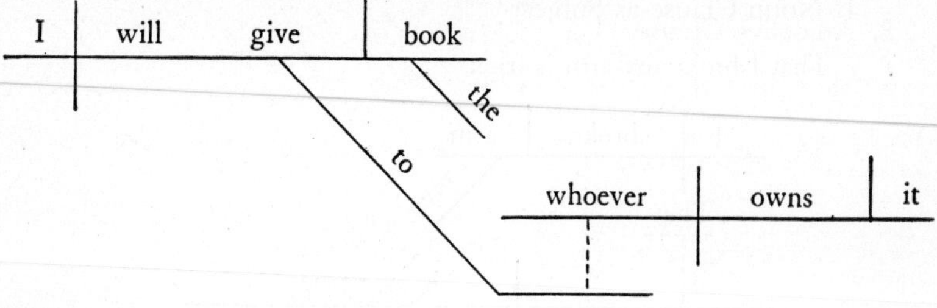

Whoever owns it is a noun clause, object of the preposition *to* and indirect object of the verb *will give. Whoever* is the subject of the verb *owns; it* is the direct object of *owns.*

5. Noun Clause as Subjective Complement (Predicate Noun)

Happiness is what everyone hopes for.

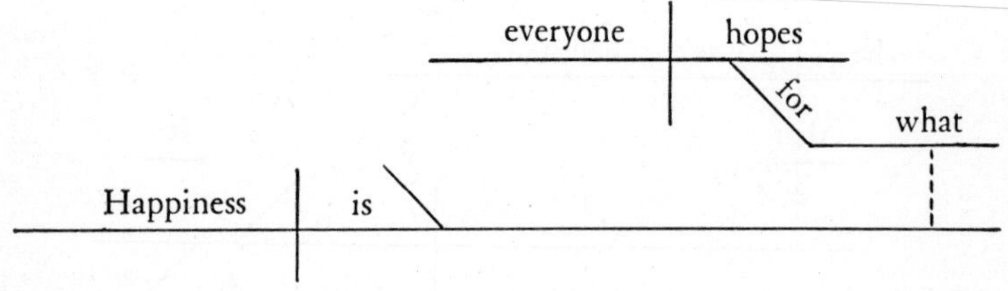

What everyone hopes for is a noun clause, subjective complement of *is. What* is a relative pronoun, linking the clause to the main clause, and object of the preposition *for*, and indirect object of *hope.*

6. Noun Clause as Objective Complement

You may call me what you wish.

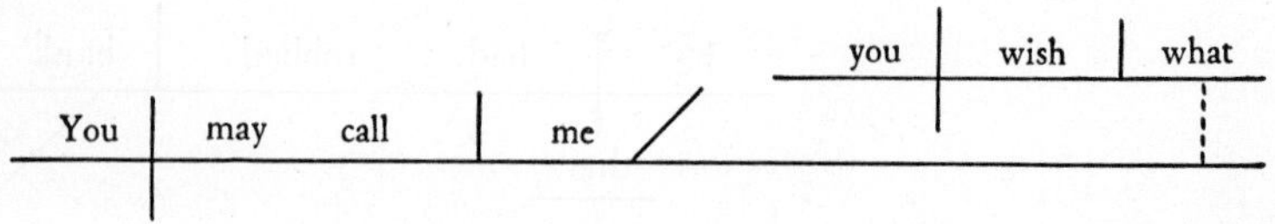

Me is the direct object of *may call. What you wish* is a noun clause, objective complement of *me* (observe the slanted line indicating this construction). *What* is a relative pronoun linking the noun clause to the main clause and serving as the direct object of *wish*.

B. Adjective Clause

1. Adjective Clause Modifying Subject

He who hesitates is lost.

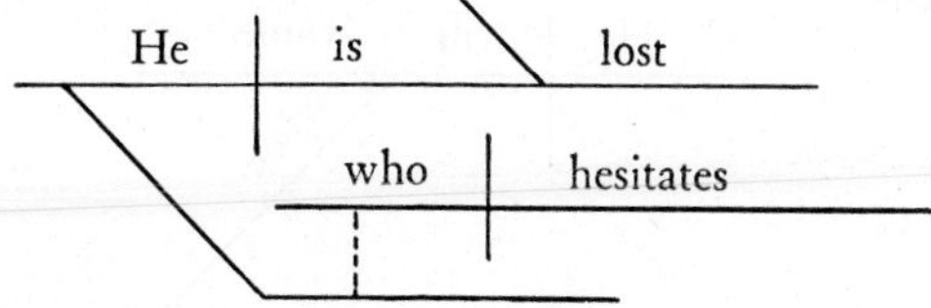

Who hesitates is an adjective clause modifying *he*.

2. Possessive Relative (Adjective) Clause Modifying Subject

The runner whose shoe came off finished last.

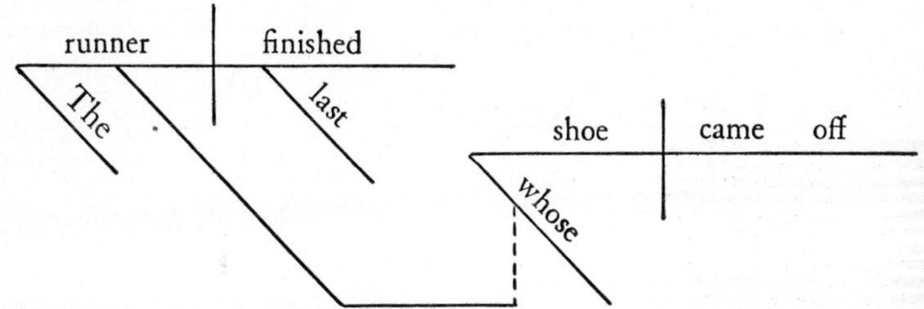

Whose shoe came off is an adjective clause modifying *runner*. *Whose* is a possessive relative pronoun, linking the adjective clause to *runner* and modifying *shoe* as a possessive adjective.

3. Adjective Clause Modifying Direct Object

I know the office where he works.

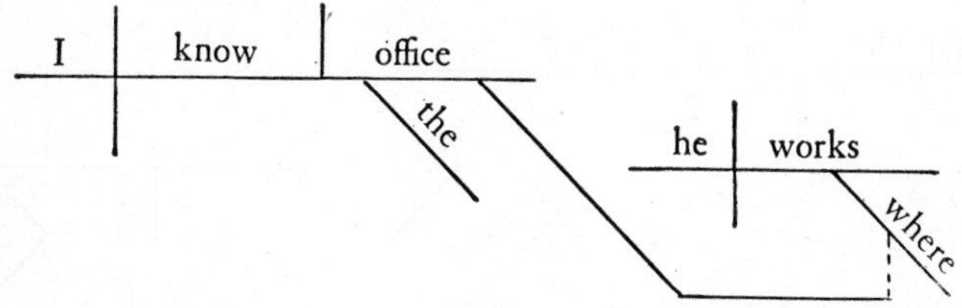

Where he works is an adjective clause modifying *office*. *Where* is a relative adverb linking its clause to the direct object (*office*) but serving also as an adverb modifying *works*.

C. Adverb Clauses

1. Adverb Clause Modifying Verb

He will come when you call.

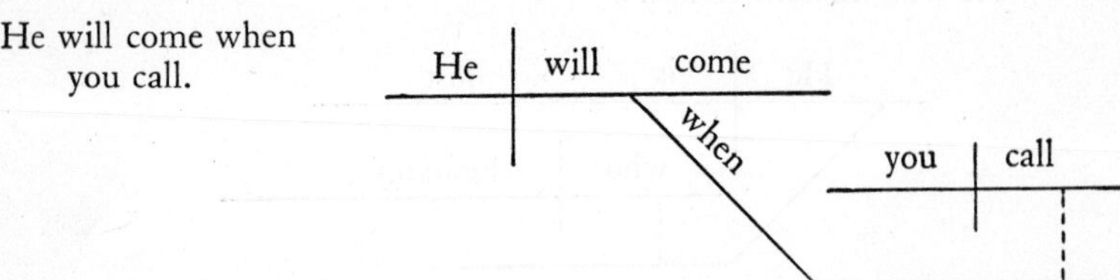

When you call is an adverb clause (of time) modifying *will come*. *When* links the adverb clause to the main clause and also modifies *call*.

2. Adverb Clause Modifying Adjective

I am happy that you are here.

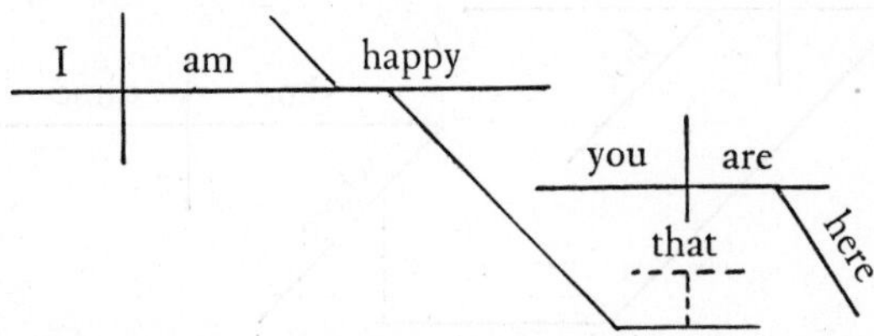

That you are here is an adverb clause of reason modifying the adjective *happy*. *That* is a subordinating conjunction linking the clause *you are here* to *happy*.

3. Adverb Clause Modifying Adverb

Winston is hitting better than he did last year.

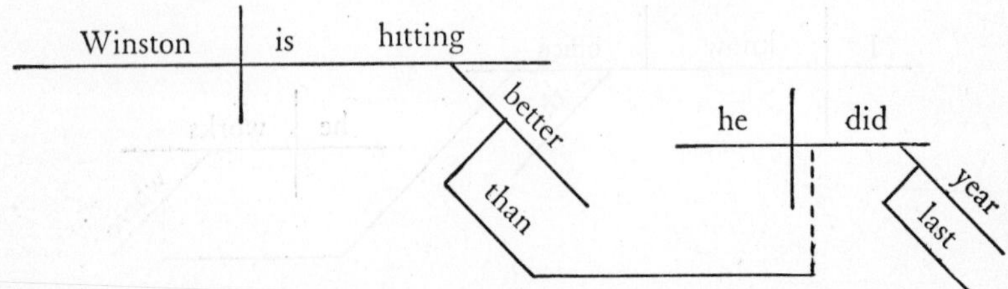

Than he did last year is an adverb clause of comparison modifying the adverb of manner, *better*. *Than* is the subordinating (adverbial) conjunction linking the clause *he did last year* to the adverb, and modifying *better*. *Last year* is an adverb noun phrase modifying *did*. *Last* is an adjective modifying *year*.

4. Adverb Clause Modifying Verb

Though he was late, he came at last.

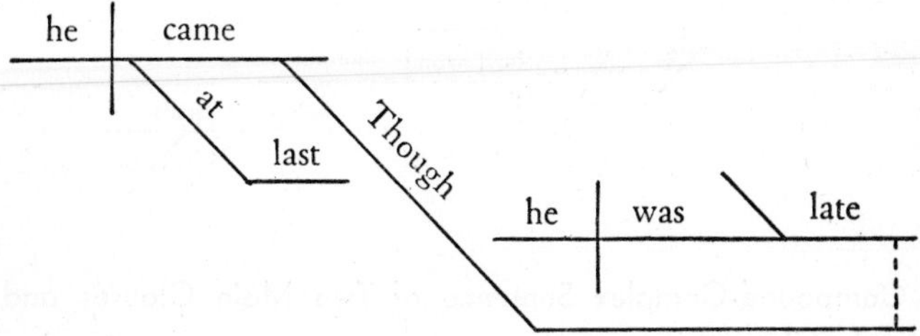

Though he was late is a concessive adverb clause modifying *came*. *Though* is a subordinating (adverb) conjunction linking *he was late* to *came*, and also modifies the adjective *late* directly as an adverb.

V. OTHER SENTENCE PATTERNS

Other sentence patterns, no matter how complicated in structure, are simply extensions of the patterns diagramed above, as the following examples will show.

A. Compound Sentence of Two Main Clauses with Modifiers

Sweeping across the lake, the wind blew hard against the flimsy cottages, and the big willows bent to the ground.

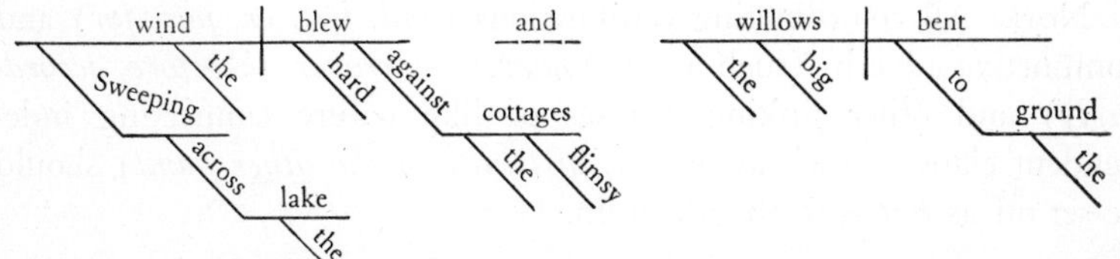

B. Complex Sentence with Main Clause and Two Subordinate Clauses

The leading contestants for the title are Jerry Brock, who represents Madison High School, and Alton Williams, who won the shot-put in the city finals.

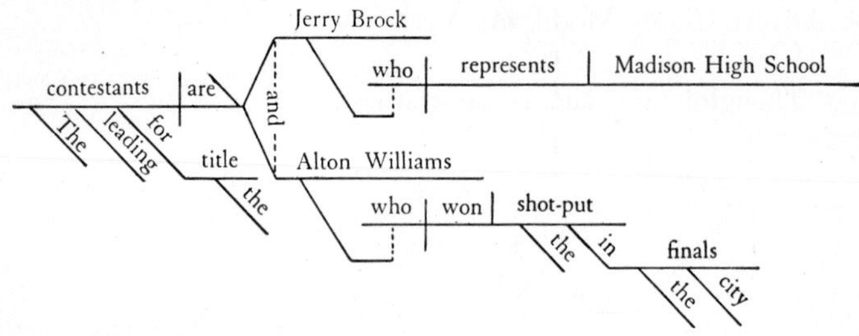

C. Compound-Complex Sentence of Two Main Clauses and Two Subordinate Clauses

The fans groaned when Smith came to bat, but when he drove the ball over the fence they swarmed from the benches and carried him from the field.

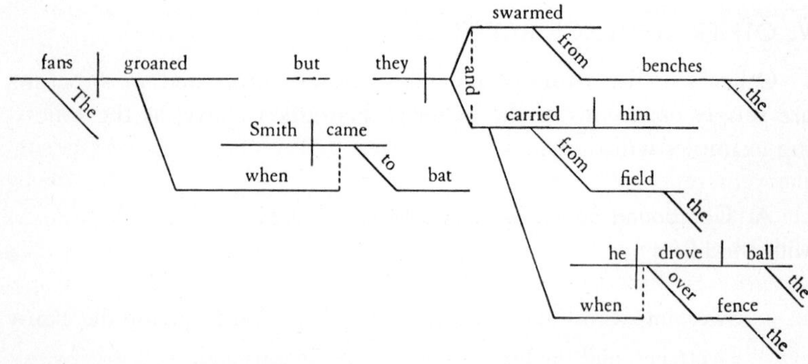

Note: All co-ordinating conjunctions (*and, but, or, nor, for*) and conjunctive adverbs (such as *so, however, moreover, therefore, accordingly*) and other linking phrases of like nature connecting independent clauses (such as *in fact, in truth, on the other hand*) should be set off as *but* is in this diagram.

D. Complex-Compound Interrogative Sentence with Two Subordinate Clauses and Modifiers

Are their humility, which seems imposed by moral principles, their shyness in relation to the extracollegiate world, derived from the ages when learning was the passion of pious brotherhoods and shut away between the walls of foundations?—EDMUND WILSON

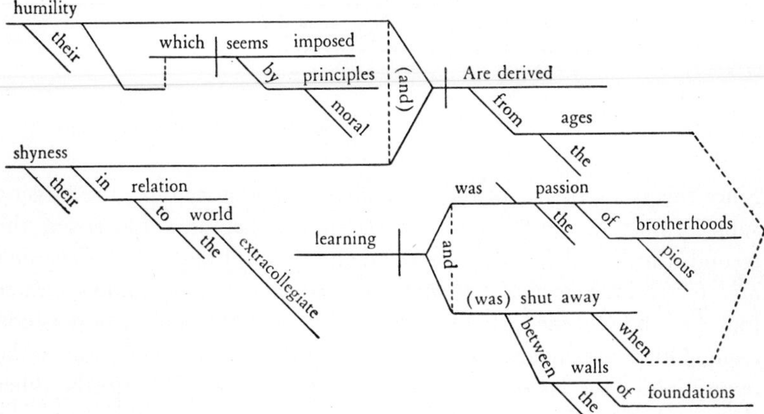

Humility and *shyness* are the compound subject of the sentence, as will be seen if the interrogative form is made into a declarative statement. *Humility* has two adjective modifiers, the possessive adjective *their* and the relative clause *which seems imposed by moral principles; shyness* is modified by the prepositional phrase *in relation* and *relation* is similarly modified. The passive verb *are derived* is modified directly by the adverbial prepositional phrase *from the ages; ages,* noun object of the preposition, is modified by the relative (adjectival) clause *when learning . . . was shut away between the walls of foundations. When* in its relative force links the clause to the noun; as a relative adverb, it modifies the compound predicate *was the passion . . . and shut away.*

E. Imperative Sentence with Parallel Infinitive Phrases

Read not to contradict and confute; nor to believe and take for granted; nor to find talk and discourse; but to weigh and consider. —FRANCIS BACON.

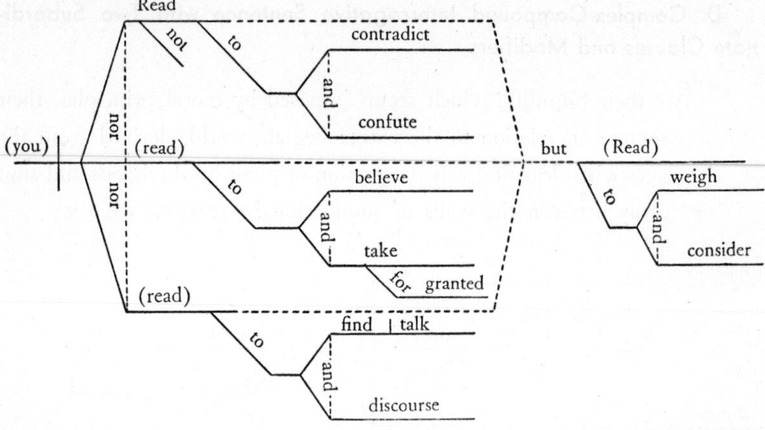

Since this is a sentence of the imperative or hortatory type, the missing subject must be supplied for the complete diagram. Moreover, the second, third, and fourth compound infinitive phrases, *to believe and take for granted, to find talk and discourse,* and *to weigh and consider* may each be regarded as elliptical predicates modifying an understood *read*. Other arrangements are possible, but this one emphasizes the opposition of the last phrase (*but to weigh and consider*) to the other three, reflecting the author's intention.

EXERCISES

1. Study the definition of the sentence and the relationship of subject and predicate as defined in Chapter 2, The Structure of Sentences, Sections 10A, B, C, F, 11A 1–4, and the illustrative diagrams above, Sections I and II. Then diagram the sentences in the exercise on p. 72. Be able to explain each of your diagrams in full.

2. Study the definitions of phrases in Chapter 2, Section 11B, and the related diagrams in Section III above. Diagram the ten sentences in the exercise on p. 74.

3. Study the definitions of clauses in Chapter 2, Section 11C, and the related diagrams in Section IV above. Diagram the sentences in the exercise on pp. 76–77.

4. Study the basic types of sentences in Chapter 2, Section 11D, and the related diagrams in Section V above. Explain the diagrams in Section V. Diagram the sentences in the exercise on pp. 79–80.

5. Diagram the paragraph in Exercise B, p. 80.

INDEX

Index

Index

Index

Index

Whole Composition	Sentence Structure and Parts of Speech		Sentence Form	Punctuation and Mechanics
1A Limiting Subject	10 Sentences	15 Verb	21 Loose Sentence	31 Comma
1B, 8A2 Title	11 Basic Structure	15C Voice	22 Periodic Sentence	32 Semicolon
2A Tone	11D Basic Sentences	15D Tense	23 Subordination	33 Period
2B Tone and Diction	12A Incomplete Sentences	15E Mood	24 Parallelism	34 Question Mark
3 Unity and Coherence	12B "and who" Fault	15G Agreement	25 Balance	35 Exclamation Point
4 Emphasis and Proportion	12C Comma Splice	15H 1 Infinitive	26 Emphasis	36 Apostrophe
5 Organization	12D Fused Sentence	15H 2 Participle	27 Economy	37 Colon
5A Beginning	12E, F "because" Faults	15H 3 Gerund	28 Variety	38 Dash
5C Ending	13 Noun	15H 4 Dangling Modifiers	29 Rhythm	39 Parentheses
6 Outlining	13D2 " is when or where"	16 Adjective		40 Brackets
7 Writing Theme	14 Pronoun	17 Adverb		41 Quotation Marks
8 Manuscript	14J Case	18 Faults in Comparison		42 Italics
9 Final Revision	14K Number	19 Preposition		43 Hyphen
	14L Reference	20 Conjunction		44 Capitals
				45 Abbreviations
				46 Numbers